Praise for *The Old Testament in the Light of the New*

"Steve Clark's *The Old Testament in the Light of the New* is a welcome and well-done contribution to the Church's ancient tradition of understanding what in the Old Testament anticipated and prefigured what is only fully realized in the New. This work helps us more clearly understand everything written in the law of Moses and in the Prophets and the Psalms, precisely in the light of Christ."

DONALD CARDINAL WUERL
Archbishop of Washington, D.C.

"Throughout the liturgical year, we are challenged to understand and present how the Old and New Testament readings fit together, not merely in the minds of those who compiled the Lectionary, but rather, in 'the mystery hidden from ages' but now revealed in Christ: God's plan of salvation. Stephen Clark helps us to see in Scripture how this plan unfolded and how we are part of it."

MOST REVEREND WILLIAM E. LORI
Archbishop of Baltimore

"One of the chief challenges of a contemporary reader of the Bible is to discern through the vast medley of books and authors one single story. Stephen Clark offers a framework that will equip the attentive reader to discover the threads of the plot that drives the narrative of our salvation."

MOST REVEREND MICHAEL BYRNES
Coadjutor Archbishop of Agana in U.S. Territory of Guam

"Stephen Clark admirably demonstrates the integral unity found between the Old and New Testaments, a unity found within the person and work of Jesus. Theologians, students and seminarians, pastors, and the laity will all benefit from Clark's book not only by obtaining a proper understanding of the relationship between the

Old and New Testaments, but also by deepening their faith in Jesus who inhabits both and is the truth that gives life to both."

"Stephen Clark has done careful, scholarly work for many years. His new book is no exception. Many Christians are perplexed about how to understand the relevance of the Old Testament to the Christian life. While the first half of the book is accessible to the general reader, the second part is included for those interested in its scholarly underpinnings. Stephen Clark has made a useful and ecumenically sensitive contribution to understanding this important issue."

"There are few subjects more important for Christians today than how to understand the Old Testament, for it is widely recognized that it is impossible to understand the New Testament without proper knowledge of the Old. This book is an enlightened and accessible guide to Jesus' Bible, and therefore a crucial source for understanding Jesus himself."

"Without the Scriptures which Jesus opened to his disciples, the message which he conveyed and embodied would be incomprehensible. Clark leads his readers on a journey like that which was taken by the two disciples on the road to Emmaus; we can all benefit by walking that road with him."

"A Lutheran reading Clark's book will come away from this Thanksgiving Table not just stuffed with biblical knowledge and satisfied that his every Lutheran itch has been scratched (e.g., law-gospel distinction, Christocentric-incarnational anti-gnostic content, the tensions arising from the theology of the Cross dialectic, and all this in a full course meal of biblical theology) but rather, better equipped and energized to follow Jesus into the world, making authentic disciples of all nations."

TED JUNGKUNTZ
Professor of Theology (retired), Valparaiso University

The Old Testament in the Light of the New

The Old Testament in the Light of the New

The Stages of God's Plan

STEPHEN B. CLARK

EMMAUS
ROAD
PUBLISHING

Steubenville, Ohio
www.emmausroad.org

Emmaus Road Publishing
1468 Parkview Circle
Steubenville, Ohio 43952

ISBN: 978-1-945125-31-7

Library of Congress Cataloging-in-Publication Data

Names: Clark, Stephen B., author.
Title: The Old Testament in the light of the new : the stages of God's plan /
  Stephen B. Clark.
Description: Steubenville : Emmaus Road Pub., 2017. | Includes
  bibliographical references.
Identifiers: LCCN 2017004605 | ISBN 9781945125317 (pbk.)
Subjects: LCSH: Typology (Theology) | Salvation--Biblical teaching. | Bible.
  New Testament--Relation to the Old Testament.
Classification: LCC BS478 .C53 2017 | DDC 221.6/4--dc23 LC record available
at https://lccn.loc.gov/2017004605

Cover images: *The Last Supper* (1592–1594) and *The Jews in the Desert*, (ca.
1593), Jacopo Tintoretto, San Giorgio Maggiore, Venice

Cover design and layout by Margaret Ryland

Contents

FOREWORD

This is an important book. Or perhaps it is better to say: this is a very fine book on an important topic.

How are Christians supposed to read the Old Testament? Is it still a book that we can use? Some critics claim that the Old Testament presents a dark view of a violent and selfish God—and we must leave behind these primitive myths and stories. Other critics seek to erect an impenetrable barrier between the Old and New Testaments, saying that we are not justified, historically or theologically, in reading the Old Testament in the light of faith in Jesus Christ.

In *The Old Testament in the Light of the New*, Stephen Clark shows us how as Christians we can (and must) read the Old Testament in the light of the New. And of course this means that we must read the New Testament in continuity with, and as the fulfillment of, the Old Testament.

This focus on reading the Old and New Testaments together with the figure of Christ as the center and focal point is entirely in keeping with Pope Benedict's approach. In his work, *Jesus of Nazareth*, Benedict writes: "You can see that the Old and New Testaments belong together. This Christological hermeneutic, which sees Jesus Christ as the key to the whole and learns from him how to understand the Bible as a unity, presupposes a prior act of faith."[1]

---

[1] Pope Benedict XVI, *Jesus of Nazareth*, vol. 1, *From the Baptism in the Jordan to the Transfiguration* (Doubleday: New York, 2007), xix.

The genius of *The Old Testament in the Light of the New* is that it teaches us how to see the narrative unity of God's plan as revealed in the Scriptures, Old and New Testament. The focus is on the beginning, the center and climax, and the end. As with a great symphony, we only understand the individual movements once we have heard the whole work, once we have grasped how everything is summed up in the final climax.

So it is with the narrative of Scripture. We need to know *God's purpose from the beginning*—and here the opening chapters of Genesis are essential. We need to know *the center and goal of the plan*—and this is Christ, the Word made flesh. But we also need to know *where God's purpose is going*—and this is eternal life with God forever, beautifully displayed as the "marriage feast of the Lamb" in the book of Revelation.

The book divides the narrative of God's plan into seven stages: (1) Adam and creation; (2) Noah and a new creation; (3) Abraham and the patriarchs; (4) Moses and the covenant on Mt. Sinai; (5) David and the foundation of the kingdom; (6) the coming of Jesus Christ and the dispensation of the Spirit; (7) the return of Jesus Christ and the new heavens and new earth. The author is respectful of other ways to distinguish the stages of God's plan, each of which brings out something important. He elects to follow these seven stages because they show in greater detail how the Lord God has fulfilled his plan in discreet stages, each of which is fulfilled in the figure of Jesus Christ.

Importantly, Clark maintains that, though the stages follow one upon the other, they are also overlapping—that is, the Lord God may continue to relate to people according to one stage even as another stage is underway. And so, even though we now live in the stage of Christ and the Spirit, God can continue to relate to non-Christian Gentiles according to the way he related to Noah and his sons (the Noahide covenant), and to the Jewish people according to the covenant on Sinai (the Old Covenant). This makes for a complex relationship between the stages: we are able to discern the discreet stages but we have to be careful about using this knowledge to make specific judgments about the work of God in history.

The Old Testament in the Light of the New makes ample use of typology in showing the interrelation of the stages. Again, Pope Benedict witnesses to the indispensability of typology as an interpretative lens to read the unified narrative of Scripture. In *Verbum Domini*, he writes: "From apostolic times and in her living Tradition, the Church has stressed the unity of God's plan in the two Testaments through the use of typology; this procedure is in no way arbitrary, but is intrinsic to the events related in the sacred text and thus involves the whole of Scripture."[2] Instructing Christians about what typology is and how it can be used to see God's plan in the Scripture (chapter 3) is a priceless component of the book.

Part II provides greatly helpful explanations on special topics and technical issues. How historically reliable is the Bible? How can we interact with modern scholarship? How does literary genre affect our interpretation of the Bible. These are the *real* questions that readers of the Bible consistently face. Clark has provided clear and readable explanations of these challenging issues.

Three qualities in particular mark the achievement of *The Old Testament in the Light of the New*. First, it provides (indirectly) a *liturgical* reading of the Bible. In the liturgy of the Mass and the liturgy of the hours, the Church adopts a typological reading of the Bible, allowing the Old and New Testaments to mutually illuminate each other, with Christ always at the center. This is precisely the kind of approach expounded here. Thus, this book provides considerable help for reading the Scripture in a way that supports active and full participation in the liturgy.

Second, this volume offers a conscious *ecumenical* reading of the Bible. Though the author writes as a Catholic, he warmly welcomes Orthodox, Protestant, and Messianic Jewish readers and contributors, because he is convinced that a unified, narrative reading of the Old and New Testaments is something that unites Christians and enables them to live and worship in greater unity.

---

[2] Pope Benedict XVI, *Verbum Domini*, Post-Synodal Apostolic Exhortation, Sept. 30, 2010, 41.

Third, this work offers a *Christ-centered but non-supersessionist reading* of Israel, the Old Testament and the Jewish people. The author combines in a remarkable way a clear and sharp focus on Christ as the fulfillment of God's plan without disparaging Israel, the place of the Law, or the ongoing role of the Jewish people. Jesus brings everything to fulfillment and there is genuine newness in him, but Israel, the Law, and the Old Covenant retain their value and importance. One could say that this is a "law-friendly" and "Israel-friendly" account of the stages of God's plan. Not only does the author see Israel before the coming of Christ in a positive light but he believes that the Jewish people continue to participate in God's ongoing plan.

In all of this, what is the final goal of God's plan that Clark perceives in the entire narrative of Scripture? It is to create a people, sons and daughters, made (and reformed) in God's image and likeness, living freely in his presence in the world, sharing a way of life together. The only-begotten Son of God became flesh and won our redemption so that we could become through the Spirit sons and daughters in the Son.

—Daniel Keating
Professor of Theology,
Sacred Heart Major Seminary

PART I:
THE STAGES OF GOD'S PLAN

INTRODUCTION TO THE TOPIC

This book concerns reading the Old Testament in the light of the New, that is, reading it with the understanding that the New Testament writings provide for us. It is a basic presentation of how the Old Testament forms part of the Christian Bible and how to read it as a Christian. Key to doing this is reading it with an understanding of the stages of God's plan, especially with the perspective that comes from understanding the future completion of God's plan.

Since the word "testament" is an older English translation of the Hebrew word for "covenant," the Old Testament is the book that contains writings that speak about the old covenant, the covenant God made with the people of Israel (2 Cor 3:14). The New Testament contains writings that speak about the new covenant God gave through his Son, Jesus Christ, when he poured out the Spirit on those who believed in his Son. The New Testament describes how the old covenant was not cancelled but fulfilled by what God did through the new covenant, as we will see more clearly farther on when we look at the meaning of "old" and "new" in the New Testament, especially in chapter 10.

We can read the Old Testament books as books directed to an old covenant audience. That can be a true reading insofar as it goes, and we will usually need to begin there. But we can also read them in the broader perspective of the whole plan of God, that is, as Christian Scriptures. That is what we will seek to do in this book. Understanding the stages of God's plan is not all that is needed for understanding how to read the Old Testament in the light of the New. There is more to the New Testament understanding of the Old Testament than is treated in this book, but the nature of the stages of God's plan is fundamental for a New Testament reading of the Old Testament.

The Christian Old Testament. In various places in the books of the New Testament we come across surprising statements about the Old Testament. Those statements claim that the Old Testament is a "Christian" book in the sense that it is a book to be used by Christians, believers in Jesus Christ. They even claim that the Old Testament contains Christian teaching, that is, teaching about Christ and what he has done for us—even though the Old Testament was written many years before the birth of Christ.

For instance, the Apostle Paul, after speaking about a series of events narrated in the Old Testament, said in 1 Corinthians 10:11,

> Now these things happened to them as a warning, but they were written down for *our* instruction, upon whom the end of the ages has come.

In Romans 15:4, after quoting from Psalm 69, he said much the same,

> For whatever was written in former days was written for *our* instruction, that by steadfastness and by the encouragement of the Scriptures we might have hope.

When he said *our* instruction, he was not denying that what was said in the Old Testaments was intended for the people in former days ("them"), not only by the human authors but more importantly by God himself; but Paul did mean that its primary purpose in God's eyes was to instruct *us*, that is, Christians. As we will see, he also held that much of the Old Testament could only be fully understood by Christians.

Perhaps the clearest statement of the way in which the Old Testament is a Christian book containing Christian instruction can be found in an exhortation in 2 Timothy 3:14–17, which says,

> But as for you, continue in what you have learned and have firmly believed, knowing from whom you learned it and how from childhood you have been acquainted with the sacred writings which are able to instruct you for salvation through faith in Christ Jesus. All scripture is inspired by God and profitable for teaching, for reproof, for correction, and for training in righteousness, that the man of God may be complete, equipped for every good work.

Since the New Testament had not been completed and put together at this point, the *sacred writings*, the *scripture* referred to here are mostly likely the Old Testament, or some parts of it. The passage is therefore saying that the Old Testament is useful for Timothy as a Christian leader both to understand salvation through faith in Christ and to know how to conduct himself.

The New Testament view of the Old Testament as a Christian book is most strikingly apparent in its understanding that much of the Old Testament is about Christ—even though Christ lived on earth after the Old Testament was written. In fact, many passages in the New Testament teach that the Old Testament explicitly speaks about Christ, at least prophetically—in the prophetic books, certainly, but in others as well. Christ, speaking to Jewish leaders, says in John 5:39,

> You search the scriptures, because you think that in them you have eternal life; and it is they that bear witness to me.

On the road to Emmaus after his Resurrection (Lk 24:25–27, 44–47), Christ said to two disciples

"O foolish men, and slow of heart to believe all that the prophets have spoken! Was it not necessary that the Christ should suffer these things and enter into his glory?" And beginning with Moses and all the prophets, he interpreted to them in all the scriptures the things concerning himself. . . .

Then he said to them, "These are my words which I spoke to you, while I was still with you, that everything written about me in the law of Moses and the prophets and the psalms must be fulfilled." Then he opened their minds to understand the scriptures, and said to them, "Thus it is written, that the Christ should suffer and on the third day rise from the dead, and that repentance and forgiveness of sins should be preached in his name to all nations, beginning from Jerusalem."

If, as Christians, we are going to come to a better understanding of how to read the Old Testament as a Christian book, we have to recognize that by Christ's own instruction it is the foundation for understanding him and his work.

Reading with the ending in view. How is it possible to make sense of the Old Testament as a Christian book though it was written before the birth of Christ? One key, as Christ himself indicated, is the conviction that Old Testament prophecies were speaking about Christ. We can see that illustrated in the story of Philip and the Ethiopian eunuch in Acts 8:27–35:

And behold, an Ethiopian, a eunuch, a minister of Candace, queen of the Ethiopians, in charge of all her treasure, had come to Jerusalem to worship and was returning; seated in his chariot, he was reading the prophet Isaiah. And the Spirit said to Philip, "Go up and join this chariot." So Philip ran to him, and heard him reading Isaiah the prophet, and asked, "Do you understand what you are reading?"

And he said, "How can I, unless some one guides me?"

And he invited Philip to come up and sit with him. Now the passage of the scripture which he was reading was this:

"As a sheep led to the slaughter
or a lamb before its shearer is dumb,
so he opens not his mouth.
In his humiliation justice was denied him.
Who can describe his generation?
For his life is taken up from the earth." [Isa. 53:7–8]

And the eunuch said to Philip, "About whom, pray, does the prophet say this, about himself or about some one else?" Then Philip opened his mouth, and beginning with this scripture he told him the good news of Jesus.

Philip was able to interpret the prophecy in Isaiah to be about Christ by telling the Ethiopian eunuch the good news about who Christ was and what he did and how that fulfilled the prophecy. As a result of the conversation the Ethiopian eunuch became a Christian.

To be able to provide a full presentation of how to read the Old Testament in the light of the New would take a presentation of how the New Testament approaches Old Testament prophecy. While we will look in this volume at some of the Old Testament prophecies as fulfilled in the New Testament, for reasons of space we will not be able to treat most of the principles behind the New Testament reading of the Old Testament prophecies. That would require another volume.

Another key for reading the Old Testament in the light of the New, however, is understanding the framework of the whole Bible as Christians have seen it. That framework can be termed "the stages of God's plan." It is this that we will be primarily concerned with in this book.

It is difficult for most Christian readers of the Old Testament to believe that they are reading a book of Christian instruction unless they understand the stages of God's plan. Otherwise the material in it seems too disparate and much of it even pointless from the Christian point of view. Only an understanding of the stages of God's plan allows us to gain a coherent view of the Bible as a whole, Old and New Testaments together.

The main outlines of God's plan can be found in the Old Testament itself, as we will see. Old Testament writers already knew that there were stages in God's plan for the human race, and they described a number of them. The New Testament writers, however, believed there was more to God's plan than Old Testament writers knew about. They believed a new stage had begun with the coming of Christ and his death and Resurrection—the new covenant stage.

The New Testament writers also believed that Christ would come again to judge the living and the dead and to bring all of creation to fulfill the purpose God has for it. That Second Coming would introduce a further stage of God's plan, sometimes referred to as "the age to come" (Mt 12:32; Mk 10:30; Lk 18:30; Heb 6:5). As a result of their further knowledge about the stages of God's plan, the New Testament writers used an understanding of the stages that was more developed than the Old Testament writers' (or modern orthodox Jewish writers'), and that included a fuller view of what God was working toward.

Most of us have had the experience of reading a novel two or more times. Unless we peeked at the last chapter during the first reading, we likely did not know what the whole story was about until the end. Then, most of the details the writer put into the story fell into place. The second time we read the story, we knew all along the significance of most of the things that were said, because we saw them in the light of the ending. We also usually noticed more of the details each time we reread it and grasped the significance of some things we originally passed over. We also appreciated much more the skill and beauty of the author's work because we could see it as a whole.

Some have pointed out that in detective stories and many novels, there is a "second narrative" at the end of the books—a synopsis. In this, the detective or chief investigator gives a summary of the events that puts everything together in a coherent way. This is usually short, much shorter than the book as a whole, and the other characters in the story had not understood fully what was going on until the end and hearing the second narrative. After reading the second narrative, it is difficult to read the first narrative in any other way. The Christian creed or rule of faith is somewhat similar to the second narrative in such books.

Christians reading the Old Testament should be guided by the creed from the start. We should know, for instance, that God has been in the process of establishing his kingdom, a reign of blessing, from the moment of creation, and that he will complete that work after the Second Coming. If we do, the account of any one step in that process—for instance, the establishment of the kingdom of Israel under David—has much greater significance than it would have if we saw it merely as the history of a successful and devout early Middle Eastern chieftain. We can also begin to understand why the bringing of the ark to Jerusalem—which enables the centering of God's people upon his presence in their midst and their worship of him—is an important part of the story.

To be sure, Christians read much of the Old Testament the way Jews do. *You shall not murder* applies to both, and mainly in the same way. The Jewish rabbinic exegesis can be helpful to Christians as well as Jews, and Jewish authors sometimes see things Christian authors miss. But since Christians read the New Testament as part of the same Bible as the Old Testament, they see some things in the Old Testament that Jews who do not believe in Christ do not see, or would not accept as being there.

The New Testament writers, then, looked at the Old Testament writings in a larger context than the Old Testament authors themselves did. They saw the realities the Old Testament was speaking about in relationship to what was to come, especially what would happen in Christ. They believed they had a better perspective on the Old Testament and the old covenant itself, because they could see it in the context of how God was completing the process he began in creation and then had moved forward, first in the old covenant and then in the new covenant. We are going to adopt the same perspective.

We are going to look at the Old Testament as a Christian book. We are going to try to understand why our Bible contains both the Old Testament and the New Testament, why both have been considered the Word of God—of one and the same God—why the Fathers of the Church and Christian teachers throughout most of Christian history have taught directly out of the Old Testament, and why Christ and the Apostles referred to many things in the Old Testament as foundational for the new covenant. In these pages, we will attempt to strengthen the use of the Old Testament as a Christian book that is fundamental to understanding the New Testament, and in addition strengthen its use as a source of Christian teaching.[1]

In the next chapters, we will focus on the Old Testament. We will particularly be looking at those sections that present the key transitions in the stages of God's plan, seeing both how the Old Testament understands them and how the New Testament sees them in a new light. At that point we will have an overview of the contents of the Old Testament as Christians should understand them. We will then look at the completion of the old covenant as the New Testament teaches it.

The Approach of the Book

There are two main parts to this book. The first part is an exposition of the stages of God's plan. This provides an overview, a synthesis, of the topic. The second part contains scholarly or methodological material that provides the underpinnings of the approach presented in the first part. The division of material is based on the conviction that the first need for understanding the topic is an overview of the

---

[1] For "Some Terms for the Nature of the Scriptures" see the glossary on p. 389. This glossary also provides a schematic outline for the nature of the Scriptures as approached in this book.

stages of God's plan, and that many issues and controversies are obscured by the lack of such an overview. Nonetheless, there are scholarly and methodological issues connected to putting together such
an overview, and many of those are discussed in the second part.

This book is not a commentary on the Old Testament, and
does not primarily focus on understanding the full Old Testament
text. It is an exposition of how to read the Old Testament in the
way the New Testament does. It is therefore selective, omitting a
large amount of Old Testament material and bypassing many issues
of interpretation, because its purpose is not to present a full commentary, much less an introduction, to the Old Testament. Rather,
it is intended to be a help in understanding the Old Testament in the
light of God's overall plan as revealed in the New Testament, with
the secondary consequence that it should be a help in understanding the New Testament itself.

This book is also not attempting a full treatment of Christianity.
The important Christian truths are referred to and discussed, but
they are not fully presented. In particular, the redeeming work of
Christ is not explained. For that I recommend my book *Redeemer*.[2]
The focus of this book, rather, is on the Old Testament, and there-
fore the two covenants as Christians understand them, not on all of
Christian doctrine.

This book is not intended to stand alone in presenting the Old
Testament in the light of the New. Hopefully there will be a second
volume on the worship types of the Old Testament—what Christians have often referred to as the ceremonial law of the old covenant. The second volume will focus on the significance of the tabernacle and the Jerusalem temple in God's plan and will also focus on
the significance of all the features of the worship of Israel that went
with them. Christians who are not messianic Jews do not believe
that they need to follow the ceremonial commandments literally, by,
for instance, keeping kosher when they eat, much less offering God
sacrifices of bulls on an altar in the temple mount in Jerusalem. But

---

[2]   Stephen B. Clark, *Redeemer: Understanding the Meaning of the Life, Death, and Resurrection of Jesus Christ* (Ann Arbor, MI: Servant, 1992), hereafter cited as *Redeemer*.

these texts about temple worship embody truths of the highest importance to all Christians and also teach us how to worship God in the only way that will fully please him.

Some ecumenical concerns. This book is intended to be ecumenically accessible. It is intended to be something that orthodox Christians of all Christian traditions and churches—Catholic, Protestant and Orthodox—can read with profit without being confronted by views that they cannot accept or perspectives that exclude them. By "orthodox" I mean here simply those who believe in the Nicene and/or Apostles' Creeds the way their authors understood them, but who also accept the Ten Commandments to be obeyed in the way the Scriptures and orthodox Christian teachers have traditionally understood them.

For this topic, ecumenical issues in the sense of issues about doctrinal differences that divide the contemporary Christian churches are not central. Where they are relevant, an explicit orientation to them is given. The ecumenical approach of the book, then, is one that attempts to follow the method that Pope John Paul II advocated, an ecumenical approach that is *"some sort of 'appendix.'* . . . Rather, ecumenism is an organic part of her life and work, and consequently must pervade all that she is and does."[3]

In the select bibliography there is a note on Roman Catholic documents on Scripture. These are useful both for Christians who are not Catholics and for Catholics as well, because they show how close the Catholic approaches to Scripture are to traditional Protestant approaches, including contemporary Evangelical ones—despite old and new polemics that seek to make the approaches seem very different.

Messianic Jews are included in this ecumenical concern. Since they represent a group of Christian believers who are Jews and who

---

[3] John Paul II, Encyclical Letter on Commitment to Ecumenism *Ut unum sint* (May 25, 1995), 20: "Thus it is absolutely clear that ecumenism, the movement promoting Christian unity, *is not just some sort of 'appendix'* which is added to the Church's traditional activity. Rather, ecumenism is an organic part of her life and work, and consequently must pervade all that she is and does; it must be like the fruit borne by a healthy and flourishing tree which grows to its full stature."

believe that they should keep the whole old covenant law, their theological concerns affect the way the material in this book is presented at various points. There is a special discussion of "Jewish Christians and the Law" in chapter 8 that deals with a number of the concerns of Messianic Jews. Even though many of them would prefer simply to be referred to as Jews who believe in the messiah (who is Jesus/Yeshua of Nazareth, the Christ), and not as Christians, they are understood to be part of the Christian people, as they themselves agree that they are part of the Christian people theologically.

"Fundamentalists" are included in this ecumenical concern. They are a group of conservative Evangelical believers who often show significant insight into Scripture and who include, and have included, good scholars. They are very commonly disdained and ignored by the "scholarly establishment," but they should be partners in the theological discussions among believing Christian teachers—at least those Fundamentalists who can accept a broader range of Christian teachers than their own.

Scholarly concerns. In part I there is little explicit reference to and discussion of particular contemporary scholarly works. Part I has been designed as a general exposition of the topic, not an extended engagement with particular theories and viewpoints in contemporary scholarship. The sources throughout the main exposition are the Scriptures themselves, and not the opinions of contemporary interpreters, although the discussion has been informed by relevant scholarly material and occasionally contemporary interpreters have been referred to when their works contain a fuller or special treatment of some matter.

The current state of biblical scholarship means that we cannot simply refer to *the* scholarly opinion on almost anything in the scriptural text.[4] It is rare that there is only one scholarly view on most of the important matters. To deal with all the exegetical issues touched

---

[4] For a brief overview of the current state of scriptural scholarship, see the methodological discussion in the section, "1. Modern Scholarship and Reading the Old Testament," on p. 432.

upon in part I would make the book very lengthy indeed. Hopefully all the opinions presented are sound and at least defensible.

Part I has not been written as an argument for a position or a set of positions. It is written with the conviction that the first need in dealing with this topic is to have an intelligible overview of what the Scriptures say about God's plan, not with a commentary that *begins* by discussing all the exegetical issues about particular passages and *then* seeks to assemble an overview. That should not imply that the particular exegetical issues are unimportant, but that the overview should not be obscured by the details.

Part I is for general readers. It only requires a basic knowledge of the Scriptures. Part II contains treatments of many scholarly discussions of the issues raised by part I. It is primarily for those who have some knowledge of the scholarly literature on scriptural interpretation. Although the material in part II is more advanced in a certain way, it presupposes the exposition in the first part, therefore part I should be read before part II. The select bibliography contains further helps to the scholarly literature on the subject.

These two parts could be seen as two books. Someone can read the first part with profit and not go on to read the second. Those used to reading scholarly literature on the interpretation of the Scriptures, however, will still need orientation to the approach taken in the first part. Therefore, both parts have been put together in one volume and are interrelated.

Practical Orientations for the Reader

At the beginning of each chapter of part I, one or more texts are listed—sometimes several chapters of the Scriptures, sometimes only a short passage. Readers may find it helpful to read these texts before reading the chapter, because they contain most of the material that the chapter will be discussing.

In the appendices there are glossaries of technical terms that are used in the text.

Throughout the book there are special exegetical discussions. They can be skipped without missing something essential to the main points of the book. For most readers, especially those for whom an extended discussion of the stages of God's plan is new, I would recommend skipping these and reading straight through the main part of the text. They can return to the special discussions afterwards or to a selection of them they would find helpful. Readers who are familiar with the subject of the book and have an interest in the technical parts of the discussion might find it more helpful to read the special discussions as they go along.

There are also technical notes in the appendices. These are referenced in the footnotes to the text when they are especially helpful. Like the exegetical discussions, they can be skipped in the first reading of the exposition and returned to later, or read when they are referred to.

The quotations from the Bible are mainly drawn from the Revised Standard Version, 1973 edition (RSV) and use the standard citations in the English–speaking world. I have chosen the RSV because it is the most widely accepted text that is ecumenically approved and has been commonly used in Christian theological discussions. Like most people who study the Scriptures in much depth, I have my own preferences for how the relevant texts should be translated, and they can differ from the RSV. I have therefore retranslated the RSV texts at the points where I judged it to be especially helpful to do so. Where I have retranslated, I have included the RSV translation in brackets.

Although the book sometimes cites the deuterocanonical/apocryphal books, it does not presuppose that all the Christian readers of the book will accept them as authoritative for establishing doctrine. Even for those who do not, they are helpful as witnesses to early Jewish tradition and as background to the New Testament.

CHAPTER ONE

GENESIS 1: THE CREATION

TEXT: GENESIS 1:1–2:4

Introduction to the chapter. The Bible begins with the words "In the beginning." That is the name of the first book of the Bible in Hebrew, because the books are named by their first words. In Greek, the name is *Génesis*, brought into English as our name for the first book as well. It means "coming to be." The book is concerned primarily with the coming to be of the covenant people of God, but also with the coming to be of the world.

Genesis is the introduction to the first five books of the Bible, the Pentateuch, and to the history of the people of Israel.[1] The bulk of Genesis is the account of the patriarchs (Genesis chapters 12–50). There we find a description of the origin of the people of Israel. But the people of Israel were not the first human beings, and human history did not begin with the events narrated in Genesis 12, the call of the first patriarch, Abraham.

The beginning of the human race is recounted in Genesis 1–11. These chapters form an "introduction to the introduction" and tell us briefly of the origins of the human race, of the fundamental realities we encounter as human beings, and of human civilization. But creation did not begin with the human race. Chapter 1 goes back to the very beginning of creation and situates the beginning of the

---

[1] For "Some Terms for Parts or Versions of the Bible," see the glossary on p. 392.

human race in that context. It tells us what was there at the outset—
God. As it says in Psalm 90:2:

> Before the mountains were brought forth,
>   or ever you had formed the earth and the world,
> from everlasting to everlasting you are God.

God with his creative power was there in the beginning, and he
was the origin of everything else.

In this chapter we will look at Genesis 1. The account of creation in Genesis 1 does not end until the first few verses of chapter
2, but for convenience, we will refer to the whole account as Genesis
1. It is here that we will begin. What comes first lays the foundation
for what comes after, and we will see that this is a repeating pattern
in stage after stage of God's plan for the human race.

One of the main questions that comes up for most readers of
Genesis 1 (and Genesis 1–11) is "how literally" to take what the
text says. The exposition of the texts in the first part of this book
simply approaches the narrations as they present themselves. The
issue of how literally to take the texts is reserved to the second part
of the book—in the methodological discussion "2. Scriptural Interpretation and Literary Genre" p. 447, where the position is upheld
that we should only take a text as literally as the text is intended to
be taken.

In that same second part of the book, we will also take up historical questions that are often raised about the account in Genesis
1. How does the account relate to what we know from modern science? Where does it fit in human history? (see "2. Scriptural Interpretation and Literary Genre," p. 447 and "9. Historical Reliability,"
p. 519).

In this book, we are not going to be mainly interested in the historical questions about the people and events we will be discussing.
We will use understandings of the events narrated in Scripture that
are historically defensible according to modern scholarly historiog-

raphy, but we will not engage in defenses of the positions we have adopted. We are interested in how as Christians we should understand these people and events. For that we will primarily rely on both testaments, including the typological and spiritual interpretations they contain.

Creation. The Bible begins with a solemn opening, one unique in human literature for its simplicity and power. The first verse states:

In the beginning God created the heavens and the earth.

There was an origin to the universe that we live in, and that origin was due to God. He created or made *heaven and earth.* This means he created everything, since *heaven and earth* is a scriptural idiom for saying "all there is." Everything other than himself, then, came into existence by God's action (Rev 4:11; Heb 11:3; 2 Macc 7:28–29). This has been traditionally described as creation out of nothing, sometimes referred to by using the Latin *creatio ex nihilo.*

Beginning with verse 3, we have the six days of God's work of creation. Each day is described within the same verbal structure, starting with *and God said,* and ending with *and there was evening and morning, [another] day.* At the end comes the seventh day. The opening in verse 1 and the closing in verse 4a[2] frame the account (marked by an inclusion):[3] Genesis 1, then, is the account of the creation of the heavens and earth, all things.

Before the six days of creation begin, the account sets the scene for God's action of creation in a way that intensifies the dramatic nature of what is to follow. The second verse says,

---

[2] Here we follow the view that Genesis 2:4 is a transitional verse, ending the previous section and beginning the new section, but expressing a unity to the two sections by the chiastic way the verse is constructed.

[3] For "chiasm," "inclusion," and other technical words for biblical style that will be used in what follows, see the glossary "Some Literary Terms for Describing Biblical Style" on p. 394.

The earth was without form and void, and darkness was upon the face of the deep; and the spirit of God was moving over the face of the waters.

The verse speaks of the earth being absent or empty—probably the former since the earth is not created until the third day—perhaps a way of saying there was no place for us. It speaks about formless waters (the *deep* or the *abyss*) that go down on and on, darkness covering everything. We are looking out, and there is no identifiable thing, no thing in particular, to be found. Moreover, there are no boundaries, no perceptible outer limits to what we see, no horizon. There is only an indistinct darkness. Then we can sense something like a breeze or a wind beginning to move. The spirit of God is starting to work.

Whether the description in verse 2 is of a pre-existent formless or unknown state as a contrast to what is to come or a way of saying that there was nothing at the outset, verse 3, the beginning of God's work of creation, presents the incomprehensible creative power of God beginning to act:

And God said, "Let there be light"; and there was light.

All of a sudden there is a blinding flash, something too powerful for human beings to imagine, something too powerful for human beings to endure.[4] We are fortunate not to be there, only to be told about it by the only one who was present.

Even in modern science, light is understood to be special—pure

---

[4] The physicist Robert Jastrow, quoted in Francis Collins, *The Language of God: A Scientist Presents Evidence for Belief* (London: Simon & Schuster UK, 2007), 67, describes the "Big Bang" by saying, "the chain of events leading to man commenced suddenly and sharply at a definite moment in time, in a flash of light and energy." Many nowadays hold, with some good reason, that Genesis 1 should not be interpreted by concordism with modern science (see the discussion of "Scriptural Interpretation and Literary Genre" on p. 447). Nonetheless it would seem strange to ignore the fact that the scientific description of the origin of the universe of which we are now confident—the Big Bang—conforms so well to Genesis 1:3, and also gives us some further understanding of what Genesis 1 so succinctly describes.

energy. We would not want to be struck by lightning. We do not want to stare at the sun. A soft candlelight would burn us if we touched it. But behind the light that entered this world was God; for *God is light* as the Apostle John tells us (1 Jn 1:5). The light that appeared at the outset of creation was directly connected to God himself, who *dwells in unapproachable light* (1 Tim 6:16).

The Apostle Paul in 2 Corinthians 4:6 quoted the words in Genesis by saying, *God…said, "Let light shine out of darkness"* or to use his next phrase *in* the darkness. He seemed to be saying that when God in Genesis said, *Let there be light,* he was not bringing light itself into existence. Rather, as many Christian Fathers and early Jewish interpreters have held, he was determining that the uncreated light of his own being shine in the nothingness and begin the process of creation.[5]

This, however, does not mean that all light is uncreated. There is, for instance, sunlight—energy of limited extent—and we exist as beneficiaries of that light. The description of the events in day 4 of creation speaks about the sun and moon and stars, created beings, as "lights." We ourselves, when we strike a match, in a certain way bring some created light into existence.

However, the existence of created lights is a participation in the uncreated light, which is God himself and his word. His light, uncreated light, enables created lights to exist and function. Like all created things, a created light truly exists as a limited being, but only because it is sustained by the Creator God and participates in, that is, draws the kind of existence it has from, his nature as light. When God said "Let there be light," his own uncreated power was bringing into existence the created order.

The shining forth of God's light into the nothingness was not just a work of power. It was also a work of wisdom (Ps 104:24; Prov 3:19–20; Prov 8:22–31; Job 28:20–28). God spoke and the created world came into existence. His speech was a word of command,

---

[5] For a fuller presentation of the view in Old Testament, Christian, and Jewish tradition that the light on day 1 was uncreated light, see Mark S. Smith, *The Priestly Vision of Genesis 1* (Minneapolis: Fortress Press, 2001), 73–77.

and as a command it stated what the result of his speech should be. It contained in itself the nature, or plan, or rationality, of the universe. God not only brought into existence the created universe, he formed it in a wise way. The word of God was not just speech, but the speech that comes from reason or wisdom or, more likely, reason itself, the divine reason, the divine wisdom. The created result of light shining forth is not an unformed chaos, but a formed or ordered whole, an intelligible structure, a whole that is structured to be something good.

For the most part, we find ourselves occupied by particular things within our experience: a meal to eat, a task assigned by our boss, a friend to help. Some people may get no further than that. But most people, at some point, are impressed by the pervasive background of their life.

Yes, there are meals, assignments, and friends. Nonetheless, there is a world in which all these occur, and this background has an unchallengeable stability. Gravity takes over when we drop something. The sun rises and sets and gives us warmth and light. At night the stars come out and go through a pattern of movement that does not change year after year.

Now, with modern science, we have a complex and vast, though still limited, description of how these things happen, and we have found more change over time than we perceive in our ordinary experience. Nonetheless, can we affect that? Can we alter it? Can we get the star Sirius to rise a second earlier or gravity to reverse direction? We know we cannot.

God could. God simply said, "Let there be light," and there was light. *He spoke and it came to be; he commanded and it stood forth*, as Psalm 33:9 says. We cannot imagine how there could be nothing or formless matter, then all of sudden a word from God, light bursting forth, and afterwards things coming into existence. But that, the opening description of Genesis tells us, is the ultimate fact about this universe we find ourselves in. In the beginning God already was, and it was his decision and his command that everything come into existence. Moreover it came into existence the way he said it should.

As children we slowly emerge to consciousness. At some point, if we are fortunate, we come to know about God and we learn that we too were created. The beginning of Genesis is not merely a description of a cause and effect relationship, a metaphysical statement about the origin of the universe that indicates the existence of a First Cause. The beginning of Genesis tells us something important about our own existence as mere creatures.

Because God created everything, he has the right to determine what everything should be and do. We can see this principle stated in Isaiah 45:9–12:

> "Woe to him who strives with his Maker,
> an earthen vessel with the potter!
> Does the clay say to him who fashions it, 'What are you
> making'?
> or 'Your work has no handles'?
> Woe to him who says to a father, 'What are you begetting?'
> or to a woman, 'With what are you in travail?'"
> Thus says the LORD, the Holy One of Israel, and his
> Maker:
> "Will you question me about my children,
> or command me concerning the work of my hands?
> I made the earth,
> and created man upon it;
> it was my hands that stretched out the heavens,
> and I commanded all their host."

A clay pot simply has to accept the decision of the potter about what it should be and how it should function. Because a father is the source of his son, a new human being, he has an authority over his son and a responsibility for him. The same is even truer of the relationship of God and his creation. The same is true of God and each one of us.

God created everything. Because he created everything, he has authority over and responsibility for everything. He is the one who knows how everything should go, because he created everything for a purpose (Is 46:8–11; Eph 1:11; Prov 16:4, etc.). Therefore, if we want to live in the way that we are made to live, we need to understand God's mind and his purpose. If we want to live within creation and in harmony with the way creation is supposed to be, then we need to cooperate with him, the one who made it.

THE CREATION OF THE WORLD

The creation. The first sections of Genesis 1 have more to tell us about the nature of creation, the world we live in. After the appearance of light and the separation of light from darkness, the account says,

> And God saw that the light was good; and God separated the light from the darkness. God called the light Day, and the darkness he called Night. And there was evening and there was morning, one day.

There is a detail here, one that is easily overlooked. It says, *there was evening and there was morning, one day.* We would be inclined to say "the first day," especially since we find the next days described as the second day, the third day, and so on to the seventh. Many traditional Jewish and Christian commentators, however, saw the difference in phrasing to be significant.

In this understanding, "one day" indicates that the first day, the beginning, was special. When light shone in the darkness, day began and all of creation came into existence. The rest of the days of creation unfolded what already had been done on the first day, the *day that the Lord God made heaven and earth* (Gen 2:4). The shining forth of light into nothingness is in principle the creation of everything.

The first three days of creation recount the beginning steps of creation. Light appears. Then heaven appears, creating a space in the middle of the waters. Then the dry land appears in that space, separating the earth and the seas. All three of these are described in terms of a division or separation. God lets the light shine in the darkness and separates the light from the darkness. God then creates the "firmament" (RSV), perhaps a "dome" (NAB) or an "expanse" (NIV), and separates the waters above and the waters below. God then creates the earth and separates the land from the seas. In all three days there is a shaping of creation into distinct realms.

The starting point is emptiness or at least formlessness. Then God steps in, and as he creates, he makes a separation here, a separation here, and a separation here, and so brings order into his creation. Creation is the bringing into existence of an ordered whole. The very word *cosmos,* the word derived from the Greek that we use for the totality of material creation, means that it is an ordered whole.

The second three days—days 4, 5, and 6—involve the creation of beings who populate the places created in the first three days. The fourth day, when the sun, the moon, and the stars were created, seems somewhat different from the fifth and sixth days. We would not think the sun, moon, and stars to be living beings in the same way as other creatures. Nonetheless, they move, even though their movement is limited to a set path. In fact, what we see in the text is a progression from the creation of things in the first three days that do not move but are the spaces in which things can move, to things that move in a set path, to things that have freedom of movement (birds, fish, and land animals), and then to things that not only have freedom of movement but also can choose how to live and so where to move (human beings).

The first three days of creation and the second three days of creation roughly correspond to one another. On the fourth day, we have the creation of the sun, the moon, and the stars. They are the beings that "rule over" what had been created on the first day, the day and the night. They are the beings that mark off the units of time, especially the times for the sacred observances within each year and from year to year, the divisions that should be the background of human life. They are also the beings that give light to the earth.

Then on the fifth day we have the creation of the fish and birds, who occupy what had been created on the second day, the sky and the sea. On the sixth day we have the creation of the animals that live on the dry land, which had been established on the third day, and the human race, which also lives on the dry land but is intended to rule over all living creatures.

The result is a habitable, limited dry land in an ordered, formed creation. But outside of that cosmos, as far as we can see, there is only darkness and the abyss. In creation, the Lord formed an ordered world of definite things, something good, in the midst of the kind of nothingness that prevailed in verse 2. As a created world, it only stays in existence, is sustained rather than falls back into nothingness, by the action of God, but, as we will see, is constantly threatened by that nothingness.

The later Scriptures indicate that from the darkness and abyss comes an opposition to God's work that produces corruption and destruction, what is described as *the kingdom of darkness* (Col 1:13). The Apostle John, speaking of the course of God's work of creation and salvation, going on even now but begun on day one, said *the light shines in the darkness and the darkness has not overcome it* (Jn 1:5). Other places in the Scriptures speak of conflict with various beings in the course of the work of creation (e.g., Ps 74:12–14; 89:8–10; Job 26:11–12; Is 51:9–11). From the abyss [RSV: the bottomless pit] can come various hostile beings (Rev 9:11; 11:7; 20:1–3).

As we shall see, at the end of this present time night shall be no more (Rev 21:25, 22:5), and the action of God will triumph and secure the existence of his good creation. But in the meantime not everything goes smoothly. In Genesis 1, however, this opposition does not appear and all is simply the good work of God. As the first chapter of the Bible this is the overriding perspective, the background within which all subsequent challenges to God's plan need to be seen (Ps 89:11).

In summary, creation is an ordered whole. Even as the creation itself is described as an imposition of order, so the narrative, the very way the creation is described, is seeking to present the creation story in an orderly fashion. The account seems to be written in a way that itself makes a point about the creation that it is describing, namely, that the creation in its initial goodness flows from God, that the creation has an order and harmony that comes from God himself, and that God's work involves actively forming and establishing the creation in the face of the alternative of chaos and nothingness.

The presence of the Trinity. There is a long-standing Christian perspective on the beginning verses of Genesis that many Christians nowadays are not familiar with, what we might call a Trinitarian perspective. To begin with, in the text of Genesis, God's creative work is connected with his word and with his spirit. Verse 3 says, *God said, "Let there be light," and there was light.* Things happen as God speaks through his almighty word. In verse 2 we also see the presence of the spirit of God: *the spirit of God was moving over the face of the waters.* The spirit of God is present and at work; the word of God goes forth; the realities of the universe are created.

This description of creation is developed further in Psalm 33, which contains a short summary of the truth stated in Genesis 1. In Psalm 33:6 we read,

> By the word of the Lord the heavens were made, and all their host by the breath of his mouth.

The word "breath" is another English translation of the words for "spirit," both in Hebrew and in Greek, and it was through God's breath or spirit and through God's word that the heavens were made.[6]

There is an obvious connection between the breath and the word. When people speak, they breathe out and form the breath into

---

[6] See also Judith 16:14, probably quoting and developing Ps 33:6: "Let all your creatures serve you, for you spoke and they were made. You sent forth your Spirit, and it formed them; there is none that can resist your voice." See also Wisdom 9:1; 16:12; and 18:15 for the portrayal of the word as an agent of creation.

sounds. The word and breath come out together from the speaker and belong to him, the word expressing the meaning or reason of his action and the breath the power behind the speaking. Psalm 33, probably based on Genesis 1, understands God's word and his spirit as his agents of creation. God acted by speaking a word, and therefore acted by sending forth his word and spirit (breath).

Many Christian teachers have seen these verses as a reference to the action of the Persons of the Trinity in creation. To some extent this view is based on Old Testament texts like Psalm 33, as we have seen, and Psalm 107:20 which speaks about God sending forth his word,

> . . . he sent forth his word, and healed them
> And delivered them from destruction

and Psalm 104:30 which speaks about sending forth his spirit:

> When you send forth your spirit, they are created
> and you renew the face of the earth.

Although the Old Testament speaks about God's word and his spirit as if they were agents of creation, seemingly somewhat separate from God, they are his own word and spirit, and therefore also divine.

In the New Testament we see even clearer statements. The Apostle Paul says in 2 Corinthians 3:6 that *the Spirit gives life*. The Spirit of God then, is a life-giver and so a creator.

The word of God is also a creator. The key place where we see this is in John 1:1–3, a commentary on Genesis 1:1, beginning with the same words as Genesis 1:1 — *In the beginning*.

> In the beginning was the Word and the Word was with God, and the Word was God. . . . All things were made through him, and without him was not anything made that was made.

This Word (of God) was the one *through whom all things were made*, or *in whom all things were created* (Col 1:16). To say, then, that the Word was the one who created all things is to say that he is divine, because the one true God is the one who created all things, and the *only* one who created all things. Therefore, the Gospel of John says *the Word was God* [RSV] or *the Word was divine*.

What was God's word when he created all things? God said *Let the light shine out of* (or *in*) *the darkness*. The Word of God was the light that shone in the darkness. This Word was "true God from true God, light from light," as the Nicene Creed puts it. This was *the Word* who *became flesh* (Jn 1:14) in Jesus Christ.

When we say that Genesis 1:1–3 contains a Trinitarian reference, we are not necessarily saying that the authors of Genesis or Psalm 33 conceived of God as three hypostases or three persons in one substance (being), to use the formulae of the early Christian creeds. We are, however, saying that now that we know about the Trinity through Christian revelation, now that we understand that there is one God in three hypostases or persons, we can go back and ask whether the Trinity was manifested at all in the Old Testament.

Many of the Fathers said that of course the Trinity was manifested, and one place we can see that is in the first verses of Genesis. When Genesis talks about God speaking (with his word and his spirit or breath), it is speaking about a threefoldness in God. We now know, as a result of the Incarnation of God's Son, the Word, and as a result of the outpouring of the Spirit, that the Trinity was being spoken about in the first chapter of Genesis. The threefoldness to which these verses refer is manifested more fully in the New Testament, and was understood better after the discussions of the early Christian Fathers that led to the creedal statements of the early ecumenical councils.[7]

---

[7] Rather than speaking about God's word as describing the agency of Christ in creation, some of the Christian Fathers said that Christ was the beginning, and all things were created in him, that is, in him who is the beginning. All of the Christian Fathers who wrote about the creation were convinced that Christ and the Spirit had to be agents in the creation, and that their presence could be traced in the text of Genesis 1.

To read the Old Testament in the light of the New, then, does not mean that we necessarily think that Old Testament authors understood things the way Christians do. Probably they did not, unless they had some special revelation. It means, however, that we now understand some things about God and his plan that they did not. As a consequence, we can see some things in the Old Testament that old covenant readers would not have seen, either because we know something more about the realities of which they speak or because we know something more about what God was aiming at. In doing so, we are not adding anything to the text or reading anything into it.[8]

To use an example, when whalers three hundred years ago said that there were great fish called whales in certain areas of the world, and their blubber gave useful oil, we know perfectly well what they were talking about and agree with what they said. However, we would not describe whales as fish but as mammals, because they take their oxygen from the air, not from the water, using lungs, not gills. Earlier, anything that swam in the waters and used fins for locomotion was called a fish.

We have changed our terminology because we have a more developed (and useful) understanding of biological structure, so we would not classify whales as fish anymore. But the whalers of old and writers who passed on what they said were talking about the same animals we are, and saying true things about them. We have no trouble in finding those animals and verifying what those older authors said about them, even though we have a more developed knowledge of the animals—and we rightly read what they said in the light of our more developed knowledge about whales.

In a similar way, as a result of the coming of Christ and of the Trinitarian discussions in the patristic period, we would now speak of the Spirit of God as a distinct hypostasis or person in the Trinity. But the human author of Genesis was talking about one and the same Spirit of God we are, and saying true things about him, things

---

[8] The question of what constitutes eisegesis (reading something into the text that is not there) is discussed more fully in the section "Eisegesis and Ideological Exegesis," on p. 507.

that we can recognize and accept. He was in fact talking about the Holy Spirit, the same Holy Spirit Christians believe in. And likewise he was talking about the same Word of God Christians believe in. So when we say that the Triune God was at work in the creation, we are not contradicting what the text of Genesis is saying or reading something into it that was not there. We understand it in a fuller way because we have more knowledge about the Spirit of God and the Word of God.

THE CREATION OF THE HUMAN RACE

The human. Day three and day six correspond to one another in the order of the account of creation because they both have two acts of creation, not just one. On day three God makes earth (the dry land) appear, separated from the sea, and then in a second action God creates plants to cover it. On day six God creates the land animals and then in a separate action creates human beings to rule the fish, birds, and animals. Days three and six seem to be a center of focus toward which the account is leading. On the third day the place of main concern, earth (dry land) covered with plants, the source of animal life (Gen 1:29–30), is created. On the sixth day, the living beings of main concern, land animals and human beings, are created. The goal of *the work of which God did in creation* (Gen 2:3) is human beings who live with animals on the vegetation-covered earth.

The completion of the work of creating material beings in Genesis 1, then, occurs in the second part of the sixth day with the creation of the human race. Not only does it describe the last act of creation, but it is also the lengthiest account and one that is special in several ways. It begins this way:

> Then God said, "Let us make man in our image, after our likeness; and let them have dominion over the fish of the sea, and over the birds of the air, and over the cattle, and over all the earth, and over every creeping thing that creeps upon the

earth." So God created man in his own image, in the image of God he created him; male and female he created them. And God blessed them, and God said to them, "Be fruitful and multiply, and fill the earth and subdue it; and have dominion over the fish of the sea and over the birds of the air and over every living thing that moves upon the earth."

Verse 26 [RSV] says, *Let us make man in our own image.* The Hebrew word translated as "man" is "*adam.*" "Adam" can be used as a corporate term in Hebrew, meaning "human race" or "humanity," as well as the proper name of an individual human being. Sometimes, in fact, the word translated in the RSV as the proper name "Adam" is translated by others as just "human," because the meaning of the name of the first human being in Hebrew is "human."

In addition, the text shifts back and forth from the singular to the plural: *Let us make man in our image, after our likeness; and let them have dominion over the fish of the sea, and over the birds of the air. God created man in his own image, in the image of God he created him; male and female he created them.* The word 'adam, then, is the antecedent of both a singular and a plural pronoun. This implies that Adam was an individual, but he also was humanity. This first individual human being sums up and represents—and begins—the whole human race.

Adam, then, is "The Human." Throughout the Scripture a name often reveals something of the identity and significance of the person (as the name Abraham means "the father of the people" and the name Joshua or Jesus means "the one who brings salvation"). So the name of this particular individual—Adam, Human—indicates who he is. He is the human race, the beginning of the human race, the head of the human race, and the father of the human race. He is, simply put, "The Human Being."

Two truths. In this text we have two facts about the way Adam is created and therefore about the way the human race is created: first, that the human race is created in the image of God, and second, that the human race is created male and female. These are the two primary truths that we are told about God's creation of the human race: *God created man in his own image . . . male and female he created them* (Gen 1:27).

These two facts are connected in a parallelism to two commands. The first command is, *Have dominion over the fish of the sea and over the birds of the air, and over the cattle, and over all the earth, and over every creeping thing that creeps upon the earth* (Gen 1:27). This first command, to rule or exercise dominion, is connected to the first fact: The reason that the first human beings can and should rule is because they are created in the image of God and so are capable of representing God. Human beings, the human race, were created to share God's rule over his creation.

We can see something of what it means to be in the image of God by looking at Genesis 5:3, where we have a reference to the birth of Seth, born as the son of Adam and described as in Adam's "image and likeness." Image and likeness, when used in regard to human beings, can be a way of speaking about sonship and so a sameness of nature. Therefore, as Seth was the son of Adam, Adam (the human race) was the son of God.

Such an understanding can also be found in the Gospel of Luke, which traces Christ's genealogy back to Adam, and then traces Adam's back to God himself. Luke makes God part of the genealogy, concluding the genealogy by saying: . . . *who was the son of Adam, who was the son of God* (Lk 3:38). The reference to image and likeness in Genesis 1:26, then, is an indication that Adam is created to be the son of God and to be like God as a son is like his father.

To see what is involved for a human to be in the image of God, we should begin by looking at what God is like in Genesis 1, the text that describes human beings as in God's image. God orders creation. He determines what things are and how they are to act. He names them and so can identify them. He speaks in a personal way to those who are capable of understanding speech. He acts with a purpose in mind, a final vision of what he is trying to bring about. The result of his action is good.

To be in the image of God does not mean that we are omnipotent, omniscient, omnipresent, that is, all-powerful, all-knowing and everywhere present, and so on. If we were, we would be God, not one of his creatures. We do not have the same (divine) nature as he has. But we are nonetheless like him. To be created according to God's image is to be like him in the ways he acts in Genesis 1, that is, to be a rational agent, an agent who can act with wisdom and understanding, deliberately bringing about a good world.

There is, however, another aspect of being in the image of God that we might miss. It does not have to do solely with intelligence and with power to do things, but also with good character. Good character is the developed orientation to seeking that the things we do are good (desirable). It especially involves seeking that the things we bring about are morally good (desirable because they uphold the good order of the universe). We can see this in the book of Colossians in an exhortation about being in the image of God:

> Do not lie to one another, seeing that you have put off the old nature [literally, old human being] with its practices and have put on the new nature [literally, new human being], which is being renewed in knowledge after the image of its creator. . . . Put on then, as God's chosen ones, holy and beloved, compassion, kindness, lowliness, meekness, and patience, forbearing one another and, if one has a complaint against another, forgiving each other; as the Lord has forgiven you, so you also must forgive. And above all these put on love, which binds everything together in perfect harmony. (Col 3:9–14)

This exhortation begins with encouragement to put off the old nature, the one we are born with, and put on the new nature. The new nature is one that is renewed after (in accordance with) the image of God. Then, when the passage continues to explain what that is like, we have a list of good character traits, moral virtues, traits that God has and that we need to have if we are in his image. Therefore, the human race, if it is renewed in the image of God, should be like him in his character and as a result make use of the power and authority that God gives to order the world in a good way, a moral way, a beneficial way. If we make use of our nature to rule but rule in a bad way, we may not have destroyed but we have certainly marred the image of God in us—as fallen human beings regularly do.

Many of the early Christian Fathers distinguished between the image and the likeness of God in human beings. They understood the image of God as the nature given us and the likeness of God as something we need to attain by growth in character. In such an understanding, we are in the image of God, but we need to grow in the likeness of God.

The extent of good human responsibility in a situation, then, depends on the extent to which we are like God in the way we exercise the responsibility we have been given. The more like God we become in the way we act, the more we do what is good, the more effectively we can govern as his representatives, bringing creation to the purpose for which he made it. Our exercise of the authority God has given us has important consequences for what happens on earth, and if we exercise this authority the way he would, we will see good results, results that will fulfill what his purpose was in creating the world in the first place.

The second command to the first human beings is *be fruitful and multiply and fill the earth*. The second command is connected to the second fact, namely that the human race is created male and female. After human beings are created male and female, they are commanded to be fruitful and multiply. The creation of sexual differentiation is connected to the command to be fruitful and multiply, or, as we might put it, a primary purpose of sexual differentiation, certainly the primary purpose according to Genesis 1, is to have children. That in turn should result in human beings filling the earth.

It is not only human beings that are created male and female. The animals are as well. Being male and female is a characteristic human beings share with the animals, a manifestation of their animal nature, because both humans and animals reproduce sexually. God, on the other hand, is not male and female. Unlike human beings and the rest of the animal kingdom, unlike Pagan gods, he does not increase and multiply. There is only one God and never will be another.

To say that human beings were created male and female is to say that they, unlike God, but like the animals, can and should have offspring in order to fulfill the purpose for which God created them. Being male and female, the second fact in this passage contrasts with being in the image and likeness of God, the first fact in the passage.[9] Both put together say that we are animals (with emphasis on the way that we, like other animals, reproduce), but at the same time transcend animality by our rationality. To use another biblical wording, we are both earthly and heavenly in the way we were created.

The second command also tells us something important about the developmental role of human beings in God's creation. God created Adam and Eve good in themselves, and he created both of them in his image and likeness. But he did not create them in a way in which they could fulfill his command to rule the earth all by themselves. They had to increase and multiply and fill the earth with a race of human beings. This would take time. In other words, the human race was made to complete God's work of creation and, in a process of development, to make his creation as a whole into what he intended it to be. The world was not created perfect or complete—although it was created good in principle—but was created to *eventually* become completely what God had in mind.

The connection of the two commands to the two facts about human nature shows us something additional about the way God's commands function. God commands us to do things that are in conformity to the way we are made. His very first two commands are not just arbitrary requirements, but follow from the nature of human be-

---

[9]   See Stephen B. Clark, *Man and Woman in Christ: An Examination of the Roles of Men and Women in Light of Scripture and the Social Sciences* (Ann Arbor, MI: Servant, 1980; East Lansing, MI: Tabor House, 2006), 11–13 (hereafter cited as Clark, *MWC*), for a general presentation of "image and likeness"; see Fergus Kerr, *Twentieth–Century Catholic Theologians: From Neoscholasticism to Nuptial Mysticism* (Oxford: Blackwell, 2007), 194–5, for important observations on how the idea has functioned in traditional and contemporary theology.

ings. We cannot say that all of God's commands can be tied precisely to the way we are created. In fact, we shall see in the next chapter of Genesis that he does give a command that does not seem to be tied to our nature. But for the most part God's law is a reflection of his creation. His commands are not usually arbitrary or simple tests of obedience. And the most important ones are not commands just to deal with a temporary situation. They are for our own good and the good of others, given to enable us to express, by how we act, the way in which we are created, and they enable us to accomplish the purpose for which we and the things around us were created.

This illustrates another important fact about God's creation. Genesis 1 could seem as if God simply does everything that needs to be done: he speaks the word and creation simply comes into existence. But Genesis 1 makes equally clear that there is more to it. The plants bring forth seeds that become more plants; the birds, fish, and other animals increase and multiply; the human beings do likewise. All his creatures take an active role in furthering the work of creation.

God brought into existence a set of creatures, a part of his creation, to represent him by ruling over that creation on his behalf. He made those creatures with an animal nature and so capable of reproducing so they could gradually *fill the earth*. And he made them capable of ruling over creation by bestowing on them his image and likeness. As the corporate son of God, the human race was to be God's viceroy in creation.

Presumably, God put the human race in such a position so that in a certain way creation could develop itself, since human beings were part of creation and could act as created beings, who could lead in the development of creation—although, of course, not without God's providential sustaining power. But he constituted them in such a way that they would not rule by their own arbitrary or selfish decision, but as his ministers, ruling according to true wisdom, the wisdom that God gives to those he made in his image and likeness to be partners with him in bringing creation to its full purpose.

Let us . . . There is another feature of the text on the creation of the human race that seems small, but that has been the source of much discussion. The passage starts off by saying, *Then God said, "Let us make man . . ."* This itself marks off the creation of the human race from the rest of creation as something of special importance. Instead of just commanding something to come to be, God addresses "us" and calls "us" to make man. This, however, raises the question: to whom is he referring when he says "us"?

There have been a number of proposals about the "us," both over the centuries and now in scholarly writings. None of these has received universal agreement, especially among modern scholars. One of the better proposals is that God is here addressing his heavenly court, made up of angels, the hosts of heaven. This has the advantage that the rest of the Bible has many references to such beings. It has, however, the difficulty that these beings have not been mentioned in Genesis 1 as either created or involved in creation. It would be strange to just refer to them as if readers—perhaps readers who are reading the Bible for the first time and start at the beginning—would understand that the members of his heavenly court were the "us." Moreover, they are never spoken of as involved in the work of creating human beings.

The Medieval theologian Thomas Aquinas, representing a common view, held that this opinion was "perverse."[10] He said this because most traditional Christian interpreters saw "us" as a reference to the Trinity. This view has the significant advantage, especially over understanding the reference being to the angels, that the "us" is involved in an act of creation, and the Hebrew verb for "create" (at least in the forms used in our passage) is only used of God. Moreover, after speaking of creating the human race in "our" image and likeness, the text speaks of the fact that the human race was created in the image of God. Such a phrasing has the consequence that the "us" was God. In other words, as Aquinas thought was important,

---

[10] Thomas Aquinas, *Summa Theologiae*, hereafter *ST*, I, 91, 4, ad 2. For one example of the main view among Christian teachers, see Ambrose of Milan, *De paradiso* (New York: Fathers of the Church Inc., 1961), 253.

the "us" has to be divine. As a result, the passage lets us know that there is some kind of plurality in God.

We do not have to see Aquinas' view as any more than a common Christian interpretation. We do not have to see it as the only one interpretation a Christian teacher can take and be a faithful Christian teacher. However, it is likely the leading interpretation in Christian tradition, deserving of special respect. More important for our purposes here, it shows the importance Christian teachers have placed upon the fact that human beings are created in the image and likeness *of God*.

God's good work. After the creation of the human race, God establishes the relationship of the human race (and of all animals) to the plant kingdom:

> And God said, "Behold, I have given you every plant yielding seed which is upon the face of all the earth, and every tree with seed in its fruit; you shall have them for food. And to every beast of the earth, and to every bird of the air, and to everything that creeps on the earth, everything that has the breath of life, I have given every green plant for food." And it was so. And God saw everything that he had made, and behold, it was very good. And there was evening and there was morning, a sixth day. (Gen 1:29–31)

This passage describes God's provision for human beings (and animals). God provides for human beings as a father provides for his children (and his domestic animals), in this case giving them food. In fact, several elements of God's fatherly care are shown in this chapter. He provides a place for the human race to live; he gives them work, the responsibility of ruling the material creation; he calls them to take his place of authority; and finally he gives them physical provision.

At the end of God's work of creation, which was accomplished in the six days, the text says, *And God saw everything that he had made, and behold, it was very good.* The results of all he did were very good, not only intrinsically worthwhile but also fulfilling the purpose he set out to accomplish.

The goodness of all creation is an important Christian (and Jewish) teaching, one that has often been a point of controversy. In the early church, one of the greatest heresies was Gnosticism, and a fundamental tenet of many forms of Gnosticism was that the created, material world was evil. However, the Christian teaching is that all creation, including the material world, was good when it first came from the hand of God. The origin of evil in human history first comes up in Genesis 3, and we will discuss that in the next chapter.

THE SEVENTH DAY

The first three verses of the second chapter of Genesis form a literary unit with the first chapter. They have the same style and also connect by content with the material in chapter 1. They describe the last day of the week of creation:

> Thus the heavens and the earth were finished, and all the host of them. And on the seventh day God [had] finished his work which he had done, and he rested on the seventh day from all his work which he had done. And [RSV: so] God blessed the seventh day and hallowed it, because on it God rested from all his work which he had done in creation.

The text then adds, as we have seen:

> These are the generations of the heavens and the earth when they were created.

The *generations of the heavens and the earth* seems to mean the elements—or elements in a series—that made up the heaven and earth.

Creation is here presented as having lasted a week. The seventh day comes at the very end of the section we are referring to as Genesis 1. When God created the world, he worked for six days until he finished his creation of heaven and earth, and then he rested (ceased) on the seventh *from all his work which he had done.*

But what did God do when he "rested" on the seventh day? With modern ideas of rest, we might be tempted to think he slept in to recover from his work week, or at least took a long nap, or perhaps headed for the beach. But a study of the use of "rest" in the Scriptures shows that it does not usually imply inactivity, much less engaging in entertainment or refreshing recreation. Therefore, here it most likely does not refer to complete inactivity but to a different sort of activity than "work" does.

"Rest," the translation of two different words in the Hebrew Bible that are rough synonyms (see Gen 2:2–3 and Ex 20:11 where the two Hebrew verbs are interchanged), is used in a somewhat different way than in ordinary English. As in English these words can be used for ceasing work, mainly for ceasing difficult or laborious work. In Isaiah 14:3, the Hebrew Bible describes a rest God would give his people as "rest from your pain and turmoil and the hard service with which you were made to serve."

"Rest" in Scripture is especially used to speak about the state in which an individual or people has become free from enemy attack, either because they have fended it off and so been victorious or because the enemy has lost the ability to be dangerous. For instance, Second Samuel 7:11 reads, *and I will give you rest from all your enemies.* Fighting, whether in attack or defense, was a very strenuous effort. To say, then, that God rested on the seventh day seems to imply that he was able to cease from what we would understand to be the difficult or burdensome work of bringing the creation he wanted into existence, perhaps with a certain amount of fighting.

"Rest," however, is commonly used in a broader way in the Bible. It is used, for instance, for the kind of rest that involves creating a space for celebration. Esther 9:17 describes the celebration after the deliverance of the Jewish people by saying, *And on the fourteenth day they rested and made that a day of feasting and gladness.* In other words, resting (from work or fighting) creates a space for feasting and gladness. Many overlook the important truth that the sabbath day in the Jewish calendar is a feast day—the primary feast day (Lev 23:1–3)—and so is not "a day off," but a day of celebrating the goodness of the Lord.

"Rest" can even be used as a synonym for delight (enjoying a good result that is finished). Proverbs 29:17 says, *Discipline your son, and he will give you rest; he will give delight to your heart.* In Genesis 1:31 we possibly see a similar indication as to what God did on the sabbath feast day. There it says, *And God saw everything that he had made, and behold, it was very good.* In other words, at the end of the sixth day, he had completed his work of creation and, so to speak, stepped back, looked at it, and was satisfied with what he had done. He then took a day to rejoice or to celebrate or to delight in what he had done. To say that God rested on the seventh day therefore seems to indicate that it was a time for God to contemplate and enjoy a successful accomplishment after striving, even fighting, to reach his goal.

Genesis 2:3 adds that God *blessed and hallowed* (made holy) the seventh day. This could mean that he set it apart for a special purpose. He made it a special day, the way he set apart feast days for special observance (cf. Neh 8:9, 11). We probably most naturally think that the phrase *blessed and hallowed* means he set the seventh day of our week apart so that we would observe it as a day of rest.

Certainly God has set apart the sabbath for a day of rest, for the Jews especially, but also for Christians. We find the commandment to do so in Exodus 20:8–11 when he requires it as part of the law. This commandment is linked to the fact that God rested on the seventh day:

> Remember the sabbath day, to keep it holy. . . . for in six days the LORD made heaven and earth, the sea, and all that is in them, and rested the seventh day; therefore the LORD blessed the sabbath day and hallowed it.

The reason for the observance provided in the text is the Lord's example, and this has been a very common reason given for God's action as described in the Genesis 1 account of creation. God, in this view, intended to give a good example of resting after a work week, and we therefore should follow that example.

But Genesis 2:1–3 does not contain a command to do likewise. It does not tell us to set apart one day in seven for a day of rest. That only comes after the Exodus, when God provided manna for his people in the wilderness (Ex 16:22–30) and then when he commanded them to observe *the seventh day as a sabbath to the Lord* (Ex 20:8–11). This likely indicates that the main significance of the hallowing of the seventh day of Genesis 1 has to do with God and not with us, even though later on it was to be taken as an example to imitate.

To *hallow* or to "make holy" or to "consecrate" or to "sanctify"— all possible translations of the Hebrew verb with slightly different connotations in English—can mean to set something created apart for God. Setting something apart makes it a holy thing, something that especially belongs to God. But something becomes holy not only when human beings set it apart for God, but also when he becomes spiritually present in it, as when he becomes present in a temple. In this case it is made holy by his presence, as the Lord, speaking of the door of the tent of meeting, said,

> There I will meet with the people of Israel, and it shall be sanctified by my glory; I will consecrate the tent of meeting and the altar. (Ex 29:43)

If this is an aspect of the meaning of hallowing the seventh day, the fact that God hallows the seventh day would indicate that he becomes especially present in it. This meaning would also go along with the fact that he *blesses* and *hallows* the seventh day. We can see in Exodus 33:14 that God's presence is a source of blessing and rest.

Making the day holy then is connected to God's rest on the seventh day. When someone or something spiritual becomes present in some place or thing, especially when they become present in an ongoing or abiding way, they are said, in the Hebrew idiom, to "rest" there. Such an idiom is commonly used of temples. When God established a tabernacle or temple, he then came to rest in it and dwell in it (Ex 40:34–35; 1 Kgs 8:10–11, Ps 132:5, 8), hallowing it, setting it apart as something that was especially his. In so doing he filled it with his presence and power, and from it came salvation and blessing for his people (Ps 132:13–18).

The fact that God rests (dwells) in a temple is significant for understanding the seventh day because in the Torah the old covenant teaching from God, the temple and the sabbath are connected. In Leviticus 19:30 it says, *You shall keep my sabbaths and reverence my sanctuary: I am the LORD,* linking the two as if they were similar holy things. The laws in Exodus about the building of the tabernacle are linked with laws about keeping the sabbath (Ex 31:12–18; 35:1–3), indicating that the two are related. The likely implication is that the sabbath is like a temple in time, that is, a time when God is especially present. It, then, is the time when the purpose of a temple is most fully achieved and the time when those who observe the sabbath receive blessing from God.

Finally, the description of the completion of the temple seems to contain allusions, or at least parallels, to the completion of the work of creation.[11] If that is so, then creation itself is intended to be a kind of temple, a place where God intends to dwell. This truth is expressed more directly in Isaiah 66:2, a passage that will be discussed in the next section. These considerations about God's seventh day rest might well indicate that the seventh day of creation is a time when God rests in his creation and makes it holy. These considerations raise the question: when did God begin to dwell in the temple of his creation?

The sabbath and the age to come. The most common interpretation of the seventh day given now by Christian teachers is as a description of God ceasing work and resting at the end of the first week of

---

[11] A summary of this understanding can be found in the technical note "Numerology, The Number Seven" on p. 419.

creation, a time in the distant past. From that is taken the understanding that we are to imitate him in observing the sabbath once a week, and he will bless our doing so. But there is another view of the seventh day in Genesis 1, namely, that it refers to something that has not yet happened: the age to come. God's work of creation is not yet completed, but will be in the age to come.

There is a special feature of the text that seems to point toward the seventh day as something that will happen in the future. All the days so far in Genesis 1 have been described by saying *there was evening and there was morning*, a limited period of time. But there is no evening and morning on the seventh day. Some traditional commentators have said that this indicates that the seventh day is an eternal day. In addition, the text, though similar, is also quite different from the texts of the previous days. It simply says three times, emphatically, without the usual features of the descriptions of the other days, that God ceased from his work, indicating that the work of creation was now all done.

Many have interpreted these things to mean that the seventh day is an image or symbol, perhaps even a prophecy, of the age to come. In such a view, we are in the sixth day.[12] And there is something yet to come, something that will last for all eternity: the day of God's rest.

This understanding seems to be stated in some places in the New Testament. Christ himself spoke about God "still working." He said, *My Father is working still, and I am working* (Jn 5:17). He said this after having healed the paralytic on the sabbath (and also having warned him not to sin again). In doing this he was imitating his

---

[12] Augustine of Hippo in *De Trinitate*, 4.4.7: "Sacred Scripture commends the perfection of the number six to us especially in this, that God completed his works in six days and made man in the image of God on the sixth day. And the Son of God came in the sixth age of the human race and was made the Son of man, in order to re-form us in the image of God. This is the age in which we are at present, whether a thousand years are assigned to each age or whether we settle upon memorable and notable personages as turning points of time. Thus the first age is found from Adam to Noah, the second from that time to Abraham, and after that . . . from Abraham to David, from David to the carrying away to Babylon, and from then to the birth of the Virgin. These three ages added to those make five. Hence the birth of the Lord inaugurated the sixth age, which is now in progress up to the hidden end of time."

heavenly Father who even on sabbaths now brings human beings into existence and judges them, as Jewish teachers of the time would admit. But, he said, *the hour is coming* (Jn 5:28–29) when there will be a last judgment. This seems to imply that after the Christ comes again and summons the dead from the tombs, God will then cease from his work—at some future time.

Likewise, Second Peter, after describing the Second Coming of Christ, which brings *the day of God*, the new heavens and new earth, concludes with a doxology to Christ,

> But grow in the grace and knowledge of our Lord and Savior Jesus Christ. To him be the glory both now and to the day of eternity. Amen. (3:18)

The *day of eternity* probably refers to the age to come that occurs after the redeeming work of Christ will be completed.

The view presented in these passages builds upon a prophecy in Isaiah. Isaiah 65:17–25 speaks of the new creation, the new heaven and the new earth to come, and then in Isaiah 66:1–2, the Lord, probably speaking of the dispensability of the earthly temple building, says:

> Heaven is my throne
>   and the earth is my footstool;
> what is the house which you would build for me,
>   and what is the place of my rest?
> All these things my hand has made,
>   and so all these things are mine, ...

In other words, the heaven and the earth are a temple in which the Lord rests, that is, a temple in which he dwells and from which he rules, seated on his throne. If the Lord speaks of heaven and earth (the cosmos) as a temple, then the seventh day of Genesis 1, the day of the completion of his creation, is the day on which he rests in the temple of the cosmos.

In such a view the seventh day then would be the day of the new creation in which God dwells or takes up his full residence in all of creation, having completed his work of bringing it into existence, filling it or ruling it, so that it is fully his and fully pleasing to him (Rev 21:1–8). It is the age to come when all of his creation is fully a holy place in a holy time, the day when he will be *everything to everyone* or *all in all* (1 Cor 15:28).

It is perhaps not common for Christians or Jews now to look at the seventh day of Genesis as a symbol or prophecy of the age to come. Many Jews, however, have done so. In the time of the second temple in Jerusalem, during the liturgy of the daily offering, "On the Sabbath they [the Levite singers] sang *A psalm: a Song for the Sabbath* Day, a Psalm, a song for the time that is to come, for the day that shall be all Sabbath and rest in life everlasting" (*Mishnah, Tamid* 7:4). Many of the Christian Fathers have done so as well. For example, Ephrem, the Syrian Church Father, said of the seventh day in Genesis, "It was given to them in order to depict by a temporal rest, which he gave to a temporal people, the mystery of the true rest, which will be given to the eternal people in the eternal world" (*Commentary On Genesis* 1.32–33.2).

We can therefore see the seventh day as the completion of God's work of all creation—when he does not just rest in a single place (a temple) or on a single day to be present to bless his people as he does in the old covenant (and in a different way in the new covenant). Rather, he rests or fills all of his creation, making it his, making it holy, and making it something that is completely according to his will, completely his kingdom, completely a realm of blessing. We will see the significance of this in chapter 11 of our study, when we look at the end of the book of Revelation.

Genesis 1 is a mysterious part of Scripture. It first of all speaks about the beginning, so it is not surprising to find it speaking in a hidden way of all of God's work of creation. But the end is the time when the beginning is fully established and complete, so it would not be surprising to find it speaking of the end as well. We might add that the first and the last together are a scriptural designation of

God as Creator of everything (e.g., Is 44:6; Rev 22:13), the one who begins all things and brings them to completion.

Moreover, as we have seen, the first chapter of Genesis is presented in the form of an orderly account. It is described as a week of seven days, and it is encoded with the number seven, the number of completeness or perfection.[13] The use of the number seven for the seventh day, then, indicates the complete and perfect order of creation and of its goodness in the way God has planned it and will complete it.

If the seventh day of creation refers to the age to come, then we can see Genesis 1 as the affirmation of God's good creative work. Whatever defects we may see now in his creation, God is not finished. When he is done, everything will be very good and his full intention will be accomplished. When Christ comes again and raises the dead, the human race will enter into a life that is life indeed. If we take this interpretation, we can see Genesis 1 as the summary of all of God's work and read the rest of the Scripture in the light of it.

There are, then, two understandings of the seventh day, one that sees it as the last day of the first week, the original creation; and the second that sees it as prophetic of the completion of all creation at the end. We do not, however, need to choose between the two understandings of the seventh day, especially if we note the significance of the sabbath day and the tabernacle/temple in this age. The sabbath and temple together in this age are the first fulfillment of the seventh day of creation. They are the feast time and holy place that are a step toward establishing what God was aiming for when he created material things. They were therefore ordained when the old

---

[13] There is also a pervasive numerology in the text that indicates we are being given a statement about the completeness (including, likely, the future completion) of the universe. In addition to the seven days that structure the account as a whole, there are seven Hebrew words in 1:1; 14 (7 x 2) in 1:2; and 35 (7 x 5) in 2:1–3. In Gen 1:1–2:3, God is mentioned 35 (7 x 5) times, earth 21 (7 x 3), heaven/firmament 21, and the phrases "it was so" and "it was good" 7 times. Seven is the number of completeness and probably also the number of divine action. It is coded into the Israelite festal calendar as well and into the account of the building of the tabernacle (see the technical note "Numerology" on p. 419). The coded numerology indicates that we are reading an account of the complete work of creation.

covenant was established on Sinai. They also, however, point toward and symbolize the completion of all creation at the end, when God will fully "rest" in this space–time world. A fuller understanding of that link will be presented in chapters 8 and 11.

Concluding comments. The first chapter of Genesis from its literary form appears to be a special work. It is highly structured, especially forming the whole around the number seven. It has strong regular features combined with variation that provides an orientation to the nature of the universe and of God's work. It is, moreover, placed at the beginning of the Torah (the Pentateuch) and therefore at the beginning of the whole Old Testament and of the whole of the Bible, the Holy Writings. It seems designed to be a statement about God's work as a perfect whole in the light of which everything else should be understood.

When we look at Genesis 1 as a whole, however, at least two things stand out. The first is that God is the Creator of the universe; he made everything by a word of command or by himself making particular things. That means that the beings the pagans worshipped—the sun, moon, stars, and the animals—are simply creatures of God. A main purpose of the Genesis account is summarized in Deuteronomy 4:15–20:

> "Therefore take good heed to yourselves. Since you saw no form on the day that the LORD spoke to you at Horeb out of the midst of the fire, beware lest you act corruptly by making a graven image for yourselves, in the form of any figure, the likeness of male or female, the likeness of any beast that is on the earth, the likeness of any winged bird that flies in the air, the likeness of anything that creeps on the ground, the likeness of any fish that is in the water under the earth. And beware lest you lift up your eyes to heaven, and when you see the sun and the moon and the stars, all the host of heaven, you be drawn away and worship them and serve them, things which the LORD your God has allotted to all

the peoples under the whole heaven. But the LORD has taken you, and brought you forth out of the iron furnace, out of Egypt, to be a people of his own possession, as at this day."

The second thing that stands out is that human beings are created in the image and likeness of God himself, and they are placed in the world to have dominion over all of material creation. They are not to worship and serve God's creatures. Rather, they are to develop creation, bringing it to the purpose for which God created it. As we will see in the next chapter, they were created to be the priests within the cosmic temple of this creation.

If we look at the New Testament references to Genesis 1, these are the main things that the New Testament picks out as well. The New Testament, however, adds an important truth: Creation happened in and through Christ by the Holy Spirit. The one true God is threefold, and the Son of God, the true image of God, took on human nature and began the human race anew, now re-created in the image of God, and he did so through the outpouring of the Holy Spirit. This, too, we will look at more fully.

CHAPTER TWO

GENESIS 2–4: PARADISE LOST

TEXT: GENESIS 2:4–4:26

Introduction to the chapter. When we read Genesis 1, we get an overview of God's creation of the cosmos. In the first six days, everything in the material universe is established to fulfill the role and work that God had in mind for it. Darkness still "exists" but it is held at bay. The sea still is capable of threatening the dry land, but it has been firmly put in its place. The cosmos is moving surely to become what God wants it to be. In the seventh day, God's work is completed. God's will is being done, and his work is good.

In Genesis 2 we see a similar presentation of part of God's work of creation. Adam, the newly–created son of God is placed in paradise with the prospect of being the one to bring God's creation to what it was meant to be. He should be able to develop and protect it, no doubt with his Father's help. We see nothing but hope for the future.

There is a problem with this picture that most readers of Genesis 1 and 2 intuitively realize. Our experience of the human race (and to be honest the rest of creation) is dissonant from this. The world around us does not seem to be made according to the will of God—unless God is not as powerful as Genesis 1 presents him, or unless he did not make everything "very good."

What we see in human history is flawed. Murder, cruelty, sexual disorder, greed, envy, and a long list of other disorders characterize human life—along, of course, with generosity, kindness, chastity, compassion, and other good human actions as well. The result, in short, is a mixed blessing. And the human race God made to develop the creation, although now having greater and greater technological mastery, does not seem to be clearly developing it toward a good end.

What went wrong? Why is the world in which we live the way it is? And where is God's guiding hand?

Genesis chapters 2–4, especially 3–4, present the root answer to these questions. The answer turns out to be disobedience to God, producing, to use the term much Christian theology has used, the Fall. Right after the description of creation comes the description of the Fall or, as some have expressed it, the Downfall. From early on the course of human life, perhaps even of all creation, has not been what God intended it to be. It is this that we will consider in this chapter.

The beginning of the human race. In Genesis 2, we read again about the Lord at work, but we get a somewhat different picture than the one in Genesis 1. We are still reading about *the day* (Gen 1:5)—*the day that the Lord God made the earth and the heavens* (Gen 2:4). In the second half of the sixth day, we are told that God himself *made man* (Gen 1:26). Genesis 2:7 builds on this verse by expanding on how God made the human race:

> then the LORD God formed man of dust from the ground, and breathed into his nostrils the breath of life; and man became a living being.

In Genesis 2 we see the Lord God on the earth he had created. We see him having personally entered into his creation. We see him at work as if he were part of it, or at least as if he were an agent within it. We see him taking some earth, *dust* [RSV], perhaps mud from a clay soil, and forming it until it comes out the way he wants it. We see him making it into a material thing that is an image of himself.[1]

---

[1] For the methodological discussion of God being described as if he were human, see "5. Anthropomorphism" (p. 475).

Then we see him personally breathing into the nostrils of that image, as if he were giving artificial resuscitation. This was, however, not resuscitation, but creation. *The man* came to life and *became a living being*. The man was earthly, dust or mud that had become flesh and blood, but he had life in him that came from God, and so he was also heavenly. He was created to rule the earth, the material creation, on behalf of his Creator.

The Lord God understood how created things functioned because he had designed and formed everything. He knew living things could not exist on their own. They needed an environment that was fitted to them. The creation of man, however, had occurred in an inhospitable environment:

> In the day that the LORD God made the earth and the heavens, when no plant of the field was yet in the earth and no herb of the field had yet sprung up—for the LORD God had not caused it to rain upon the earth, and there was no man to till the ground; but a mist went up from the earth and watered the whole face of the ground—then the LORD God formed man of dust from the ground, and breathed into his nostrils the breath of life; and man became a living being. (Gen 2:4–7)

There are various views, traditional and modern, of the meaning of verses 5 and 6 and how they relate to what is said in Genesis 1.[2] Perhaps the most common understanding is that these verses describe the state of affairs on the sixth day. At least it seems clear that the account is setting the stage by describing the earth before the human race and paradise began, that is, in a wild state, a state in which human beings cannot live well. Possibly the phrase *of the field* means that there was no tilled or planted ground. One view is that these verses might be based on a description of the marshy ground

---

[2] For the methodological discussion of the relationship of Genesis 1 and 2 with special attention to the views of source critics, see "4. Genesis 1, Genesis 2, and Source Criticism" (p. 467).

around the head of the Persian Gulf in ancient Mesopotamia—the *land* [RSV: the earth] to which the account is referring, a traditional candidate for the location of the garden of Eden—before it had been drained and turned into agricultural fields.

Once again, the Lord God took a personal hand in the work and provided what was needed:

> And the LORD God planted a garden in Eden, in the east; and there he put the man whom he had formed. And out of the ground the LORD God made to grow every tree that is pleasant to the sight and good for food, the tree of life also in the midst of the garden, and the tree of the knowledge of good and evil. (Gen 2:8–9)

The Lord God made in Eden a garden or a *paradise*, the anglicized version of the Greek translation of the Hebrew word for the garden. He made it a good and pleasant home for the son he had created for himself. In so doing, he gave him what the Scripture later describes as an inheritance, that is, a place where he could live with land that would provide for his needs. The garden God planted was a place that would make it possible for human beings to live well, which would be an indication that they were living in fulfillment of what they had been made for.

The Lord God also gave his human son work to do, so that he could contribute something:

> The LORD God took the man and put him in the garden of Eden to work it and guard it [RSV: to till it and keep it]. (Gen 2:15)

The ability to engage in work and make a contribution was an aspect of being in the image of God the creator and a source of dignity through partnership in the work of creation. Turning the ground into fruitful fields required people *to work the ground* (Gen 2:5, 15). Set before the newly created human being was the task of bringing the human race into existence and gradually extending paradise, eventually making the whole earth into a paradise, worked and also guarded by human beings.

We have already adverted to the fact that human life as we experience it is less than perfect. We should also advert to the fact that the rest of creation is in the same condition. There is a common discussion that surfaces from time to time among Christians (and no doubt others) that begins with the question, "Why did God make X?" (fill in the blank with mosquitos, horseflies, bubonic plague bacteria, and whatever else). Why did he?

Perhaps he did not do so. Perhaps these things were originally in his intention more obviously perfect. Perhaps he never intended the things he made to prey upon one another. Perhaps this is all the work of Satan and demons who perverted God's perfect creation. "An enemy has done this" (Mt 13:28). But that answer just pushes the question a step further back. Why did God let an enemy in and let the enemy have his way with all of creation?

There is no one clearly accepted answer to this question that Christian teachers have presented and now present. But there is a background understanding that we can give. First, God's creation (and not just the human part of it) is not what he intends. The goal, to use the words of the prophecy in Isaiah 11:46–7, is for *the wolf to dwell with the lamb*. And his plan was to create someone (Adam, the Human) who could perfect his creation by ordering it and developing it in a good way, eliminating its defects.

We can, in fact, see that human beings have an inborn capacity to re-order creation. We can see it, for instance, in the fact that they have eliminated the deadly killer smallpox (declared by the World Health Organization in 1980 as completely eliminated). Could they not therefore eventually radically change the way non-human creation functions? The answer is perhaps yes, making disease, parasites, tornadoes things of the past.

Yet, we notice something else. In the midst of making what we would regard as improvements, we also see humans making things worse (e.g., "ecological disasters") or even watching their improvements fall back (as malaria seemed largely eliminated, but then recurred). In short, from God's point of view, the issue is with the being God created in his image and likeness, and why that being both does and fails to do *at the very same time* what God might have wanted.

The creation of the garden, fresh from the hand of God, seemed perfect for the flourishing of the human race. It contained an abundance of food and other necessities. It showed signs that it could be extended to accommodate as many human beings as there were. It seemed thoroughly secure with God watching over it.

But there is more to the story. The newly created human being not only needed to work but also to *guard the garden*.[3] Something from the outside could apparently mar the new creation.

Moreover, God put one item, *the tree of the knowledge of good and evil*, off bounds. God, like a good parent, foresaw a potential problem and sought to forestall it by commanding his obedient but young son not to eat of the fruit of that tree—and attached a severe warning.

> And the LORD God commanded the man, saying, "You may freely eat of every tree of the garden; but of the tree of the knowledge of good and evil you shall not eat, for in the day that you eat of it you shall die." (Gen 2:16–17)

Something apparently could go wrong. Very wrong.

THE HUMAN IN PARADISE

The holiness of paradise. At the end of the first section of Genesis 2 (verse 17) we find the first human being in paradise. The Old Testament contains another account of the creation and life of the first human being, one often overlooked because it occurs in a diffi-

---

[3] Guarding of the temple was a priestly role in the old covenant. See Num 1:53; 3:7–8, 10, 32; 8:25–26; 18:3–7; 1 Sam 7:1; 2 Kings 12:9; 2 Chron 34:9; Ezek 44:14–16.

cult passage—Ezekiel 28:11–18—sometimes known as the Lament on the King of Tyre. In that passage, the fall of the king of Tyre is presented as being similar to the Fall of Adam. Paradise there is described as being *the garden of God*, built on a *holy mountain* and protected by a *guardian cherub*, and the king is described as wearing jewel-studded priestly garments.

From this description we can see that paradise was a temple, a place where Adam had access to God's presence the way a priest in a temple would. Genesis 3 confirms this understanding by speaking of paradise as a place where God walked and talked with Adam and later Eve. It also speaks of paradise as a place from which Adam, when he profaned himself by his disobedience, was driven; a place with access on the east side, which was the side of the entrance to the Jerusalem temple, another detail that likely indicates the nature of paradise as a temple. In addition it was defended by the cherubim who were responsible for guarding the holy presence of God. Paradise was a place in which God was present (Gen 4:16). This same understanding of paradise can be found in the last chapters of Revelation. The city of God, which is a paradise (Rev 21:22), is presented as a temple on a holy mountain in which God and his people commune together and where none who have profaned themselves by practicing evil without having repented of it are allowed (Rev 21:8, 27; 22:14–25).

In one way, God is present everywhere, omnipresent. He keeps everything in existence. But in another way, he is only present from time to time and from place to place. When the Scriptures in later passages speak of God's special presence, they often use the Hebrew word for *face*. When we worship him in the temple, we come *before his face* (RSV: before him; e.g., Ps 22:27). In other words, when God becomes present to us, he turns to us in such a way that we know that he is looking at us. He becomes personally present to us.

We could walk into a room where a friend of ours is, who did not notice us, and he would be physically present to us. If he looked up and saw us, he would also be personally present to us. God's presence to us is similar.

God is not, however, personally present to us except when he chooses to be. When he does not choose to be, it might seem that he was absent if we did not realize that all that we are and all we can do depend on him and that he is everywhere and knows everything. In the sense of his personal presence, coming "before his face," however, we are not with him until he becomes present to us. To use another scriptural expression, he *draws near* to us (Ps 69:18).

When God enters into a good relationship with us, a communion with us, he allows us to also *draw near* to him (Is 48:16). We are allowed to interact with him. Genesis 3:8 describes God as walking in the garden and talking in a fatherly and familiar way with Adam and Eve. When first created, human beings had regular access to the presence of God, perhaps like young children or adolescents with their father.

Adam's garments in Ezekiel's depiction of humanity at the beginning (Ezek 28:13) have a significance that we might miss. We tend to see clothing as an external protection or adornment. In the Scripture, clothing is more significant. If properly used, it is understood to be an outer manifestation of a certain status or a certain character. Kings, for instance, wore special garments, robes of state, whenever they held court, and the ministers who served them did as well, so that those who entered knew they had come to a solemn event and an encounter with very important people.

In the passage from Colossians we looked at in the previous chapter (3:9–14), we saw Paul exhort the Christians to "put on" or "clothe themselves" in good character traits that were manifestations of the image of God. A character trait is visible in behavior, but also rooted in the inner person. Those who meet Christians should know, by the way Christians receive them and by their character-clothing, that they are being received by the sons and daughters of God. The clothing spoken about in the Colossians text does not just refer to something external, but also refers to an inner character disposition that is manifested externally.

The priests in the temple wore different clothing depending on how they would minister. Their clothing corresponded to the degree of holiness of each part of the temple. The high priest, when he ministered within the tabernacle or temple, wore clothing that had the kind of jewels that Adam was described as having in Ezekiel 28 (see Ex 28:17–20; 39:10–13). Adam was to be the high priest of creation with a special access to God, and his covering was a manifestation of the image of God in him.

Some later passages in Scripture, as well as rabbinic writings and works of Christian Fathers (e.g., Ps 8:6; *Genesis Rabbah* 20:12; John Chrysostom, *Homilies on Genesis 16.14*), speak of Adam as being covered or clothed in glory, the glory that manifested the good inward nature and character he was created with, an inner power that allowed him to live in a good way, in holiness. Like God, in whose image he was, he was *clothed with honor and majesty, [having] covered himself with light as with a garment* (Ps 104:1–2). In such a view, the first human beings who were without the kind of clothing we wear did not have to be ashamed of their nakedness, because their glory, due to their participation in God's nature (image), covered them in light and therefore in honor and not shame.[4]

The picture we get of Adam and of paradise from Ezekiel 28 and from Genesis 3 corresponds to that of Genesis 1. God made creation to be a temple to his glory. But that creation had to develop into such a temple. So he began by creating paradise as a temple, an initial version of what the earth and eventually all material creation was to become. And he created Adam as the priest of that creation. As a priest he was to be a minister to the king of the universe, with the responsibility to bring more and more of creation into the holy state of paradise.

There has been much discussion by Christian teachers about human nature as God originally created it, some holding that Adam was created with almost superhuman perfection, others that he was created as a child, needing to grow up into maturity (an understanding partially based on Genesis 2:25). For our purposes, we only need to see that Adam and Eve were created different from us in that

---

4 For a fuller treatment of the glory of the first human beings had, see *Redeemer*, chap. 1 "What God Wanted."

they had an inner capacity that would allow them to actually live the way God wanted the human race to live. The various ways of speaking about the newly created Adam all point to this conclusion. He was in the image and likeness of God. He had priestly garments. He was filled and covered with glory.

This does not mean that Adam and Eve had reached the full perfection human beings could attain. As we will see, the presence of the two trees in the garden probably indicated that God intended to develop their nature. But the first human beings had some clear advantages over us. They were able to live free from the futility and frustration so common in our lives, which seems to be rooted in an interior weakness that there is no indication they shared.

The picture of the first human being in the Lament on the King of Tyre makes more explicit the background to the severity of God's warning to Adam and the fate that would befall him if he ignored that warning. Paradise was not just a nursery or a playground, but a temple. It was a place that belonged to God and existed for his glory. Adam was not just a son, but also was created to be a high priest whose responsibility included the care of the temple and the guarding of its holiness. God is a loving Father, but also the holy Lord of all, whose holiness cannot be profaned, especially by disobedience, without severe consequences. As the king of Tyre was *cast as a profane thing from the mountain of God* because of his *iniquity* (Ezek 28:16), so could Adam be.[5]

The command. These truths provide perspective on the instruction God gives the first human being. He opens the paradise to him freely, but he also prohibits him from eating of the tree of the knowledge of good and evil. This was an expression of his fatherly care. God was in so many words saying, "Don't play with fire." He was instruct-

---

[5] For an exposition of this view from the works of Ephrem the Syrian, see Gary A. Anderson, *The Genesis of Perfection: Adam and Eve in Jewish and Christian Imagination* (Louisville: Westminster John Knox, 2001), 56–57. For a fuller exposition of Ephrem's understanding of paradise, see Sebastian Brock's introduction to St. Ephrem the Syrian, *Hymns on Paradise* (Crestwood, NY: St. Vladimir's Seminary Press, 1990), 49–57, which contains a summary of early Christian views on paradise.

ing his newly created son how to live, how to conduct himself, in the first years of his life in order to arrive at the place God intended for him, and arrive safely.

There are two main interpretations given by commentators, both ancient and modern, of *the tree of the knowledge of good and evil*. The first interpretation holds that the tree simply represents wisdom, knowledge of good and evil, or perhaps more broadly good and bad. God prohibited the eating of the fruit of the tree because Adam and Eve were not yet ready for it.

The second interpretation holds that the tree is named for its consequences. If Adam and Eve disobey and eat of the tree, they will experience evil for the first time and so also experience the meaning of goodness by its loss. A variety of this interpretation holds the view that the tree was put in the garden simply to be a test of obedience, with the consequence of evil for disobedience.

The first main interpretation is more likely the right one. First, the knowledge of good and evil is interpreted throughout the account (as we can see in verse 3:6) as that which makes one wise. There is no necessary implication in the account that the tree gives evil knowledge or produces intrinsically evil consequences. It simply says that human beings get wisdom from eating of this tree. Moreover, further on in Scripture, the knowledge of good and evil or good and bad is seen in the same light. Someone who has the knowledge of good and evil is a wise person, like an angel or a man who is mature (Is 7:15; 2 Sam 14:17; 1 Kings 3:9; Heb 5:14).

This provokes the question, "What is wrong with that? Why should human beings not eat of the tree of knowledge of good and evil if it is intrinsically good?" It is the very question that the serpent tried to get Eve to ask, although she knew the most important answer: "God said that we should not." Why God forbade them to eat from the fruit of the tree, however, is not obvious from the account.

Most likely God had his way of giving the man and woman the knowledge of good and evil that they needed. He knew that knowledge could be dangerous and that human beings need some level of maturity to handle higher levels of wisdom. He would let them eat of the fruit of the tree when they were ready, but not until then. In the meantime, he would instruct them.

God's prohibition of eating the fruit was like the action of a parent who forbids a child to cross the street, but not because there is anything intrinsically wrong with crossing the street. In fact, the parent wants to teach the child how to do that as soon as safely possible. The first truth the child needs to learn, however, and that the first human beings needed to know, is the importance of obedience, because "the fear of the Lord is the beginning of wisdom" (Prov 1:7). They could acquire wisdom safely only through obeying God's instructions as they learned.

There was also the tree of life in the garden. We can see later on in the account that if Adam and Eve ate of the tree of life, they would *live forever* (Gen 3:22). The fruit of the tree would give a special kind of life, a higher life, a life that could not be destroyed by death. Adam and Eve had a natural life, but they could have had a spiritual life that would be eternal. Many Christian Fathers identified this with the life Christ came to give us.

Later on, we find that Adam and Eve had not eaten of the tree of life. Why was that? Various answers have been given, but perhaps the best was given by the Christian teachers who saw a link between the tree of the knowledge of good and evil and the tree of life. This link is already spoken about in the Old Testament. The book of Proverbs says that wisdom "is a tree of life to those who lay hold of her" (Prov 3:18), and it has wisdom say "He who finds me finds life" (Prov 8:35). The book of Sirach seems to teach as much when it says, "The knowledge of the Lord's commandments is life-giving discipline, and those who do what is pleasing to him enjoy the fruit of the tree of immortality" (Sir 19:19). Because they had not yet eaten of the tree of the knowledge of good and evil and because they had not yet developed a tested obedience, they were not allowed to eat of the tree of life.[6]

---

[6] An exposition of this view can be found in the second-century Christian writing, the *Epistle of Diognetus*, "Indeed, there is a deep meaning in the passage of Scripture which tells how God in the beginning planted a tree of knowledge and a tree of life

Some of the early Christian Fathers, like Ephrem the Syrian (for instance, *Hymns on Paradise*, III, 13–17), explained the link between the two trees in terms of paradise being a temple. The tree of life was in the holy of holies and was itself all holy. The tree of the knowledge of good and evil was also holy, but was like the veil of the temple. It protected the tree of life from those who were not fit to partake of it. Behind this is the truth that wisdom leads to life, and those without enough wisdom are not yet ready to receive a life they cannot handle, especially a life that involves a participation in the divine life of God himself.

This understanding gives us a further perspective on the command God gave to Adam. God said that *in the day that you eat of [the tree of the knowledge of good and evil] you shall die.* This could mean that God would immediately put Adam to death. Eating of the fruit of the tree would work the way touching a live wire would; namely, instant execution by electrocution. But the phrase about dying could be translated *you will be doomed to die.* The passage in Ezekiel 28 points the same way: Adam would be cast from paradise because he had profaned it. In other words, the command of God is not a warning of instant physical death, but of a spiritual death that would come as a consequence of what had been done, a death that would come from being deprived of paradise, the place of true life, and from the hope of eating of the tree that would give immortal life—therefore also an eventual (and unnecessary) physical death. This would involve the positive consequence of a chance for repentance before death came to pass.

But what about paradise itself? Could we find it somewhere on

---

in the midst of paradise, to show that life is attained through knowledge. . . . And so the two trees were planted close together" (sec. 12). A similar statement of this can be found in Ephrem the Syrian, *The Hymns on Paradise*, XII, 15: "Two trees did God place in paradise, the tree of life and that of wisdom, a pair of blessed fountains, source of every good; by means of this glorious pair the human person can become the likeness of God, endowed with immortal life and wisdom that does not err." For an exposition of Ephrem's full views on the two trees, see Brock's introduction to *The Hymns on Paradise*, 57–62, which also discusses Ephrem's understanding, shared with other early Christian writers, that the tree of life was fulfilled in Christ.

earth? We know we cannot. Certainly now when human beings have explored the whole earth, we know it is nowhere to be found. God removed it from the earth, if it ever was simply *on* the earth. Perhaps this was part of his mercy in order to remove us from temptation.

Commonly it has been held that paradise was removed into heaven, and it has not been accessible to human beings now living on the earth, although certain human beings have been allowed to enter it at times (cf. 2 Cor 12:2–4). Christ's death and Resurrection, however, reopened paradise to the human race. We will be able to enter it fully in the age to come, as we can see in the book of Revelation.

We might be able to summarize the meaning of paradise by saying that it is the place and state where human beings live in the holy relationship with God that he intended when he created them. Before the Fall, it was in some way on the earth, although it did not yet convey the fullness of what God ultimately intended for the human race. As a result of the Fall, it was removed from earth and human beings no longer have had regular access to it. At the end of time, it will be reunited to earth; in fact, it will be co-extensive with the whole earth, and bestow the true life for which human beings were made (Rev 22:2).

We should add that since paradise is the life-giving place that is the temple of God, human beings have been granted certain foretastes of it. The old covenant temple was one. The new covenant temple of the Holy Spirit is another. These we will look at in the next chapters. But the fullness of paradise will not become available for the human race until the age to come.

Genesis 2 presents us with a picture of the first man in the place God made for him. It contains elements that are described but not explained, especially the meaning of the two trees and the reason for the initial command. It looks to a future development for the human race and for the rest of creation. Some of the elements become clearer in the early Genesis chapters that follow. Only in the course of the rest of the Old Testament and in the New Testament does the whole story become clear.

THE FIRST WOMAN

The next section of Genesis 2 contains the account of the creation of the first woman.[7]

> Then the LORD God said: "It is not good that the man should be alone; I will make him a helper fit for him." So out of the ground the LORD God formed every beast of the field and every bird of the air, and brought them to the man to see what he would call them; and whatever the man called every living creature, that was its name. The man gave names to all cattle, and to the birds of the air, and to every beast of the field; but for the man there was not found a helper fit for him. So the LORD God caused a deep sleep to fall upon the man, and while he slept took one of his ribs and closed up its place with flesh; and the rib which the LORD God had taken from the man he made into a woman and brought her to the man. Then the man said,
>
> > "This at last is bone of my bones
> >   and flesh of my flesh;
> > she shall be called Woman,
> >   because she was taken out of Man."
>
> Therefore a man leaves his father and his mother and cleaves to his woman [RSV: wife], and they become one flesh. And the man and his woman [RSV: wife] were both naked, and were not ashamed. (Gen 2:18–25)

As we have seen, God's plan was to have a human race that would fill the earth and transform it into a paradise. In this opening line of Genesis 2:18–25, God recognizes a defect in what he has done so far. He has indeed created a human being who should be able to

---

[7] For a fuller exposition of the material in this section, with scholarly references, see Clark, *MWC*, chap. 2.

fulfill the task set before him, but so far he has not created any more than one, and one would not be enough. It was not good for Adam to be all by himself, because he would not be able to fulfill the purpose for which he had been created. It would take a whole race.

God then brought animals before Adam *to see what he would call him*. This expresses human rule of the animal kingdom, or at least the part of the animal kingdom that could become part of his domestic household. Naming in this sense is a ruling function. A name could be individual (Fido) or general (a dog). Here Adam probably is giving a general name to differing species of living creatures and that name is based on his understanding of how they can and should function and so of their place in the order of things.

There was a further purpose to Adam's inspection of the animals. No helper fit for Adam was found. No doubt many if not all of the animals brought before Adam could be of help in various ways: as oxen, sheep, dogs and others could certainly be. But none was fit for what Adam needed. There was no partner of "his own kind" with whom he could "multiply and fill the earth" (Gen 1:28).

God then took one more step to create the human race, and made a woman from Adam himself. When he saw her, Adam recognized that she was what was needed. She was of the same species he was, of a different sex, and together they could have children. Whatever she was like in various respects, she was a human being, unlike the animals, but like him. And she was human because she was taken from him.

Then follows the saying, *Therefore a man leaves his father and his mother and cleaves to his woman* [RSV: wife] *and they become one flesh* (Gen 2:24). This is obviously not about Adam himself, because he had no father and mother. Rather it is about man and woman and marriage. Some have held that this is a comment by the author of the text, giving the meaning of the creation of the woman. Some have held that this was a prophecy about the place of the male-female relationship in human life. Either way, it is a foundational statement about marriage.

The word *cleave* is one that is used a number of times in the

Old Testament. Sometimes the word is translated "cling," but this translation now easily creates a misleading view of the husband-wife relationship. Better English translations are "join oneself to" or "adhere," so the man joins himself to his woman. The Hebrew word expresses a committed personal relationship; in this case, a covenant relationship (Mal 2:13). To say that the man cleaves or joins himself to or adheres to his woman means the man enters into a committed personal relationship with her. The Hebrew word for the man's partner is literally "woman" and is the normal Hebrew word for wife, so his wife is "his woman" and he is "her man." They belong together as male and female.

In the husband-wife relationship, the two *become one flesh*. In the New Testament, "becoming one flesh" with a woman is used to describe having a sexual relationship with her (see 1 Cor 6:16). The phrase was understood in this way among Jewish teachers, as rabbinic sources also indicate. Some modern writers understand it as "one person," but the phrase more likely indicates what we sometimes refer to as the result of the consummation of marriage, that is, the completing of the establishment of the husband-wife relationship by physical (sexual) union. Although it does not always establish a long-term family relationship when there is no binding commitment, sexual intercourse is an integral part of establishing a family relationship between a man and woman.

In verse 2:18 God had said, *it is not good that the man should be alone*. The solution to the aloneness was not only the creation of a woman, but the beginning of a family that could be produced through the creation of a woman. The aloneness is not overcome by having one constant companion, but by having the man and the woman together bring into existence a community of people, a race. The woman, of course, would be a special companion for her husband, but God seems to be mainly concerned here about the lack of a community and his intention to establish the human race. The husband and wife needed to be able to have children to achieve that purpose. For that reason, as we have seen, when God created the human race, he gave them the command to *be fruitful and multiply* (Gen 1:28).

When it says God created *a helper fit for* the first human being, *helper* probably means something practical, rather than primarily emotional, as people today might be inclined to interpret it. In fact, Scripture presents a practical view of the husband-wife relationship (Prov 31:10–31). The husband and wife lived together, had children together, and shared a household life, often with other relatives. There was an economic dimension to it—keeping flocks, running a farm, or carrying on some kind of business. The wife did part of the work, a different part than the man did. She especially managed the home (cf. 1 Tim 5:14), while his responsibilities were more outside the home and caring for the family as a whole. No doubt it was a personal support for him to have her, but that is not likely the point of the passage. The point, more likely, was that the man and woman were to be partners in forming a family and ultimately a race, as the rest of the text makes clear.

When Genesis 2 indicates that the woman was created as a helper fit for the man or when Paul in 1 Corinthians 11:8–9 commenting on this passage says that the woman was created for man, this does not mean that the first woman was simply created to be an instrument for the first man's welfare or personal fulfillment. One of the main points of the passage is that the woman is a human being like the man and that she too was created in the image and likeness of God (Gen 1:27). She too was to share in the dominion of the human race over creation, bringing God's creation to fulfill its purpose.

Rather, the first man and the first woman, Adam and Eve, were to be partners in forming a family and ultimately a race. The man was the head of the family and had an ordering role in the family, and so had an overall responsibility for the family and its welfare. The woman was his partner in making family life. Moreover, she did not exist solely to do whatever he told her, but she had her own role as the wife and mother, and that included a responsibility for the management of the household. The roles of men and women are a very controversial area nowadays, and it cannot be treated adequately in a book like this whose focus is elsewhere. But Genesis puts before us the importance of family in the human race and the importance of the human race being created *male and female* with their complementary roles.[8]

The stage is now set. Adam and Eve, husband and wife, are together in paradise, beginning their newly created life. God has provided for the man what he needs to fulfill the task he has given him. The central drama of the passage is about to begin.

DISOBEDIENCE

The act of disobedience. Following on the creation of woman comes the central event or turning point of our passage, the Fall of the human race (Gen 3:1–7):

> Now the serpent was more cunning [RSV: subtle] than any other wild creature that the LORD God had made. He said to the woman, "Did God say, 'You shall not eat of any tree of the garden'?" And the woman said to the serpent, "We may eat of the fruits of the trees of the garden; but God said, 'You shall not eat of the fruit of the tree which is in the midst of the garden; neither shall you touch it, lest you die.'" But the serpent said to the woman, "You will not die. For God knows that when you eat of it your eyes will be opened, and you will be like God, knowing good and evil." So when the woman saw that the tree was good for food, and that it was a delight to the eyes, and that the tree was to be desired to make one wise, she took of its fruit and ate; and she also gave some to her husband, and he ate. Then the eyes of both were opened, and they knew that they were naked; and they sewed fig leaves together and made themselves aprons.

The account in Genesis 3:1–7 is about a serpent and a woman and a man. At the very least the serpent is a very unusual serpent,

---

[8] A fuller description of the scriptural view of the roles of husband and wife can be found in Clark, *MWC*, chap. 3.

able to speak, and in fact to be persuasive. But what he says is ominous. He seeks to persuade Eve, and through her Adam, the guardian of the garden, to distrust God and as a result to disobey him. We discover here that God's creation of the human race in paradise is not secured against all danger. God's provision for protecting paradise was the vigilance of the man he put in charge of it, and this is now at issue.

Later on in Scripture the serpent is identified as Satan or at least being the one through whom Satan spoke (Rev 12:9; see also Wis 2:24). Moreover, Satan is identified as a heavenly being whose fall and opposition to God must have occurred before his appearance in Genesis 3. Satan entered into the serpent, and it is Satan in the body of a serpent who had the discussion with the woman. Outside of the order of God's creation there was darkness and the abyss, and outside of the earth were the seas with the potential for destruction. In addition, we are now seeing the first appearance of a being who can command destructive force to do evil, although he does not begin by using force but rather by using persuasion and deception.

The serpent asked the woman, *Did God say, "You shall not eat of any tree of the garden"*? The answer she gave was, "No, God did not say that. He said we could eat of all of the trees except for the tree of the knowledge of good and evil, and we should not even touch that one." It is clear from her discussion with the serpent that she knows the command even though she probably was not there when it was first given. She is not blindly ignorant of what is going on. She gives the serpent the right response by explaining God's decree.

But the serpent said to the woman, "You will not die. For God knows that when you eat of it your eyes will be opened, and you will be like God, knowing good and evil." Satan said to her in so many words, "You cannot trust God. He is trying to keep you in a subservient position. He does not want you to eat from this tree because this is the tree that gives wisdom, and when you get that wisdom you will be like him and he can no longer treat you as children." It is a line of thought common nowadays and not just nowadays: "You should not be kept as children, but should have autonomy and independence."

The woman then accepted what Satan said, and the text describes the consequence by saying, *So when the woman saw that the tree was good for food, and that it was a delight to the eyes, and that the tree was to be desired to make one wise, she took of its fruit and ate; she also gave some to her husband, and he ate.* In describing the woman's eating of the fruit, the tree is described here not only as a tree that gives knowledge, but knowledge of good and evil, that is, the kind of knowledge that would make one wise.

The woman ate the fruit because she desired to be like God, because she desired to have a position that was not yet given to her by God. She transgressed the commandment in order to get wisdom that she believed would place her in a higher position. Though there was an element of sensual pleasure involved, the Fall was fundamentally and most importantly an act of pride, that is, an act of self-exaltation, an act of reaching for a position not given by God. The woman was reaching for something good in itself (wisdom), but she reached for it in order to have a higher position, one that was either higher than God intended her to have or at least higher than God was ready to give her at that point.

Eve took the fruit and ate, and then gave some to her husband, and he ate also. Eve was the first to eat, but she immediately involved her husband. Rather than exercise the right kind of authority and responsibility in this situation, he yielded to his wife and ate. This, too, is a common human pattern.[9]

The consequences of disobedience. After the disobedience of Adam and Eve, the account in Genesis presents the encounter they had with God:

> And they heard the sound of the LORD God walking in the garden in the cool of the day, and the man and his wife hid themselves from the presence of the LORD God among the trees of the garden. But the LORD God called to the man,

---

[9]   For a fuller exposition of the nature of the disobedience of Adam and Eve, see the section "The 'Model' Sin" in *Redeemer*, 42–59.

and said to him, "Where are you?" And he said, "I heard the sound of you in the garden, and I was afraid, because I was naked; and I hid myself." He said, "Who told you that you were naked? Have you eaten of the tree of which I commanded you not to eat?" The man said, "The woman whom you gave to be with me, she gave me fruit of the tree, and I ate." Then the LORD God said to the woman, "What is this that you have done?" The woman said, "The serpent beguiled me, and I ate." (Gen 3:8–13)

This scene takes place in the garden, because as we have seen the garden is the place where the Lord God was present and where there was personal interaction (fellowship, communion) between God and human beings. When God came to the first human beings in the garden, he recognized that they had some kind of knowledge that he had not given them. In response to God's questioning, Adam puts the blame on Eve—and on God, for it was God who gave him this woman as a companion. In turn Eve puts the blame on the serpent for persuading her. Neither Adam nor Eve accepts responsibility for their disobedience, even when being confronted by their heavenly Father and being given a chance to repent. Rather, they seek to put the blame on someone or something outside of themselves. This too is a common human pattern.

After Adam and Eve were caught in their disobedience, God stated some of the bad consequences. He began with the serpent, the originating cause of the trouble.

The LORD God said to the serpent,
   "Because you have done this,
      cursed are you above all cattle,
      and above all wild animals;
   upon your belly you shall go,
      and dust you shall eat
      all the days of your life.
   I will put enmity between you and the woman,

> and between your seed and her seed;
>   he shall bruise your head,
>   and you shall bruise his heel." (Gen 3:14–15) [10]

First the serpent was condemned to crawl upon the ground. Then there is a statement that there would be a conflict between the serpent and a human being, a conflict in which the serpent inflicts damage, but in which the human being triumphs. In the New Testament (Rom 16:19–20) and subsequent Christian teaching, the second part of this pronouncement is understood to refer to an enmity between the human race and Satan, eventually resulting in Satan's defeat by Christ.

Many Christian Fathers understood this to be the first annunciation or preaching of the Gospel (the *"proto-evangelium"*). God was foretelling, obscurely, that Satan would bruise Christ's heel in the crucifixion, and Christ would destroy the power of Satan. In other words, Satan had defeated the first human beings by causing them to sin and so bring upon themselves the consequences of sin. God, however, promised redemption—that he would rescue the human race through one of the descendants of Eve.

God then turned from the serpent to the woman and then to the man, and he predicted the consequences that would follow for them.

> To the woman he said,
> "I will greatly multiply your pain in childbearing;
>   in pain you shall bring forth children,
> yet your desire shall be for your husband,
>   and he shall rule over you."
> And to Adam he said,
> "Because you have listened to the voice of your wife,
>   and have eaten of the tree
> of which I commanded you,
>   'You shall not eat of it,'

---

[10] For an explanation of the word "curse" (and its opposite "blessing") see the technical note on p. 397.

cursed is the ground because of you;
>   in toil you shall eat of it all the days of your life;
thorns and thistles it shall bring forth to you;
>   and you shall eat the plants of the field.
In the sweat of your face
>   you shall eat bread
till you return to the ground,
>   for out of it you were taken;
you are dust,
>   and to dust you shall return." (Gen 3:16–19)

The second consequence affects man and his work. In the beginning, he had been given work to do in the garden. Work, then, was not a result of the Fall. Now, however, because of the Fall his work became toilsome and burdensome. In addition, he had lost the chance of earthly immortality.

To the woman, God said, *I will greatly multiply your pain in childbearing.* The word *pain* is the same word translated as *toil* in what he said to Adam (Gen 3:17). The consequence for the woman, then, is similar to the consequence for the man. For the man, the misfortune affects his work; while for the woman, it affects childbearing. People most commonly interpret the term "the pain in childbearing" narrowly to mean the physical pain that a woman has when giving birth to a child, but it can be taken in the broader sense of the toil she has in her family life and in raising children.

God then adds, *In pain you shall bring forth children, yet your desire shall be for your husband, and he shall rule over you.* The word *yet* could also be translated "and." The more common interpretation of this line is that the woman's relationship with her husband will become problematic and also burdensome. A second interpretation is the reverse, namely that her relationship with her husband will be a consolation and source of strength for her in the difficulties of her childbearing and raising children. A third interpretation is that this is the point at which woman becomes subordinate to the man, and that subordination is a result of the Fall, and can be overcome in Christ. This third one is common among feminists and is at odds with the New Testament understanding of the text (1 Cor 11:8; 1 Tim 2:8–9; Eph 5:21–24).[11]

Although there are some uncertainties in how to interpret everything that God says as a result of the disobedience of Adam and Eve, we can see an important pattern, one that occurs throughout the rest of God's dealings with the human race as we read about them in the Scriptures. God makes covenants with human beings. When he makes a covenant, he gives a set of commandments. Good consequences come from keeping the commandments, and bad consequences come from disobeying the commandments. The bad consequences are just (righteous) punishments. Such an understanding provides the framework for this section of Genesis 3.

Many hold that there was an explicit covenant between God and Adam in which God gave a command about the eating of the tree of the knowledge of good and evil. But even without taking the view that God made an explicit covenant with Adam, we can see that God clearly expected Adam and Eve to keep his commandment, with good consequences (blessing) to follow obedience—or bad consequences (curse) to follow disobedience. As their creator, he had the right to expect obedience from them.

After God's judgment, we have the last step in the Fall. Adam and Even are put out of paradise:

> The man called his wife's name Eve, because she was the mother of all living. And the LORD God made for Adam and for his wife garments of skins, and clothed them.
>
> Then the LORD God said, "Behold, the man has become like one of us, knowing good and evil; and now, lest he put forth his hand and take also of the tree of life, and eat, and live for ever"—therefore the LORD God sent him forth from the garden of Eden, to till the ground from which he was taken. He drove out the man; and at the east of the

---

[11] For a fuller discussion of the approaches to this text, see Clark, *MWC*, 31–36.

garden of Eden he placed the cherubim, and a flaming sword which turned every way, to guard the way to the tree of life. (Gen 3:20–24)

We see here that the garden is the place where God's original intention for man was to be realized, the place where Adam was to enjoy God's presence and live in fellowship with him. As a result of his sin, Adam was exiled from the place that God had originally intended for him. He did not lose all relationship with God, but he was distanced from him and lost the immediacy of access he once had.

Adam had to be put out of the garden because he had disobeyed and marred the image and likeness of God that he had been given. As Ezekiel 28:16 says, he had profaned himself, that is, he had made himself unworthy to live in God's presence. Losing paradise, the place God created for him to live and have access to himself, was the greatest evil brought on the human race by the Fall—a true spiritual death.

Before they were expelled from the garden God clothed the man and his wife. They had lost their original glorious covering. Now God clothed them in skins. He showed his fatherly care for them in being willing to make them clothing when they did not know how to clothe themselves adequately. The clothing, however, must have been made out of the skins of dead animals, probably indicating that they now wore mortality, only a temporary protection against death, perhaps symbolizing the flesh they now lived in, deprived of their original glory.[12]

Cain and Abel and Seth. Genesis 4 continues the account in Genesis 2 and 3. Although it is somewhat common in Christian teaching to end consideration of the Fall of the human race with chapter 3, chapter 4 presents a fuller view of the Fall. There we see that the first-born of Adam, Cain, turns out badly, and his descendants go from bad to worse. The disobedience of Adam and Eve, especially

---

[12] For an exposition of the significance of the garments of skin, see Anderson, *The Genesis of Perfection,* chap. 6.

Adam, the head of the human race (Rom 5:12), results in the consequences of the first sin passing on to the descendants of Adam. In the previous section, we considered the Fall of Adam and now in Genesis 4, and in a fuller way in Genesis 4–11, we will see that the Fall of Adam led to the Fall of the human race.

"The Fall" has become a common term in Christian teaching to describe the origin of the mixture of good and bad in human life that we all experience. There are many questions connected to understanding the Fall. Some of these center around the guilt that might be due to individuals because of it. Some of these center around how corrupt or depraved human nature is because of it. Here we simply need to see that there is something wrong with the human race, especially in its relationship with God. And we can speak of that as due to the Fall and see the consequences beginning in Genesis 4 and the account of the first children of Adam and Eve, Cain and Abel.

First John 3:12 says that Cain was a murderer who violated the law of love of neighbor in one of the worst possible ways—by killing his brother—out of envy. The difficulty began with the sacrifices that Cain and Abel brought to God. The human race had not fallen so far that the first human beings stopped offering sacrifice to God. Genesis 4:4–5 says that the sacrifice of Abel was accepted, but the sacrifice of Cain was not. It does not clearly say why the sacrifice of the one was acceptable, but not the other. The two main views are that Cain's sacrifice was done the wrong way, a way that was not acceptable to God, or that Cain's inner disposition was not right.

From this we can see that not all sacrifice or worship is acceptable to God. A common modern mentality takes the view that "as long as you are religious, you are alright," and that any kind of prayer or worship makes you automatically commendable. But both the Old Testament and the New Testament are very strong on the opposite. It is important to offer the right kind of worship, because the wrong kind of worship is not acceptable and can get us into spiritual trouble. It is better not to worship than to worship in a wrong way. In this case, the fact that Cain's sacrifice was not accepted and Abel's was provokes Cain to kill Abel.

After Cain murdered his brother, God addressed him in a similar way to the way he addressed Adam and Eve after the Fall. He said, *the voice of your brother's blood is crying to me from the ground* (Gen 4:10). Abel's blood, in other words, cried out for punishment of the crime. This is probably a way of saying that certain kinds of sin objectively demand punishment. Just as Adam and Eve had to be cast out of paradise because they had profaned themselves and so could not be allowed to remain in a holy place, so Cain had to be punished because he was guilty of murder.

What happened to Cain and Abel is the consequence of Adam and Eve's sin. Cain was driven even further away from God's presence than Adam as a result of his murder, but we can see by the way the account is constructed that Cain's sin is a consequence of Adam's sin. Transgression against love of God leads to transgression against love of neighbor. Rebellion against God leads to murder. Disorder in one area leads to disorder in the other. We see these consequences spelled out in chapters 1 and 2 of the letter to the Romans.

The children of Cain turned out to be wrongdoers as well. They were cultured, and they brought forth many important things into the world. But they were like their father Cain—even worse. Lamech is the end of Cain's line, and his violence is sevenfold that of Cain's. The line of Seth, the next son of Adam and Eve, on the other hand, does much better, at least for a while. They seem to worship the true God (4:26), apparently unlike the descendants of Cain. Moreover, Noah eventually comes from the line of Seth and brings a new hope. The image of God was marred or wounded by the Fall, but the human race was not all evil. It came out as a mixed blessing with the possibility of doing better.

Genesis 1 and Genesis 2–4 go together. God's good work of creating is followed by human disobedience. That disobedience leads to the loss of much of the blessing brought about by God's work. That in turn is part of a pattern that continues throughout the Scriptures. The Fall narrated in Genesis 2–4 is repeated in the middle of the building of the tabernacle by the fall involved in the making of the Golden Calf (Ex 32–33). It is repeated in the middle of the first accepted sacrificial offering by the fall involved in the profanation of Nadab and Abihu (Lev 9–10). It is repeated again and again as we will see. But also, as we will see, God is not deterred but keeps moving the human race on from stage to stage until he achieves his purpose: the completion of a perfectly good creation.

Concluding comments. Genesis 2–4 says that the way human beings live now is not the way God created them to live. If we look around, we can see traces of what God intended—there is much goodness in human life. But we do not see human life as God planned it. Genesis 3 lets us see that human transgression, the disobedience to God's command, caused something to go very seriously wrong. The Apostle Paul says that through human disobedience came sin, and through sin death came into the world (Rom 5:12). God did not set it up that way; human beings are responsible.

God's intention for the human race did not just get derailed by the bad consequences of how human life was being lived. It also got derailed by the failure of the human race to gradually bring about God's intention for all of creation so it would *be set free from futility and from its bondage to decay* (Rom 8:20–21). The interaction between God and the human race portrayed in Genesis 2 was not only the cause of the problems of the human race to come, but also the cause of the failure of the human race to develop all of creation in the way God wanted.

To be sure, the first human pair were tempted to fall. They did not come up with the idea of disobedience on their own. Rather they yielded to a source of evil that pre-existed them. They were not the originators of evil. Nonetheless by agreeing to be disobedient, they were responsible for the evil that came into their own life and indirectly into all of creation. That truth points to what human beings can do to begin the work of restoring creation to the full goodness God intended for it—turn to God in repentance and seek to obey him.

Paradise and Christian Symbols and Types

A scriptural "type" is something past or present that corresponds to something in the future. In other words, it shows us something about what is to come. Most commonly, it is something described in the Old Testament that shows us the meaning of something in the New Testament. The next chapter will consider the nature of types and how they function in scriptural interpretation.

A "symbol" is anything that stands for something else. Once we understand the meaning of the symbol, we can understand what is being communicated by the use of the symbol. As we will see, types can be used as symbols.

The earliest Christians were familiar with the first chapters of Genesis, and the various elements of the creation account functioned as symbols and types in Christian instruction. The most significant understandings in the first chapters of Genesis are as follows:

Adam: The first human being and at one point the embodiment of the whole human race, a type of Christ as the beginning of the new (redeemed) human race, who reversed what Adam did

Eve: The first woman and the mother of the human race, a type of Mary the mother of Christ, who by her obedience and trust in God reversed what Eve did, and a type of the church

Paradise: The garden that was the blessed home for the human race, a type of the new Jerusalem

The tree of life: The source of immortal life, a type of Christ and the Cross of Christ

The tree of the knowledge of good and evil: The source of wisdom, a type of the Scriptures and the teaching of God's wisdom

Adam's garments: Originally garments of glory and high priesthood, a type of Christian character traits and of the glorified nature of Christ and human beings

The garments of skin: The garments that Adam and Eve wore after the Fall, a symbol of their mortality

CHAPTER THREE

Spiritual Interpretation

Introduction to the chapter. In this chapter we are going to take a different approach than we have so far. We are not going to look at a passage or section in the Scriptures and understand it in the context of the stages of God's plan. Rather, we are going to look at some of the principles that will guide our interpretation of Scripture as a whole, especially how we can put together in a good way what the Scriptures are teaching.

In this chapter we will discuss a foundational principle in the New Testament approach to the Old Testament: typological interpretation. The use of typological interpretation is perhaps the main reason why the New Testament interpretation of the Old Testament is so distinctive. Some Christians in trying to understand how the New Testament writers use the Old Testament go so far as to say that the New Testament approach is from "a whole different world." By that they mean that people in our culture would not read the Old Testament in such a way. In this they are mostly right. If, however, we can understand the typological principle, we can understand much of how the New Testament authors use the Old Testament writings—and why.

We will then look at the question of spiritual interpretation. We want to *understand the gifts bestowed on us by God* as Paul says to the Corinthians, by being *taught by the Spirit* (see 1 Cor 2:12–13). We will seek to understand how to read the Scriptures in a spiritual way.

This chapter provides a basic introduction to what this book calls theological exegesis. This will raise many technical questions of scholarly method. Those are addressed more fully in part II of the book.

The Spirit and God's plan. The Apostle Paul had to defend his work as an apostle at various times, and we learn a great deal from the defenses we can read in several of his letters. In the second chapter of First Corinthians, he tells us some important things about his teaching:

> Yet among the mature we do impart wisdom, although it is not a wisdom of this age or of the rulers of this age, who are doomed to pass away. But we impart a secret and hidden wisdom of God, which God decreed before the ages for our glorification. . . . But, as it is written,
>
>> "What no eye has seen, nor ear heard,
>> nor the heart of man conceived,
>> what God has prepared for those who love him,"
>
> God has revealed to us through the Spirit. . . . Now we have received not the spirit of the world, but the Spirit which is from God, that we might understand the gifts bestowed on us by God. And we impart this in words not taught by human wisdom but taught by the Spirit, interpreting spiritual truths to those who possess the Spirit. (1 Cor 2:6–13)

Before this passage, Paul had just finished explaining how he preached the Gospel to new people, and brought them to faith in Christ. Here he turns to how he teaches *the mature*, that is, people who have a basic Christian formation, including those who are hearing this letter read. He says that he *imparts wisdom*, that is, teaches new Christians a fuller understanding, an understanding of how God had decided to act *before the ages*, that is, before he began to create the world. God's goal was *our glorification*, as we will see more clearly when we get to chapter 11. In other words, Paul taught the new Christians about what we are referring to as the stages of God's plan.

God's plan has turned out to be greater and better than anything human beings before Paul's time had even conceived. Paul, and now his audience of new Christians, have found out about this by the Holy Spirit. The Spirit of God not only gives us the revelation of God's plan, but also gives us the understanding of what is involved in the plan. We will return to this later in this chapter, but we need to begin by understanding the nature of the task we are engaged in. We are trying to acquire a wisdom that no human beings ever came up with solely by using their minds. We are trying to understand a revelation that has come to us by the work of the Holy Spirit.

TYPOLOGY

The nature of typology. The technical term "typology" was invented by Scripture scholars about one hundred fifty years ago to speak about one way Christian writers read the Old Testament in the light of the New. It refers to a method of scriptural interpretation that sees many things in the Old Testament as corresponding to things in the New Testament. "Typology" is the most common way now to describe this approach. Since *figura* was the standard Latin word for "type," we very often also describe things in the Old Testament as "prefiguring" those in the New, and this method of reading is sometimes termed "figural reading."

The terms "type" and "anti-type" are anglicized forms of two Greek words used in the New Testament. "Type," an important term in Greek thought, in Scripture, and in the Fathers, is also translated as "pattern" and sometimes as "form" or "figure." A type is something with a certain form that shapes something else.

We used the term "type" for the letters on a typewriter because they are shaped in a certain way, and when we hit their key, they make an impression on the page that is of the same shape or form (and significance) as the type. A dress pattern could be described as a type, because it is used to make dresses of a certain shape or form.

A type comes before an anti-type. The anti-type corresponds to the type in its form, and the type had a role in shaping it. "Anti" here does not mean "against," but "corresponding to." The letter on the paper as an anti-type corresponds to the shape of the type, the key on the typewriter.

We find the word "type" in Romans 5:14, which says, *Adam, who was a type of the one who was to come. The one who was to come* is Christ. This passage refers us to the texts in Genesis 1–5 that speak about Adam, and tells us that they teach us something about Christ. There is, in other words, a correspondence between Christ and Adam. They are like one another and have the same significance in one important respect. Christ fulfilled a similar role or function to the one Adam had: beginning humanity, in this case beginning a *new* humanity, the new covenant people of God.

Another place we find this word is in 1 Corinthians 10:6, a passage that speaks about the events of the Exodus as corresponding to Christian initiation (Baptism and Eucharist). It goes on to speak about how the Israelites were punished for their disobedience to God, even though they had come into a relationship with him similar to that which Christians have through Christian initiation. Therefore, Christians should take care not to disobey.

In the course of describing the results of their disobedience, the passage says, *Now these things are warnings for us, not to desire evil as they did.* A more literal translation would be, "Now these things are types for us, not to desire evil as they did." Though the RSV translation of the word as "warning" accurately conveys an important part of the meaning, it is an interpretive or idiomatic translation. The literal word here is "types," and it indicates that the similarity of the old covenant events and the new covenant events means that the old covenant events can be used to instruct us in how God set up and now approaches the new covenant events.

Another example is found in Hebrews 9:24: *For Christ has entered, not into a sanctuary made with hands, a copy of the true one, but*

into heaven itself, now to appear in the presence of God on our behalf.
The word "copy," here, is an alternate translation of the Greek word
for "anti-type." The type in this case is heaven. The word "anti-type"
signifies the thing that corresponds to the type. In this case, the
earthly tent (tabernacle) or temple is an anti-type of heaven, because it is formed or laid out to be like the heavenly temple. This
passage next refers to the Greek Septuagint translation of Exodus
25:40, *And see that you make them* [all the things in the tabernacle]
after the pattern for them, which is being shown you on the mountain.
"Pattern," or in other versions "model," is a translation of the word
"type" in the Greek, which reads more literally "make them after
the type which is being shown you on the mountain."[1]

The final example is 1 Peter 3:21. Here, Baptism is seen as an
anti-type of the Flood in the time of Noah. The Flood is the type;
Baptism is the anti-type. The translation in the RSV is *Baptism,
which corresponds to this, now saves you.* But if we translate the passage more literally we get, "Baptism, which is an anti-type of this,
now saves you." This means that Baptism functions in a similar way
to the Flood by destroying sin—as we will consider in chapter 4.
From these passages we see that the word "type" along with the cor-
relative word "anti-type" is used somewhat commonly in Scripture.

The Scriptures sometimes use the words "shadow" and "substance" as a way to understand typology. For instance, Colossians
2:16–17 says,

> Therefore let no one pass judgment on you in questions of
> food and drink or with regard to a festival or a new moon or
> a sabbath. These are only a shadow of what is to come; but
> the substance belongs to Christ.

Hebrews 8:5 and 10:1 use the same image. While relating to the
shadow of something is not directly relating to the thing itself, the
shadow has a close connection to the thing. If we relate to a shadow

---

[1]   For the Septuagint, see the technical note "Some Terms for Parts or Versions of the
    Bible" on p. 392.

that we see on a window shade in order to figure out who or what is in the room behind the shade, we are also relating to the things in the room. In relating to a type—the Passover lamb, for instance— old covenant people were already being oriented by God to what he would be doing in Christ, because Christ would fulfill the function of the Passover lamb in a fuller and more effective way (a more "substantial" way, to use the RSV term in the Colossians passage).

While the word "type" highlights the similarity between the two things being compared, the word "shadow" highlights the difference. The shadow has less reality than that which casts the shadow. It is merely a reflection of the real thing. This is easiest to see when the phrase "the shadow" is used to describe earthly realities as reflections of heavenly realities, as in the book of Hebrews. Sometimes, as in the Colossians passage above, the real thing is in the future, and casts its shadow into the past. In such a case the implication is that the new covenant reality is greater than the old covenant reality, which, in God's intention, was shaped to prepare for and lead to the new covenant reality. The new covenant reality more fully contains and exemplifies what God is working toward.

There is yet another New Testament way of speaking that expresses the same idea, a way that can be surprising or misleading to contemporary English speakers. We can see it in Hebrews 9:24, where it says,

> Christ has entered, not into a sanctuary made with hands, a copy of the true one, but into heaven itself, now to appear in the presence of God on our behalf.

And we can see it in Hebrews 8:2, where it speaks of,

> a minister in the sanctuary and the true tent which is set up not by man but by the Lord.

Hebrews uses the word *true* here in a way unusual to us. Surely, if either tent is a "true" tent, it is the earthly tent, not heaven itself.

Heaven is not "truly" a tent at all. This unexpected way of using the word "true" in Hebrews, however, is an indication that "true" is being used in a special sense. In these passages, "true" means something like "having full spiritual reality" and is contrasted with "having partial or weaker spiritual reality."

Heaven is the true tent, but not because it is a tent and the earthly one is not. The contrast here is not between true and false, so that the earthly temple is a false temple the way an idol is a false god in contrast to the one true God because it is not a god at all. Rather, both the earthly and heavenly tents have the same reality, the reality of being the place of God's indwelling presence. Heaven, however, has that reality more fully than the earthly tent that Hebrews is referring to, that is, the tent of meeting which went with the Israelites in the wilderness. Heaven is more truly where God dwells (see 2 Chron 6:18–20). "True" here, then, has much the same meaning as "in substance" in contrast with "in shadow" in Colossians 2:16–17.

In the Gospel and Epistles of John, the words "true" and "truth" are often used to speak of new covenant realities as related to old covenant realities. Christ is the true bread (Jn 6:32), not because he is more really bread than the manna was, but because he brings with fuller reality what God was aiming at in giving the manna—life. He is the true vine (Jn 15:1), not because he produces better grapes, but because his disciples are more fully God's planting than the leaders of the old Israel were. Jesus is the "true light" (Jn 1:9; 1 Jn 2:8), not because he physically shone brighter than John the Baptist, but because, compared to Jesus, John was partial or weaker in the spiritual light he could give.

Christ, in fact, is in his own person truth itself (Jn 14:6), the full spiritual reality, the full presence of God, and the full life God ultimately intends for us. To belong to him is to receive the full gift God wishes to give the human race. He, in fact, brings "truth" in a way the Old Testament law did not (Jn 1:17). The law brought types, shadows—the reality in a less substantial form. Christ, the incarnate Word, brings the fullness of what God wants to give his people.

Typological thinking or typological interpretation is employed much more often than in the passages where these words are used. For instance, the Passover lamb is a type of Christ as a sacrificial victim. We cannot find any place in the New Testament that says that the lamb is a type of Christ, but from the way in which the Passover lamb is spoken about in relation to Christ in the New Testament, we can nevertheless see that it is. For instance, First Corinthians 5:7 simply says, *For Christ, our Paschal Lamb, has been sacrificed,* as if it were straightforward to see Christ as our Passover lamb.

Typology has to do with the correspondence between two existing things. A type is not just a symbol, although a type can function as a symbol. David, for instance, can function as a symbol of kingship in general or of effective kingship. We might say of Saint Wenceslas, the Medieval Bohemian king, "he was another David," and mean that he was an instance of the kind of kingship that David represents. We might also say that "he was another Aragorn," a king in Tolkien's *The Lord of the Rings,* and mean that he was an instance of the kind of kingship that Aragorn represents. David, however, was more than a symbol, much less a literary figure like Aragorn. He was someone who existed historically. Nonetheless, he is a type, because in God's plan he shows us something about what Christ would be, and is now, as king.

Typology is not the same thing as allegory, according to most modern definitions of allegory.[2] In an allegory, as understood by many modern scholars, the correspondence is actually written into

---

[2] In the ancient Greco-Roman world, "allegory" was used more broadly than it is commonly used now. It could refer to any example of speech where "one thing is spoken about, another thing is meant" (Quintilian, *Institution,* 8.6.44), including scriptural typology. For a discussion of allegory in patristic writings, see Robert Louis Wilken, "Allegory and the Interpretation of the Old Testament in the 21st Century" in *Letter & Spirit,* vol. 1 (2005). See also Mark Edwards' discussion referred to in note 6. In Christian writings subsequent to the patristic period, "allegory" has been used more narrowly as a term for one of the three spiritual (typological) senses. For a description of the four senses of Scripture, a commonly used way of speaking about typology in Christian tradition, see the technical note "The Four Senses of Scripture" on p. 414. In later patristic writings it was common to use the term *theoría* instead of *allegoría* (see John J. O'Keefe and R. R. Reno, *Sanctified Vision: An Introduction to Early Christian Interpretation of the Bible* [Baltimore, MD: Johns Hopkins University, 2005], 15).

the text itself by the human author and an allegorical interpretation gives us the author's own intention of the meaning of the text. Matthew 13:3–4, 18–19 is an allegorical interpretation of a parable in this sense.

John Bunyan's *Pilgrim's Progress* is another example of allegory, in this case a whole book. In the episode of the pilgrim (the Christian) falling into a bog, we are given a description of the market fair the pilgrim is going to, called Vanity Fair, and a description of the bog the pilgrim falls into on the way, the Slough of Despond. The market and the bog are imaginative ways the author uses to present the concepts of vanity and despond (sadness, depression, discouragement). The whole book is an allegory, and the events are not intended to describe what happened, or even just to tell a story, but to represent abstract ideas in concrete form. If we understand the word "allegory" to refer to the way *Pilgrim's Progress* is written, an allegory is a text written to describe ideas under the guise of a story.

Typology, on the other hand, is a correspondence of two actual events that are described by a text. To say that the Passover lamb is a type of Christ as sacrificial victim is to say that there was a Passover lamb, and there was also a man named Jesus Christ, and that there was a similarity between them. Christ, when he died on the Cross, accomplished something similar for the human race to what the Passover lamb accomplished for the Israelites in Egypt. To say that one is a type of the other is not primarily to interpret a text but to specify a relationship or a correspondence between the two realities spoken about in the text. That correspondence allows us to read the Old Testament text in reference to the new covenant reality, and vice versa, and so to understand both of them better.

At times scholars use the term "typology" more broadly than to speak about the correspondence between Old Testament and New Testament realities, and commonly hold that the New Testament writers derived their approach to typology from the Old Testament. For instance, they sometimes describe the correspondence between the exodus from Egypt and Israel's return from exile in Assyria that we can see in Isaiah 43 as a typological understanding. These are both Old Testament events, and so a broader view of typology would include typology within the Old Testament, or even a typological relationship between biblical and extra-biblical realities. Most commonly, however, when we speak about types or typology, we are discussing the relationship between old covenant events, people, and institutions and new covenant ones.

The fundamental truth behind typology is the unity of God's work in human history. When God set out to create, he had in mind what he was trying to accomplish with the human race—ultimately to save it and bring it once again into a relationship with himself. He kept that purpose in mind all the way through the process of salvation. He was always working toward it, so everything he did was a step toward what he did later on and therefore something of what he was aiming at.

The fullness of what God is aiming at will be clear when Christ comes again. However, God was working toward the same sort of thing in Adam, Abraham, and David that he was working toward in Christ in his first coming, and that he will be bringing about when Christ comes again. There is a similarity in pattern or form between the earlier events and the later events, so that frequently we can understand the later events better by understanding the earlier events and vice versa.

There is, however, more to a typological relationship than simply a similarity in pattern. There is a connection between the two corresponding events or people involved. God worked in the earlier event to *prepare for* the later event. The later event brings about in a fuller or more effective way what God was aiming at. They are two steps in a process that God was and is moving forward. For this reason, the new covenant realities are often spoken about as the fulfillment of the old covenant realities (e.g., Jn 19:36 speaking about Christ's death on the Cross as a fulfillment of the Passover sacrifice, even without an explicit prophetic indication of the connection).

This understanding does not imply that the earlier type no longer has a function. Many messianic Jews believe that various Old Testament institutions, practices, places, and times, even if they have a new covenant fulfillment, should still be followed by Jewish Christians, as we will consider in chapter 8. Nonetheless, here we simply need to understand the nature of typological fulfillment.

Two examples of typology. We will now look at a couple of passages about types to get a better sense for how typology works. In a passage to which we have already referred, Paul writes:

> I want you to know, brethren, that our fathers were all un-der the cloud, and all passed through the sea, and all were baptized into Moses in the cloud and in the sea, and all ate the same supernatural food and all drank the same super-natural drink. For they drank from the supernatural Rock which followed them, and the Rock was Christ. Neverthe-less with most of them God was not pleased; for they were overthrown in the wilderness.
> Now these things are warnings [types] for us, not to de-sire evil as they did. (1 Cor 10:1–6)

Paul then goes on to list some of the examples of how the Israelites were judged by God for doing evil. This should warn Christians that just being baptized into Christ or fed with Eucharistic food is not enough to guarantee God will be pleased with them. They also have to obey him.

In the passage, Paul is saying that the children of Israel were bap-tized and given supernatural or, more literally, "spiritual" food and drink. The baptism happened when the Israelites went through the Red Sea with the pillar of cloud covering and protecting them, as described in Exodus 14. The supernatural food refers to the manna first given in Exodus 16 (also referred to in a similar way in John 6). The supernatural drink refers to the spring of water that flowed out when Moses struck the rock, as described in Exodus 17. Passing un-der the cloud or going through the Red Sea are types or foreshadow-ings of Christian baptism, and the manna and water from the rock are types or foreshadowings of the Lord's Supper, or Eucharist.

Paul says that the rock was Christ. There was a Jewish tradition at the time of Paul that the rock actually followed the people of Israel in the wilderness. He is perhaps referring to that tradition and identifying that rock with Christ. He was more likely seeing the rock as a type of Christ, and probably also saying that Christ was the one at work in the rock to give the water. Either way, by saying the rock *was* Christ, he was saying that the rock was a type.

Paul at least is saying that the cloud, the sea, and the food and drink of the wilderness wandering are foreshadowings of what happened later with Christ and so can instruct us about them. According to some, Paul might, however, be saying something stronger. He might be saying that in some way the children of Israel in the wilderness participated in what Christ would later accomplish. In an incomplete shadow-form they were participating in the redemption that Christ won on the Cross and in his Resurrection.

These two views illustrate two different understandings of the nature of the typological relationship. The fact, however, that Paul explicitly says that the Israelites were baptized *into Moses* indicates that they were baptized into the old covenant, not into the new covenant. On the other hand, as we have seen, by relating to the shadow (the type), they were in fact relating to the new covenant reality by relating to something that gave them a relationship with God similar to that which the new covenant would bring, and probably some participation in advance in that reality. We will consider the relationship between the old covenant order and the new covenant order in chapter 10.

Now we can take another look at what Paul says about Adam in the passage in Romans 5:12–17 and see a somewhat different kind of typological relationship:

Therefore as sin came into the world through one man and death through sin, and so death spread to all men because all men sinned—sin indeed was in the world before the law was given, but sin is not counted where there is no law. Yet death reigned from Adam to Moses, even over those whose sins were not like the transgressions of Adam, who was a type of the one who was to come.

But the free gift is not like the trespass. For if many died through one man's trespass, much more have the grace of God and the free gift in the grace of that one man Jesus Christ abounded for many. And the free gift is not like the effect of that one man's sin. For the judgment following one trespass brought condemnation, but the free gift following many trespasses brings justification. If, because of one man's trespass, death reigned through that one man, much more will those who receive the abundance of grace and the free gift of righteousness reign in life through the one man Jesus Christ.

Paul states that Adam is a type of Christ, and he then goes on to develop the correspondence between the type and the anti-type. He focuses on how much of a change one man's action makes for all those who come after him. The act of Adam, the father of the human race, changed the future in regard to sin. The obedience of Christ, the father of the new human race, changed the future in regard to the redemption from sin of those who follow him.

We have here a typological relationship that is partly the same and partly a reversal. Christ is like Adam in being the head of the human race, but not like Adam in that Adam's disobedience led to the reign of sin and death while Christ's obedience led to the reign of righteousness and life. There is a correspondence between Christ and Adam because they both have the same role as head of the human race. Both pass on their nature to their offspring. On the other hand, there is a difference between them because Christ is successful in bringing the human race to what God intended it to be, and Adam was not. Moreover, both in the similarity and the difference, there is a connection between them, since Christ was appointed to make up for what Adam did by starting humanity over again. Therefore, Adam was a type of Christ.

We can give similar interpretations for other types in the Old

Testament. The point, however, should be clear. When we read the Old Testament, we need to see that much of it, all of it in a certain way,[3] was fulfilled in the new covenant. We need, therefore, to read it typologically, that is, we need to see what it is moving toward. Such a perspective is one of the keys to deriving full Christian profit from the Old Testament.

THE NEED FOR SPIRITUAL INTERPRETATION

The New Testament authors at times use the word "spiritual" to speak about the Christian way of reading the Old Testament (or the New, itself). Most often in using this word, they are indicating not that something is immaterial but that it pertains to or is produced by the Holy Spirit. For instance, First Peter 2:4–5 uses this word to characterize new covenant realities:

> Come to him . . . and like living stones be yourselves built into a spiritual house, to be a holy priesthood, to offer spiritual sacrifices acceptable to God through Christ.

The passage is speaking of the Christian community as a temple. The word "house" here refers to a temple as in the phrase "the house of God" (e.g., Judg 18:31; Ps 135:2). The verse does not mean that the house, in this case the Christian community, is immaterial. No body of Christians on this earth is immaterial. Rather, the text is saying that the Christians are a temple formed by the Spirit and so are different in nature than the temple building in Jerusalem. Likewise, it is saying that Christian worship contains sacrifices formed by the Spirit and so they are different in nature than the animals, cereals, and oils used in the Jerusalem temple sacrifices.

The book of Revelation, speaking of Old Testament realities, uses "spiritual" in a related way. When we look at the role of the city

---

[3] For discussion of the fulfillment in Christ of the Old Testament as a whole, see the methodological discussion "10. Spiritual Transposition" (p. 543).

of Rome (the most likely referent of "Babylon") in the persecution described in the book of Revelation, we are told that, literally translated, Rome is "spiritually" called Sodom and Egypt (Rev 11:8), that is, identified as the current example of the worldly city that is hostile to God's people, as Sodom and Egypt were. By the revelation or insight that the Spirit gives, we can see that Rome plays the same role in God's plan.

Many Christian writers over the centuries have spoken of the spiritual interpretation of the Scriptures and contrasted it to the literal or historical one. Some have been explicit in connecting the literal or historical meaning with the intent of the human author, or at least with what he might have been able to understand in his context at the time.[4] They then saw spiritual interpretation as allowing us to get at the fuller meaning of the Old Testament (sometimes referred to as the *sensus plenior*, the Latin for "fuller meaning").

There are different ways to get at the fuller meaning of Old Testament texts like the text of Genesis. Because of the light that has been revealed to us in Christ, we have a fuller view of what God was about at different points in human history than Old Testament writers did. We know much more about God's purpose in creating Adam and Eve than the people who first heard the account knew, because they did not know about Christ or about the coming of the kingdom in the age to come. If we read the Old Testament in the light of what we know about the stages of God's plan, we can understand better what God was about in creating Adam and how Christ fulfilled that intention. That, of course, is the main focus of this book.

The example of the Trinity in Genesis 1 is somewhat different. The early Church Fathers who wrote that when God said, "Let us make man in our own image and likeness," he was referring to his Trinitarian nature when he said "us" probably did not say it on the basis of a reflection on the stages of God's plan. Rather, they said it

---

[4] For a further discussion of the spiritual interpretation of the Scriptures as traditionally understood, see the "Technical Note: The Four Senses of Scripture" on p. 414. For a discussion of the intent of the author and the ways the phrase is understood in scholarly literature, see "The Intent of the Author(s)" in part II on p. 499.

on the basis of what they knew about the reality being spoken of. They knew that God is Trinitarian because of Christian teaching, and therefore they thought that if "we" made man in "our" image and likeness, that probably was a reference to God and therefore in some way to the Trinity.[5]

Christian teachers who took this position did not necessarily expect the Old Testament author explicitly to know that it was so. But they believed they knew it was so because they understood something about the nature of God that the Old Testament authors probably did not. Strict adherence to an historical method that focuses exclusively on the knowledge of the original human author rules out knowledge we have of what is being said, when we now know more about the reality the original author was writing about. This is not especially helpful unless we are concerned with a solely historical view.

Moreover, in the traditional Christian method of exegesis, what we can call a theological method of exegesis, it is the subject matter, the Incarnation or sexual morality, for instance, which on the whole controls the process rather than the literary or historical character and antecedents of the text. A text is primarily related to other texts on the same subject or to anything else known about that subject.[6] This does not mean that what we see in the text has to be fully explicit in the text or it is not there at all. As we saw, even in matters that are not especially theological, we could explain what Old Testament authors said about "great fish" by using the knowledge we have of whales that they did not have. In fact, it is not rare for teachers who engage in theological exegesis to observe that a particular text does not seem to teach or to clearly teach something that is more fully known about the subject from another source.

---

[5] Trinitarian references in Genesis 1 are discussed more fully in chapter 1, both in the section "The Creation of the World" and the section "The Creation of the Human Race."

[6] See Mark Julian Edwards, *Origen Against Plato* (Aldershot, Hants, England; Burlington, VT: Ashgate, 2002), 144 for a description of how patristic writers (in this case, Origen) use texts with similarity of subject matter as the primary way of interpreting a given text.

A theological approach to exegesis is "spiritual." It is at least spiritual in the sense that it is the approach of the New Testament authors, writers inspired by the Holy Spirit, and of Christ himself. But it is also spiritual in the sense that the Holy Spirit works in human beings to know God and especially to know God in Christ. The focus of a spiritual understanding is God himself, not history or literary method, as useful as these may be in understanding Scripture.

To be able to give a valid theological exegesis of a text based on theological knowledge that comes from another source than the scriptural text we are considering, we have to be able to refer to sources that convey reliable theological knowledge. For the most part these are other scriptural texts, because these are inspired by the Holy Spirit and therefore spiritual writings. In the case of the Old Testament, the New Testament plays a major role. Orthodox Christian teachers will normally also refer to creedal definitions, including the Nicene Creed. Although not usually considered inspired, these are recognized as spiritual interpretations (Acts 15:28).

Christian teachers will also stand in a theological tradition, whether they recognize that they do or not. Those formed in a certain tradition will use certain theological sources and prioritize them in a certain way. Increasingly now they will also let ecumenical considerations influence how they do theology. Of course when orthodox Christians use the same or a similar theological method, they will not necessarily all agree on everything, any more than historians who use similar methods will agree with one another in all their conclusions. Nonetheless, they are seeking the mind of Christ, which the Holy Spirit reveals to us (1 Cor 2:10–11, 16).

The fact that spiritual (theological) exegesis focuses first and foremost on the subject being discussed is one of the keys to why spiritual exegesis allows the Old Testament to be used by Christian teachers. If our method is historical, especially if it is secular historical, we only see the text in its relationships to historical facts (e.g., what we know about the conditions or events of the time, what previous writings influenced it, what gave rise to it, what the human author's understanding of its content was). If our method is literary, we only see the literary features of the text (e.g., stylistic devices, unifying techniques, rhetorical techniques). If, however, our method is spiritual exegesis and the text is about God and the things of God, we are able to speak about its true significance, including its Christian significance, when we speak about its content.

Spiritual interpretation also treats the words of the Scripture as inspired. The entire Scripture was written under the inspiration of the Holy Spirit in the first place. "Inspiration" is not the same as revelation. The letter to the Philippians is inspired Scripture. In it Paul says he was in prison. He must not have needed revelation to know he was in prison. But when he wrote Philippians, God's hand was enough in what led up to the letter that we know the letter as a whole is God's word, God's communication to us, and it contains things we need to know to be saved, including how God wanted Paul to approach his imprisonment. For that reason it was accepted into the canon, even though only some of it was revealed truth (although all of it was written under the inspiration of the Holy Spirit).

Moreover, frequently people have only a partial understanding of everything the Holy Spirit inspires them to speak, so there could have been a fair amount of content in Genesis that went beyond the understanding and therefore the intent of the author. A classic example is that of the high priest Caiaphas in John 12:49–50, who gave his opinion that it was expedient that "one man should die for the people," without realizing that God was speaking through him to indicate that Jesus of Nazareth had to die to save the children of God from perishing due to their sins. The Scripture is the inspired Word of God, even if not everything in it came through the conscious understanding or intention of the human author, whether acquired by human knowledge or by revelation.

Moreover, there is a spiritual gift of interpretation that allows us to understand Scripture as a work of the Holy Spirit and understand what he was doing in the Old Testament. Not only is there a shortcoming in the modern emphasis on what the human author intended, there is also a shortcoming in a secular methodology that prohibits a spiritual interpretation of the Scripture. First Corinthians 2:12–18 presents forcefully the need of a spiritual interpretation:

> Now we have received not the spirit of the world, but the Spirit which is from God, that we might understand the gifts bestowed on us by God. And we impart this in words not taught by human wisdom but taught by the Spirit, interpreting spiritual truths to those who possess the Spirit.
>
> The unspiritual man does not receive the gifts of the Spirit of God, for they are folly to him, and he is not able to understand them because they are spiritually discerned.

Paul, in other words, is teaching here that unless we are spiritualized people—people who have received the gift of the Spirit, which puts us into contact with spiritual realities and allows us to understand them, and who have let our minds be formed by spiritual teaching—we will not be able to understand the full meaning of the Old Testament, or the New Testament for that matter.

When Christians, whether ordinary believers or scholars and teachers, have received the gift of the Spirit in an experiential way, they come to understand who God is by acquaintance and not just by report or through studying texts. They also come to understand "the things of God," *spiritual truths*. They know the holiness and goodness of God in ways that they cannot fully put into words or fully grasp by concepts. They "see" the transcendent majesty of God in a way that makes it impossible to confuse him with the gods of pagan mythology or any other human idol, and this "seeing," this spiritual insight, compels them to understand his words in ways that point them to something beyond this world. They can *understand spiritually* [RSV: *discern spiritually*].

Spiritual interpretation also allows us to go beyond what the Old Testament authors had in mind when we apply the Scripture to our own lives or circumstances. The human author of the book of Revelation was enabled to see that Rome played the same role as Sodom or Egypt. The Roman Empire is gone, but we can be guided by the Spirit to see a similar application to some people or corporate entities in our own world. We may be able to spiritually and truly say some city or nation is Sodom and Egypt today, without, of course, claiming the same inspiration as the writers of Scripture. We are enabled by the Holy Spirit to see spiritually.

When someone takes the historical method as the *only* way of getting at the meaning of a text, they have cut themselves loose from a genuine Christian interpretation of the Scripture. An unspiritual person cannot reach a Christian interpretation. It is not available to a secular mind, because genuine Christian interpretation has to be reached the same way the Scripture was written; namely, by the Spirit of God.

CHAPTER FOUR

GENESIS 5–11:
NOAH AND THE FLOOD

Introduction to the chapter. As we have said, the first eleven chapters of the book of Genesis constitute a prologue to the whole book of Genesis and therefore the prologue to the beginning of the old covenant. These chapters are not intended as a history of the whole race up to the time of Abraham. There is no attempt in them to narrate a consistent sequence of events that describes a coherent history. Rather, they are a sequence of incidents, each telling something about the human race before God began his special work of redemption. This prologue therefore also tells us something about the human race even now. At least it tells us something about the part of the race that has not become part of God's redemptive work, whether by being part of the old covenant or the new covenant.

This long prologue is written in a different style from what follows it. Each incident has a certain narrative unity that makes a point. One of the features of its style is what we might call "holes" (*lacunae*) in the account as a whole. Perhaps the paradigm example of such a hole is expressed in the question: "Where did Cain get his wife from, if Cain and Abel were the two children of Adam and Eve?" We can certainly make various guesses, and the history of exegesis of the story of Cain and Abel provides us with many such guesses. However, the text itself provides no help, and a guess is just a guess. That should let us understand that we are mainly to pay attention to what the text tells us, because that is the key to the meaning of the passage, not what the text does not tell us, however interesting the attempt to solve that puzzle might be.

The first chapters of the book of Genesis indicate the stages of God's plan by the use of genealogies of ten generations each.[1] The first of the genealogies occurs in chapter 5:1–32. That genealogy takes us from Adam to Noah. In the chapters 2 to 4, therefore, we have looked at the first stage, the stage of the sons (descendants) of Adam. We learned both of God's intention for the human race, and of the Fall of humanity that has so far prevented the intention from being fully realized. The key turning point was disobedience to God, and disobedience to God leads to bad consequences. One of the main bad consequences is a recurrent propensity to evil.

We now need to consider the second stage, the stage of the sons (descendants) of Noah, treated in chapter 6 to the end of chapter 11, concluding with the genealogy tracing the descendants of Noah. In this section we see how God deals with the evil in human life and works to bring good out of evil, even in what we would describe as pagan or secular society. This section lays an important foundation for the following history of the old and then new covenant people of God, especially in their relations with those who do not belong to God's people. It focuses on a special event, the Flood, and a special set of human beings, Noah and his immediate family. It contains an account of God's response to the fallen state of the human race, and gives us foundational elements of his strategy to overcome the effects of the Fall and bring the human race to the state he intended it to be in from the beginning.

Creation being destroyed. The beginning of Genesis 6 contains a description of the human race having reached rock bottom. Early in the account, we read the following verses:

> The LORD saw that the wickedness of man was great in
> the earth, and that every imagination of the thoughts of his

---

[1] For a discussion of the various roles that genealogies play in biblical writings see the technical note on p. 406.

heart was only evil continually. And the LORD was sorry that he had made man on the earth, and it grieved him to his heart. So the LORD said, "I will blot out man whom I have created from the face of the ground, man and beast and creeping things and birds of the air, for I am sorry that I have made them." But Noah found favor in the eyes of the LORD. (Gen 6:5–8)

The human race so little expressed the purpose of God in creation, so little expressed the image and likeness of God in the way it lived and acted, that it almost seemed like a mistake to have brought it into existence in the first place.

There was, however, an exception—Noah—and next comes a brief description of the people who will play the key role in what is to follow: Noah and his three sons.

These are the generations of Noah. Noah was a righteous man, blameless in his generation; Noah walked with God. And Noah had three sons, Shem, Ham, and Japheth. (Gen 6:9–10)

Then there is a restatement of the problematic situation of the human race, a somewhat similar description to that found in Genesis 6:5.

Now the earth was corrupt in God's sight, and the earth was filled with violence. And God saw the earth, and behold, it was corrupt; for all flesh had corrupted their way upon the earth. (Gen 6:11–12)

What some have termed "the call of Noah" follows.

And God said to Noah, "I have determined to make an end of all flesh; for the earth is filled with violence through them; behold, I will destroy them with the earth." (Gen 6:13)

Here God speaks to Noah about his view of the situation of the human race, "all flesh," and tells him that he is about to destroy them all, along with the earth—a radical remedy. Noah, however, is to build an ark, and that ark is to contain Noah and his family along with representatives of the animals, so that there will be a future for the human race and the rest of creation.

We find two statements of the human problem in chapter 6, and the different features of both are instructive. The statement in Genesis 6:5 describes the human race as committing great wickedness, and states that the wickedness was rooted in the inclination of their thoughts toward evil. The problem is both in the external actions of the human race but even more significantly in their interior inclinations. This tells us what the root difficulty is.

The second statement in Genesis 6:11 describes the human race as filled with "violence," as it is translated in the RSV. Others translate this as "outrageous behavior" or something similar. The evil actions of the human race had become flagrantly bad. The evil that was manifested in Cain's murder of his brother had become characteristic of the human race as a whole.

This second statement of the problem contains another key feature of the problem. It says that the earth *was corrupt,* and it was corrupt because *all flesh,* all human beings, *had corrupted their way,* the way they lived (6:12). God's response then is that he needed to *destroy all flesh* (6:13). "To be corrupt," "to corrupt," and "to destroy" are translations of different forms of the same Hebrew verb. This probably means that the earth was being destroyed because human beings had already been destroying the moral goodness of their life, and as a result God decided to complete the destruction of the human race. As Revelation 11:18, puts it, he had to "destroy the destroyers of the earth."

This second statement gives us an important understanding of the nature of God's judgment. Wickedness, evil, outrageous behavior ruins human life or at least produces a process of ruin. God did not have to do anything for sinful behavior to produce very bad consequences. Rather, God's judgment in the Flood sped up the process that was already going on. It did so because he decided to remedy the situation. A radical remedy was needed.

To understand God's approach, we need to see not only the destruction caused by the Flood but also the other feature of what happened. The Flood completed the destruction of what had become an intolerable situation, but most of the account is not about the Flood. It is about God's remedy. The remedy centers upon one human being.

The Lord had one man of whom he could approve, one who had *found favor in [his] eyes*. This was a man who was *righteous*, who was *blameless in his generation*. That latter phrase may indicate that he was righteous for the stage of God's plan he was in (the meaning of which will be discussed further on in this chapter). He was a man who had not corrupted his way on earth. He was also a man who *walked with God*, a man who lived in a good relationship with him. This was a man who could make a new beginning for the human race. He was there when he was needed.

God chose Noah to make that new beginning by telling him to build an ark. He explained to him that he was going to destroy the earth by bringing a flood upon it. He wanted Noah, however, to preserve every kind of living thing in the ark, to bring them through the destruction. He would then make a covenant with Noah and his descendants.

When God finished telling Noah about what he was supposed to do, there is one simple line of Scripture that follows. *Noah did this; he did all that God commanded him* (Gen 6:22). This line is repeated after the Lord tells Noah that the time had come and he should enter the ark (Gen 7:5). Noah's response was simply to obey whatever the Lord told him to do, in contrast to Adam. Noah's obedience enabled him to take the role God was giving to him.

The New Testament in Hebrews 11:7 adds a further perspective to what we are told in Genesis:

By faith Noah, being warned by God concerning events as yet unseen, took heed and constructed an ark for the saving of his household; by this he condemned the world and became an heir of the righteousness which comes by faith.

Noah heard God speak to him and tell him something that he had no way of knowing about except through faith in God's word. God gave Noah instructions that only made sense if in fact what God said was true. Noah believed God, and his faith was expressed in obedience.

Hebrews 11:7 adds the important point *by this he condemned the world.* This probably does not mean that Noah pronounced judgment on the world. Rather, it means that his faith and obedience revealed that it would have been possible for human beings to respond to God the same way Noah did. Obedience to God was not beyond the capacity of the human race, however much Noah, and other human beings who pleased God, needed God's grace to be obedient. The fact that Noah obeyed God, in contrast to the rest of the human race, who did not, meant that Noah and his obedience made clear the guilt of most of the human race.

In the whole account of Noah and his role in the Flood (Genesis 6:9 to 9:19), Noah does not say anything. Nothing in the account helps us to know what he thought or felt when God spoke to him and gave him such an unusual commission. Noah's lack of speaking has the effect, however, of centering attention on what Noah did. He obeyed God with regard to building and using the ark because he believed God had spoken to him and told him what needed to be done. And afterwards, as we shall see, when God had delivered him and his family and the animals, he offered sacrifice to thank God.

The account of Noah and the Flood provides a foundational "type" for Christian teaching. It presents a basic pattern for how God deals with the human race, especially its fallenness, the state brought about by the Fall of Adam and Eve that manifests itself not only in immoral behavior, even flagrantly bad behavior, but also in an inner inclination to do evil. And it presents an important background for understanding the work of Christ and the new covenant. The story of Noah is a story of judgment, but even more it is a story of a new creation, and in that it prefigures the redemptive work of Christ.

THE FLOOD

The Flood. The Flood is described in Genesis 7–8 in a way that brings out its significance. The sequence of the number of days is not accidental. There were seven days of waiting for the Flood, then a second seven days of waiting, then forty days of flooding, then one hundred fifty days of the waters prevailing. Then there were one hundred fifty days of the water subsiding, enough for the ark to rest on Mount Ararat, then forty days of further subsiding, then seven days of waiting, then another seven days of waiting.[2]

At the turning point, when the Flood had reached its crest, there is a simple line: *But God remembered Noah* (Gen 8:1). The word *remembered* here is a Hebrew idiom. It does not imply that God had forgotten about Noah's existence (and now all of a sudden remembered him). Rather, it means something more like "called to mind" or "paid attention to" (and acted on the basis of). He now considered Noah and decided to act because of Noah. And the account says he did that at the turning point of the Flood. In other words, because of Noah, the man God had chosen, the man who exemplified what God wanted human beings to be like, God caused the Flood to subside and dry land to appear again. He caused the whole process to be reversed step by step, symbolized by the reverse order.

Noah was not alone. After the Flood came and the old order on earth was destroyed and after the Flood subsided, the account says,

> So Noah went forth, and his sons and his wife and his sons' wives with him. And every beast, every creeping thing, and every bird, everything that moves upon the earth, went forth by families out of the ark (Gen 8:18–19).

The book of Sirach contains a comment on this passage:

---

[2] For an explanation of the chiastic pattern in the Scriptures exemplified in this scriptural text, see the technical note on p. 409.

Noah was found perfect [blameless] and righteous;
    in the time of wrath he was taken in exchange;
therefore a remnant was left to the earth
    when the flood came. (Sir 44:17)

In the time of judgment *a remnant was left* and that remnant made
it possible for God to make a new beginning. The human race was
not totally destroyed but a faithful man was found. He and his descendants formed a remnant that God could work with. We see this
pattern again and again throughout the rest of the Old and New Testaments.

We easily miss another feature of the account of the Flood:
the description of the Flood is a description of the reversal of creation followed by a re-creation. In Genesis 7:11, the beginning of
the Flood is described by saying *the fountains of the great deep burst
forth, and the windows to the heavens were opened.* This is a reversal of
what happened on the second day of creation, when God separated
the waters, the waters of the abyss, so that there was a "firmament,"
a dome or expanse that created an open space between the waters
above the heavens and the waters below the heavens. This had given
him space on the following day to bring forth "dry land." Now those
waters began to return and bury the dry land.

Moreover, Genesis 8:1, the beginning of the account of the subsiding of the Flood, begins with a "wind" [RSV], the word that can
be translated "breath" or "Spirit," the same word used in Genesis
1:2. In other words, the breath or spirit of God passes over the water,
the waters once again are separated, and the dry land appears.

If we read the account of the Flood in comparison with the account of the original creation, we can see that the subsiding of the
Flood is being described as a re-creation. A renewed earth appears.
This new earth has the chance to be the place for new life and a new
human race that can fulfill the purpose of the original creation.

A careful reading of the account of Noah and the Flood, then,
lets us see something that modern readers often find surprising. To
be sure, the account is a story of judgment. Sin, wrongdoing, fla-

grantly wrong behavior needs to be condemned and eliminated, and God is determined to do so. However, the account is even more an account of re-creation as the way to eliminate sin.

Sin is corrupting; it is destructive of the goodness of human life and of creation as a whole. God's response to it is primarily to renew creation. He needs to destroy sin, and that often involves putting sinners to death. But his strategy more fundamentally is to take what is good, the faithful human being and the remnant people, and re-create human life according to his original purpose for it. In regard to the corporate process of the curing of the human race, he is like a doctor, faced with a broken leg that set badly, who first breaks the leg again, seemingly making it worse, so he can reset it in a better way, the way it is supposed to be. In relation to his creatures, God is first and foremost a creator—a creator of a race—and a creator who is determined to bring his creation to the purpose he has for it.

Noah, the Flood, and the New Testament.[3] Before we talk about what happened after the Flood, we will first look at the New Testament understanding of the Flood. The Flood is a very important event in the history of God's dealings with the human race. The New Testament (along with much of early Christian tradition) paid considerable attention to it.

Christ himself referred to the Flood in Luke 17:26–27 (and Mt 24:37–39). He was there talking about the Second Coming:

> As it was in the days of Noah, so will it be in the days of the Son of man. They ate, they drank, they married, they were given in marriage, until the day when Noah entered the ark, and the flood came and destroyed them all.

In this passage the account of Noah and the Flood is an example and a symbol for sudden judgment and the destruction of evil. The wa-

---

[3] For a full exposition of the Flood as a type, with special attention to patristic exegesis, see Jean Daniélou, S.J. *The Bible and the Liturgy* (Notre Dame, IN: University of Notre Dame Press, 1956), chap. 4.

ters of the Flood are waters of destruction. The Lord was also drawing a parallel between himself and Noah, and we will return to that.

Much the same description of the Flood as waters of destruction and Noah as key to the preservation of the world is found in 2 Peter 2:5 and 9, where Peter says,

> if he did not spare the ancient world, but preserved Noah, a herald of righteousness, with seven other persons, when he brought a flood upon the world of the ungodly . . . then the Lord knows how to rescue the godly from trial, and to keep the unrighteous under punishment until the day of judgment.

A third New Testament passage on the Flood can be found in 2 Peter 3:5–7, where the letter, speaking about disbelievers in the Second Coming, says,

> They deliberately ignore this one fact, that by the word of God heavens existed long ago, and an earth formed out of water and by means of water, through which the world that then existed was deluged with water and perished. But by the same word the heavens and earth that now exist have been stored up for fire, being kept until the day of judgment and destruction of ungodly men.

There is a parallel between the waters of the Flood that destroy the earth and the future judgment not by water but by fire, which will be like a flood of destruction. Again the waters of the Flood are described as waters of destruction. In all three passages, the Flood is a type of the last judgment, the one yet to come.

The next passage, 1 Peter 3:18–22, is harder to understand, but contains a key to seeing how the early Christian writers viewed the Flood. Peter is giving an example of how someone ought to go through persecution, following the example of Christ.

> For Christ also died for sins once for all, the righteous for
> the unrighteous, that he might bring us to God, being put to
> death in the flesh but made alive in the spirit; in which he
> went and preached to the spirits in prison, who formerly did
> not obey, when God's patience waited in the days of Noah,
> during the building of the ark, in which a few, that is, eight
> persons, were saved through water. Baptism, which corre-
> sponds to this, now saves you, not as a removal of dirt from
> the body but as an appeal to God for a clear conscience,
> through the resurrection of Jesus Christ, who has gone into
> heaven and is at the right hand of God, with angels, author-
> ities, and powers subject to him.

Here, too, the Flood is a type, but this time, surprising to many, it
is treated as a type of Christian Baptism. When the passage says,
baptism, which corresponds to this, now saves you, a more literal translation is "baptism, which is an anti-type to this, now saves you." The
Flood, then, is the type and Baptism is the anti-type, and the correspondence between them is important.

In considering this passage, our purpose is only to look at the
parallel that is being drawn between the Flood and Baptism. Often
when people talk about Baptism, they explain the waters of Baptism
as waters that wash the sin away, waters of purification. That is an
aspect of it, but that idea cannot be connected to what happened to
Noah and his family in the Flood. The story of Noah and the Flood
does not contain the notion of washing. Noah did not take a huge
bath, but mainly avoided a bath by being in the ark. Not only did he
not get cleaned in the ark, he probably emerged from the ark dirtier
than before. A symbolic washing away of sin is not the significance
of water in the story of Noah.

In Baptism, as in the Flood, the waters are waters of destruction,
waters of judgment. The water in Baptism signifies that something
is destroyed or put to death, namely our sinful nature.[4] This is con-

---

[4] Basil of Caesarea, *On the Holy Spirit*, 15:35: "The water into which the body enters as
into a tomb symbolizes death."

nected in this passage to Christ's death and Resurrection. We should understand Baptism in the light of the truth expressed in Romans 6:3–4 and other passages in the New Testament,

> Do you not know that all of us who have been baptized into Christ Jesus were baptized into his death? We were buried therefore with him by baptism into death, so that as Christ was raised from the dead by the glory of the Father, we too might walk in newness of life.

Baptism, then, signifies that our old human nature was buried, put to death, and we were raised to new life. This occurs because we are joined to Christ, who himself died and was raised to new life, and we now, as part of his body, share in what happened to him.

As the passage in 1 Peter 3 indicates, the same kind of thing happens in Baptism that happened in the Flood. Something (us, or at least the old "us" in this case) is put to death. There is a destruction of the sinful way of life, and there is a new beginning, a new life. The willingness to undergo Baptism is a willingness to die spiritually with the confidence that we will be able to live in a new way, a sin-free way. Just as the new life, the new creation after the Flood came as a result of the work of one righteous man, Noah, the new life in Baptism comes from one righteous man, Christ.

There is one more incident in the New Testament that has a typological connection with the account of Noah and the Flood, and that is in the passages recounting the baptism of Christ. There is a brief description of Christ's baptism in the Gospel of Mark:

> In those days Jesus came from Nazareth of Galilee and was baptized by John in the Jordan. And when he came up out of the water, immediately he saw the heavens opened and the Spirit descending upon him like a dove; and a voice came from heaven, "You are my beloved Son; with you I am well pleased." (Mk 1:9–11)

When he was baptized, Christ was manifest to the world as the Son of God. The appearance of the dove that descended upon him was the anti-type to the dove Noah sent out into the world after the Flood. As in the account of the Flood it symbolized the Spirit that passed over the waters to bring forth a physical renewal of creation, so now in the baptism of Christ it manifested the same Spirit bringing a spiritual renewal of creation.

Christ's baptism in the Jordan, his immersion in and passing through the waters, was a figure of his real baptism, his real fulfillment of the type of Noah passing through the Flood, namely his death on the Cross and his Resurrection to glorified life. He himself predicted his death by describing it as his baptism, *I have a baptism to be baptized with; and how I am constrained until it is accomplished!* (Lk 12:50). Christ's baptism in the Jordan was symbolic of his future passing through destruction, in his case, the destruction of the fallen human nature, and beginning in his person the new creation. He would pass on the result of that new creation to those who would believe in him, who were to be buried with him in Baptism and raised to newness of life in him through receiving the gift of the Spirit.

The ark, mentioned in the text from 1 Peter 3:18–22 quoted above, also plays an important role in the story of Noah and the Flood. In it, the eight persons, the remnant, are carried to safety. They, then, are the seed from which the new creation of the human race comes. Although the typological correspondence is not stated explicitly in the New Testament, the patristic discussions of the story of the Flood identify the ark with the Church.[5] It is in the Church that the new human race, the Christians, are protected and brought to a new life in Christ. Perhaps we are also to draw the conclusion that the final judgment will not happen until the ark, the Church, is ready to bring people safely through the judgment (1 Pet 3:20).

The New Testament passages present to us a view of the account of Noah and the Flood with a repeated central feature, the waters

---

[5]   There is another common patristic interpretation of the ark, namely, as typological of the wood of the Cross. See Daniélou, *The Bible and the Liturgy,* 79–84.

of the Flood. They are understood to be the description of the destruction of a sinful world, the sinful human race. They are the main scriptural type of the judgment and destruction of wickedness and unrighteousness. But they are even more an element in the type of the new creation of the human race in Christ. The new creation can only occur through death, the death of the old, so that something new might come into existence. This is made possible by the work of one righteous man, Noah—and Christ—who bring a faithful remnant through the waters of destruction and through re-creation by the Spirit of God moving over the waters.

THE RE-CREATION OF THE RACE

The renewed race. At the end of the Flood, when the waters subsided and the dry land appeared as it had on the third day of creation, God sent Noah and his family from the ark to live on the refashioned earth and to re-establish the human race. The account goes on to describe what happened next.

> Then Noah built an altar to the LORD, and took of every clean animal and of every clean bird, and offered burnt offerings on the altar. And when the LORD smelled the pleasing odor, the LORD said in his heart, "I will never again curse the ground because of man, for the imagination of man's heart is evil from his youth; neither will I ever again destroy every living creature as I have done. While the earth remains, seedtime and harvest, cold and heat, summer and winter, day and night, shall not cease." (Gen 8:20–22)

After the Flood was all over, the first thing Noah did as a righteous man was to worship God by making offerings to the Lord. He probably gave the offerings to God as thanksgiving for the deliverance from the judgment. These were not yet the offerings of the old covenant ceremonial law, which will be discussed in chapter 8, but the kind of offering that has been common among all human beings who recognized the hand of God in their lives.

The result of Noah's righteous worship, an expression of his loyal and obedient relationship with God, was a blessing upon him from God. That blessing is described in the next verse.

> And God blessed Noah and his sons, and said to them, "Be fruitful and multiply, and fill the earth." (Gen 9:1)

As we have seen, in the original creation God said to the first human beings, *Be fruitful and multiply, and fill the earth* (Gen 1:28). God now said the same thing to Noah and his sons. They were supposed to renew the human race. They were to begin a renewed creation throughout the earth.

Noah was given the role of Adam in the renewed creation. There is, however, a difference between Noah's role and Adam's. When God smelled the pleasing odor of Noah's sacrifice, he then said, *I will never again curse the ground because of man, for the inclination* [RSV: *imagination*] *of man's heart is evil from his youth; neither will I ever again destroy every living creature as I have done* (Gen 8:21).

There is a note of resignation in this statement. As a result of being propitiated by the sacrifice and obedience of Noah, a human being, God saw that the human race is capable of good. However, he also accepted the fact that there is an evil inclination in human beings and that it is not about to change—at least not until he sends "the new Adam." We might describe this inclination as our fallen human nature. God then proceeded to give some instructions, which provided for this human fallenness.

First he determined that the animal kingdom would fear the human race and the human race would be able to take animals for food. This seems to be an indication that the new creation is not a complete renewal of the original creation. In Isaiah 11:1–9 and 65:17–25 there are connected prophecies that speak about a new creation in the latter days when the harmony between human beings and the animals will be completely restored. That likely indicates that the complete restoration of the original relationship between human beings and animals will not happen until the end times. The restoration after the Flood is incomplete.

God then gave Noah, and through him the human race, a set of commandments. The first is linked to God's previous statement:

> Only you shall not eat flesh with its life, that is, its blood. (Gen 9:4)

Although human beings may eat the meat of animals, they may not feel free to relate to animals badly or indiscriminately. Perhaps the best understanding of this verse is that they may neither eat living animals, as Ephrem, the Syriac church father said, nor parts of living animals, as Maimonides, the rabbinic theologian said, but need to slaughter them humanely and drain the blood (life) from them.

God then went on to make a still more important determination. He gave the following commandment:

> For your lifeblood I will surely require a reckoning; of every beast I will require it and of man; of every man's brother I will require the life of man. Whoever sheds the blood of man, by man shall his blood be shed; for God made man in his own image. (Gen 9:5–6)

This was likely a response to the prevalence of murder in the human race after the Fall, as exemplified in the account of Cain and his descendants. God not only forbade murder, as the human race should have known without being told (Gen 4:10), but he explicitly determined that there should be retribution for it. Those who commit murder are themselves to be executed.

Finally, he gave a foundational reason for this commandment. *God made man in his own image.* The human race—and the individual members of the human race—was made in God's image to be the Son of God and take responsibility for all of material creation to bring it to the purpose for which it was created. Here too the account explicitly echoes what was said in the creation account (Gen 1:26). God may have conceded some ground as to the standards of behavior he would uphold after the Flood, but he has not given up on his fundamental purpose for the human race. The account continues in verse 7 to repeat what God said when creating and also when re-creating human beings—they are to be *fruitful and multiply,* [to] *bring forth abundantly on the earth and multiply in it* (cf. Gen 1:28; 9:1).

God then went on to make a covenant with Noah. God promised to never again destroy the earth (Gen 9:11). The implication seems to be that although God will need to handle human sin and fallenness, he will stop short of destroying the whole race (cf. Gen 8:21–22).

The account of Noah and the Flood is the first time that the word *covenant* is used in the Scripture. "Covenant" can be used for many kinds of promises or agreements between human beings. It is, however, commonly used for what could be termed "relationship agreements," that is, the establishing of ongoing relationships between human beings, normally across family lines, or, in this case, between God and human beings.[6]

There are two kinds of relationship covenants: two-way (bilateral) covenants, such as a marriage covenant or an alliance (cf. Gen 21:22–34; 26:26–33; 31:43–54), in which both parties make promises and call upon God by swearing oaths to judge them if they do not keep the covenant, and one-way (unilateral) covenants. In one-way covenants a ruler or lord, in this case God, gives the covenant and the subordinate accepts it. The covenant may be a grant of a favor for good service or an acceptance of the subordinate into a protected client or vassal status, a kind of peace treaty. God's covenant with Noah was a one-way covenant, possibly as a grant of favor to Noah and through him the human race, possibly as something like a peace treaty with the human race.

We see here a fundamental pattern of God's dealings with the

---

[6] We will consider the nature of covenants more fully in chapter 8.

human race; namely, that God undertakes to restore and establish his relationship with human beings by means of a covenant. It is through the covenant with Noah that God re-established something that was lost, and that covenant was used as the foundation for a relationship and a new way of working with the human race. The covenant with Noah, as a new father of the human race, is a universal covenant with all human beings, not just a particular covenant like the one God later made with the people of Israel on Sinai or with individuals like Abraham and David. The sign of the covenant was put in the sky, probably to indicate that the covenant covers the whole earth and the race that lives on it.

When we read the story of Noah we tend to view in a limited way the covenant God makes, as if the only thing God is doing is promising never again to destroy the earth by means of water. But in context we can see it more broadly as the re-establishment of the human race (who are Noah's descendants: Gen 9:9) and God's commitment to work with human beings, even when sinful. This covenant, then, is foundational for God's dealings with the human race. He will not wipe out the human race, evil as its behavior may be at any given point (cf. Gen 8:21; Is 54:9–10), but will deal with it according to his steadfast love and faithfulness, often expressed in his willingness to forgive or his willingness to start over again with some of them.

The universal moral law. In this context, we can see that the commandment about not murdering takes on a greater importance. It is a commandment that goes along with the covenant and applies to the whole human race. Murder is the paradigmatic sin against love of neighbor, the sin that involves the destruction of the whole human being. Therefore, as God promises to preserve the human race as a whole, he requires human beings to preserve the lives of one another as well.

Although murder may be the chief crime against the human race, it is not the only provision in the moral law. Because of this section of chapter 9 rabbinic teachers have talked about the Noahide (or Noachic or Noahidic) commandments. These are the fundamental commandments given to the whole human race, the most basic requirements for living an acceptable human life, and are likely the commandments that Noah kept, making him *blameless in his generation* (Gen 6:9). These include not to be idolatrous (not to worship false gods), not to blaspheme the name of God, not to murder, not to steal, and not to commit adultery. The people of Israel, the Jews, were given a further body of commandments, the law of Moses, and they would be judged by those as well. The other nations, the Gentiles, however, would mainly be judged by whether or not they kept the Noahide commandments.

Such a line of thought is probably behind the first two chapters in Paul's letter to the Romans, where Paul teaches that the human race should know "by nature" the basics of the moral law (Rom 2:14), and would be judged by whether they kept it or not (1:32; 2:1ff). The Christian Fathers, Eastern and Western, consistently taught that there was a moral law that all human beings knew by nature.[7] Later on, Christian teachers presented this understanding by using the terms "the law of nature" or "the natural law."

Whatever the terminology and conceptuality, the indication is clear that God is expecting all human beings to keep the laws he gave in Genesis 9:4–7. He expects them to keep others in addition to those in Genesis 9, because the first human beings were penalized or even destroyed for various kinds of wickedness, since they should have known better. Rabbinic teachers believed that most of the Noahide commandments had somehow been given to Adam, perhaps by innate moral knowledge, and therefore because of their human nature, as we read through Genesis 3–11, it seems clear that the human race knew something about basic morality, and that God could justly hold human beings to it.

Each commandment, of course, had its positive side. The commandment not to murder implies the requirement to save the lives

---

[7]   For a summary of this patristic teaching see Stanley Samuel Harakas, *Toward Transfigured Life: The* Theoria *of Eastern Orthodox Ethics* (Minneapolis, MN: Light and Life, 1983), 127–131.

of human beings when they are endangered, because the purpose of the commandment is to safeguard the lives of human beings. The Noahide commandments that were stated in a prohibitive (negative) way, therefore, implied positive requirements to honor God the Creator, and to care for the welfare of those created in his image. In the offerings Noah made to God, we can see the action of a righteous man who was keeping the Noahide commandments not just by avoiding idolatry but by positively offering worship to God.

There are a couple of versions later Jewish teachers gave of the Noahide commandments. In the most commonly accepted list of the Noahide commandments, some rabbis taught that in Genesis 9 God added one commandment to the basic ones that had been given to Adam (cited above); namely, the command about not eating blood (verse 9:4). Other rabbis taught that God was making explicit the basic law against murder (verses 5–6) but also adding the requirement that human beings punish it. Many have interpreted this as meaning that he was requiring the human race to establish a system of justice—a criminal system. Both are reasonably seen to be implied in the text, and they seem to be related to one another.

The requirement to establish a system of justice tells us something more about what is happening in the account of Noah and the Flood. God was coming to terms with human fallenness, with the fact that the *inclination of man's heart is evil from its youth*. Rather than trying—at this point—to root out human wickedness, he established a regime to contain it and limit its destructive effects.

THE AFTERMATH

Two further events. Genesis continues by describing the aftermath, beginning in verse 9:20. The first is a story about Noah and his sons. This is a difficult story and there is no space here for an adequate explanation, and some elements can probably no longer be understood with certainty. The main current scholarly consensus seems to be, however, that this is a story about incest.[8]

The account of Noah and his sons fulfills something of the same function as the story of Cain and Abel, in the sense that it shows the consequences of the preceding events. The characteristic disorder of the first stage of the human race was murder. The characteristic disorder of the second stage was to add sexual immorality, especially unnatural (not just uncontrolled) sexual activity. With this description of unloosed fallenness the account of Noah comes to an end.

The second narrative—after a genealogy listing the nations of the known world who descended from Noah—is the account of the tower of Babel or, as some Jewish teachers have termed it, the account of the "Generation of Division." It is an account of human civilization, what some books in the New Testament might have termed a "worldly" civilization (cf. 2 Cor 2:12; Eph 2:2; 1 John 2:15; 5:19). The civilized human race was united and spoke one language. And they had reached a certain level of technological capability, especially in the construction of buildings.

> They then said, "Come, let us make ourselves a city, and a tower with its top in heaven [RSV: the heavens], and let us make a name for ourselves, lest we be scattered abroad upon the face of the whole earth." (Gen 11:4)

This determination contains an echo of the determination of Eve to eat the fruit the serpent offered her and to "become like God." The tower was probably a ziggurat, a Mesopotamian temple. The plan seems to have been to build a tower to mount to heaven and perhaps to treat with God as if in some way equals with him.

Instead of these human beings reaching up to heaven, God *went down* to them (Gen 11:7). He saw what they were doing and decided to put a stop to it. He *confused their language*, meaning that he turned the common speech into a variety of human languages

---

[8]   Scott Walker Hahn and John Sietze Bergsma, "Noah's Nakedness and the Curse on Canaan (Genesis 9:20–27)," *Journal of Biblical Literature,* 124.1 (Spring 2005): 25–40.

so that the human race could not all understand one another. He divided them, in other words, into various peoples—peoples who could not communicate with each other and so tended to develop a certain hostility to each other. As a result, he scattered them over the face of the earth.

The account of the tower of Babel is in a certain way a repeat of the Fall. It expresses a further feature of the consequences of the Fall—human disunity. Henceforth the human race would be divided into nations that would often be at war with one another. Then, beginning at Genesis 11:20, there is a transition to a new stage of God's dealing with the human race.

Concluding comments. The account of Noah and the Flood stands between the account of Adam and Eve and that of the patriarchs who were the ancestors of the people of Israel and of all the people of God. Noah can be seen as a new Adam, someone who re-founded the human race. He was the one righteous man "in his generation" (6:9) whom God used to restore a very bad situation. In this he was like Christ. Some have described him as the type of what some Jewish rabbis called the righteous Gentile, the man who lives a basically good life without the benefit of the law of Moses—or, Christians would add, the Gospel of Christ—the man who prevents a world without God from falling into complete ruin. Noah did not, however, bring the human race back to paradise. The restoration after Noah at best brought the human race to a contained fallenness, a fallenness whose bad behavior was at least to some extent restrained.

Many Christian teachers have seen Noah as a type of Christ, spoken of in the New Testament as an anti-type of Adam. He is not, however, explicitly described that way in the New Testament. The New Testament rather seems to see the Flood and the events connected to it as a pattern for Christ's re-creation of the human race. Christ brings in a new human race, not just a contained fallenness. However, as the one righteous man whom God used to renew the human race, it is reasonable to see Noah as a type of Christ.

This allows us to see something else important about typology. It is not a strictly defined, precisely stated exegetical practice. There is a range of approaches among solid Christian teachers. As long as we can state the nature of the correspondence we are looking at, we are on good ground when we describe someone or something as a type.

We spoke earlier of God's response to the human race as "containing a note of resignation" and of "coming to terms with human fallenness." That, of course, although probably implicit in the text, is an anthropomorphic way of describing the situation. It might be better to say that the story of Noah and the Flood manifested the fact that even the destruction of the human race would not cure the basic disease of human fallenness. To make a fundamental change God needed a different strategy. Rather than trying to deal with the race as a whole, he would bring into existence a new and different people and work with them to cure the disease.

Chapter 12 of Genesis recounts the beginning of the new strategy.[9]

THE FLOOD AND TYPOLOGY

The earliest Christians were familiar with the story of Noah and the Flood, and various elements of that story functioned as symbols and types in Christian instruction. The most significant understandings are as follows:

> **The Flood**: The waters that destroyed sinful human beings as a judgment from God, a symbol of judgment of evil and a type of the waters of Baptism
>
> **Noah**: The man who brought the human race through the destruction and so began the human race anew, a type of Christ
>
> **The ark**: The specially designed boat Noah built to bring the

---

[9]   The various narratives in Genesis 1–11 are framed by genealogies. For their function, see the technical note on p. 406.

remnant of human beings and their animals through the Flood, a type of the Christian Church

The dove: The bird that went forth to hover over the waters until dry land appeared, a precursor of the dove at Christ's baptism and a type of the Holy Spirit

Babel: The city of Babylon, a symbol of all worldly cities that oppose God's plan and his people, especially symbolized in the book of Revelation as the whore of Babylon

The tower of Babel: The temple mount (ziggurat) that the Babylonians built in their city, a symbol of human efforts to achieve equality with God

CHAPTER FIVE

THE STAGES OF GOD'S PLAN:
THE ELEMENTS

Introduction to the chapter. The stages of God's plan are not explicitly spoken about in Genesis, but the first ones are drawn from Genesis. Genesis 1–4 talks about the stage of the creation and Fall, Genesis 5–11 talks about the stage of Noah and his descendants, and Genesis 12–50 talks about the stage of the patriarchs. The movement from one stage to another is marked by genealogies of ten generations, and in each stage God has handled things somewhat differently. We can add further stages as we look at the rest of the Scriptures.

When we understand God's plan we can understand many things about Scripture better, especially how various things God said and did go together. As Augustine put it, "Distinguish the ages, and the Scriptures harmonize." Or, as we might say: understand the stages of God's plan and you can see God's work as a harmonious whole.

In this chapter we will present an overview of God's plan and the principles behind it, before considering the rest of the stages. One of the main goals of the book is to present an overview of the stages and to see the unity in God's work in creation in the light of the New Testament. That will provide an important foundation for reading the Old Testament in the light of the New.

Variations in God's approach. Christians reading the Scripture are often puzzled by what seem to be contradictions. Why, for instance, did God allow polygamy at one time but then forbade it at another?

Why did God at one time direct some people to raise an army and to kill their enemies and then tell others not to raise an army but to try to save their enemies?

Christ dealt with a similar question in Matthew 19:3–9. He was responding to some Pharisees who were seeking to trap him. They asked him a question about divorce in order to maneuver him into taking a position that would lose him support. We are not at this point concerned about what he said about divorce, but in how he established his response.

Christ appealed to two texts, one in Genesis 1, which describes how God made human beings male and female, and one in Genesis 2, which describes how God created a man and his wife to be one flesh. He concluded by saying that God does not want divorce:

> He answered, "Have you not read that he who made them from the beginning made them male and female, and said, 'For this reason a man shall leave his father and mother and be joined to his wife, and the two shall become one flesh'? So they are no longer two but one flesh. What therefore God has joined together, let not man put asunder." (Mt 19:4–5)

His opponents then raised a difficulty. They said that Moses gave a procedure for divorce in Deuteronomy, implying that therefore divorce must be acceptable to God in some circumstances. In response Christ said,

> "For your hardness of heart Moses allowed you to divorce your wives, but from the beginning it was not so." (Mt 19:8)

By *the beginning* Christ meant what was described in Genesis 1 and 2, the time of the original creation.

There are a couple of important things to see here. One is that Christ appealed to the very beginning as allowing us to understand this area of human life. He was referring to the time before sin entered creation. Since we find out about the beginning in the first and second chapters of Genesis, those chapters teach us important principles. They reveal to us truths about God's purposes for the human race. The way God originally created the race expressed something of his intention for it. That is a foundational understanding not only for Christian teaching on marriage but also for Christian teaching in general.

Christ's allusion to Israel's hardness of heart alerts us to something else of importance. We have to see what place an event or law has within the plan of God in order to understand what God is seeking to accomplish through it. In effect, Christ taught that God has handled divorce and other matters somewhat differently at different times. In *the beginning*, that is, when God created the human race, he created human beings without allowing a possibility of divorce. Then, after the Fall, when Moses was giving the law to the Jews who had shown themselves to be stubborn and disobedient in the wilderness, God prescribed a way that divorce could happen so that it would cause less harm. It was a way of containing human fallenness, an interim measure. But now, in Christ, God is offering grace to human beings and expecting that they should be able to live up to his original intention, although there are some differences among the Christian churches about what can be expected of all Christians.

We are here only interested in the changing way God has handled his teaching as illustrated by the case of divorce. We can notice two things. First, God's view has never changed in regard to divorce. He said through the prophet Malachi, *I hate divorce* (Mal 2:16), and he has hated it, that is, not wanted it or chosen it, from beginning to end. He created marriage so that the couple would remain united all the days of their lives.

But his intention had to face an obstacle as a result of the situation caused by sin and the Fall. "An enemy has done this" (Mt 13:28), and consequently God had to come up with a new approach after the Fall. Now step-by-step he is in the process of bringing the human race to be what it was supposed to be from the beginning. As a result, he has handled various areas somewhat differently at different times.

At a certain point, then, God made a concession. He treated the human race the way parents often need to treat children: he allowed them to live in a less mature way until he could train them out of it. For instance, parents usually work right from the start to get their children not to fight with one another, but they expect to live with some amount of fighting. However, at a certain point, they simply require their children not to fight any more and to deal with their disputes in a more mature way. The goal is the same, but the approach is different, depending on the level of maturity of the children. God's plan for the human race is developmental in a similar way. He has had a plan for how he would save people and bring them to the place he always wanted them to be, and that plan has varied over time.

GOD'S PLAN

The word *plan* here comes from the New Testament (see Eph 1:10; 3:9, RSV). The scriptural word behind it is sometimes translated "economy." Often when we speak of a plan, we have in mind an action plan or business plan. With such plans there is a goal or a set of goals with specified concrete steps to arrive at those goals. First do A, then do B, then do C, and then the goal will be reached. God's plan, rather, is more like a plan of operation. It is the way someone who is responsible for an area, someone who holds an office or position, goes about getting things done.

New farm managers or city managers, for instance, will often bring a new approach to getting their newly acquired responsibility handled. "Things change" when a new manager is appointed. The requirements of the job do not change, but the way the situation is being handled to "get the job done" often does change. To use the scriptural word, we could say the new manager comes with a new plan (of operation). Working within that plan, he likely also comes up with a variety of action plans to get particular things accomplished.

Plans of operation often have a developmental aspect. New managers usually do not change everything all at once the first day on the job. Rather, they work toward instituting the approach they want to use. Sometimes it takes them quite a while to get that approach in place, and they often need to work toward it stepwise. The word we use in this book for the main developments in the way God handles human affairs is *stages*. Each major new approach he takes is a different stage in his plan.

A scriptural word that often is used to speak about the stages of God's plan is the word *age* (cf. Mt 12:32; 28:20; Mk 10:30; 1 Cor 2:6; Eph 1:21, etc.). The Greek word for "age" can also be translated "era." Modern English speakers would be more likely to use the word "era" than the word "age." They would most readily speak of, for instance, the "era" of industrialization, as in the sentence "the invention of the steam engine brought in a new era."

When we use such a sentence, we mean several things by the word *era*. First, we mean that a new period of time has begun. But we mean something different by "period of time" than when we speak of the tenth century as a period of time. The tenth century is nothing more than a convenient division of time, while an era is not only a period of time but also involves some important human development. A new era is a period in which things work in a new way. The era of industrialization is a period of time in which people handled life quite differently than they had before.

It is helpful to note, moreover, another difference between a period like the tenth century and an era like the era of industrialization. The tenth century began everywhere in the world at the same time and ended everywhere at the same time. The era of industrialization did not. Historians have said that Japan entered the industrial era in 1853. But in 1853 Britain had already been in the industrial era for more than fifty years. Two different eras or ages are even able to coexist in the same place. An anthropologist once said about living in a village in New Guinea, "I was living in the modern age, but they were still living in the Stone Age."

"Age" can sometimes also be translated in English as *world* (Lk

16:8, RSV) because a new age creates a very different situation. Things are done so differently in the Stone Age and in the modern age that our Stone Age New Guinean and our modern anthropologist live in "completely different worlds." Most of the time when "world" appears in the English Scripture, however, it does not translate the Greek word for age but a different word (*kósmos*), which is a synonym for universe or perhaps material creation.

The scriptural term "age," then, commonly refers to an era of God's work. The New Testament often speaks of "this age" (1 Cor 2:6, RSV) or "the age to come" (Lk 18:30, RSV). These phrases concern the changes in the eras of human history introduced by the two main comings of Christ.

Another word that can be used to describe a stage of God's plan is the word *dispensation*. This word too comes from the Scripture, although it is used less commonly. Paul speaks of the "dispensation of death" and the "dispensation of the Spirit" (2 Cor 3:7–8). To "dispense" means to "serve up" or "give out." God "served up" or "gave out" his grace in different ways during different eras of history. According to Paul, the age that came to us in Christ is the age in which the Spirit, the Spirit of life, is given out to God's people instead of death being given out as a result of the sin of Adam.

"Dispensation," then, can also be used to describe what happens in the different stages of God's overall plan of operation. Among contemporary Christian teachers, the main stages of God's plan are commonly described as the different dispensations of God's plan. Some teachers are even called "Dispensationalists" because of how they have understood God's plan in a special way that emphasizes certain differences between the stages or dispensations. Not all orthodox Christian teachers would agree with their special interpretations but all would accept the importance of the differences in the stages of God's plan.

On the next page is a chart that outlines the stages of God's plan. As we go through the rest of this book, the chart can provide an overview of God's plan, a kind of map. It will make it easier to follow the development the Scripture gives us.

THE STAGES OF GOD'S PLAN: THE ELEMENTS

Stages	Founders	Events	People	Covenants	Inheritance
I Sons of Adam	Adam	Creation	Human Race	Sonship	Paradise
Fallen		The Fall		Exile	Paradise Lost
II Sons of Noah	Noah	The Flood The Ark	Human Race	Noahide Covenant	Settlements
III Patriarchs	Abraham (Isaac) (Jacob)	Call of Abraham Making Covenant	Sons of Abraham (Israel)	Covenant of Friendship	Promise of the Land
IV Dispensation of Sinai	Moses & Aaron (Joshua)	Exodus Giving of the Law	Sons of Israel	Covenant of Sinai	Land of Canaan
V Kingdom of Israel (Exile)	David (Solomon)	Anointing of David Building the Temple	Jerusalem Zion	Covenant of Kingship	Full Kingdom
VI Dispensation of the Spirit	Jesus Christ (His Apostles)	Crucifixion & Resurrection Pentecost	Church of Christ	New Covenant	Life of the Spirit
VII Glory	Jesus Christ	Second Coming Completion of All Things	New Jerusalem	New Covenant	New Earth (Heaven on Earth)

THE STAGES

In this section, we will give a quick overview of the stages of God's plan. Two of them we have already discussed. The rest we will discuss starting in the next chapter.

On the chart on the previous page, the central column shows the people, because God's plan is a plan for the creation and then restoration of the human race, the people he created in his image and likeness. The first stage is the stage of the sons of Adam, the human race as it began, created the way God wanted it to be and then fallen. The second stage is the stage of the sons of Noah. As a result of the judgment through the Flood, God re-created the human race working through Noah, a new beginning, but also with some new elements intended to contain the fallenness in human beings. The first two stages are the stages of God's working with the human race as a whole.

The third stage is the stage of the patriarchs, which begins with the call of Abraham. In this stage God starts to work with a particular group: the descendants of Abraham, Isaac, and Jacob, and their descendants. They have been chosen to begin something new in God's plan for the human race. Then, after they settle in Egypt, they are brought out of Egypt and are given the law on Sinai. That brings them into the fourth stage of being a people with a way of life. Finally, in the fifth stage, they are created as a kingdom, the kingdom of Israel, and enter into the stage of being a nation among nations, led by a king and able to rule over the surrounding nations. These three stages (III, IV, and V) are the stages of the old covenant people of God.

The sixth stage begins the new covenant. Through the Incarnation of Christ and his death and Resurrection followed by the outpouring of the Holy Spirit, the dispensation of grace—the dispensation of the giving of the Holy Spirit—creates the new covenant people of God. When the same Christ comes again, the new covenant people of God and all creation with it will be glorified and brought to the completion toward which God has been working (the seventh stage).

There are seven stages in God's plan, but they are grouped into three main divisions. The first is that of God's working with the whole human race. The second is that of God's working with the old covenant people of God, the Israelites or, as later they became known, the Jews. The third is that of God's working with the new covenant people of God, the Christians.

Charts give a simplified view of reality. The chart we are using easily leads to thinking that God works with one stage at a time. After completing his work with the human race he goes on to work with the old covenant people of God. Then he stops working with the old covenant people and begins working with the new covenant people. That view is, however, misleading. We live in stage six. Although the new covenant people of God are those through whom he will work to bring the human race to fulfill his purpose, he has not stopped working with the human race as a whole in the framework of the Noahide covenant, nor with the Jews in the framework of the old covenant.

The column of the founders and the column of the events are what bring the people into existence. Usually when God does something new and significant, he begins with an individual that he has chosen, a *founder*, or sometimes with a couple of individuals. He began the human race with Adam and recreated it with Noah. He began the old covenant people of God with Abraham, followed by Isaac and Jacob. He began the dispensation of the law with Moses, aided by Aaron and followed by Joshua. He began the kingdom of Israel with David, followed by Solomon. Finally, he began the new covenant with Jesus Christ, with his Apostles continuing his work, and he will bring it to glorification when he comes again.

Three of the founders are fathers of a people: Adam of the human race, Abraham of the old covenant people, and David of the kings of Israel. Noah is a father, but as a re-creator of the human race, not as its originator. Moses was special as the prophet who gave the law, assisted by Aaron the father of the priests of Israel. Joshua and David were both saviors, bringing God's people into their inheritance, and David was the father of all the legitimate kings of all

Israel. Jesus Christ was special as the Son of God who is the image of God and the savior in whom all the promises of God and hopes of human beings are embodied and fulfilled.

The *events* are also very important for the establishment of God's people in each of its stages of development. The first stage came about through the creation and Fall, producing a human race created in God's image but impaired in its likeness to him. The second stage came about through the Flood of judgment on the human race and the ark that brought the remnant through to begin the race anew. The third stage came about through the call of Abraham and the making of the covenant of friendship. The fourth stage came about through the exodus from Egypt and the giving of the law on Sinai. The fifth stage came about through the call and anointing of David as king and then the establishment of Israel's order of worship of God and the building of the temple, the center of the worship. The sixth stage came about through the death and Resurrection of Christ and the outpouring of the Holy Spirit. The final stage will begin with the Second Coming of Christ and the bringing to completion of all of God's creation.

When we understand the role of the founders and the purpose of the events, we understand what God is trying to accomplish in moving into each stage. These are foundational elements that make possible the development of God's people. The last two columns are elements that result from what God does to establish the people listed in the middle column.

The *covenant* column of the chart does not refer so much to the making of the covenant as to the relationship established by the covenant. Covenants, at least certain covenants including the ones God makes with human beings, establish a certain kind of relationship. As we have already seen, some Christian teachers have held that there was a covenant of Adam, the covenant of sonship; others that God's relationship with Adam was simply established by his creation as son. Sonship was the natural state of the human race, a state that God in his fatherhood is seeking to establish according to his purpose for the human race, despite the disobedience and sinfulness of men. The original relationship of sonship was followed by the covenant with Noah, by which God established a long-term relationship with the human race while seeking to contain its fallenness.

The next three covenants are progressive stages of the old covenant. With Abraham, God established a covenant of friendship, that is, of good relationship and partnership. Then on Sinai God established the covenant that made the descendants of Abraham, Isaac, and Jacob into a people with a way of life, giving them the law. Then he established a covenant of kingship with David and his descendants. Through the kings' rule the people of Israel would be a kingdom, a nation among nations, even ruling over other nations.

Finally, for the next two stages there is only one covenant, the new covenant. This is the covenant in the blood of Jesus Christ. It would come into existence by the two comings of Christ. The first of these two stages would be characterized by the redeemed, spiritualized relationship with God now, and the second by the glorified relationship after the Second Coming.

The inheritance is what God provides for his people so that they can have life. An inheritance is the resources people have, but especially through much of human history, the land from which they can live. Initially the inheritance was the gift of the earth to Adam, begun by putting him into the especially prepared piece of earth in paradise. This was lost through the Fall.

With the old covenant, the inheritance was a definite piece of land. For Abraham it was promised but not possessed. Moses and Joshua brought the people of Israel into possession of that land. David brought them into the full kingdom, ruling over the nearby nations, and established its center in the city of Jerusalem and on what would become the temple mount.

Finally, in the new covenant there was a change. The inheritance was no longer a piece of land, but was primarily the gift of the Spirit and the life that gift provided. It allowed the new covenant people of God to live everywhere on earth, not as possessors but as sojourners or resident aliens, maintaining their citizenship in heaven. At the end, after the Second Coming, their inheritance will be the new earth or the new land, glorified by being united to the new heaven and by the glory of God transfiguring his material creation in the new Jerusalem.

God's purpose for his creation was to be accomplished through the forming of the human race. The human race was to be his son, sharing his rule over all creation, acting as priest on behalf of all creation, returning glory to God. Adam fell and disrupted the relationship God had given him, with evil consequences for the human race, indeed, for all of creation. God, however, responded first by containing the damage, then by restoring his relationship with human beings—initially with one people, the Israelites, the old covenant people of God, then with all who would turn to him in Christ, the new covenant people of God.

At each stage, God has entered into a new relationship with human beings. He has saved them, and has blessed them with his presence and with true life in him. At the end, he will restore everything in Christ, and the glory of his everlasting kingdom will be manifest to all. As we understand God's purpose and plan, we learn to read all Scripture in a way that applies to us as people who live in the first stage of the new covenant in Christ.

EXPLANATION OF THE ELEMENTS CHART

Look at the chart "The Stages of God's Plan: The Elements" on page 133. It sketches the main stages of God's plan. They are as follows:

I. The first stage, the stage of **The Sons of Adam**, is that of the creation and Fall. God's plan, originally designed for human beings as he created them, became in this stage a plan for dealing with a fallen, sinful human race.

II. The second stage, the stage of **The Sons of Noah**, is the one following the Flood. The human race reached a point in which God judged it and then re-created it through Noah, and in doing so took more of a "contain the problem" approach to fallen people.

III. The third stage, the stage of **The Patriarchs**, is the one in which God worked with the patriarchs and their descendants to form them into a special people among other peoples on the earth, a people that was ready to be the vehicle to move the human race forward spiritually, the old covenant people of God.

IV. The fourth stage, the stage of **The Dispensation of Sinai**, is the one in which God gave the descendants of Israel a law and a way of life so that they might be a priestly people. This is the second stage of the old covenant.

V. The fifth stage, the stage of **The Kingdom of Israel**, is the one in which the children of Israel were ordered as a kingdom under David and so would be ready to receive the king to come, the son of David. This is the third stage of the old covenant.

VI. The sixth stage, the stage of **The Dispensation of the Spirit**, is the stage in which Christ comes to bring new life and salvation to those who receive him. This is the stage in which those of us who are Christians live and is the first stage of the new covenant.

VII. The seventh stage, the stage of **Glory**, is the final stage, the completion of God's work after the Second Coming of Christ when the redeemed human race and all creation will be brought to the glory God has for it. This is the second stage of the new covenant.

There are in addition two grey spaces in the chart. They show the way the stages are grouped together. The first section (the first two stages) indicates the way God deals with the fallen human race. The second section (the next three stages) indicates the old covenant. The third section (the final two stages) indicates the new covenant.

Look now at the five vertical columns: the founders, the events, the people, the covenants, and the inheritance. Each presents a different aspect of the relationship that God sets up with the human race in each stage:

> **The People**: those who are the vehicle of God's purpose are described in this column. This is the central column because the people are the object of each of the stages of God's plan as he works to bring human beings to the fulfillment of his purpose for them.
>
> **The Founder**: most of the new stages begin with one human being through whom God works to begin something new. Sometimes that person works together with one or two others. This column lists these people.
>
> **The Events**: there are a few decisive events, actions of God, by which he establishes a new stage. This column lists some of these.
>
> **The Covenant**: a covenant in this sense is an agreement to enter into a relationship of a certain sort. This column describes the various covenants God makes with people.
>
> **The Inheritance**: God provides for his people something that can be the source of life for them. This is their inheritance, sometimes material, sometimes spiritual. This column lists the changing form of the inheritance God gives people.

Special Exegetical Discussion:
Alternate Understandings of the Stages

There can be different understandings (conceptualities) of various matters in Scripture without their constituting contradictions.

There are different approaches to the stages of God's plan. Some approaches can be found in the Scripture itself. Most notably, the Letter to the Hebrews conceives of the typological relationships between the stages in a different way than the rest of the New Testament books do. Some other approaches can be found in later Christian teachers, who synthesize the stages in somewhat different ways. Still others can be found in modern Scripture scholars and theologians, who often are averse to synthesizing the different materials in the Scriptures into a unity, especially a harmonious unity. In this discussion, we will look at some of these differences.

Typology in Hebrews. The approach to typology in the Letter to the Hebrews is distinctive from that found in other New Testament writings. First of all, when it speaks about the old covenant ceremonial realities (temple, priest, sacrifice, etc.), it describes them as "anti-types," not as types. They are the copies.

The old covenant ceremonial realities are, to be sure, not copies of the new covenant realities, which did not yet exist, but they are copies of heavenly realities. The earthly old covenant sanctuary was a copy of heaven itself (Heb 9:5). Heaven itself is the type (8:5), the true tent (9:24). The earthly old covenant sacrifices and rites of purification are shadows that are shaped by and so point toward the future sacrifice of Christ, the blood of which will be offered in heaven by a heavenly high priest (8:1–3), in order to purify heavenly things (9:23).

Second, in the Letter to the Hebrews the new covenant realities are spoken of as the heavenly realities of the age to come. Speaking of what we have received and are now involved in as new covenant people, Hebrews 12:18–29 says,

> For you have not come to what may be touched, a blazing fire, and darkness, and gloom, and a tempest, and the sound of a trumpet, and a voice whose words made the hearers entreat that no further messages be spoken to them. For they could not endure the order that was given, "If even a beast touches the mountain, it shall be stoned." Indeed, so terrifying was the sight that Moses said, "I tremble with fear." But you have come to Mount Zion and to the city of the living God, the heavenly Jerusalem, and to innumerable angels in festal gathering, and to the assembly of the first-born who

are enrolled in heaven, and to a judge who is God of all, and to the spirits of just men made perfect, and to Jesus, the mediator of a new covenant, and to the sprinkled blood that speaks more graciously than the blood of Abel.

See that you do not refuse him who is speaking. For if they did not escape when they refused him who warned them on earth, much less shall we escape if we reject him who warns from heaven. His voice then shook the earth; but now he has promised, "Yet once more I will shake not only the earth but also the heaven." This phrase, "Yet once more," indicates the removal of what is shaken, as of what has been made, in order that what cannot be shaken may remain. Therefore let us be grateful for receiving a kingdom that cannot be shaken, and thus let us offer to God acceptable worship, with reverence and awe; for our God is a consuming fire.

The above passage is speaking about the situation of Christians, and it is contrasting it with the situation under the old covenant, particularly with the giving of the old covenant law on Sinai. It is, however, describing Christian life as participation in heaven in the age to come. We have come to the heavenly Jerusalem, populated by angels, by old covenant saints, and by Christ himself. Christians still living on earth have come to heaven.

In this, Christ himself preceded his followers. In his Resurrection, he became a priest and entered the sanctuary of heaven itself (9:11–12). There he offered his sacrifice, the sacrifice of his blood, on the heavenly altar. There he sat down on the throne of God (10:12), and it is to him in heaven that we now relate. Moreover, it is his heavenly priesthood that allows us to draw near to the true, heavenly sanctuary (10:19–22).

It is clear in the Letter to the Hebrews that there is to be a Second Coming of Christ (10:25). When that happens, we will receive in its fullness the kingdom that cannot be shaken, freed from its wrappings in the things of his age (12:27). Nonetheless, Hebrews speaks as if what we experience now is the same as what we will experience then, because the realities are in fact identical. When we live in the new covenant, we are in touch with heaven and the things of heaven, and we are already participating in the age to come.

Such an overview explains why Hebrews does not talk about old covenant realities as being types of new covenant realities. It talks about them as shadows and copies of heavenly realities (8:5). The new covenant realities are, in fact, the heavenly realities. They are the real thing, the fullness of spiritual truth that Christians now have, even though they do not yet experience them fully. Hebrews teaches that the new covenant is better than the old, precisely because it is heavenly, because it brings us into a better relationship with the true and eternal spiritual realities for which we were created and that we will someday experience in their fullness.

The use of typological terms in Hebrews, then, is different than in most writings of the New Testament. The question this poses is whether this means that Hebrews sees the realities being talked about (the theological facts, "the data") differently or not. The answer is no. The teaching in Hebrews supports the presentation in the section on typology above. There is no doctrinal contradiction, although there is a difference in presentation and the use of terminology.

Why, then, does this difference exist? Is it merely accidental, due to a different background or tradition that the author was formed in? Perhaps. But perhaps it is deliberate, although we have no indication in Hebrews that the author was making a deliberate choice in contradiction to the more common way of speaking about the area.

At least we can see that the conceptuality in Hebrews highlights a truth, namely that the new covenant realities before and after the Second Coming are the same, so that new covenant people are already participating in heavenly realities. Correspondingly, there is less emphasis on the correlate truth: namely, that we do not yet have the fullness of what God intends to give us—although that truth is not missing. The nature of the "already and not yet" will be treated more fully in chapter 10.

Alternate divisions of the stages of God's plan. The chart on the stages of God's plan in this book gives seven stages. There are, however, various ways of dividing up God's plan.

One common way centers on the division between the two covenants. The old covenant includes stages III, IV, V; the new covenant VI and VII. The decisive change is the coming of Christ. In this view, the first two stages (I and II) are preparation or background to God's work of restoration and are the stages for all humanity. This way of dividing up the stages of God's plan highlights the importance of the relationship between the two covenants, the old and the new.

A second common way of dividing God's plan is the division between "figure," "grace," and "glory." Stages I, II, III, IV, and V are the stages of "figure" or "type" in which New Testament realities are prefigured. Stage VI is the age of grace, the stage in which Christ gives the Holy Spirit so that human beings might live a new life. Stage VII is the completion of Christ's work in glory. This way of dividing up the stages of God's plan highlights the importance of what Christ has done for us after he was born on earth and will do for us when he comes again in glory. It focuses on how we interpret the words we find in the Scripture, especially those drawn from Old Testament vocabulary.[1]

---

[1]   Note: there are other smaller differences in marking off the stages:

- Some people would see little difference between the stage of the sons of Adam and the stage of the sons of Noah and so make them one stage.
- Some would see little difference between the dispensation of Sinai and the kingdom of Israel, because the establishment of the kingdom simply completed what Sinai began.
- Some, on the other hand, would divide the first stage into two, with the Fall opening a new stage of God's plan.
- Others would divide stage V into two, beginning another stage with the exile and diaspora, as the genealogy in the Gospel of Matthew does (Mt 1:17).
- While most would end up with seven stages, some would recognize eight and would see the final stage as the consummation of all the previous ones, and so outside the "week of ages."

These different ways of dividing the stages of God's plan are all legitimate and each can be helpful for different purposes.

These two alternate ways of dividing up the stages show us that the seven stages on the chart are not equal in importance. The changes from stages II to III or from stages V to VI, for instance, are more noteworthy than the change from IV to V. On the other hand, seeing all the stages helps us to observe the whole development in more detail and especially to read the significance of different periods in the Old Testament more clearly.

There are also various views of how the stages go together. For the most part, we do not have to be concerned with the differences between these views, because we only have a single purpose in mind. We want to learn how to read and use the Old Testament as Christians.

For instance, we want to pray the Psalms. The Psalms were written in stage V. We live in stage VI. God's plan is quite different in stage VI than it was in stage V. Yet we, like Christ and the Apostles and Christians through the ages, use prayers composed by old covenant people to express a new covenant relationship with God. When we pray we use the same words as old covenant people, but we understand them in a somewhat different way—we understand them as fulfilled in Christ (stage VI) and pointing to the glory to come (stage VII). To do this we need to understand the differences between the stages of God's plan—how different elements in the earlier stages prefigure the later ones and how those differences give us principles for using the Old Testament writings as Christians.

The fact that there are more ways than one to divide the stages of God's plan illustrates the nature of theological conceptuality, and human conceptuality in general. The primary data is what we find in the Scripture. As we have seen, the Scripture gives us markers for changes in the way God works in human history: the genealogies, especially those in Genesis and the genealogy at the beginning of the New Testament in Matthew; the indicators of "this age" and "the age to come" in the New Testament; the indicators of "old" and "new" used in the prophets and the New Testament; and so on.

Christian teachers using these markers are able to classify the different stages in different ways. Each way reveals or highlights different features of how God works in history. As long as the data is preserved, different classifications are legitimate and even helpful, although it is also possible to evaluate the different classifications as more or less useful or insightful and some as unfounded in the data or inadequate as a summary of all the data. Usually different conceptualities are adopted in order to further some purpose, and each potentially can let us see more clearly a different aspect of the realities we are seeking to understand.

Some scholarly conceptualizations. There is a tendency among some recent Scripture scholars to search for the differences in scriptural material, especially the differences that cover the same subject matter or same events. Once noted, they hypostatize those differences into different sources (e.g., J, E, D, and P in the Pentateuch) or different theologies (e.g., the Priestly theology and the Deuteronomic theology; or the theology of Paul and the theology of John) or in other ways, as we will have occasion to notice further on in this book. These approaches go, in other words, from observed differences in the Scriptures to hypothetical entities that cannot actually be observed, but only inferred.

It is one thing to see that different scriptural writings have different approaches to their teaching or their presentation of their material; it is another thing to decide on that basis that there are different sources, especially if those sources are conceived as pre-existent documents that were then put together into a new document (the one, it turns out, that we now have). It is one thing to observe differences in the way Paul and John speak about Christian truths, another thing to decide that Paul and John each developed his own "theology" and perhaps knew they were disagreeing with one another in doing so and even engaging in a dialectical development or perhaps forming their communities in deliberately different ways. It is yet another thing to decide that the communities the Apostles founded or worked in developed their own, differing theologies and then attributed those to their founding Apostles.

Certainly differences can be observed between different bodies of material in the New Testament. But then to go on to create the existence of different "theologies" is a step of conjecture. In this case, except for some theories of the development of the Synoptic Gospels, there is no postulating of different documents (the theologies are found in and shape different New Testament books). However, problematically there is rarely, if ever, a coherent attempt to define what is "a theology" and when we have two different ones. Nor does anyone establish that the New Testament writers ever developed "a theology" of their own (in fact, New Testament writers seem on the surface to be averse to the attempts of their contemporaries who come up with "different doctrines"). In short, a new entity ("a theology") is postulated without a convincing rationale for needing such an entity to explain anything in the data.

To evaluate the different scholarly views of these hypothetical entities goes beyond the scope of this book. They have the advantage of highlighting certain different patterns or elements in the way various bodies of teaching in the Scripture are presented. They have the disadvantage that they challenge the standard rule of intellectual methodology known as Occam's Razor: entities should not be multiplied more than necessary.[2]

Such efforts are not necessarily harmful. Normally they are simply examples of scholarly overreach. They become harmful when differences in scriptural texts are turned into contradictions or opposed "antitheses" sponsored by different early Christian groups who were teaching against one another. The worst result occurs when differences in formulation or conceptualization that most orthodox Christian teachers have found compatible are presented as irreconcilable contradictions or at least orientations opposed to one another.

On the other hand, there are undeniable differences to be found in the scriptural material. Any synthesis, like the one in this book about the stages of God's plan, has to take note of them and decide what is the most helpful way to put them together so that we have

---

[2] For a discussion of a similar approach, the use of models, see the methodological discussion "6. Analogical Discourse" on p. 479.

a unified view of God's plan and can teach on that basis. And such a synthesis needs to take note of as much of the data as it can and unify that data without distorting it in order to do so. The result is, hopefully, to provide greater insight into the Scriptures as we have them.

CHAPTER SIX

GENESIS 12–25(50): ABRAHAM AND FRIENDSHIP WITH GOD

TEXT: GENESIS 12–25

Stages	Founders	Events	People	Covenants	Inheritance
III Patriarchs	Abraham (Isaac) (Jacob)	Call of Abraham Making Covenant	Sons of Abraham (Israel)	Covenant of Friendship	Promise of the Land

Introduction to the chapter. Beginning with chapter 12, the book of Genesis describes a new stage of God's plan: stage III on the chart, the stage of the patriarchs, the first stage of the old covenant. Here the plan of God no longer focuses on the human race as a whole, but God is beginning to work with a particular people in a special way. He did that in part so that they could receive Christ, his Son, and so bring to birth the new covenant people of God and the new life in Christ and then bring the human race as a whole into the life of the age to come.

In the chapter on Noah and the Flood we ended with the tower of Babel in Genesis 11. Chapter 11 then contains a genealogy that brings the account from Noah to Abraham, and so is a transition section, moving us from the further fall, narrated in the account of the tower of Babel, to God's new beginning in Abraham. Just as Noah had been the one who began the second stage of God's plan, Abraham is the one who begins the third stage of God's plan. Most commonly

Genesis 12 is referred to as the beginning of the story of Abraham, which goes on to chapter 25 and narrates the death of Abraham. The book then is completed by the accounts of Isaac and Jacob and his sons, the patriarchs of the old covenant people of God.

When we discussed the chart of the stages of God's plan, we saw that they were not successive periods of time, but eras of the way God worked with people. As a result, an earlier era did not just cease when a new era began. Rather, old covenant people lived in a new era of God's plan, even though the nations around them lived in the previous era, the era of the way God worked with the human race as a whole before he began to redeem the fallen race. God was beginning a new dispensation of his plan—and of his favor—first with one person, Abraham, then with his descendants, the people of Israel.

Abraham and his seed. The account of Abraham himself begins in the transitional genealogy in chapter 11:26–32. There we find that Abraham was the oldest son of Terah, the last of the genealogy from Noah through his son Shem. Terah seems to have been a Semitic nomad, one of those who was scattered from the center of civilization in Mesopotamia. Although headed to the land of Canaan, he settled in Haran, in what is now southeastern Turkey. With his son Abraham—or Abram as he was called before God changed his name—the account of the old covenant people of God begins.

In the beginning of chapter 12 we read a brief description of the call of Abraham. God simply spoke to him. How he spoke to him we are not told. Why he chose him we are not told, although after reading the account of Abraham's life we can make a good guess that God chose him because of the kind of man he was. To use the phrase that gives the reason why God chose David, Abraham was *a man after God's own heart* (1 Sam 13:14), that is, a man who wanted to obey God. In this he was like Noah.

What God said at that point was foundational to everything God intended to do to bring the human race to the purpose for which he created it:

Now the LORD said to Abram, "Go from your country and your kindred and your father's house to the land that I will show you. And I will make of you a great nation, and I will bless you, and make your name great, so that you will be a blessing. I will bless those who bless you, and him who curses you I will curse; and in you all the families of the earth will be blessed."[1] (Gen 12:1–3)

When God calls people, he chooses them for a purpose and communicates to them why he has chosen them. The purpose of God's call to Abraham is blessing for the whole human race. But the first step is for Abraham to be the father of a great nation, a particular people who will be described later on as the people of Israel.

In order for God's purpose for Abraham to be fulfilled, Abraham had to take a concrete step. His situation was similar to that of Noah, whom God had also intended to be a source of blessing for the whole human race, but who had to take what might seem like a trivial step; namely, to build a boat. Abraham had to move and leave his country and his people, his family of origin. He had to go to where God wanted him to be and begin something new, and to do that he had to leave his family, his relatives, and his previous life behind.

The account then goes on to say, *So Abraham went, as the LORD had told him.* This was very similar to the line in the account of Noah, *Noah did this; he did all that God commanded him.* As in the case of Noah, Abraham obeyed God's word to him. Obedience made God's plan possible, or at least it made possible the participation of the person called by God to take a certain role.

As also in the case of Noah, Abraham's obedience was a response of faith. The section in the Letter to the Hebrews that describes Noah's faith goes on to say something similar about Abraham:

---

[1] The Revised Standard Version of the Bible gives two possible translations for verse 3. The Hebrew sentence can be rendered either "by you all the families of the earth shall bless themselves" or "in you all the families of the earth shall be blessed." The second of these is the one used in the Septuagint and in the New Testament.

> By faith Abraham obeyed when he was called to go out to a
> place which he was to receive as an inheritance; and he went
> out, not knowing where he was to go. (Heb 11:8)

Abraham, in other words, had to believe God's word, and he had to
believe it without seeing anything that would help him make sense
of it. He had to move step by step until God said, "stop here" in the
land of Canaan. At the outset when he heard God's word, he did not
even have the advantage of looking at the land that God intended
for him. He had to have faith in what was promised, not in what he
could see. Faith, in fact, was so characteristic of Abraham's response
to God that the Apostle Paul called him "the father of those who
believe" (Rom 4:11).

Abraham left Haran in obedience to God and came to the land
of Canaan. Then God appeared to Abraham and said, in effect, "This
is the place. This land is the inheritance I will give you":

> then the LORD appeared to Abram, and said, "To your de-
> scendants I will give this land." So he built there an altar to
> the LORD, who had appeared to him. (Gen 12:7)

In response to God's appearance and promise, Abraham worshipped
God, as Noah had when he was given dry land to live on—the
thanksgiving of a godly man who had received a blessing. There was,
however, one important difference. For Noah, the newly restored
earth was an accomplished fact. For Abraham, the land he would
have was still only the promised land, not the possessed land.

God promised Abraham two things. First, he promised him a
land to inhabit, a place that would provide for him and his people
what they needed to live. "Land" and "earth" are two English translations of the same word in Hebrew. God was giving Abraham a piece
of the earth to live in. The Letter to the Hebrews, using Old Testament vocabulary, also calls it *an inheritance*, because an inheritance
is something that is the possession of a family and that is passed on
from generation to generation.

God secondly promised descendants, or to use the more literal translation of the word in the Hebrew text, *seed*. Abraham would be the father of a people, a family, and that people would take an important place in God's plan to bless the whole human race, all nations. This people would be his seed, and therefore he would be their father.

God treated Abraham much as he had Adam. When God created Adam to be his son, he created him for a purpose: to fill the earth and to bring it to the perfection he intended for it. To do that, he first gave him paradise, a piece of the earth, to live in and tend. He also gave him a woman, another human being of a different sex, so that he could increase and multiply. His plan was to create a race, a people, who would fill the earth.

God now promised Abraham that he would do something similar with him. He would use him to bless the whole human race, in effect the whole earth. He promised that Abraham, who was married but childless, would have many descendants, that he would increase and multiply. And he promised him a land, a piece of the earth. But there is an important difference between what he said to Adam and what he said to Abraham. The land he promised Abraham was only part of the whole earth. Moreover, his descendants would not be the whole human race. God was taking a first step by working with one man and through him a particular people in a particular land. He had a new strategy. He had begun a new stage in his one plan.

To bring about his plan, God made a covenant with Abraham.

THE COVENANT WITH ABRAHAM

The first version of the covenant. Abraham prospered as he wandered in the land of Canaan, the land God directed him to. He was what we would call a nomadic chief, with a band of servants who made up a substantial fighting force and with many livestock that he and his servants lived from. He had become a rich and powerful man. But he had a serious concern: what the Lord had promised him—especially descendants—did not look like it was going to be fulfilled, and he was getting old.

Once again the Lord appeared to Abraham and made him the promise of a great reward (Gen 15:1–6):

> After these things the word of the LORD came to Abram in a vision, "Fear not, Abram, I am your shield; your reward shall be very great."

This promise Abraham seemed to think was too general to meet his developing concern. Abraham responded by bringing up the first aspect of his concern, the fact that he had no son and so had no prospect of being the father of a people. To all appearances his heir looked to be Eliezer of Damascus, one of Abram's servants, the steward of his house, and probably the man adopted to be his son if Abraham did not have a natural heir:

> But Abram said, "O Lord GOD, what will you give me, for I continue childless, and the heir of my house is Eliezer of Damascus?" And Abram said, "Behold, you have given me no offspring; and a slave born in my house will be my heir." (Gen 15:2–3)

To this concern he got a response:

> And behold, the word of the LORD came to him, "This man shall not be your heir; your own son shall be your heir." And he brought him outside and said, "Look toward heaven, and number the stars, if you are able to number them." Then he said to him, "So shall your descendants be." (Gen 15:4–5)

The Lord began by reconfirming his promise of descendants to Abraham in what might have seemed to Abraham an extravagant way. His descendants were to be as numerous as the stars of heaven. Despite the fact that Abraham was now old, and his wife had been barren, God insisted that Abraham would have a son to carry on the inheritance, and through that son would come a numerous people. Abraham's response was:

> And he believed the LORD.

This was a response of faith, once again in the absence of seeing anything that humanly was hopeful. The account goes on to say,

> and he [the LORD] reckoned it to him as righteousness. (Gen 15:6)

Abraham's faith in the Lord's word was enough to establish him in "righteousness." We might say that as a result of his faith he was established in a good relationship with God, one that fulfilled what God was looking for from him. This statement was quoted several times in the New Testament (Gal 3:6; Rom 4:3; Jas 2:23). As we will see, it was important for understanding Abraham's role in God's plan.

There was a further aspect to Abraham's concern. This one was connected to the other element of what God had promised him, the land. He had been living on the promised land, but he did not possess any of it, and it looked unlikely that he ever would. The Lord spoke to him about this as well.

> And he said to him, "I am the LORD who brought you from Ur of the Chaldeans, to give you this land to possess." But he said, "O Lord GOD, how am I to know that I shall possess it?" (Gen 15:7–8)

As a confirmation of his promise, God made a covenant with Abraham. He began by instructing Abraham to prepare the needed sacrifices for the making of a covenant. After Abraham prepared the sacrifices, the narrative says,

As the sun was going down, a deep sleep fell on Abram; and lo, a dread and great darkness fell upon him. Then the LORD said to Abram, "Know of a surety that your descendants will be sojourners in a land that is not theirs, and will be slaves there, and they will be oppressed for four hundred years; and I will bring judgment on the nation which they serve, and afterward they shall come out with great possessions. As for yourself, you shall go to your fathers in peace; you shall be buried in a good old age. And they shall come back here in the fourth generation; for the iniquity of the Amorites is not yet complete." (Gen 15:12–16)

God revealed to Abraham something that he had perhaps been intending to spare him. He would not be given the land, but neither would his immediate descendants. In fact, they would end up living in a land not their own (Egypt) and would be oppressed. They would not get the promised land and live in prosperity without a struggle that would involve years of perseverance.

The Lord ended by giving the underlying explanation for why the land would not be coming to Abraham's descendants for a good while to come—*the iniquity of the Amorites is not yet complete*. In other words, at a future time the Amorites, here meaning the Canaanites, the current possessors of the land, would be at a point where they would deserve to be destroyed, much like the generation of the Flood in Noah's time. Then the land could be given to the descendants of Abraham.

Such a statement is both enlightening and mysterious. It implies that God determines much of human history according to a moral standard. It also, however, leaves unsaid some of the things we would most like to know. It does not tell us the criterion for judgment on a nation or the timescale involved in determining the moment of judgment.

The account, however, does not stop at that point. God was not just re-affirming his promise, but providing a more definite assurance that he would keep his word. The account goes on to say,

> When the sun had gone down and it was dark, behold, a
> smoking fire pot and a flaming torch passed between these
> pieces. (Gen 15:17)

To understand this we need background about one ancient way of
making a covenant (see Jer 34:17–19). An offering would be taken
and cut in half, and usually both parties would pass between the two
parts as if to say to each other, "If I do not keep the promise, let the
same thing that has happened to this animal be done to me," that is,
let me be cut into pieces. It is clear that this is what the Lord was
doing, because the next verse then says,

> On that day the LORD made a covenant with Abram, say-
> ing, "To your descendants I give this land." (Gen 15:18)

Abraham saw *a smoking fire pot and a flaming torch* pass between
the pieces. The Lord, in other words, manifested his presence in
cloud and fire and passed through the pieces of the animals to indicate that he was making a covenant with Abraham to give Abraham's
descendants the land. Even more, he was committing himself to keep
it—to the death.

The Lord passed through the pieces but did not require Abraham
to do so as well. He was making a one-way covenant to confirm his
promise. As a result, Abraham could count on God's promise to him
being fulfilled. Even though it would take generations for the land to
come to Abraham's descendants, it would come, because God was
guaranteeing that the promise would be fulfilled regardless of what
the people of Israel did. The burden to see it fulfilled was on God.

The second version of the covenant. Time passed, and no son was
born to Abraham and Sarah. Sarah lost heart, and she persuaded
Abraham to make use of what was a customary practice at that time;
namely, to conceive a child with the wife's maid, in this case Sarah's
maid Hagar. They did get a son Ishmael that way, but he was not the
one God had in mind.

As a response to this, God renewed or re-established the covenant with Abraham and explicitly included Sarah in it. The first part of the renewal is described in the beginning of chapter 17:

> When Abram was ninety-nine years old the LORD appeared to Abram, and said to him, "I am God Almighty; walk before me, and be blameless. And I will make my covenant between me and you, and will multiply you exceedingly." Then Abram fell on his face; and God said to him, "Behold, my covenant is with you, and you shall be the father of a multitude of nations. No longer shall your name be Abram, but your name shall be Abraham; for I have made you the father of a multitude of nations. I will make you exceedingly fruitful; and I will make nations of you, and kings shall come forth from you. And I will establish my covenant between me and you and your descendants after you throughout their generations for an everlasting covenant, to be God to you and to your descendants after you. And I will give to you, and to your descendants after you, the land of your sojournings, all the land of Canaan, for an everlasting possession; and I will be their God." (Gen 17:1–8)

So far, what the Lord said was not much different than he had said in Genesis 15, although it was fuller. In this statement, it is clear that God was not just guaranteeing descendants and the inheritance of the land to Abraham, but he was establishing a special relationship with Abraham himself, a relationship that would be passed on to his descendants. As an indication of the importance of this covenant relationship, God changed Abraham's name from Abram to Abraham. As we will see again, God sometimes gave those he called a new name, and that name expressed the role he intended for them in his plan.

This version of the covenant began with a command to Abraham about his life as a whole. He needed to do more than just believe God's promise and obey particular instructions. He needed to walk before God, that is, live in relationship with him; and be blameless, that is, live what we would call a good life, religiously and morally, once again like Noah. We can presume that Abraham was expected to be blameless at least according to the standards of the Noahide commandments. There is, then, a certain difference between the covenant in Genesis 15 and in Genesis 17. The former is purely promise. The latter brings in the requirements of a right response.

God then made clear that this relationship would not only be with Abraham, but also with his descendants. Here he includes a phrase that is repeated often later on. *I will establish my covenant . . . to be God to you and your descendants after you.* Later on when God was speaking to the descendants of Abraham this is expressed as, *I will be your God and you will be my people* (Ex 6:7; Jer 7:23, 11:4, 30:22; Ezek 36:28). In other words, the covenant established an on-going relationship between God and a particular people. They were to be able to count on him to be their God and defend and provide for them. He, in turn, intended to be able to count on them to serve him and live a life in accord with his commandments.

God then added an important provision to the covenant that he was making, namely, the custom of circumcision.

> And God said to Abraham, "As for you, you shall keep my covenant, you and your descendants after you throughout their generations. This is my covenant, which you shall keep, between me and you and your descendants after you: Every male among you shall be circumcised. You shall be circumcised in the flesh of your foreskins, and it shall be a sign of the covenant between me and you." (Gen 17:9–11)

This covenant is sometimes called the covenant of circumcision, because it included circumcision as the sign of the covenant.

God then established the way this covenant would relate to Abraham's family. The relationship established by the covenant of circumcision and its blessing was to pass through Sarah. She was to have a natural birth and bear Abraham a son, Isaac. Isaac, not Ishmael, would be the son of the promise, although God would also bless Ishmael. As a sign of this, he changed Sarah's name from Sarai to Sarah.

Then Abraham obeyed God and fulfilled the provisions of the law of circumcision that God gave him by circumcising the males in his household. That indicated that his household, all those who lived with him, were in a covenant relationship with God by virtue of their relationship with Abraham. Their circumcision was a sign of that relationship.

A covenant relationship with God. The covenant with Abraham was a relationship covenant, a covenant that established a stable relationship with a particular person or people. This is sometimes called a covenant of friendship, although "friendship" here does not mean simply acquaintance with some regular interaction but rather refers to an ongoing relationship of mutual commitment. We might be more inclined to say it creates a family-like or kinship relationship, because most of our friendships lack the element of ongoing commitment and mutual obligation. The covenant with Abraham established a new stage of God's relationship with human beings.

A covenant of friendship between God and human beings has two further important aspects. Friendship involves a mutual confidence, at least when it is a good friendship. That confidence was expressed in the way both partners were to relate to one another, God on the one hand and Abraham and his people on the other. We can see this in the following incident.

One day "three men" came to Abraham. After receiving Abraham's hospitality, God told Abraham why they had come:

The LORD said, "Shall I hide from Abraham what I am about to do, seeing that Abraham shall become a great and mighty nation, and all the nations of the earth shall bless themselves by him? No, for I have chosen him, that he may charge his children and his household after him to keep the way of the

LORD by doing righteousness and justice; so that the LORD
may bring to Abraham what he has promised him." Then the
LORD said, "Because the outcry against Sodom and Gomorrah is great and their sin is very grave, I will go down
to see whether they have done altogether according to the
outcry which has come to me; and if not, I will know." (Gen
18:17–21)

The Lord decided that he needed to explain to Abraham what he
was about to do; namely, judge the complaints that had come to
him about the outrageous behavior of Sodom and Gomorrah, where
Abraham's nephew Lot was living—although not without investi-
gating the situation first to make sure he would be judging justly.
He needed to explain these things to Abraham because of the relationship he had with him and the relationship he would have with
Abraham's descendants.

As a result of the covenant God made with Abraham, Abraham
had become a friend of God (cf. Is 41:8, 2; Chron 20:7; and Jas
2:23). He was in a committed relationship with God, a certain kind
of partnership, and consequently he had the right to know God's
mind, at least as much of God's mind as was relevant to his affairs.
As with Abraham, God has to reveal his mind to those in covenant
relationship with him so that they can fulfill the purpose he has
given them.

But there is a corresponding responsibility of those in relationship with God. Abraham had to get his children, his household, and,
by implication, his descendants to *do righteousness and justice*, that
is, to live good lives. Otherwise they could not continue the work of
Abraham.

This truth is expressed in an even more forceful way later on in
Genesis 22. There God told Abraham that he had to sacrifice his
son Isaac, the son of the promise. In other words, he had to give him
back to God. According to all human understanding this would wipe
out the promise being fulfilled by Isaac, the promised son. Abraham
started to obey, giving a supreme example of obedience to God. But

before Abraham could sacrifice Isaac, the Lord stopped him and provided a substitute. Then we read,

> And the angel of the LORD called to Abraham a second time from heaven, and said, "By myself I have sworn, says the LORD, because you have done this, and have not withheld your son, your only son, I will indeed bless you, and I will multiply your descendants as the stars of heaven and as the sand which is on the seashore. And your descendants shall possess the gate of their enemies, and in your descendants shall all the nations of the earth be blessed [RSV: by your descendants shall all the nations of the earth bless themselves], because you have obeyed my voice." (Gen 22:15–18)

God told Abraham that because he had proven faithful, because he had given back to God what God had given to him, Abraham would indeed receive the promise and receive it in its fullness, not just the land but also being a blessing to the nations through his descendants. As some have held, this passage corresponds to God's call in Genesis 12. In Genesis 22, the promise is renewed and definitively confirmed because of Abraham's response to the call.

Abraham's willingness to sacrifice Isaac, the son whom he loved, but also the son who was to fulfill the promise of innumerable descendants, was a spectacular example of faith that issues in obedience, costly obedience. Many have also seen in Isaac a willingness to be sacrificed that matched the faith of his father. The whole story has been called "the binding of Isaac," and both Jewish and Christian teachers have seen it as the seal on God's call to Abraham.

Christian writers, beginning with the Letter to the Hebrews (11:17–19), have seen more in the binding of Isaac. They have seen it as a prophetic promise by God. God saved Isaac by providing a substitute, a lamb for the sacrifice. That lamb was a foreshadowing of God's willingness to sacrifice his own Son in the death of Christ and to receive him back in his Resurrection. The faithfulness of

Abraham to his call was matched by God's faithfulness to his promise in providing the sacrifice that would save those who believe in him and establish an eternal covenant of blessing.

There is an unconditional and also a conditional aspect of one-way relational covenants like the one God established with Abraham and his descendants. This is portrayed in the chart on p. 178. First of all, the covenant relationship is established by God's initiative. He speaks to human beings, individually or corporately, and offers such a relationship. Human beings then need to respond to him to enter into that covenant. There is an initial response of acceptance, shown by their faith in his promises and by obedience to his commands. But there is also an ongoing response by which the recipients of the offer continue in that relationship. We have seen both in the story of Abraham. The result is a stable relationship with God, a union or a friendship between God and human beings.

God speaks both promises and commandments. When he offers a relationship, he promises what he will do as a result of the relationship. He also gives commandments, provisions of the covenant relationship that we need to keep to be faithful to the covenant relationship once we accept it and enter into it. The promises are both blessings if we keep the commandments, and curses if we do not, as we have seen in chapter 2 and will see even more clearly in chapter 8. Our response to God needs to be faith in his promises and obedience to his commandments. The failure to keep the covenant by failing to obey God's commandments brings bad consequences, just as keeping the covenant faithfully brings enjoyment of the blessings of the covenant.

A covenant relationship with God, then, is both unconditional and conditional. It is unconditional in the sense that God simply establishes the covenant because of the purpose he has. We have the option of entering into the relationship God is offering or not entering in. The conditional aspect of the covenant consists in the fact that, once in the relationship, we do not get the blessing of the covenant unless we keep the covenant by obeying the commandments. Rather, we will be penalized for our unfaithfulness.

This is a covenant of friendship, but it is not a friendship be-tween equals. God is God, and he establishes the covenant and de-termines its terms. We are his creatures and we need to submit to him and obey him as God.

By the time of the death of Abraham, his son Isaac had a wife, Rebekah, and would continue the line of the patriarchs (Gen 24–25). Also, Abraham came to own a piece of the promised land, the cave of Machpelah, as a burial place (Gen 24). Both the marriage of Isaac and the purchase of the land were pledges of the future fulfill-ment of God's covenant promises. Despite the earthly odds being against what God was intending, and despite some unfaithfulness of God's covenant people, God was at work bringing about the pur-pose for which he offered the covenant relationship. That, too, is an unconditional aspect of the covenant relationship. God is faithful to covenants he makes.

Abraham and the New Testament

Abraham is a very important figure in the New Testament and in New Testament teaching about Christianity. Noah is seldom men-tioned, and mostly in passages that are not central to New Testament instruction. We were able to review all the New Testament passages about Noah and about the Flood. Abraham, however, is mentioned much more often. It would take too long to cite all of the New Tes-tament passages about him and explain their significance, but we can easily grasp the main features of what the New Testament says about him.

First, as in many Old Testament passages, Abraham is very often mentioned in association with his son Isaac and his grandson Ja-cob (or Israel as God had renamed him). These three are commonly referred to as "the patriarchs." The promised covenant relationship and blessing descends through Isaac and Jacob to the people of Is-rael and does not descend to Abraham's other descendants, like his son Ishmael or his grandson Esau. Hebrews 11:9 describes Abraham, Isaac, and Jacob as *heirs of the same promise*, since they shared in the relationship Abraham had in the plan of God. The sons of Jacob, whose story is narrated in the last section of the book of Genesis, are also called patriarchs—the twelve patriarchs (Acts 7:8)—because they were the ancestors of the twelve tribes of Israel and they established the people of the promise.

Second, the New Testament writings do not present Abraham as a type of Christ, although some subsequent Christian teachers did. There were two important types of Christ in Genesis 12–25 mentioned in the New Testament. One is Melchizedek, who is a type of Christ as the king who is also a priest. The book of Hebrews (especially chapter 7), based on Psalm 110, identifies Christ's priesthood as a priesthood "according to the order of Melchizedek."

More significant for understanding Abraham's role in God's plan and the covenant relationship that was established with him is his son Isaac. He, too, is a type of Christ. We can see this in the typological story of Hagar and her son Ishmael, and Sarah and her son Isaac (Gal 4:21–31). Isaac is "the son of the promise," as is Christ (and as are Christians through Christ). Isaac appears more clearly as the type of Christ in Hebrews 11:19, where Abraham receives him back in a figurative resurrection. Here Isaac is a type of Christ and Abraham is a type of God the Father.

In the New Testament, Abraham himself is not significant as a type of Christ, but as the one who is in a relationship with God through a covenant through promise and through faith, and a father of those who would inherit that covenant and its blessings. As a result of that covenant and the relationship with God that it established, as well as by his response of faith and obedience, Abraham became the father of the people of God, both the old covenant people of God and the new covenant people of God.

It is not difficult to see Abraham as the father of the old covenant people of God, the people of Israel, since he was physically their ancestor. It is more difficult to see him as the father of the new covenant people of God, especially the new covenant people of God who are not Jews but who have come "from the Gentiles" and are not physical descendants of Abraham. Nonetheless, this is an important truth presented in the New Testament.

We can see an initial reference to the principle on which non-Jews can be sons of Abraham in the preaching of John the Baptist, where John says to the Jews,

> "Bear fruits that befit repentance, and do not begin to say to yourselves, 'We have Abraham as our father,' for I tell you, God is able from these stones to raise up children to Abraham." (Lk 3:8)

Christ says much the same in John 8:39–40.

Both of them were warning the Jews that they would not inherit the blessing of Abraham without repentance. For John the Baptist and Christ, physical descent from Abraham is not enough to constitute someone a spiritual son of Abraham and receive the spiritual blessing promised to him. True sons of Abraham are like Abraham both in his obedience and in his faith in the word of God. This implies, as we will see, that some Jews might not be sons of Abraham in the true spiritual sense while some Gentiles might be (cf. Rom 2:28–29).

The solution to the need for repentance and change for the Jewish people in order to receive the blessing of Abraham was the coming of the messiah, Jesus Christ. This was prophesied in the Song of Mary (often called the Magnificat), where Mary explicitly connects the conception of Christ with God's faithfulness to his covenant promise to his people Israel, a promise given by the word spoken to Abraham (Lk 1:54–55). It was also prophesied in the Song of Zechariah (often called the Benedictus), where Zechariah explicitly connects the birth of Christ to God's faithfulness to his covenant promise to Abraham (Lk 1:72–73). Both Mary and Zechariah thank God for the birth of Christ as an expression of God's "mercy" or "steadfast love," the love that is an expression of covenant faithfulness.

Finally, in Acts, when preaching to the Jewish leaders and people, Peter refers to the blessing of Abraham:

> "You are the sons of the prophets and of the covenant which
> God gave to your fathers, saying to Abraham, 'And in your
> posterity shall all the families of the earth be blessed.' God,
> having raised up his servant, sent him to you first, to bless
> you in turning every one of you from your wickedness."
> (Acts 3:25–26)

We already saw in Genesis 17 and 18 how the descendants of Abraham had to live righteous and blameless lives to inherit the promised
blessing (17:1; 18:19). Out of God's steadfast love and faithfulness
to his covenant with the Jewish people, he sent his Son, the messiah,
first to them to pour out his Spirit upon them and turn them from
their wickedness so that they could enjoy his blessing in the new covenant made in the blood of his Son (Lk 22:20). That in turn would
put them in a position to bless the rest of the human race through the
Apostles of the messiah.

The blessing of Abraham. The key texts that teach about the connection of the covenant with Abraham to the new covenant salvation and life can be found in Paul's letters. We will mainly look
at what Paul said in Galatians 3, supplemented by what he said in
Romans 4. Both chapters are centrally about Abraham and the inheritance he passes on. Both are chapters with complex arguments,
often expressed with a rabbinic mode of argumentation. All we can
do here is pick out some key assertions that Paul made in the course
of his discussion about the role of Abraham.

In Galatians 3, Paul was trying to establish that a good, life-giving relationship with God, what Paul terms "righteousness," does not
depend on being circumcised as a Jew and keeping the law of Moses
as a whole. Rather, a good, life-giving relationship with God—for
both Jew and Gentile—comes through receiving the grace of God
through faith in the Gospel of Christ, and through what Christ does
for believers through his death and Resurrection and the outpouring of the Holy Spirit. In this Abraham plays a key part.

Paul begins Galatians 3 by appealing to the experience of Christians who had received the gift of the Spirit and who had seen the working of miracles. This had occurred by their coming to faith in the Gospel of Christ, not by having followed the old covenant law. He then makes his key presentation of Abraham and the giving of the covenant blessing:

> Thus Abraham "believed God, and it was reckoned to him as righteousness" [Gen 5:16]. So you see that it is men of faith who are the sons of Abraham. And the Scripture, foreseeing that God would justify the Gentiles by faith, preached the gospel beforehand to Abraham, saying, "In you shall all the nations be blessed." So then, those who are men of faith are blessed with Abraham who had faith. (Gal 3:6–9)

Abraham was justified—established in righteousness, a right relationship with God—through faith. Paul concluded from this that the way to become sons of Abraham and receive the same kind of relationship he had with God is the same way Abraham did: through faith. Those who are like Abraham in this are truly his sons.

Paul then referred to the promise given to Abraham at his call in Genesis 12:3 and reaffirmed several times (Gen 18:18; 22:18; 26:4; 28:14; and Ps 72:17). The words "Gentiles" or "nations" in the above passage are two different translations of the same Greek (and Hebrew) word.[2] The promise to Abraham was that all the nations of the earth would be blessed through him, and this could not happen through physical descent from Abraham. It had to happen through faith. In fact, it had to happen through faith in the Gospel message. The promise to Abraham was an original version of the Gospel message, a message Abraham believed. As a result of that belief, God accepted him as in a good relationship with himself, and also considered that those who believe in that message likewise to be would be in a good relationship with God and so blessed in the covenant with Abraham.

---

[2]   For an explanation of the word "Gentiles," see the technical note on p. 426.

Paul then goes on to say something more about the blessing that was promised to Abraham and that would come to all the nations. He said that Christ died (for the Jews as well as the non-Jewish nations) so that,

> in Christ Jesus the blessing of Abraham might come upon the Gentiles, that we might receive the promise of the Spirit through faith. (Gal 3:14)

The blessing of Abraham, the blessing promised to Abraham and through him to the nations, the Gentiles, is the gift of the Holy Spirit. As we will see, the reception of the Spirit is an initial sharing in the life of the age to come. This has been given to Gentiles who have faith in the Gospel of Christ, as it has been given to the Jews who have the same faith.

Starting with Galatians 3:16 Paul then spoke about the passing on of the promise to the Gentiles. There Paul said the promise was made to Abraham and his *offspring* following several statements of the promise, most notably the one in Genesis 22:18 and the one in Psalm 72:17. *Offspring* is a translation of a Hebrew word and its Greek equivalent that the RSV has translated *descendants*.

Both words, *offspring* and *descendants*, as we have already seen in the case of the Hebrew text, are translations of the Greek and Hebrew words that literally mean *seed*. They are grammatically in the singular, although they could refer to a collective entity and so at times could be translated by a plural word. This Paul sees as an important textual point. The promise was not made to the "seeds" of Abraham in the sense of many offspring, but to one seed. And that seed is Christ. The promise then is not primarily about the establishment of the old covenant people of God, although they were to have a share in it and a role in passing it on, as we will see, but about Christ. It is not an accident that the New Testament begins with the title: *The book of the genealogy of Jesus Christ, the son of David, the son of Abraham* (Mt 1:1).

Paul was saying that the promise to Abraham was fulfilled in Christ, the physical descendant of Abraham. Those who believed the Gospel about Christ and had faith in it (and him) could be joined to Christ. In him they would receive a good relationship with God and the covenant blessing of the gift of the Spirit. As a result, they would be sons of Abraham, because they were in Christ, the promised offspring of Abraham.

Paul summarizes the upshot of his presentation at the end of Galatians 3 and the beginning of Galatians 4:

> for in Christ Jesus you are all sons of God, through faith. For as many of you as were baptized into Christ have put on Christ. . . . And if you are Christ's, then you are Abraham's offspring, heirs according to promise. . . .
>
> But when the time had fully come, God sent forth his Son, born of woman, born under the law, to redeem those who were under the law, so that we might receive adoption as sons. And because you are sons, God has sent the Spirit of his Son into our hearts, crying, "Abba! Father!" So through God you are no longer a slave but a son, and if a son then an heir. (Gal 3:26–27, 29; 4:4–7)

By being joined to Christ, we become Abraham's descendants, sons and daughters of God, adopted in Christ, and receive the gift of the Holy Spirit, the blessing that was promised to him. Even the Jews, who are physical descendants of Abraham, do not receive the full blessing and inheritance that is promised to the descendants of Abraham without believing in Christ and so being given the Holy Spirit. This does not mean that Jews now who do not believe in Christ do not receive any blessing as the seed of Abraham, as we will discuss later on. Nonetheless, now all the true descendants of Abraham become Abraham's offspring and receive the full blessing by being joined directly to the Son of the promise, the seed of Abraham, Christ.

When Paul argues for the Gentiles, the uncircumcised ones, being children of Abraham in Christ, he goes back to the two versions of the covenant with Abraham in Genesis 15 and 17.

Is this blessing [the blessing of forgiveness of sins] pronounced only upon the circumcised, or also upon the uncircumcised? We say that faith was reckoned to Abraham as
righteousness. How then was it reckoned to him? Was it before or after he had been circumcised? It was not after, but
before he was circumcised. He received circumcision as a
sign or seal of the righteousness which he had by faith while
he was still uncircumcised. The purpose was to make him
the father of all who believe without being circumcised and
who thus have righteousness reckoned to them, and likewise
the father of the circumcised who are not merely circumcised but also follow the example of the faith which our father Abraham had before he was circumcised. (Rom 4:9–12)

In Genesis 15, God's covenant is solely about his promises to Abraham, and the condition for entering into that covenant relationship
was Abraham's believing God and so having "righteousness reckoned to him." In Genesis 17 the covenant with Abraham includes
circumcision, and being circumcised is a condition for entering
into the covenant. Righteousness, Abraham's good relationship
with God, came before he was circumcised. It therefore is open to
people who have faith in the Gospel. The circumcised also have
righteousness if they have the kind of faith Abraham did. Abraham,
then, is father of both circumcised and uncircumcised believers.

The force of Paul's arguments here can be missed. They are not
much use in convincing a Jew, who does not believe that Jesus was
the Christ, that non-Jews could be offspring of Abraham, and Paul
did not use them for such Jews. Rather, they are directed to Christians, to people who believe in Christ and who know that both Jews
and Gentiles have been given the Holy Spirit—who have seen the
effects of the gift of the Spirit in both Jews and Gentiles. His arguments are intended to show that Gentile believers in Christ do not
need to be circumcised and become Jews—however much value it
was to be a Jew (Rom 3:1–4; 9:4–5). And the arguments are meant
to show how some of the things God said to Abraham and did with

him can only be fully understood in the light of the outpouring of the Spirit on the Gentiles.

In reading about Abraham, then, we are reading about Christianity as well as about Judaism. Abraham is the man in a covenant relationship with God, as Christians are. He is the father of the new covenant people of God, who are heirs to the righteousness that comes from faith. He gives them a model of faith, faith in the promises of God, and obedience, faithfulness to the covenant and the difference it makes (Rom 4:18–25; 10:8–10). He is the father of a new stage in how God deals with the human race, making possible all that comes afterwards, both the old covenant and the new covenant.

The family principle. As we have seen, the New Testament begins with a heading that describes Christ as "the son of Abraham." In many other places Abraham is referred to as "father Abraham" or "our father Abraham." "Father" is his most common and most significant title. As we have also seen, those who are like him in having faith are his sons. But that raises a question that we so far have not discussed very directly; namely, why can a father have such a role?

Many people raise this question in relation to Adam. Why does Adam's sin affect us? We should also raise it on the positive side. Why does Abraham's faith affect us? After all, most of us belong to a very individualistic culture. We tend to think we should be able to stand on our own two feet and be evaluated on our own merits. Some of us are wise enough to hope for something better than what we can claim on our own merit; but few nowadays would instinctively put their hope in their status in some corporate entity—people begun by some father in the past—as the key to doing well in life. Yet, the Scripture tells us that this is really the only hope we have. Abraham needs to stand in our spiritual ancestry.

We are also confronting in the Scriptures a mentality that is somewhat at odds with the related modern principle of equality, that everyone should basically have the same lot in life and the same opportunity. This is a new principle in human history that has come from an Enlightenment mentality, even though, as we will see, there was an earlier Jewish and Christian value put on a certain equality. Nonetheless the Scripture operates primarily on a principle that was seen as common sense by almost all peoples before the Enlightenment—and perhaps most peoples even now—the family principle.

The family principle is the basic principle by which God works. In contrast to the principle which egalitarian individualism holds as ideal, God does not work by equal opportunity for all individuals. Rather, he operates by choosing different people for different things, and by having them be born to different people. Even more challenging, the reasons for his choices go beyond our understanding and wisdom.

We can, however, with a little thought, recognize that the scriptural approach is a matter of common sense about human nature. If we are born into a certain family, then that family shapes what we are like. If we are born into a certain race or a certain people, then that also shapes what our life is like and the way things go for us. If we are born Chinese, many things are going to be true about us just because of our parents and people. We are going to do many things just because we will (unconsciously) imitate those we have been raised with. But even more, we get our very position in life from our family. If our family is middle class, we are likely to be. If our father is a professional, we are likely to be. This is less true than it used to be, but it still is true.

Even more, we rarely can escape completely from what our father or our parents are like. "Like father like son." We inherit a certain amount of our personality and character from our parents. When the writers of Scripture want to describe someone's nature or character, they at times use expressions such as "son of righteousness" or "son of disobedience." Behind this is likely the analogy that we inherit our human nature from our father, but also much of our personality and character, and so when we have a certain character trait we can be said to be the "son of" or "descended from" that character trait.

This sounds somewhat deterministic. It sounds like we can have no hope of being better than our parents, and sometimes that does not seem so good. The Scriptures, of course, do provide hope. Even the Old Testament teaches, *The son shall not suffer for the iniquity of the father, nor the father suffer for the iniquity of the son. The deeds of each shall be upon himself* (Ezek 18:20), and old covenant people did not have to simply follow in the bad ways of their fathers, as people like Asa or Hezekiah or Josiah showed. Even more, the New Testament teaches that the new covenant provides a religion of new beginnings, where people can turn away from *the futile ways inherited from your fathers* (1 Pet 1:18). It is a religion of new births.

More important for this chapter, the family principle operates not only by blood descent, but also by covenant. A covenant is able to establish a relationship that is equivalent to the relationship that comes from blood descent. In fact, in God's dealings with Abraham, the covenantal aspect is even more important than the blood descent. In the old covenant, Jews who do not belong to a family that has observed the rite of circumcision do not benefit from their blood ancestry (Gen 17:14). Even more, Gentiles with no Jewish blood can become part of the old covenant people of God by circumcision. Still more, everyone can come into the people established by the new covenant in the blood of Christ by faith and baptism and so have a spiritual life that they never could have had outside that covenant.

When we acknowledge Abraham as a father, then, we are recognizing that he is a father-founder. He is the one who began a new people, a number of new peoples in fact. Most significantly for this chapter, he began the old covenant people of God, who in turn made possible the new covenant people of God. His old covenant descendants were enabled, because of him and what he began, to have a relationship with God that eventually would lead to the full salvation of the human race through Christ and the new covenant.

THE STAGE OF THE PATRIARCHS

Abraham was the beginning of a new stage of God's dealing with his people. The first stage began with Adam and the second stage with

Noah. Putting the two stages together the human race as a whole proved to be sons of Adam, following him in his fallenness, although with restraint by God. Rather than trying something again with the whole human race, God then inaugurated a significant change in approach. He decided to take one man and through him to establish a people in whom all the nations of the earth would be blessed. That man was Abraham.

Abraham, then, was one who began a new stage of God's dealing with man. He was in a covenant relationship with God, and through him God began a people in covenant relationship with himself. In this stage, God first began to establish a special relationship with certain human beings; special not in the sense of especially good, although it was that, but special in the sense of being only with certain human beings instead of with the whole human race, like his relationship with Adam and Noah.

The stage God began is often termed the age of the patriarchs. This is a stage that reached a small part of the human race. The lives of the patriarchs are described in Genesis 12–50, and by the end of the book of Genesis the family of the patriarchs only contained seventy people (Ex 1:5). What God did with the patriarchs, though, is foundational for everything that came afterward in his plan.

As we have seen, there are three main patriarchs—Abraham, Isaac, and Jacob—with the sons of Jacob sometimes also being called patriarchs, the twelve patriarchs. The three gave birth to a number of nations, including Arab tribes and the people of Edom. Nonetheless, by God's choice, the heirs of the blessing were from only one of the sons of Abraham, Isaac, and one of his descendants, Jacob, who was renamed Israel. The blessing then passed to all the descendants of Jacob. So at the end of the patriarchal age, God had a people who were heirs to the blessing, the sons, or children, of Israel.

God referred to this people of Israel as his son (Ex 4:22–23; Hos 11:1; cf. Rom 9:4). Adam had been created the son of God, and his descendants were intended to be corporately the son of God. Now a new people came into existence who were created to be the son of

God. This is probably intended to indicate to us that Israel was to be the people who would restore the human race. They were to be the source of blessing to all the nations, so that they, too, would be able to be the sons and daughters of God they were created to be. It turns out, as we have seen, that the way that blessing would be given to the nations would primarily be through one of the descendants of Abraham, Jesus Christ, an Israelite who was fully the Son of God, who would make it possible for the nations to join the Israelites to be together in him sons and daughters of God.

The patriarchs, including the first generation of the children of Israel, were nomads. They had been given a land by God, but only in promise. They had begun to increase and multiply and showed the prospect of becoming a great nation. But their significance is much greater than that. They were the people God chose and put into a covenantal relationship with himself. They were the first people of a new stage of God's plan.

From one perspective (Mt 1:1) the four most significant figures in human history are Adam, Abraham, David, and Jesus Christ. There is a fuller list of important individuals that includes Noah, Isaac, Jacob, Joseph, Judah, Moses, Aaron, Joshua, Solomon, and the Twelve Apostles, but the four are the most important of them all. Adam is the beginning of the human race; Abraham is the first man in a covenant relationship of friendship with God; David is the man who established the kingdom; and Jesus Christ is the new Adam, the son of Abraham and the son of David in whom God's plan is fulfilled. Abraham, therefore, is a new beginning, the most significant person in God's dealing with the sons of Adam until Jesus Christ.

The Patriarchs and Typology

The various elements of the account of the patriarchs have functioned as symbols and types in Christian instruction throughout the centuries.

Isaac: The son promised to Abraham, a type of Christ

Melchizedek: The king of Salem (Jerusalem) who was a priest, a type of Christ

Abraham: The first of the patriarchs, a type of God the Father in Genesis 22

Jacob/Israel: The third patriarch, the father of the people of Israel and a symbol of the old covenant people

Joseph: The son of Jacob who was sold into slavery but became the chief minister of Egypt, a type of Christ who was put to death and so went ahead of his people to preserve life (Gen 45:5)

The land of Canaan: the promised land; see "The Exodus as a Type" on p. 207

Circumcision: The sign of the covenant with Abraham in Genesis 17 and of the people of Israel (the Jews) and a symbol of putting off the flesh (unredeemed humanity) and obedience to God (cf. Deut 10:16; Rom 2:25–29)

A Covenant Relationship with God

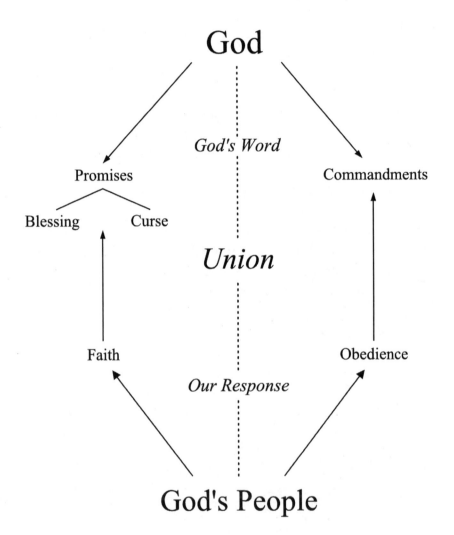

CHAPTER SEVEN

EXODUS TO JOSHUA: THE EXODUS

TEXT: EXODUS 1–24; JOSHUA 1–6

Stages	Founders	Events	People	Covenants	Inheritance
IV Dispensation of Sinai	Moses & Aaron (Joshua)	Exodus Giving of the Law	Sons of Israel	Covenant of Sinai	Land of Canaan

Introduction to the chapter. So far we have looked at the book of Genesis. The bulk of the book was the account of the patriarchs, Abraham, Isaac, Jacob, and the twelve patriarchs, the sons of Jacob. God's work with them was the first stage of his plan to have a covenanted people, and we considered it in the previous chapter.

Now we are going to look at the second old covenant stage of God's plan, the dispensation of Sinai. We are going to consider how God takes the descendants of Jacob from their oppression in Egypt and gives them a covenant on Sinai, a covenant that includes the law, that is, provisions for how they can live with him as his people. The result is the establishment of the old covenant people of God under the leadership of Moses and Aaron. This is narrated in the rest of the Pentateuch: Exodus, Leviticus, Numbers, and Deuteronomy.

The story does not, however, end with the establishment of Israel as a people with the giving of the law. The Israelites go on to take possession of the promised land. That result is primarily narrated in the book of Joshua, where the account of the taking of the land under the leadership of Joshua is told. The descendants of the patriarchs, the twelve tribes of Israel, at last began to receive their inheritance. The book of Joshua is therefore closely related to the Pentateuch, and often all those books together are described as the Hexateuch (the six scrolls), the Pentateuch plus the book of Joshua.

In this chapter we will be looking at the Hexateuch. We will consider the events from the deliverance out of Egypt to the entry into the land of Canaan. In so doing we will present an overview of the flow and significance of those events. In the next chapter we will consider the law given to the old covenant people so that they could live the life God intended for them. For that we will only need to consider the Pentateuch. The two chapters together will give us the main outlines of the establishment of the dispensation of Sinai and its nature.

Moses and the Exodus. The book of Genesis ends with seventy descendants of Jacob living in the land of Egypt at a healthy distance from the land that had been promised to them by God. At first they prospered there, because Joseph had become the chief minister of Pharaoh, the quasi-divine king of Egypt, or, at least in the more likely time of Joseph's life in Egypt, king of the northern part of Egypt. And Joseph had set up his Semitic relatives well in the delta of northern Egypt.

The book of Exodus begins with a very different situation for the descendants of the three patriarchs Abraham, Isaac, and Jacob. The people were still in Egypt and their patron brother, Joseph, was dead and forgotten by the Egyptians. The people of Israel had become very numerous and the Egyptians began to fear them. They therefore sought to gradually eliminate them:

> And the Egyptians were in dread of the people of Israel. So they made the people of Israel serve with rigor, and made their lives bitter with hard service, in mortar and brick, and

in all kinds of work in the field; in all their work they made them serve with rigor. (Ex 1:12–14)

And the people of Israel groaned under their bondage, and cried out for help, and their cry under bondage came up to God. And God heard their groaning, and God remembered his covenant with Abraham, with Isaac, and with Jacob. And God saw the people of Israel, and God knew their condition. (Ex 2:23–25)

God had made his people prosperous in Egypt for a long time, and they grew in numbers. But then there was a reversal in their fortunes and their situation became bitter. God, however, *remembered his covenant with Abraham, with Isaac, and with Jacob.* As we saw in the case of God remembering Noah, this does not mean that God had forgotten his covenant or lost track of it. Rather, the phrase *remembered his covenant* is a Hebraic idiom meaning that he acted on the basis of his covenant when special action was needed.

During the persecution of the people of Israel, God had preserved an Israelite boy, Moses, who had been rescued by Pharaoh's daughter, adopted by her, and raised in the court of Pharaoh. Witnessing an Egyptian mistreating an Israelite, he killed the Egyptian. His deed was discovered and he needed to flee the country. He lived with an Arab tribe, the Midianites, married, and seemed to have settled down among the Midianites, but one day the Lord appeared to him. His appearance is described in a passage sometimes termed "the call of Moses,"

And he said, "I am the God of your father, the God of Abraham, the God of Isaac, and the God of Jacob." . . . Then the LORD said, "I have seen the affliction of my people who are in Egypt, and have heard their cry because of their taskmasters; I know their sufferings, and I have come down to deliver them out of the hand of the Egyptians, and to bring them up out of that land to a good and broad land, a land flowing with milk and honey, to the place of the Canaanites, the Hittites, the Amorites, the Perizzites, the Hivites, and the Jebusites. And now, behold, the cry of the people of Israel has come to me, and I have seen the oppression with which the Egyptians oppress them. Come, I will send you to Pharaoh that you may bring forth my people, the sons of Israel, out of Egypt." (Ex 3:6–10)

The Lord had prepared Moses, who was an Israelite by birth but also a member of the Egyptian ruling class. Now he appeared to him, as he had appeared to the patriarchs before him, and announced to him that he was the God of his fathers. He had *come down to deliver them.* And he was sending Moses to *bring forth* [his] *people, the sons of Israel.*

Moses was wise enough to realize this was no easy assignment and that he ran the risk of being put to death by Pharaoh. However, he eventually acquiesced and was sent back to Egypt equipped with a rod that would allow him to do signs and wonders and was given the promise of the help of his brother Aaron. So begins the story of the Exodus, recounted by the people of Israel from generation to generation, and also by the Christian people from generation to generation. For both it is the story of their redemption.

Sometimes by focusing on the deliverance and nothing further the story of the Exodus is told as a story of freedom, freedom from slavery and oppression. The result of such presentations is often that the Exodus is seen as the model of getting the freedom to do what we want; to live the kind of life we want without being dictated to by others. It is even seen as the model of the freedom that comes through political liberation. However, the account of the Exodus does not present us with those kinds of freedom as the goal. Rather, it is about the freedom to live the life God wanted his people to live under his rule, and is about God making his old covenant people into a body of people who could do so.

More broadly it is the account of how God is bringing the human race to live the kind of life he created them to live.

The Deliverance and Sinai

The Exodus has several parts to it. The first part is the deliverance from Egypt: the ten plagues, the Passover sacrifice, and the crossing of the Red Sea with the destruction of Pharaoh's army. At the end of these events the Israelites were across the frontier of Egypt. Often when teachers speak about the Exodus, this is all they are referring to.

More happens, though. The people journey through the wilderness to Mount Sinai. There the old covenant is established; they are given the law and they build the tabernacle. They then journey through the wilderness, and after many trials they begin to receive the promised land by warfare. As a result of all these events, the descendants of Abraham, Isaac, and Jacob became a people in a land of their own. This was, in fact, the goal of the deliverance from Egypt.

When we speak of the Exodus here, we will be concerned with this whole process of how God took the people of Israel from their bondage in Egypt and brought them to where he wanted them to be, the promised land. To see that, we cannot stop with the Israelites on the opposite shore of the Red Sea from the Egyptians and the Egyptian army, nor with the Israelites on Sinai. We need to go on to see the Israelites receiving their inheritance in the land of Canaan. And we need to look at what God told them on the way about how they were to live in the promised land. The deliverance from Egypt does not have its true significance except in the light of what it led to.

The deliverance from Egypt. As we have seen, the account of the deliverance from Egypt begins with the Israelites being oppressed by the Egyptians and their Pharaoh. The first stage of that deliverance had three very important elements: the ten plagues, the Passover sacrifice that saved the Israelites from the tenth plague, and the crossing of the Red Sea with the destruction of the Egyptian army. Each of these played an important role.

In chapter 3 the Lord appeared to Moses in the burning bush in the Sinai, told him what he was about to do, and sent him back to Egypt to confront Pharaoh and lead his people out of Egypt. After being rejected by Pharaoh, who thereupon made the Egyptians' treatment of the Israelites even more oppressive, the Lord spoke to Moses again and reaffirmed his intention. After describing how he had established his covenant with Abraham, Isaac, and Jacob and how he had made himself known to them and had promised them the land of Canaan, the Lord then said,

> "Moreover I have heard the groaning of the people of Israel whom the Egyptians hold in bondage and I have remembered my covenant. Say therefore to the people of Israel, 'I am the LORD, and I will bring you out from under the burdens of the Egyptians, and I will deliver you from their bondage, and I will redeem you with an outstretched arm and with great acts of judgment, and I will take you for my people, and I will be your God; and you will know that I am the LORD your God, who brought you out from under the burdens of the Egyptians.'" (Ex 6:5–7)

The Lord was planning to use his divine power to deliver his people because of the commitment he had made, [his] *covenant* with Abraham, Isaac, and Jacob. The central events of the previous stage of God's plan are foundational for what he was now going to do.

This passage reveals much of the significance of the upcoming ten plagues. Although God is speaking to Moses as the human leader who is going to lead the people out, the Lord is the one who will actually deliver his people, working through Moses. He uses the phrase *with an outstretched arm*, a way of referring to the fighting a powerful warrior does in hand-to-hand combat. We usually understand the word "plague" to mean a kind of disease. The meaning of the Hebrew word, however, was "blow," and the ten plagues were blows God delivered in the fight to redeem his people, only some of which were plagues in our sense.

The Lord described the plagues as his work of *redemption*. His people were slaves in Egypt and oppressed by the Egyptians. When slaves were purchased, they were said to be redeemed—either so they could be set free or so they would belong to a new master. Those who emphasize the Exodus as a story of liberation see the redemption as simply setting the people free. In the case of the Exodus, however, the Israelites were redeemed from slavery to the Egyptians so that they could belong to God and serve him. They were receiving a new master—their God—instead of Pharaoh and the gods of Egypt.

The Lord also described the plagues as *acts of judgment*. God was judging the Egyptians for the way they treated the Israelites, but probably even more so for their unrighteousness as a people, especially their pervasive idolatry. These were not just acts of force, of superior (divine) power. They were righteous acts decided upon by a righteous king (God himself) for a good reason.

Further on in the book of Exodus, when speaking about the final plague, the Lord asserted that his judgment was not just against the Egyptians and their Pharaoh, but even more against their gods.

> "I will pass through the land of Egypt that night, and I will smite all the first-born in the land of Egypt, both man and beast; and on all the gods of Egypt I will execute judgments: I am the LORD." (Ex 12:12)

God did not make a distinction between a nation and its gods at that point, because the nation was the servant of its gods, as the Egyptians well knew. The deliverance from Egypt was a conflict between the God of the Israelites, the one true God, and the false gods of the Egyptians and the spiritual forces behind them (the demons, "the spiritual armies of evil in heavenly places" as Ephesians 6:12 puts it). The ten plagues, then, were blows in a fight between the one true God and false gods and the nation and their ruler who served those demonic gods and oppressed God's people. They were, in fact, an early skirmish in the liberation of the human race from the oppressive power of Satan and his forces.

At the end of the passage from Exodus 6 quoted above, the Lord promised that he would take the people of Israel to be his own people. The purpose of the deliverance from Egypt was for the Lord to have a people for himself through whom he could work. He used the phrase, *I will take you for my people, and I will be your God,* the phrase we have already looked at that describes the nature of the committed relationship that he wanted to have with them, a covenant relationship. All the way through the account of the plagues, the Lord *made a distinction between the Egyptians and Israel,* those he was choosing to be his people (Ex 11:7).

The Passover sacrifice. The second main element in the deliverance was the Passover sacrifice, which occurred just before the tenth plague. The Lord instructed the Israelites through Moses:

> "Tell all the congregation of Israel that on the tenth day of this month they shall take every man a lamb according to their fathers' houses . . . and you shall keep it until the fourteenth day of this month, when the whole assembly of the congregation of Israel shall kill their lambs in the evening. Then they shall take some of the blood, and put it on the two doorposts and the lintel of the houses in which they eat them. . . . The blood shall be a sign for you, upon the houses where you are; and when I see the blood, I will pass over you, and no plague shall fall upon you to destroy you, when I smite the land of Egypt." (Ex 12:3, 6–7, 9, 13)

There were two aspects of the Passover sacrifice: the slaughter of the Passover lambs with the placing of the blood on the doorposts of the houses of the Israelites, and the eating of the lamb in a sacrificial meal.

The blood played an important role. When the destroying angel saw the blood, he passed over the Israelites and slew the first-born of the Egyptians. The blood of the sacrifice of the Passover allowed the Israelites to escape the judgment on the Egyptians, among whom they lived, and the judgment on the gods of the Egyptians.

The meal also was important. As is the case with many sacrifices, the meat of the lambs offered in the Passover was eaten by those who offered the sacrifice and was a symbolic way of sharing in the benefit of the sacrifice. The eating of the Passover meal, however, had a future significance beyond the actual event of the Exodus. The Lord commanded the Israelites to observe the Passover feast as a way of commemorating the Exodus. It was a way of celebrating what God had done and reminding them of it every year, so that they would always keep in mind that the deliverance from Egypt in the past was their own deliverance as well. As it is said in the Jewish Passover celebration to this day, "In every generation one must look upon himself as if he had personally come out of Egypt."

The crossing of the Red Sea. The third main element in the deliverance was the crossing of the Red (Reed) Sea. After the final plague, in which the first-born Egyptian sons were killed, Pharaoh seemed finally convinced that no good could come of his conflict with Moses and the Lord. He sent the Israelites away, and they went toward the wilderness, to the Red Sea on the border of the land of Egypt.

Pharaoh then changed his mind again, sent out his army and pursued the fleeing Israelites. The people found themselves seemingly caught between the Egyptian army and the Red Sea. At that point Moses said to the Israelites:

> "Fear not, stand firm, and see the salvation of the LORD, which he will work for you today; for the Egyptians whom you see today, you shall never see again. The Lord will fight for you, and you have only to be still." (Ex 14:13–14)

Again Moses followed the Lord's instructions. The Lord had given him a special rod, and he had used that rod to get many of the plagues to happen. Now he stretched out that rod and the waters of the Red Sea parted. The Israelites marched through on dry land. Then Moses stretched out his rod again, and the pursuing Egyptians were drowned in the Red Sea. The people of Israel held a victory celebration on the other bank of the Red Sea and sang what was afterwards called The Song of Moses:

> "I will sing to the Lord, for he has triumphed gloriously;
>   the horse and his rider he has thrown into the sea."
> (Ex 15:1)

It was the Lord himself who accomplished the deliverance of his people from Egypt. He did it by winning a victory over the oppressors of his people and over the spiritual forces from the kingdom of darkness who were behind those oppressors. He did it by destroying them and their power. The Lord worked through Moses, especially through the use of the rod he had given Moses, but in the final analysis, it was the Lord who delivered his people, or, as the Scripture often phrases it, *redeemed* his people. The departure from the land of Egypt was, however, only the beginning. The Lord now had to bring them to the place of his dwelling, Sinai, the mountain of God.

The journey through the wilderness. There are two parts to the journey of the people of Israel through the wilderness. The first part of the journey was from the Red Sea to Sinai. The second was from Sinai to the land of Canaan. Each has a different character in the life of the people of Israel. In the first one, his people suffered deprivation, and the Lord provided for them. In the second one, in a similar set of events, the Lord provided for them but rebuked them for their manifestations of lack of faith, the faith they should have learned already. We will consider here some of the important features of the first part.

Once delivered from Egypt, the people of Israel were to go first to the mountain of God to worship the Lord and receive his instructions. After crossing the Red Sea, however, they were now on their own, and they were out in the wilderness, a relatively deserted and arid land. At least in the land of Egypt there was plenty of food and water available. In the wilderness, they could not count on those things. To get to Sinai, they needed to survive, going from oasis to oasis until they could encamp at Sinai.

First of all, we are told that the Lord himself went with them and led them on their way through the wilderness:

> The LORD went before them by day in a pillar of cloud to lead them along the way, and by night in a pillar of fire to give them light, that they might travel by day and by night; the pillar of cloud by day and the pillar of fire by night did not depart from before the people. (Ex 13:21–22)

Although there are some different views on the subject, it seems likely that there was one pillar, a column of fire covered by a cloud of smoke. During the day, only the cloud was visible, but it was probably a bright cloud due to the fire inside. During the night, the light of the fire shone through the cloud so it looked like a pillar of fire.

The pillar was a manifestation of the presence of the Lord. It was a material object on earth that behaved in an unusual way. Pillars of cloud or fire do not wander around the earth. It was clear to the Israelites that this cloud was something special and it was connected to the Lord being with them. The pillar appeared right after the night of the Passover, and it accompanied the Israelites from the time they left their homes in Egypt, through the Red Sea, and then on as they journeyed through the wilderness.

On the way, there were three things the people of Israel needed if they were going to make it to Sinai: food, water, and protection from enemies. Each of these the Lord provided for them in a manifest form.

First of all, the Lord provided food for them. He said to Moses, *Behold, I will rain bread from heaven for you* (Ex 16:4). The bread he rained down was manna. He provided just enough manna each day for the people to live on, and on the sixth day he provided twice as much so that they could keep the sabbath on the seventh day and be able to eat without having to work gathering the manna.

The Lord also provided water for them. When they reached the oasis at Rephidim, they found that it was dry or at least almost dry. The Lord then had Moses use his rod to strike a rock—an unlikely source of water—and water came out. That allowed the people and their animals to drink and to survive.

Finally, when the Amalekites, a hostile people, attacked the Israelites with intent to destroy them, the Lord instructed Moses what he was to do. Moses had his assistant Joshua lead the army of Israelites, while he himself took his rod and raised it up toward heaven over the battle. As long as Moses held up the rod, the Israelites prevailed in battle, and eventually they defeated the Amalekites.

Very often when people read accounts of the Israelites in the desert, they see it primarily as a time of trial, and it was. But there was something more important about it than the trials and how the Israelites responded to them. It was primarily a time when God provided for his people—provided food and drink and protection from enemies. This was a time when his people could not provide for themselves using normal human means, so God provided for them directly. It was a manifestation of the kingdom of God, when the Lord showed himself to be the king of his people and showed himself a king who could provide for his people. And it was the last part of the deliverance from Egypt, because the Lord was bringing his people to the mountain of his dwelling place, Sinai.

The Covenant at Sinai. Fifty days after they left Egypt the Israelites arrived at Mount Sinai, "the mountain of God" (Ex 3:1), a special place of God's presence. There they encamped. The book of Exodus then describes what happened next:

> And Moses went up to God, and the LORD called to him out of the mountain, saying, "Thus you shall say to the house of Jacob, and tell the people of Israel: You have seen what I did to the Egyptians, and how I bore you on eagles' wings and brought you to myself. Now therefore, if you will obey my voice and keep my covenant, you shall be my own possession among all peoples; for all the earth is mine, and you shall be to me a kingdom of priests and a holy nation. These are the words which you shall speak to the children of Israel."

So Moses came and called the elders of the people, and
set before them all these words which the LORD had commanded him. And all the people answered together and said,
"All that the LORD has spoken we will do." (Ex 19:3–8)

This was the point at which the Lord offered a covenant to the
Israelite people. The Lord had not just compassionately delivered
his people from oppression and then left them to live life as they
could and would. He did so in order to bring them to himself, and
that involved making a relational covenant with them.

The people of Israel were now familiar with the Lord and what
he could do. He had redeemed them from bondage and brought
them to Sinai, his holy mountain. He was here offering them the
committed covenant relationship that could be summarized in the
phrase, *You will be my people and I will be your God.* They needed to
keep the covenant and obey him. The result is that they would be *a
kingdom of priests and a holy nation.* He, in turn, would continue to
provide for them and protect them.

This covenant was a development of the covenant with Abraham and the patriarchs, but different in one important way. God had
promised Abraham that he would make his descendants a great nation and give them a land to live in. Now he was addressing himself
to those descendants and offering them a relationship as a people.
This is what we would call the old covenant, and it was the covenant
by which the Israelites *corporately* became God's people.

The making of the covenant involved more than simply the initial agreement. In the fourth chapter of Deuteronomy, while speaking to a new generation of the people of Israel, Moses described the
central event in the making of the covenant:

"On the day that you stood before the LORD your God at
Horeb, the LORD said to me, 'Gather the people to me, that
I may let them hear my words, so that they may learn to fear
me all the days that they live upon the earth, and that they
may teach their children so.' And you came near and stood at

the foot of the mountain, while the mountain burned with fire to the heart of heaven, wrapped in darkness, cloud, and gloom. Then the LORD spoke to you out of the midst of the fire; you heard the sound of words, but saw no form; there was only a voice. And he declared to you his covenant, which he commanded you to perform, that is, the ten commandments; and he wrote them upon two tables of stone. And the LORD commanded me at that time to teach you statutes and ordinances, that you might do them in the land which you are going over to possess." (Deut 4:10–14)

Horeb is another name for Sinai. The Lord had Moses gather the people before the holy mountain, prepared to meet him. He then descended upon the mountain. His arrival must have looked like a volcanic explosion, although Sinai is not a volcano. The mountain *burned with fire* covered by a cloud of smoke. The Lord appeared the same way he did in the pillar of cloud and fire, but in a much more imposing form, one that put great fear into the people.

The Lord then told them the content of the covenant, *the ten commandments*. The commandments laid out what the Israelites were to do to keep the covenant and so have the relationship with the Lord that he was offering. The Lord also added statutes and ordinances to the ten commandments, as chapters 20–23 of Exodus describe. In the next chapter we will return to the ten commandments and the rest of the law and their significance.

There was one more event that was part of this initial making of the covenant, the offering of sacrifice. As we have seen, serious covenants were sealed with a sacrificial meal. The people first committed themselves to obey the covenant the Lord had made with them. They then offered burnt offerings and peace offerings. The offering was completed by Moses sprinkling the blood of the offerings onto the altar, to give them to God, and also onto the people, as an expression of the unity between God and the people established by the covenant, sealed with the sacrifice. Then he said,

"Behold the blood of the covenant which the LORD has made with you in accordance with all these words." (Ex 24:8)

Moses, Aaron and two of his sons, and the elders (the representatives of the people) then went up the mountain to eat the sacrificial meal before the Lord:

> Then Moses and Aaron, Nadab, and Abihu, and seventy of the elders of Israel went up, and they saw the God of Israel; and there was under his feet as it were a pavement of sapphire stone, like the very heaven for clearness. And he did not lay his hand on the chief men of the people of Israel; they beheld God, and ate and drank. (Ex 24:9–11)

The Israelite leaders were, in other words, given the privilege to *see* *God* in some way, enthroned in heaven above the mountain. At the same time, they partook of the sacrificial meal as an expression of their new communion with God.

The Lord then had Moses come up the mountain to receive the rest of the law. The Lord himself wrote down the ten commandments on two tablets of stone. He also explained to Moses what more he and the people needed to do, instructions referred to as *statutes and ordinances* (Deut 4:1; Ex 21:1). He especially gave Moses the instructions to build a tabernacle, a tent that was a dwelling place for God in the midst of the people, one built in such a way that they could carry it on their journeys. God then would be present in the tabernacle. There they could worship him and would be assured that he was with them. His presence with them enabled them to be *a kingdom of priests and a holy nation* (Ex 19:6).

The golden calf. Moses remained on the mountain for forty days and nights. This was apparently more than the people had expected. While he was on the mountain, the people persuaded Aaron to make an idol for them, the golden calf. This was in direct violation of the covenant they had just committed themselves to. Ironically it also happened at the very same time that Moses was receiving directions from God for establishing true worship.

God then decided to judge his people for their disobedience and breaking of their commitment. Moses, however, interceded for them, much as Abraham had interceded for Sodom and Gomorrah. As a result, God agreed to forgive them. He had Moses come up to the mountain again and rewrote the ten commandments on the tablets of stone. He also added a set of ceremonial prescriptions to the statutes and ordinances he had originally given (Ex 34:11–26).

The incident of the golden calf was a very serious matter. Some of the rabbis (e.g., *Genesis Rabbah*, 32) took the view that God had been establishing a relationship with the Israelites like the one Adam would have had with God before the Fall, but as a result of the incident of the golden calf he saw that that would not work, and so he decided on a more distant relationship with his people. Once again, God had to work to contain human fallenness.

As we will see, some New Testament writings include the understanding that the old covenant relationship with God was not the full restoration of individual sonship with God. It was only a servant relationship, designed to keep the Israelites at something of a distance until God could further repair the situation. And many scholars think this approach was caused not only by the incident of the golden calf but also by subsequent instances of disobedience in the wilderness.

God's giving of the covenant and law on Sinai is the center of the Pentateuch. This is the point at which the people of Israel became God's people. This is the point where God agreed to come and live in their midst in the tabernacle, which later on was refashioned into the temple. This is the point where God taught them how to live a life of holiness. This is the point where God reversed the Fall enough to have a part of the human race come into a relationship with him so that they would not worship other gods, but where the one true God would be their God and they would be his people.

Sinai was a turning point in moving the human race toward

God's purpose. There was however, a shadow over it. There is a certain parallel in this respect to the account of the creation and the account of Noah and the Flood. God moved his plan forward, but he still had to contain the fallenness of the human race that was still very much in evidence in the people he was working with. The old covenant was a major step forward in God's plan. But something more needed to happen.

JOSHUA AND WINNING THE INHERITANCE

The Exodus and the entry. The Pentateuch ends at an ironic place. It is the collection of books in which the law is given, the law that explains to the people of Israel how they are to live as God's old covenant people in the land that God will give them. And yet at the end of it the people of Israel have not yet received the full promised land or begun living the life the law lays out.

Even more ironically, the two main leaders of the Exodus, Aaron, the first high priest, and Moses, the great prophetic lawgiver, do not get to go with the people into the promised land. Aaron died at the edge of the promised land, and the Pentateuch ends with Moses being given the consolation of looking at the full promised land, but dying before he could enter, or enter the main part of it, depending on how one understands the promise. At the end of the establishment of the old covenant and the work of Moses, the plan of God for the old covenant is incomplete, and incomplete because of the failure of the people of Israel and of their leaders to respond in obedience to God.

Moreover, at the end of the Pentateuch, the Exodus itself is incomplete. In the book of Deuteronomy, Moses gave the Israelites something to say to their children to explain the Exodus, and in it are the following words:

> We were Pharaoh's slaves in Egypt; and the LORD brought
> us out of Egypt with a mighty hand; and the LORD showed

signs and wonders, great and grievous, against Egypt and against Pharaoh and all his household, before our eyes; and he brought us out from there, that he might bring us in and give us the land which he swore to give to our fathers. (Deut 6:21–23)

The children should understand that the Lord *brought us out* in order that he might *bring us in*.

The word "exodus" comes from a Greek word (éxodos) meaning "exit" or "departure." There is a corresponding Greek word (eísodos) meaning "entrance" or "entry." The departure from Egypt, then, was not complete until the entry into the promised land was mainly successful. For an account of that we need to look at Joshua and the book of Joshua, the last book of the Hexateuch.

In the book of Sirach, written in the second century BC, we get a summary account of Joshua and his significance. It reads as follows:

Valiant leader was Joshua, Son of Nun,
    assistant to Moses in the prophetic office,
Formed to be, as his name implies,
    the great savior of God's chosen ones,
To punish the enemy
    and to win the inheritance for Israel. (Sir 46:1)

Joshua was an important person in the Exodus.

At the beginning of the Exodus Joshua played a subordinate, but already important, role. He was Moses' minister, possibly even his chief minister. He was his personal attendant on Sinai (Ex 24:13; 32:17), going up to assist him as he received the revelation of the law. He was given charge of the tent of meeting (Ex 33:11). He was the main military commander of the Israelites, especially commanding the army in battle against the Amalekites on the journey to Sinai (Ex 17:8–16; cf. v. 14). He was one of the Israelites sent to spy out the promised land (Num 13–14), and he and Caleb were the two who upheld the Lord's plan. As a result, he was able to survive the death of the first generation of Israelites and live on to enter the promised land.

Moses ordained Joshua to be his successor, in obedience to the divine choice (Num 27:18–23). God himself charged Joshua with the responsibility just before Moses' death (Deut 31:14, 23). He was to succeed to Moses' position and relationship with God. God said *as I was with Moses, so I will be with you* (Josh 1:5; 3:7; 4:14)—although Joshua had a significantly different role in God's plan. Where Moses was the prophetic lawgiver but never a leader in war, Joshua was the commander who led the entry into the promised land, the one who brought Moses' work to completion.

Joshua was one of those who had his name changed by God—from Hoshea to Joshua (Num 13:16), which means "the Lord (YHWH) saves"—to indicate the importance of the role he would be taking and the change he would be introducing. And lastly, he was one of those who had a book of the Bible named after them, in this case not because he wrote it but because of the importance of his deeds narrated in the book.

The entry into the land of Canaan, then, is the point at which the Israelites receive their inheritance as God's people, the old covenant children of Abraham. As the completion of the Exodus, the entry shows direct parallels to the events of the deliverance from Egypt, although parallels with a significant difference. The entry begins with the crossing of the Jordan, which corresponds to the crossing of the Red Sea, although the crossing of the Jordan was the beginning of the entry to the promised land as the crossing of the Red Sea was the end of the exit from the land of bondage.

In both events the water was stopped and the people passed through on dry ground. There was, however, the notable difference that in the crossing of the Red Sea God was present in the midst of the waters by the pillar of cloud, while in the crossing of the Jordan he was present in the midst of the waters by the ark of the covenant, built by his instructions on Sinai for his ongoing presence among his people.

At the end of the crossing of the Jordan, the parallel is made explicit. Joshua instructs the people to remind their children about the crossing, and he says,

> "you shall let your children know, 'Israel passed over this Jordan on dry ground.' For the LORD your God dried up the waters of the Jordan for you until you passed over, as the LORD your God did to the Red Sea, which he dried up for us until we passed over, so that all the peoples of the earth may know that the hand of the LORD is mighty; that you may fear the LORD your God for ever." (Josh 4:22–24)

There is also a parallel in the events of the entry in regard to the Passover sacrifice. Once the Israelites had crossed the Jordan, the men were all circumcised, in accordance with the provision of the law that said circumcision was required for the eating of the Passover (Ex 12:48). This established them fully as a people in covenant with God and therefore a people as a whole who could claim the promise of God for an inheritance (Gen 17:7–12). Those who left Egypt had been circumcised, but those born during the wandering in the wilderness had not been (Josh 5:4–7), and the circumcision of the second generation was likely an indication that the penitential years of wandering were over and the Israelites were ready to obey God under the leadership of Joshua. Some patristic authors saw this as a symbol of Baptism, which confers circumcision of the heart.

The Israelites then kept the Passover on the day it was supposed to be kept. Once again there is also a difference. The original Passover was kept before the crossing of the waters, this one was kept afterwards. This Passover commemorated the beginning of the Exodus, and it possibly included the first commemoration of entering the promised land now that the Exodus was being completed.

The account of the entry then adds something that might seem like a detail but was in fact also a significant event:

> And on the morrow after the Passover, on that very day,
> they ate of the produce of the land, unleavened cakes and
> parched grain. And the manna ceased on the morrow, when
> they ate of the produce of the land; and the people of Israel
> had manna no more, but ate of the fruit of the land of Ca-
> naan that year. (Josh 5:11–12)

The manna had been the provision for God's people while they
lived in the wilderness, their "way-bread" or "bread for the journey."
Now they were able to eat from the provisions the promised land
would give them. They had begun to enter their inheritance. They
no longer needed to look for provision directly from heaven, but
would be able to harvest the food themselves from their own land.

There then followed an incident that was parallel to the incident
of the burning bush. Joshua was *by Jericho*, probably in advance of
his people, considering what needed to be done. Then *a man stood
before him with his drawn sword in his hand.* He announced himself
as *commander of the army of the Lord* and told Joshua the same thing
Moses heard from the voice in the burning bush: *"Put off your shoes
from your feet; for the place where you stand is holy"* (Josh 5:15).

Here, too, there was a significant difference. The event happened after the crossing of the Jordan and the celebration of the
Passover. It signaled a completion of the process of entry. But *the
man* appeared not as a promised deliverer; rather as a commander of
an army giving the order to attack. Some have held Joshua was seeing Michael, the commander of the angelic armies. More likely, giv-
en the parallel with the incident of the burning bush, he was seeing
the Lord himself, but the Lord taking a new role as the commander
in war.

The fact that the events at the beginning of the entry were parallel to those of the beginning of the Exodus but in reverse order
follows the chiastic pattern commonly used in the Scriptures.[1] Both
sets of events point toward a central event, in this case the establish-

---

[1] For the fuller description of the chiastic pattern, see p. 409.

ment of the old covenant, including the giving of the law on Mount Sinai and the construction of the tabernacle. One set leads up to Sinai and one leads away from it. The difference in the two sets of events indicates the difference the central event has made. The Israelites had become an ordered people with the ongoing presence of God dwelling in the tabernacle and seated over the ark of the covenant in their midst, a people now able to provide for themselves and to fight effectively under the direction of their God. What made the difference was the covenant at Sinai.

The taking of Jericho. The entry into the promised land follows, and it begins with the taking of Jericho. The taking of Jericho was symbolic of the whole taking of the land. It was the first piece of the promised land that the Israelites conquered and as such a pledge of what was to come.

The taking of Jericho happened in a special way. The ark of the covenant was carried around the city for seven days, preceded by the army of Israel and seven priests blowing seven trumpets. This happened daily for six days and then was repeated seven times on the seventh day. When the trumpets were sounded the seventh time on the seventh march on the seventh day, the army shouted and the walls fell. This symbolized emphatically that the Lord, the Creator of all, was going before the Israelite army to make a complete victory possible.

However, the Israelite army this time played a significantly different role both in giving the battle shout before the fall of the walls and in taking the city. When the Egyptian army was destroyed, the Lord accomplished the task without the Israelites lifting a finger against the Egyptians. Worse, they were in faithless fear, pleading to God for deliverance, and murmuring against Moses who had promised deliverance (Ex 12:10–14). When the walls of Jericho fell, the Israelite army first gave the battle shout in response to the command of Joshua: *Shout for the Lord has given you the city*, and then the army *went up into the city, every man straight before him, and they took the city* (Josh 6:16, 20).

The Lord had said beforehand that he had *given* the city *into your hand* (Josh 6:2), but they had to take it. And they had to take the rest of the land by fighting, as well as destroy the armies opposing them by pursuing them when they fled. The result of the Exodus was that now the people of Israel were no longer a disorderly and helpless group of refugees fleeing from the army of their enemies, but they had become a disciplined and effective fighting force, capable of handling themselves and putting to flight their enemies—*if* they followed the Lord.

There then followed the "conquest" (as some put it) under the leadership of Joshua. Often people read the account of the fighting in the book of Joshua as the Israelites taking over the land of Canaan, driving out or killing all the old inhabitants, and settling the allotments listed in chapters 13–21. Some scholars, participating in the scholarly debate about the nature of the Israelite settlement of the land, see the account in the book of Joshua in a similar way as the narrative of a complete conquest and a supplanting of all the former inhabitants. They then find such a description to be in contradiction with the archaeological data and so historically inaccurate.

These views are a mistaken reading of an ancient form of writing. To be sure, the success of the Israelites under Joshua is put in emphatic terms, some would say in an epic form, and it would be easy to think there were no Canaanites left at the end of the book of Joshua. Victory accounts in the ancient world were not usually put in carefully qualified form, modestly acknowledging all limitations and shortcomings, but were celebratory of what had been attained, in this case what had been attained in the entry to the land under Joshua.[2]

When we read the first two chapters of the book of Judges and certain statements in the book of Joshua (Josh 13:1; 14:13; 15:63;

---

[2] For presentations of the stylistic similarities between the narratives in Joshua and Near Eastern texts of the time, see James K. Hoffmeier, *Israel in Egypt: The Evidence for the Authenticity of the Exodus Tradition* (New York/Oxford: Oxford University Press, 1996), 38–43 and K. A. Kitchen, *On the Reliability of the Old Testament* (Grand Rapids, MI: Eerdmans, 2003), 160–164, 168–174, 179.

16:10; 17:12–13, 16–18; 18:3; 23:5, 7, 12–13), we can see that the campaigns of Joshua established a predominance of Israel in the land, mainly the highlands, disabling or at least subduing the chief powers in the higher parts of the land. Nonetheless, the full occupation of the land, supplanting the earlier inhabitants, was a somewhat long process that had to follow and seemed to involve successes and failures.[3] It possibly only finished under David and perhaps not even then. More importantly, the relevant biblical texts indicate it only succeeded as the Israelites obeyed the instructions of the Lord. Nonetheless, the campaigns under Joshua were the beginning of the taking of the land, a real entry into the inheritance the Lord wanted them to have and that they could begin to enjoy, a land that was really now their own—and the Lord's.

The Israelites at war. Modern people are often scandalized by the fact that the Lord had the Israelites drive the Canaanites out, even killing many of them. Some say this is not what Christ did later. Such a view involves conveniently omitting the driving of the money changers out of the temple or the descriptions of the last battle in the Second Coming or the various statements like that in 1 John 3:8 that Christ came for spiritual warfare, that is, to "destroy the works of the devil," or the statement in Matthew 10:34 and Luke 12:51 that he "did not come to bring peace but a sword." But there were important reasons for what the Israelites did.

To begin with, we are looking at the early Iron Age. Human society at that time (and for much of human history and, most people would admit, even now) was violent, unpredictably violent. At any time there might be raiding parties like the Midianites coming for plunder or aggressive neighbors like the Philistines conquering and exacting tribute (Judg 2:14).

Sometimes defeat meant being taken over, usually by having all adult and adolescent males slaughtered and the women and children taken and assimilated, and at times by having everyone slaugh-

---

[3]   In addition to the material in the previous note, see Baruch Halpern, *The First Historians: The Hebrew Bible and History* (San Francisco: Harper and Row, 1988), 182.

tered. This complete slaughter was, for instance, the fate of part of the Israelites in Transjordan at one point in their history—according to the inscription by Mesha, the king of Moab, on the Moabite Stone:

> And Chemosh [the Moabite god] said to me, "Go, take Nebo from Israel!" So I went by night and fought against it from the break of dawn until noon, taking it and slaying all seven thousand men, boys, women, girls and maid-servants, for I had devoted them to destruction for (the god) Ashtar-Chemosh.[4]

This makes clear a further factor in the situation, namely, the gods of the nations surrounding the Israelites often incited their worshippers to destroy the Israelites, probably in opposition to the Lord, an example of the conflict between the Lord and other gods that we have seen in the account of the plagues during the Exodus from Egypt. We should add that failure to somehow disable an enemy nation—whether destroying them, taking them over, driving them out, or somehow subduing them—could mean exposure to revenge on their part and possible destruction in turn.

Having two nations peacefully co-existing in a narrow land like Palestine at the time was not very feasible. Fighting was a condition of survival (Judg 3:2). Pacifism, had anyone then seriously thought about it, would have been national suicide.

Some have held that God's approach was to have all the Canaanites or any other enemy nation in the land slaughtered. They quote Deuteronomy 7:2 (or Deut 20:17) that says the Israelites should "utterly destroy them [RSV]." That is, however, an interpretive translation, in this case misleading. A more literal translation is "put them under the ban." The ban did not automatically mean destroying something (cf. Josh 6:24). It could at times involve putting people to death, for reasons we have seen, especially

---

[4] *Ancient Near Eastern Texts Relating to the Old Testament*, James B. Pritchard, ed., 2nd edition (Princeton, NJ: Princeton University Press, 1954), 320–321.

in conditions of warfare, but that was not its primary meaning.

The ban meant putting something off limits, taking something out of ordinary use, separating from it, making it prohibited (taboo) in some sense. The context of Deuteronomy 7:2 indicates that as a result of the ban the Israelites were not to make restrictive alliances or take prisoners in battle (having soon to free them to fight again), or intermarry (a senseless prohibition if all of the enemy people had been slaughtered). The last was, in fact, the way the ban against the peoples of the land was understood in Ezra 9:1–2. The Israelites were in addition to destroy all idolatrous objects in the land (Deut 7:1–5).[5] We could add that in later biblical, Jewish, and Christian history, the ban was understood to mean some form of excommunication for immorality, not physical execution but social excommunication (e.g., Gal 1:8–9; 1 Cor 16:22).

The accounts of taking over the land indicate that the Israelite armies did not deliberately try to exterminate all enemy people, partly because it was beyond their capacity, but mainly because the goal was somehow to separate a god-fearing people from all idolatry and the worst sorts of immorality like child sacrifice. The parallel passage in Exodus 23:23–33 indicates that the primary strategy (the one that God enjoined) was to have many of the enemy driven out or to have many assimilated to become part of the Israelite people, as the prominent example of Rahab and her family shows (Josh 6:25). It also indicates that the purpose of the strategy was to keep the idolatrous nations from influencing the Israelites to idolatry or immorality (Lev 18:8; 18:24–30). Moreover, as we have seen in the previous section, the separation of the Israelites from the influence

---

[5]   For a fuller treatment of this word, see R. W. L. Moberly, *Old Testament Theology: Reading the Hebrew Bible as Christian Scripture* (Grand Rapids, MI: Baker Academic, 2013), 58–62, who also makes the important point that most scholars now would hold that the Israelites never attempted to kill all the non-Israelites (pp. 64–67). A similar point is now sometimes made by scholars about the phrase, "Joshua smote them with the edge of the sword and utterly destroyed every person in it," which taken literally sounds like complete extermination, but must mean something like "scored a decisive victory over," because many of the cities remained to be taken only later by the Israelites (e.g., Josh 10:37 with Judg 1:10, and Josh 10:39 with Judg 1:11). See also the references in note 2.

of idolatrous nations was, and was intended by God to be, a gradual process (cf. Ex 23:28–30).

There also seems to have been, as we have seen (Gen 15:16), a matter of spiritual judgment on God's part. The Lord wanted the land to be free of Canaanites (at least to have them subdued or assimilated) because of the "iniquity" of the Canaanites, their immoral practices—especially their sexual immorality but also their idolatrous practices, including their practice of human sacrifice (e.g., Deut 9:4–5; 12:31; 18:9–14). Moreover, he gave them a period of time to change, although during that time they seemed to get worse. In the biblical phrase, they had *completed* their *iniquity* when the Israelites entered the land (Gen 15:16; see also note 6). We might add that this was a land of God's special possession, as we will see in the next chapter, and they were there without permission. They were only squatters on his special property.[6]

There is another important reason. To have a holy people, a people with a holy temple who were free from idolatry, there was need of a holy land, a place where only a holy people lived. Others who lived in their midst (at least as full participants in their society) would ensnare the Israelites and lead them into idolatry. The history of Israel shows that this happened often enough (Judg 2:11–14). As

---

[6] This view of the complaint against the Canaanites is presented at some length in chapter 12, verses 3–11 of the book of Wisdom:

Those who dwelt of old in your holy land you hated for their detestable practices, their works of sorcery and unholy rites, their merciless slaughter of children, and their sacrificial feasting on human flesh and blood. These initiates from the midst of a heathen cult, these parents who murder helpless lives, you willed to destroy by the hands of our fathers, that the land most precious of all to you might receive a worthy colony of the servants of God. But even these you spared, since they were but men, and sent wasps as forerunners of your army, to destroy them little by little, though you were not unable to give the ungodly into the hands of the righteous in battle, or to destroy them at one blow by dread wild beasts or your stern word. But judging them little by little you gave them a chance to repent, though you were not unaware that their origin was evil and their wickedness inborn, and that their way of thinking would never change. For they were an accursed race from the beginning, and it was not through fear of any one that you left them unpunished for their sins.

some scholars have held, it was very unlikely that an early Iron Age people could live with others in their midst without having their way of life corrupted and their dedication to God diluted.

We are looking at a period in which there was no overarching empire, like the Persian or Roman Empire, maintaining peace between the nations they ruled over and relatively tolerant of their ways of life. In the early Roman Empire, when Christianity began, there was then a possibility to establish a people who could maintain their way of life, including their exclusive worship of the one true God, while living peacefully in the midst of others. But they had to be as ruthless in keeping themselves free from idolatry and immorality as the old covenant people were supposed to have done. The old covenant pattern was a typological model for what was to come, but a model that could be modified in important ways throughout the centuries, as we will see.[7]

Ultimately, God views war the way he views many other human practices that do not reflect his complete plan:

> in the latter days . . . he shall judge between the nations . . .
>   and they shall beat their swords into plowshares
>   and their spears into pruning hooks;
>   nation shall not lift up sword against nation,
>   neither shall they learn war any more. (Is 2:4)

When God fully establishes his kingdom and he himself justly settles all disputes, there will no longer be a place for war.

The role of the people in the Exodus. There is still another spiritual truth in the way the Israelites brought about the winning of the inheritance. Sometimes Christian teachers speak about redemption as the Lord doing it all. In an important sense that is correct. If the Lord had not done all in the Exodus, there would have been no redemption (or winning of the inheritance). On the other hand, the

---

[7]   For more background to this discussion, see the special exegetical discussion "The Sociological Stages of God's People" on p. 334.

role of the people is significantly different before and after the establishment of the covenant and law on Sinai.

At the outset of the Exodus the Lord did all the fighting and "the people" (everyone, but especially the Israelite warriors) did hardly anything other than follow Moses. In the entry to the land of Canaan, the people did the fighting. In a similar way, when wandering in the wilderness, the people needed the Lord to provide food they could not otherwise get. After the entry, they harvested food from the land the Lord had given them. The Lord continued to work and fight in and through his people, but not without their action, including working and fighting when needed. Moreover, he required their faithful perseverance for success, and he required them to faithfully follow his instructions in how to carry out their part. The work of the Lord in redemption is a matter of bringing his people to the point where they can do what is needed—in, with, and through him.

THE EXODUS AS A TYPE

The Exodus as a whole. In the 15th chapter of Acts, the Christian leaders in Jerusalem are discussing the Gentiles who have become Christians: After hearing Peter speak, James says, "Simeon has related how God first visited the Gentiles, to take out of them a people for his name" (Acts 15:14). James is alluding to what happened in the Exodus; namely, that God visited the Israelites when they were in bondage in Egypt so that he might bring out a people for himself (his name). James was saying that what was happening among the first Christians was the same, bringing out a people for himself, but now happening to Gentiles as well and not just Jews.

The Exodus as a whole, then, is a type of the establishing of the new covenant people of God. We can see this in a number of other places in the New Testament. First Peter is a chief place where the typology of the Exodus is important. In verse 1:17, we read,

And if you invoke as Father him who judges each one impartially according to his deeds, conduct yourselves with fear throughout the time of your exile. You know that you were ransomed from the futile ways inherited from your fathers, not with perishable things such as silver or gold, but with the precious blood of Christ, like that of a lamb without blemish or spot. (1 Pet 1:17–19)

Those who are "in exile" are people who are not living in a land of their own. That is the condition of all Christians in this age and was the condition of the Israelites living in Egypt in the book of Exodus, away from the promised land of Canaan. The death of Christ on the Cross is like the sacrifice of the Passover lamb, which ransomed the Israelites from the oppressed life they were forced to live in Egypt and began the process of acquiring their inheritance, the promised land. The sacrifice of Christ allows Christians to journey toward the true promised land.

In First Peter 2, there is another reference to the events of the Exodus, in this case even clearer since it is based on a quote from Exodus 19:

Come to him, to that living stone, rejected by men but in God's sight chosen and precious; and like living stones be yourselves built into a spiritual house, to be a holy priesthood, to offer spiritual sacrifices acceptable to God through Jesus Christ. . . . you are a chosen race, a royal priesthood, a holy nation, God's own people, that you may declare the wonderful deeds of him who called you out of darkness into his marvelous light. Once you were no people but now you are God's people; once you had not received mercy but now you have received mercy. (1 Pet 2:4–5, 9–10)

The passage behind verse 9 is one we have already looked at, Exodus 19:5–6:

Now therefore, if you will obey my voice and keep my covenant, you shall be my own possession among all peoples;
for all the earth is mine, and you shall be to me a kingdom of
priests and a holy nation.

The phrases in Exodus 19:5–6 reappear in First Peter 1:9 in a
slightly different order and with some changes in wording. The
most significant change is the addition of *a chosen race*. This may
have been included because many of the Christians were not the
physical descendants of Abraham, but both Jews and Gentiles constituted a people in Christ by the choice of God and the new birth
in the Spirit.

We will return in the next chapter to the importance of the
Christian people as *a spiritual house*, and *a holy priesthood*, who *offer spiritual sacrifices*. These, too, refer to something in the Exodus
account. Most important, however, for the subject in this chapter,
is the ending of the First Peter passage above. The end result of the
new covenant exodus is similar to that of the old covenant Exodus. It
brought into existence a people who are *God's people*. The old covenant Exodus was not an end in itself, but a step in God's plan to have
a people, and it was a type of the new covenant exodus that brought
into existence the new covenant people of God.

There are other allusions to the Exodus in the New Testament.
The fullest one is a passage from First Corinthians we have already
looked at (p. 90):

I want you to know, brethren, that our fathers were all under
the cloud, and all passed through the sea, and all were baptized into Moses in the cloud and in the sea, and all ate the
same spiritual food, and all drank the same spiritual drink.
For they drank from the spiritual Rock which followed
them, and the Rock was Christ. Nevertheless with most of
them God was not pleased; for they were overthrown in the
wilderness. Now these things are warnings for us, not to desire evil as they did. (1 Cor 10:1–6)

We looked at the first part of this passage in chapter 3, because it contains the Greek word for "types," translated above as *warnings*. The passage is a typological warning to the Christians that just because they have been joined to Christ, especially through Baptism and the Eucharist, they cannot be disobedient to God's commandments without being condemned.

Here we can see another example of how the Exodus as a whole functioned in bringing into existence a people for God. Paul said being *in the cloud and in the sea* resulted in the Israelites being *baptized into Moses*. The Jewish teachers never used this phrase, but Paul did, to draw the typological parallel. He is saying that the Israelites went through a kind of baptism, *Moses* here standing for the old covenant and the law. In a similar way, Christians are baptized into Christ, and so become part of the new covenant people of God, the body of Christ. The redemption in Christ is like the redemption of the old covenant people from Egypt; enough like it that the Exodus teaches us how God relates to people who have been baptized and partaken of the Eucharist, but who disobey God.

The full Exodus and the events that are part of it are types of Christian redemption. As such, they can be used for Christian instruction, and were used this way in the early church. The Exodus as a whole is seen in the New Testament and in the Fathers of the Christian Church as a type of the redemption in Christ. It was a pattern, the archetype, for the way God delivers and redeems people and brings them into a covenant relationship with himself.[8] A summary of the main features of the Exodus events and their role as types of the establishment of the new covenant can be found at the end of this chapter on p. 219.

The Passover. Paul in 1 Corinthians 10:1–14 is primarily concerned with two aspects of the Exodus—the fact that the Israelites were joined in the old covenant relationship to God in the events that led them to Sinai and the fact that their disobedience after Sinai led to

---

[8] For a full exposition of the Exodus as a type, with special attention to patristic exegesis, see Jean Daniélou, S.J., *The Bible and the Liturgy,* chaps. 5 and 10.

being "overthrown." There are two other features of the Exodus that receive prominent attention in the New Testament: the Passover sacrifice that made possible the Israelites' deliverance from the last plague on the Egyptians, and the establishment of the old covenant with the giving of the law on Sinai.

The sacrificing and eating of the Passover lamb is a central type for understanding the New Testament view of the redemption in Christ. When we looked at First Peter 1:17–19 at the beginning of this section, we saw the connection between the blood of the sacrificed lamb in Exodus and the blood of Christ. The typological connection is made more clearly in First Corinthians 5:7 where Paul says, *"Christ our paschal lamb has been sacrificed." Paschal* is an adjective form of "Passover," so the passage is saying that Christ is the Passover lamb for the new covenant.

The connection between the Passover lamb and Christ goes back to the Lord himself, who celebrated a Passover meal with his disciples on the evening of his death and then went to his crucifixion. The celebration of that meal involved an explanation of his imminent death. Christ spoke about the blessed bread as *his body given* [i.e., offered] *for you* (Lk 22:19) and the blessed cup of wine as *the new covenant in his blood . . . poured out* [i.e., offered] *for you* (Lk 22:20). In other words, he died during the Passover season so that he could redeem his people from sin *by the sacrifice of himself* (Heb 9:26) and establish the new covenant relationship with God for them, and that sacrifice was the fulfillment of the Passover sacrifice.

As we have seen, the Passover sacrifice during the Exodus made it possible for the Israelites to escape the last plague, the death sentence upon the first-born of Egypt. The blood was put on the houses of the Israelites and the destroying angel passed over them and let their first-born live. In a similar way, the sacrifice of Christ on the Cross makes it possible for Christians to escape the coming judgment on the human race. Those who, as the book of Revelation puts it, have *washed their robes . . . in the blood of the lamb* (7:14; 22:14) will be delivered from the bondage of sin, made part of the redeemed people in the new covenant, and be protected in the last judgment.

Sinai. The events at Sinai were also a central type in the New Testament. This can be seen most clearly in Acts 2, the description of the day of Pentecost. In the time of Christ, the Jewish feast of Pentecost—the same as what the RSV and other translations call the "Feast of Weeks" in the Old Testament—was the celebration of the giving of the covenant and law on Mount Sinai, which occurred about fifty days after the Passover, and was the end of the Passover season. As we have seen, the deliverance from bondage (the negative side) was not complete until the Lord achieved the purpose for the deliverance; namely, the establishment of a committed relationship with himself in the old covenant (the positive side).

Most Christians are vague or ignorant about the connection of Pentecost with Passover and with Sinai. They do, however, usually know that Pentecost is the day the Holy Spirit was first poured out upon the disciples. Putting the two together, we can see that the outpouring of the Spirit on the day of Pentecost described in Acts 2 was the new covenant fulfillment of the establishing of the old covenant and the giving of the law on the day of Pentecost at Sinai.

We will return to the connection of the Spirit and the old covenant law. Here it is enough for us to see that the gift of the Spirit on Pentecost is the new covenant fulfillment of the central event in the Exodus, the giving of the covenant and law on Sinai. That understanding indicates that the outpouring of the Holy Spirit on Pentecost completed the process of our redemption in Christ by completing the establishment of the new covenant relationship with God as the events of Sinai had completed the establishment of the old covenant relationship with God.

Moses and Joshua as types. As a type the Exodus is mainly a type of the new covenant process of redemption. The people in the Exodus, however, especially the leaders, also have a role as types. Here we need to look at the role of Moses and Joshua, and secondarily of Aaron.

Sometimes Christian teachers, including some of the writers of the patristic era, speak about Moses as a type of Christ himself.

The connection is an easy one to make and Moses does foreshadow Christ in various ways. Nonetheless, Moses is not directly present-ed as a type of Christ in the New Testament, but is most commonly presented in a certain contrast to Christ. The contrast was not one of opposition or of someone whose work needed to be reversed, but of someone whose work was foundational but needed to be completed.

We can see this contrast expressed directly in a few texts in the New Testament, most notably in John 1:17:

> For the law was given through Moses; grace and truth came through Jesus Christ.

We see a similar contrast in chapter 3 of Hebrews where it says,

> He was faithful to him who appointed him, just as Moses also was faithful in God's house. Yet Jesus has been counted worthy of as much more glory than Moses as the builder of a house has more honor than the house. . . . Now Moses was faithful in all God's house as a servant, to testify to the things that were to be spoken later, but Christ was faithful over God's house as a son. (Heb 3:2–3, 5–6)

From these passages, and others, we can see that the roles of Moses and Christ in God's plan have a certain correspondence, but that there was an important difference—Christ surpassed Moses and in so doing altered Moses' work for the better.

If we see Moses as a typological predecessor of Christ, he was primarily so as a prophet, but as a particular kind of prophet. He was, first of all, different than the other prophets we read about in the Old Testament. God spoke to them in visions and inspirations, but he spoke to Moses *face to face*:

> And [the LORD] said, "Hear my words: If there is a prophet among you, I the LORD make myself known to him in a

vision, I speak with him in a dream. Not so with my servant
Moses; he is entrusted with all my house. With him I speak
mouth to mouth, clearly, and not in dark speech; and he beholds the form of the LORD." (Num 12:6–8)

And there has not arisen a prophet since in Israel like Moses,
whom the LORD knew face to face. (Deut 34:10)

Moses, then, was a prophet who had unique access to the Lord and
so was able to receive from him foundational revelation.

In the Gospel of John especially, when we see the people spec-
ulating about who Jesus of Nazareth was, they sometimes guessed
that he was the messiah, and we will look at this in chapter 9. But
many of them thought he was *the prophet* (not just *a* prophet):

When they heard these words, some of the people said,
"This is really the prophet." (Jn 7:40)

The same thing was said in John 1:21, 25; 6:14; and perhaps in Matthew 21:11. The same thing was said about Christ after the Resurrection (Acts 3:22–16; 7:37).

The view that Christ was *the prophet* was based on Deuteronomy 18:15–19, a passage where Moses predicts that a prophet like
himself would be raised up and speak to them in such a way that they
would not have to hear the voice of the Lord as they did on Sinai:

"The LORD your God will raise up for you a prophet like me
from among you, from your brethren—him you shall heed—
just as you desired of the LORD your God at Horeb on the
day of the assembly, when you said, 'Let me not hear again the
voice of the LORD my God, or see this great fire any more,
lest I die.' And the LORD said to me, 'They have rightly said
all that they have spoken. I will raise up for them a prophet
like you from among their brethren; and I will put my words
in his mouth, and he shall speak to them all that I command

him. And whoever will not give heed to my words which he
shall speak in my name, I myself will require it of him.'"

We can miss the significance of this when we primarily see
prophets as people who predict the future. Prophets are, however,
God's "mouthpieces" (spokespersons), and they often give teaching,
especially new teaching that God wants his people to have. When we
read about Moses' prophetic speech in the Pentateuch, we find him
time and time again passing on instruction from God. Moses was
a prophet in the sense that *the law was given through Moses*, and he
mainly is referred to in the New Testament in connection with the
law, which is at times called the law of Moses, and so closely identified with Moses that it could simply be referred to as *Moses* (e.g., Lk
24:27; Acts 21:21; 1 Cor 10:1; 2 Cor 3:15).

Rather than speak directly to his people, God spoke to them
through Moses and gave them the old covenant law. Without Moses
there would be no old covenant. He is the prophetic lawgiver. And
Christ honors him as such. This we will consider more fully in the
next chapter. But just as he was the essential one in establishing the
old covenant, there would be a more important prophet to come,
and that would be Christ himself.

Some see Christ seated on the mountain in the Sermon on the
Mount as directly taking the role of Moses. He is the prophet like
Moses. He is giving a teaching that is not a cancellation of the law, but
an interpretation of its application to the lives of his disciples and a
fulfillment of it (Mt 5:17). However more significantly, he is teaching
directly, not passing on something God has told him. He is a prophet
who will teach people how God wants them to live, but he will do
that in a way that surpasses Moses. He is *the builder of the house*, the
son (Heb 1:2), who speaks God's word directly, *as one who had authority and not as the scribes*, who were commentators and scholars.
He speaks God's word directly as the *Holy One of God* (Mk 1:21–28).

Moses was probably not the main type of Christ in the events of
the Exodus. Joshua likely is. Joshua is presented in a paradoxical way
in the New Testament. First of all, he is hardly ever mentioned. Even

in the two places he is mentioned (Heb 4:8 and Acts 7:45), he does not play a very important role. That raises the question: why is he not prominently mentioned?

Scripture scholars and writers tend to hold one of two positions. The first is that the New Testament writers, and therefore the early Christians, did not see Joshua as very important, and those who hold this view have given a variety of speculations as to the reason. The view has the great difficulty connected to it that, as we have seen, Joshua did play a very important—a crucial—role in the success of the Exodus, and it would be hard to think that the New Testament writers simply missed it. Moreover, there is no good reason to think they might want to play it down.

The alternate position has to do with Joshua's name. In the Greek Bible, the name of Joshua is Jesus (*Iesoûs*), as it has been anglicized. Those who can read the Bible in Greek often are surprised when they find themselves reading the Old Testament "Book of Jesus" and find "Jesus" doing many things. If we reverse the process and read the New Testament substituting the name "Joshua" (in its later Hebrew version, "*Yeshua*"), we find the New Testament Joshua doing a remarkable set of things, including leading a war against the kingdom of darkness. Christ was deliberately named Joshua, which, as we have seen, means "the Lord (YHWH) saves," because he was the one who would *save his people from their sins* (Mt 1:21), their true enemies, along with the powers of darkness behind them.

For a variety of reasons, Joshua presents a closer parallel to Christ than Moses and therefore was more fitted to be a type of Christ. He succeeded where Moses did not. He was presented as sinless in his chief trial (Num 14:4–10), while Moses did not enter the promised land because of a personal sinful failure based in unbelief (Num 20:12). Joshua was formed by Moses, and then became his successor, as Christ was also formed by Moses (the old covenant law), and became his successor in God's plan. Perhaps even more important, Moses did not complete his work, but Joshua completed it for him, as Christ did. The second position about Joshua in the

New Testament, the more likely one, then, is that Joshua was not mentioned prominently in the New Testament because the whole New Testament is about the work of the Joshua of whom the old covenant was just a foreshadowing.[9]

Joshua was engaged in the work of taking the promised land, the work by which the inheritance of the Israelites was given to them, the land that allowed them to live and be a people. The entry to the land itself foreshadowed the work of Christ in the New Testament, especially his work of casting out demons and healing. He was about destroying the reign of darkness and bringing in the kingdom of light. *The reason the son of God appeared was to destroy the works of the evil one* (1 Jn 3:8). As with the old covenant conquest, the work of Christ created a certain hegemony of the Christian people over the kingdom of darkness, even though it was not so complete that evil spirits were deprived of all influence or that the Christian people did not need to continue to fight against them to secure their inheritance. Christ, then, allowed people to enter into their inheritance: the life of the Spirit.

The work of Christ comes in two stages. In his earthly ministry, he was primarily delivering people from sin and making them a people for God. He came to undergo a baptism, a death that was a transition to a more glorious life. He came to be the Passover lamb, whose sacrifice would enable the salvation of the human race. But he is also to come again in glory, completely destroy the work of Satan, and establish the full reign of God over the earth. In this he will fulfill what Joshua did, not just with a piece of earth or land in the Middle East, but with the whole earth.

The entry into the land of Canaan, then, foreshadowed both the attaining of the new covenant life now and the life of the age to come. "Jericho," the strength of this world, has fallen, and we now can, and need to, fight fully to enter into our new covenant inheri-

---

[9] Daniélou, *The Bible and the Liturgy*, 101–102, argues for this, giving supporting patristic citations. A fuller discussion is found in Daniélou, *From Shadows to Reality* (Westminster, MD: Newman, 1960), 229–243. A full discussion can also be found in O'Keefe and Reno, *Sanctified Vision*, 74–78.

tance. On the other hand, in a fuller way, Jericho has yet to fall (cf. Rev 18–19), and we look forward to the day when the true Joshua will come and lead his armies (us) to destroy the kingdom of Satan and enter into the heavenly life.

A type of Baptism. Joshua's work of winning the inheritance began with the crossing of the Jordan, and the meaning of this provides a further challenge in typological interpretation. The early Christians saw the crossing of the Jordan as a type of Baptism. For many of them this followed from the fact that Christ himself was baptized in the Jordan, and that made it possible for him to enter upon his ministry. The results of his ministry were passed on to new covenant people by Baptism, which was an imitation of and participation in the baptism of Christ.[10]

We have, however, already seen that the crossing of the Red Sea was a type of Baptism. We have also seen that the crossing of the Red Sea and the crossing of the Jordan were deliberate parallels. What then is the relation of the two in regard to new covenant realities? The answer is that we have two types of Christian Baptism that are similar to one another. We have three if we add the Flood, which we have seen is also a type of Baptism. All three of them coincide in giving us the same pattern: passing through judgment and death to new life.

There are often many Old Testament types of each new covenant reality, and as we put them together, we are instructed as Christians about the new covenant. The Flood especially indicates that sin needs to be judged and put to death, as it is in conversion to Christ and Baptism. The crossing of the Red Sea especially indicates that people need to be freed from the forces of darkness, sin, and Satan, as they are in conversion to Christ and Baptism. The crossing of the Jordan indicates that people need to and can go on to a conquest of their inheritance. This indicates that Baptism should be a beginning, an entry into the new life that God has for his people.

---

[10] For an exposition of the crossing of the Jordan as a baptismal type, see Daniélou, *The Bible and the Liturgy,* chap. 6.

All these types point to the fact that there needs to be an important transition of leaving behind an old life and entering into a new life that involves a covenant relationship with God and the possession of the inheritance he wishes to give us.

In the book of Revelation, we are given an anticipatory vision of the triumph of faithful disciples after Christ comes again (Rev 15:2–4). We find them standing in front of the throne of God *with the harps of God in their hands. And they sing the song of Moses, the servant of God, and the song of the Lamb.* They sing the song that the Israelites sang to celebrate the crossing of the Red Sea and their deliverance from Pharaoh's army. But now it is also the *song of the Lamb.* The Exodus is a foreshadowing of the death and Resurrection of Christ, but also a foreshadowing of the Second Coming of Christ, when the Exodus will be completely fulfilled in the final victory of the Lord over the forces of the kingdom of darkness.

THE EXODUS AS A TYPE

The earliest Christians were clearly familiar with the Exodus and the use of it for Christian instruction. In the patristic period, the events of the Exodus were laid out and interpreted as a standard instruction or catechesis about the redemption in Christ. The most significant interpretations are as follows and they provide a good summary of the Christian understanding of the Exodus.

> **Egypt**: The land of bondage, a type of the world in the sense of unredeemed society
>
> **Pharaoh**: The ruler of Egypt, a type of Satan
>
> **The armies of Pharaoh**: A type of the demonic spirits, the armies of hell, usually manifested in various kinds of sin
>
> **The Passover**: The sparing of the people of Israel, a type of God's sparing of us through the work of Christ
>
> **The Paschal lamb**: The sacrifice that made the sparing possible, a type of Christ, the lamb of God

The blood of the lamb: The blood on the doorposts which caused the destroying angel to pass by, a type of the blood of Christ's sacrifice which atones for our sins

The pillar of cloud and of fire: The visible sign of God's presence, a type of Christ or of the Holy Spirit or both

The crossing of the Red Sea: The destruction of Pharaoh's armies and the transit out of Egypt, a type of conversion and Baptism, the destruction of the hold of Satan on us and deliverance from the life of sin

The water from the rock and the manna (the bread from heaven): God's provision of life in the wilderness, a type of the life of Christ given through the Spirit and of the Lord's Supper or Eucharist

Sinai: The place of the establishing of the old covenant, involving the giving of the law and the establishment of the people, which were types of Pentecost and the full establishing of the new covenant in Christ

The promised land: The inheritance of the people of Israel, a type of the presence of the Holy Spirit and living of a spiritual life in the new covenant now, and a type of the glorified life of the age to come

The wars: Beginning with the Amalekites and ending with the wars of the entry under Joshua, a type of the spiritual warfare against the attacks of the kingdom of darkness, especially including temptation to sin

Moses: The leader in the deliverance from Egypt and the prophetic teacher who brought the law from God, a type of Christ

Joshua: The leader in winning the land and a type of Christ who will lead us into a true spiritual life now and the glorified life of the age to come

CHAPTER EIGHT

EXODUS TO DEUTERONOMY: THE LAW

Stages	Founders	Events	People	Covenants	Inheritance
IV Dispensation of Sinai	Moses & Aaron (Joshua)	Exodus Giving of the Law	Sons of Israel	Covenant of Sinai	Land of Canaan

Introduction to the chapter. In the previous chapter we looked at the main books of the Pentateuch, the books from Exodus to Deuteronomy, and the book of Joshua, which is a completion of the Pentateuch and with it comprises the Hexateuch. We have seen in it a remarkable transition, the transition of the people of Israel from bondage in Egypt to the beginning possession of a land of their own where they can be what God wanted them to be, a people in covenant relationship with him and a people who could live a godly life.

Jewish teachers at the time of Christ and afterwards did not neglect the account of the Exodus as a transition from Egypt to the promised land. They did not, however, study the book of Joshua the same way they studied the Pentateuch. They studied the Pentateuch intensively, because it contained the old covenant law, the way of life they were supposed to live to please God. While the Pentateuch was the collection of books that contained the law, the book of Joshua did not contain any laws and simply described how the old covenant people of God received their inheritance, not how they were now to live. Hence the book of Joshua was not studied the same way.

We now need to look again at the books from Exodus to Deuteronomy and consider the instructions or teaching it contains on how the old covenant people of God should live, and what that tells us about being Christians. As the Letter to the Romans puts it,

> For whatever was written in former days was written for our instruction, that by steadfastness and by the encouragement of the Scriptures we might have hope. (Rom 15:4)

This applies not only to the account of the departure from Egypt and the entry to the promised land, but also to all the provisions of the old covenant law. In this chapter, we will consider how that is the case.

Israel at Sinai. The arrival of the Israelites at Sinai, the mountain of God, is described at the beginning of Exodus 19:

> On the third new moon after the people of Israel had gone forth out of the land of Egypt, on that day they came into the wilderness of Sinai. And when they set out from Rephidim and came into the wilderness of Sinai, they encamped in the wilderness; and there Israel encamped before the mountain. And Moses went up to God, and the LORD called to him out of the mountain, saying, "Thus you shall say to the house of Jacob, and tell the people of Israel: You have seen what I did to the Egyptians, and how I bore you on eagles' wings and brought you to myself. Now therefore, if you will obey my voice and keep my covenant, you shall be my own possession among all peoples; for all the earth is mine, and you shall be to me a kingdom of priests and a holy nation. These are the words which you shall speak to the children of Israel." (Ex 19:1–6)

In this passage we can see that as soon as the Israelites encamped at Sinai, Moses went up to the mountain to hear what the Lord had to say to him, and that turned out to be a statement of what he, the Lord, intended to do for this people.

The Lord began by summarizing what he had done so far for the Israelites. He said, *You have seen what I did to the Egyptians, and how I bore you on eagles' wings and brought you to myself.* The phrase *what I did to the Egyptians* refers to the deliverance from Egypt, including the plagues and the destruction of the Egyptian army at the Red Sea. *Bearing you on eagles' wings* refers to God's provision for his people as they went through the wilderness. *Bringing you to myself* refers to bringing them to Mount Sinai, the mountain where God was especially present. They were there at Sinai because the Lord had brought them there, and in the course of that they had already experienced God's deliverance and provision, and knew what he could do.

He then said, *Now therefore, if you will obey my voice and keep my covenant, you shall be my own possession among all people, for all the earth is mine; and you shall be to me a kingdom of priests and a holy nation.* God, then, was going to make the people of Israel *his own possession*, his people among all the other peoples. There was to be a special relationship between God and this people. They were to be his people in a way that other people were not. They were going to be a *kingdom of priests and a holy nation.* They were, as a nation, to be holy in the sense of being set apart for the Lord and to be priests to God, the ones especially responsible for the worship of God among all the peoples of the earth.

The Lord began his promise to them by saying, *Now therefore, if you will obey my voice and keep my covenant.* In saying this, he indicated that he was going to give them a covenant. That covenant needed to be kept, obeyed because God gave it.

These few sentences contain foundational truths. God was going to give the Israelites a covenant, a covenant that would establish a relationship, much the same as the covenant he gave to Abraham in Genesis 15 and 17. In this case, though, the covenant was given to the people as a whole so that they would be made a holy and priestly nation, especially belonging to God. To use the phrase that summarizes a covenant relationship, if they accepted, *he would be their God* and *they would be his people.*

In one way, the covenant was simply given to them by the Lord without their meeting any condition. It was his idea, not theirs; and it was announced to them as something that was "news to them" (good news). It was a one-way covenant, like the covenant with Abraham. It was given by God and accepted by the people. At the same time, the covenant had a condition. Its purpose would not be realized if they did not obey God and keep the covenant he had given them. This meant that they had to keep "the law." The response of the Israelite people to this offer was then described in Exodus,

> So Moses came and called the elders of the people, and set before them all these words which the LORD had commanded him. And all the people answered together and said, "All that the LORD has spoken we will do." (Ex 19:7–8)

In the next section we will look at how covenant, law, and being a people go together.

SINAI: COVENANT, LAW, AND PEOPLE

The Law and the Covenant. As we have seen, God brought the Israelites to Mount Sinai. There he manifested himself to them in a very dramatic way. As Exodus 19:18 describes it: *Mount Sinai was wrapped in smoke, because the LORD descended upon it in fire . . . and the whole mountain quaked greatly.* It was the kind of manifestation of the Lord's presence that we saw in the pillar of cloud and fire, but much more spectacular.

The Lord then spoke to the people from out of the fiery cloud with a voice that sounded like thunder:

> "I am the LORD your God, who brought you out of the land of
> Egypt, out of the house of bondage.
> You shall have no other gods before me.
> You shall not make for yourself a graven image . . .
> You shall not take the name of the LORD your God in vain . . .
> Remember the sabbath day, to keep it holy. . . .
> Honor your father and your mother . . .
> You shall not kill.
> You shall not commit adultery.
> You shall not steal.
> You shall not bear false witness against your neighbor.
> You shall not covet . . ." (Ex 20:2–17)

The Lord spoke to them what we call the Ten Commandments, more literally in Hebrew *the ten words*.

The account then describes the effect on the people. They were *afraid and trembled,* and asked Moses to be the one to speak to God for them, instead of God speaking to them directly. Then Moses said,

> "Do not fear; for God has come to prove you, and that the
> fear of him may be before your eyes, that you may not sin."
> (Ex 20:20)

The Lord was not exactly threatening them, but he was warning them. He was in earnest that they should obey the words he spoke to them.

Moses then went up to the Lord, and the Lord gave him a set of *statutes and ordinances* (Ex 21:1; Deut 4:14). Scholars call this "the covenant code," because they were given at the same time the covenant was made. When Moses returned to the people, they responded in unison,

> "All the words which the LORD has spoken, we will do." (Ex
> 24:3)

There followed the covenant sealing service we have already looked at in which the Israelites offered sacrifices to the Lord, and then the elders, representing the people, participated in a sacrificial meal with the Lord. This concluded the establishing of the old covenant. From this point on the Israelites were a people covenanted to the Lord, so that he would be their God and they would be his people.

Contemporary Christians often find the account puzzling. Many especially do not quite know what the Ten Commandments have to do with the covenant. The description of this same event in Deuteronomy 4, however, makes the connection explicit:

> "And you came near and stood at the foot of the mountain, while the mountain burned with fire to the heart of heaven, wrapped in darkness, cloud, and gloom. Then the LORD spoke to you out of the midst of the fire; you heard the sound of words, but saw no form; there was only a voice. And he declared to you his covenant, which he commanded you to perform, that is, the ten commandments; and he wrote them upon two tables of stone. And the LORD commanded me at that time to teach you statutes and ordinances, that you might do them in the land which you are going over to possess." (Deut 4:11–14)

The Ten Commandments, or ten words, actually were integral to the agreement involved in being in the covenant relationship. They began with a preface that stated who the Lord was and what he had done for his people, and that he was giving the covenant. They then stated what the people needed to do to keep the covenant. They then were followed by statutes and ordinances that explained how the Ten Commandments were to be kept. The people committed themselves to keeping them, and the agreement was sealed with a sacrifice and sacrificial meal.

There is a structure to a covenant relationship with God, one that we have already seen in the covenants with Noah and Abraham. The relationship is not one of two equal parties who have made a mutually beneficial contract. Rather, God chooses the people and benefits them, then makes a commitment to them involving more benefits, and requires certain things from them in turn.

The two words that are commonly used to summarize God's commitment are *promise* and *commandment*. God makes a set of promises and gives a set of commandments. The promises include both blessings and curses (see especially Lev 26 and Deut 28, summarized in Deut 11:26–28). To these the people need to respond with faith and obedience. If they believe and obey the Lord's voice and keep his covenant, they will receive blessing. If they do not, they will receive judgment and penalties according to the terms of the covenant.

The scene we have looked at is often referred to as the making of the covenant with the people of Israel—the covenant of Sinai—and is also referred to as the giving of the law. The rest of Exodus, Leviticus, Numbers, and Deuteronomy contain a narrative of the events the people of Israel went through in the wilderness, especially a back-and-forth interaction with the Lord, but they also contain more statutes and ordinances. These together make up the old covenant law—along with the few laws already given in Genesis—and the Pentateuch was described simply as "the law," because it contained the covenantal law that the people of Israel were to live by.

The law is in some ways a misleading translation, probably used in English because the word in the Greek Bible that was used to translate it (*nómos*) has been normally translated "law" in English. The Hebrew word is *torah*, and it is sometimes also translated "teaching." As should be clear by this point, the books that are described as "the law" (the *torah*) contain more than commandments, statutes, and ordinances. They also contain descriptions of who God is, what he is like, and what he is trying to accomplish. In addition, they contain narratives of the individuals and people who are in relationship with him, of their responses to God, and of the consequences of those responses.

Nonetheless, the actual commandments, statutes, and ordinances are very important, as we have seen in all the covenants with

God that the Pentateuch describes. They lay out a way of life for the people in a covenant relationship with God. The Lord is working to create a human race in his image and likeness to be his sons and daughters, and each time he makes a relationship covenant, he teaches some of what has to be involved in that.

There is a connection between a people and a way of life. We live in what sociologists sometimes call "a mass society." Modern human societies, as distinguished from traditional ones, are a mass of individuals, usually without a definite way of life they would all accept as their own. Although such societies always have a large amount of laws and regulations for the public sphere, each individual is theoretically free to develop his or her own private way of life.[1]

But human beings do not form a people unless they have a common way of life. That binds them together and allows them to relate to one another in a commonly accepted way. The Lord was engaged in having a people for himself, a people that would be in relationship with him and worship him, as well as in good relationship with one another, and for that to happen, that people needed to have a common way of life. For that reason, he gave the Israelites "the law" (the *torah*), which Christian teachers commonly have also called "the law of Moses" or "the old covenant law."

The worship. There is another aspect of the covenant relationship that is also very important. The people of Israel were to become *a holy nation*, and *a kingdom of priests*. They were not just to be a people with a way of life, more or less the same as other nations on earth, with—like all the others—its own peculiarities. They were to be a special people, a people in relationship with the one true God, the people on earth that would worship him and witness to him. To be that, they needed a way of life that was appropriate to people in relationship with the true God and established in the worship of and witness to God.

After the covenant-sealing ceremony, Moses went up on the

---

[1]   For a fuller development of these points, see Clark, *MWC*, chap. 18.

mountain again for forty days and forty nights. There the Lord showed him either his own throne room in heaven or a model of it. He then explained to Moses that he was to see that a tabernacle (literally dwelling place) would be built on earth that was like the heavenly throne room (Ex 25:8–9).

The tabernacle was a tent that the people of Israel could carry with them through the wilderness (Ex 25–31; 35–40). It was a portable temple, the kind nomads needed, similar in construction to the tents kings lived in when they led their armies or went on royal visits. It had two rooms, the holy place in front and the holy of holies at the back. In the holy of holies was the ark of the covenant, a wooden chest with two figures of cherubim on it, and in the ark were the two tablets on which the law had been written—the covenant. In the holy place was one altar, the altar of incense, along with a lampstand and a table with the bread of the presence on it. Around the tabernacle was a court. In that court was another altar, the altar of sacrifice, in front of the entrance to the tabernacle.

Modern Christians tend to think of a temple building, or in this case a tabernacle, as an assembly hall for the people to gather in and hold a service. The Israelites, however, did not gather in the tabernacle, but in the court in front of the tabernacle. Only the priests were allowed in the tabernacle and then only when they were performing certain ceremonies. The tabernacle itself was not for the people, but for God. It was his "dwelling place," the place of his presence. The ark was the footstool of his throne, and he was enthroned invisibly above it.

The Israelites did not think of God as contained in a space (see the dedication prayer for the temple in 2 Chron 6:18–21). He transcended space and time and so was everywhere (omnipresent) and eternal. But he did become present in a special way in certain places, as we saw in chapter 2, and human beings could have special access to him there, more effective access than they could otherwise have had.

The Jews later described his special presence as his *shekinah*, that is, his act of dwelling. He "dwelt" or was especially present in the pillar of cloud and of fire, and he was especially present in the holy of holies, enthroned above the ark of the covenant in the tabernacle. There the Israelites could come to make contact with him for certain purposes, especially to offer sacrifice and to ask for his help. What made the Israelites special was that God was present in their midst as their king (Ex 33:14–16), and during the Exodus, the tabernacle was the place of that presence and went with them.

In this the temple was connected to the creation itself. As the creation was intended to be a place where God dwells, as we saw in chapter 1, so was the temple.

> He built his sanctuary like the high heavens,
>> like the earth, which he has founded for ever.
> (Ps 78:69)

The temple was to be a kind of image of all creation, and especially a foretaste of the age to come. It was also, as we saw in chapter 2, a foretaste of paradise, which would be restored fully to earth in the age to come.[2] It would be the place where God would begin to restore his rule or kingdom to all his creation.

Some of the law contained specifications of how to build a tabernacle that would be acceptable to God and in which he would dwell. There were, however, other provisions in the law for how the holy people of Israel should worship God in an acceptable way. There were, first of all, provisions about priests and Levites (Ex 28–29, 39; Lev 8–10, 21–22; Num 8). These were God's ministers—that is to say, servants of God, the king of the universe—who attended him when he was present, and who served him as he reigned over his people.

There were also provisions for sacrifice (Lev 1–7, 23; Num 28–29, 15; Lev 22:1–16). Modern Christians tend to think of "a sacrifice" as something killed or destroyed. But a sacrifice in the old covenant was primarily a gift, something made over to God as an offering to him, a gift given to him to establish or strengthen re-

---

[2] It was likely for this reason that the temple was decorated with images of garden-like plants: 1 Kings 6:18, 29, 32, 35; 7:18–19.

lationship with him. Animals given in sacrifice were killed, their
blood poured out on the altar, and their bodies or part of their bodies burned on the altar. This was done as a way of giving them as
an offering to God, who did not have a physical body resident on
earth. Something similar was true for the grain, the wine, and the
oil that were offered to God in sacrificial ceremonies—they were
poured out or burned as a way of giving them to God. The sacrificial
ceremony was symbolic of giving something to God, a being who
transcended our earth.

In many sacrifices, the ones called peace offerings (RSV) or
communion offerings (NAB), the sacrificial offering concluded
with a meal (Lev 3:1–17; 7:11–36; 19:5–8; Ex 20:2; Num 10:10;
etc.). The Passover sacrifice itself was a special peace offering.
The sacrificial meal was an important way in which the old covenant people took part in old covenant sacrifices of this kind (1 Cor
10:18). What they gave to God, God gave back to them to share in a
feast, a festal meal with him. This was an indication of the way they
shared in the benefits that came from whatever kind of sacrifice they
offered (thanksgiving offerings, votive offerings, devotional offerings). And so they were strengthened in their relationship with God
and made holy, renewed in their consecration to God. The meal was
a ceremonial meal (like the Passover meal) and included blessings
of what was to be eaten or drunk to thank God for his goodness to
his people.

Modern Christians tend to think of the priest as someone who
gave the offering to God and who slaughtered animals for sacrifice.
That was true for certain sacrifices, especially those for the people
as a whole or for the priests themselves, but for other sacrifices,
perhaps the greater part, it was the ordinary Israelite who gave the
sacrifice to God and who slaughtered the animal, if it was a sacrifice
involving animals (Lev 1:5, 11; 3:2, 8, 13; 4:4, 15, 24, 29, 33). The
role of the priest was to bring the sacrifice to God, usually by burning part or all of it or pouring it out on the altar. He was the minister
or servant of God in the transaction, receiving the gift from the
people and passing it on to God, the king of all, and then mediating

the blessings God gave the people in response to their sacrifice.

The law contained ceremonies of consecration (Ex 28–29, 40; Lev 8–10; Ex 24:8; 19–20). When someone or something was taken from ordinary life and dedicated to God, usually for worship, they underwent a ceremony of consecration that could involve washing for purification, anointing, and sacrifice. The people were consecrated through circumcision and, later on, through proselyte baptism. The priests and Levites were consecrated through rites of ordination. The temple, the furniture of the temple, the priestly garments, and the altars were likewise consecrated in special ceremonies. Whatever was consecrated was thereafter holy, something that especially belonged to God.

The law also contained ceremonies of purification (Lev 12, 14, 15, 16, 17; 22:1–9; Num 19; Ex 30:17–21). Various things in the course of life made the people ceremonially unclean or defiled them, that is, made them unfit to be in God's presence. The law prescribed what would defile someone, but it also prescribed the way to purify oneself. Often these included the offering of a sacrifice.

Finally, the law contained a pattern of worship (Lev 23; Num 28–29; Ex 29:38–46). It prescribed daily services, weekly observance of the sabbath with special worship, an observance of the beginning of each month at the time of the new moon, and a yearly cycle of feasts. The feasts included the three great pilgrim feasts— Passover, Pentecost, and Tabernacles—when the people of Israel were to go up to Jerusalem to worship the Lord together. It also included various other feasts, most notably the Day of Atonement.[3]

Much of the law described the ceremonies of the old covenant that allowed the people of Israel to worship their God and to be in good relationship with him. But much of the law prescribed how the Israelites were to live and relate well to one another and to God. Much of it also described how they—especially their leaders— were to conduct the corporate life of Israel. The effect of it all was to make them a holy people, a people who belonged to God, who

---

[3] For a summary of the festal calendar, see the technical note "Numerology, the Number Seven" on p. 419.

worshipped him, and who lived in a way that reflected his character. They were a people who were to *be holy, for I the Lord your God am holy* (Lev 19:2). Their greatest blessing was to have been chosen by God to be his people and to have him dwelling with them (Ex 33:14–16).

We would not think of the land of Israel as being part of the worship. Yet, in a certain way it was. It was the place where the people of Israel, the holy people, were to dwell and from which they were to draw their sustenance (Lev 26:3–6). Connected to that, it was the place where God himself dwelled and where he would walk (Lev 26:11–12; Num 35:34). The land, like the people, was holy, that is, in a special way it belonged to God (Lev 25:23; Deut 11:12; Josh 22:19; 1 Sam 26:19–20). Moreover, certain laws concerned special behavior for those living in the land. The most obvious ones were those about the sabbath and jubilee years, the years when the land had to be given its rest, along with the people (Lev 25:4). But also the laws of tithing applied only to the produce of the land (*Mishnah, Qiddushin* 1:9).

All of these things had to do with holiness. God, of course, was himself holy, thrice holy. "Holiness" is perhaps the word in Hebrew that best expresses God's transcendent greatness and with it his omnipotence. It also, however, is used to describe those things that belong to God: God's people, the priests and Levites among the people as his ministers, the tabernacle/temple, the furnishings of the tabernacle/temple, and sacrificial offerings and other gifts that had been made over to him. It also is used to describe those places where he dwells and/or that are close (near) to him: the holy of holies, the holy place, the temple, the temple mount, the city of Jerusalem, and the land of Israel. A chart that summarizes the rabbinic understanding of the Old Testament teaching on the degrees of holiness can be found on page 257.

There is, however, also an unsuccessful side to the events of the Exodus and the giving of the law. We already saw it in the previous chapter where Paul went through a list of times when the Israelites had transgressed against their relationship with God. The consequence was that most of them were *overthrown in the wilderness* (1 Cor 10:5).

One of the chief transgressions, as we have seen, occurred right after the making of the covenant. While Moses was up on the mountain, receiving the instructions for a tabernacle that would allow God to dwell in their midst in an ongoing way, the people, with the acquiescence of Aaron, the brother of Moses who was to be their high priest, formed an idol or image and worshipped it. This was a major violation of the law that God had given them and that they had solemnly committed themselves to. It was perhaps the archetypical example of the old covenant people transgressing God's law—and such violations often seemed to occur right after God had shown his people special favor.[4]

As a result of this and perhaps of further acts of disobedience (cf. Gal 3:19), a distance between God and the old covenant people was built into the old covenant worship. The ceremonial law contained provisions that seemed to be designed to keep people at a safe distance. They were not allowed to simply come into God's presence, but could only come so far and no farther, and they needed to purify themselves before doing that if they had become ceremonially unclean. Moreover there were ceremonies of atonement for sin, remedies for wrongdoing, but ones that only pointed to a future atonement and did not suffice to attain a full atonement (Heb 10:1). The result was that they were not brought into the full relation of being individually sons and daughters, but were left in what Paul described as "a yoke of servanthood" (Gal 5:1).[5]

This raises the question of the reasons for the old covenant cere-

---

[4] For a fuller summary of this pattern and the way the sin of the golden calf fits into the broader pattern of the way God and his people have interacted over the centuries, see Anderson, *The Genesis of Perfection*, appendix A. For the central importance of the sin of the golden calf, see Krister Stendahl, *Paul Among Jews and Gentiles* (Philadelphia: Fortress, 1976), 19–20.

[5] For a summary of patristic approaches to the reason for many of the ceremonial provisions of the law, see Michael Patrick Barber, "The Yoke of Servitude: Christian Non-Observance of the Law's Cultic Precepts in Patristic Sources," *Letter & Spirit* 7 (2011): 67–90.

monial law, both as seen by Jewish teachers and Christian (patristic) teachers. Two aspects of that question are discussed in the following special exegetical discussions. For the topic here it is enough to see that the old covenant ceremonial law had a purpose in establishing a good relationship with God, better than that of the pagan nations, but it also had aspects that kept the old covenant people at a safe distance from God's holiness, not yet in the full relationship God had in mind for the human race.

Nonetheless, the greatest blessing, the source of pride for the Israelites, was their relationship with God, and this included their worship. When Paul in the Letter to the Romans describes the things the Israelites could be proud of, he says,

> They are Israelites, and to them belong the sonship, the glo-ry, the covenants, the giving of the law, the worship, and the promises; to them belong the patriarchs, and of their race, according to the flesh, is the Christ, who is God over all, blessed forever. Amen. (Rom 9:4–5)

Antinomianism. Most Christians today do not have trouble seeing most of the items on Paul's list in Romans 9 as genuine blessings God gave to the Israelites. The main item they often have trouble with is *the giving of the law.* They also sometimes have problems with *the worship*, that is, the formal ceremonial worship of the old cove-nant tabernacle/temple, with the priesthood, sacrifices, and purifi-cation ceremonies. These they associate with the law, and they often see themselves as having a less formal, even casual worship, which they see as superior to the old covenant worship, because it is "freer."

Many Christians today are inclined to draw a simple contrast: "The law was for the old covenant. Christ has come and the whole thing is abolished. We do not have to be concerned with the law. In fact, it probably makes little sense to even read it." They might add, "And we are well rid of it." For many modern Christians the law has no value, and possibly never did.

Until very recently, however, that is not the way Christians have viewed the law given on Sinai. That the law of Sinai has no place in the new covenant would be a recent Christian heresy (actually, a revival of some features of the heresy of Marcionism, which was condemned in the second century). It is based partly on the difficulty of knowing how the old covenant law can be reconciled with Christian teaching. We will consider that issue in the next section of this chapter.

The issue of the value of the old covenant law is raised in a more serious way by modern antinomians and the antinomian temper of modern society. The word "antinomian" means "against law." There were some antinomians among the early Christians. There were some antinomians at the time of the Reformation. But antinomianism seems to be a special characteristic of modern society.

In general, our present society is somewhat negative on law, commandments, requirements, and standards. They are seen as an imposition on human freedom. "Law" and "freedom" are commonly set at odds with one another. Our society is, however, not absolutely negative on these things.

It is more accurate to see our society as ambivalent about law, requirements, and standards. Most Western societies have very thick law codes and an abundance of regulations. People cannot smoke in airports under pain of very serious disapproval and fines, and they cannot throw out their garbage except following complex recycling regulations. They can, however, kill their own children—if they are still in the womb, and in some places even afterwards—and engage in almost every sort of sexual perversion—if they only do so with consenting adults or by themselves.

The key to understanding our ambivalence has to do with understanding modern individualism and the distinction between public and private spheres. Ideally, according to most modern people, individuals should be as free as possible from requirements and standards. They should only have to do what they really want to do. They should, however, not be allowed to restrict others' freedom or harm others in any way. Therefore, in their own private lives they should be allowed to do whatever they want to, but in the public sphere, the place where they affect others, they should be regulated, even strictly regulated. Some would add that they should also be conditioned in their private life so they behave well—in other words, so that they would want to do even in private what those doing the regulating and conditioning want them to do.

Untangling the way modern society approaches law, requirements, and standards is rather complicated. Nonetheless, there is clearly an ideal of freedom from such things. All restrictions are commonly seen as only necessary evils to keep us from being harmed by others or even by ourselves. When possible, though, we should be able to do what we want to do, consulting only our own desires. This view is applied to "religion" as well. Religion is a matter of individual preference, and belongs to the private sphere. The best religion is one that allows us to do what we want in religious matters. Hopefully that means we should be religious ("spiritual"), but we should be religious without external constraints, especially without laws—including, for many, laws about what gods we should worship and what evil spirits we might consort with. Modern Christians, living in and influenced by an antinomian society, often see law as something negative. Christians previously, however, valued law very highly. They wanted to be law-abiding people who were instructed by the law, especially the moral law, in the best way to live.

Surprising to many people, orthodox Protestants in the Reformation times also saw the antinomians of their day as heretics and strongly condemned those who were against law as having any place in the godly living of redeemed people (e.g., *The Apology of the Augsburg Confession*, IV, 257; Luther, *Against the Antinomians*; Calvin, *Institutes*, II, vii, 12–15). In fact, they were the ones who coined the term "antinomian" to describe those who erroneously thought that they were freed by grace from the obligation to observe the moral law. They may have thought Catholics were legalists because they sought to earn their salvation by keeping laws, but they were quite positive toward law and observance of the commandments for those who wanted to live as Christians. We therefore need to consider how Christians, including Protestants, Catholics, and Orthodox, have in previous centuries approached the old covenant law, the law of Moses.

"The Law" and New Covenant People

The Law and God's will. God created the earth and the human race for a purpose. In order to fulfill that purpose, human beings have to live according to his image and likeness and so be like him in their character and conduct. God did not make them and then abandon them, like unwanted children, leaving them to run wild and do anything they might be moved to do. Rather he taught them to live in a way that would fulfill the purpose for which he made them. As the Scripture often puts it, they should "do his will" and live in a way that is "pleasing to him."

His will is expressed in commandments. We often understand commandments to primarily be restraints. And in a way they are, because if we follow them, there are some things we will not do, even when we desire to do them. Most of the commandments, however, are not primarily restraints, but instructions. They instruct us in a good way to live. As Psalm 119 puts it,

> Oh, how I love your law!
>   It is my meditation all the day.
> Your commandment makes me wiser than my enemies,
>   for it is ever with me. (Ps 119:97–98)

Moreover, insofar as they are restraints, they are intended to keep us from harming ourselves or others.

As we have seen, God gave Adam commands right from the beginning. He was told to increase and multiply, to fill the earth and subdue it. He was told not to eat from the tree of the knowledge of good and evil.

Adam was also expected to know more of what he should and

should not do than was expressed in explicit commands in the early chapters of Genesis. He and his descendants were expected to know the basic laws of universal human morality. As we saw in chapter 4 in the section on "the universal moral law," rabbinic teachers have called these the Noahide commandments, and Christian teachers have often referred to them as the "law of nature" or the "natural law," the law that human beings should know because of their human nature, the way they were created. We saw from the book of Genesis that the human race, even before the giving of the old covenant law, was expected to know basic morality. As the Lord put it in the account of Cain and Abel and in the account of Sodom and Gomorrah, there are human actions that cry out for penalization (cf. Gen 4:11; 18:20–21). Even the pagans were supposed to know that these and other things were wrong.

Law and commandments are integral to morality and are not phased out by the new covenant. Christ said to his disciples, *If you love me, keep my commandments* (Jn 14:15). Paul talked about *the law of Christ* (Gal 6:2) and stressed that there are things Christians cannot do and still enter the kingdom of heaven (e.g., 1 Cor 6:9–10). He also said that Christians needed to *submit to God's law* (Rom 8:7). The book of Revelation ends up showing that those engaged in serious immorality will not be allowed to enter the new Jerusalem at the end of time (Rev 21:8; 22:15). There are many more statements along the same lines.

The old covenant law is a stage in God's work of teaching human beings how to live, which always involves teaching them through law and commandments. It is, however, a special stage. The old covenant law contains provisions that not all new covenant people are expected to observe. The question, then, is how to understand the special place of the old covenant law in God's plan, what it was designed to accomplish, and how to determine what provisions in it all Christians need to follow.

The old covenant law and new covenant people. To begin with, there is a potential confusion in the term "the law." At various times, the

New Testament, especially Paul, says that Christians are *discharged from the law* (Rom 7:6) and *not under the law* (Gal 3:23; Rom 6:14). Subsequent Christian teachers have said the same thing.

Some interpreters of the Scriptures have understood the term "the law" or "law" in New Testament writings to mean law (requirements) in general, or at least the requirements that come from God. Based on such an understanding, they have understood the Pauline teaching of Christians not being "under the law" as meaning that Christians do not need to keep any law to receive salvation, nor can they keep the law so well that they thereby receive salvation. Rather, they simply need to believe the Gospel about Christ's redeeming work and put their faith in that. Most who follow this interpretation, however, do not hold that Christians can now disregard the requirements of the moral law.

Others, and this seems to be the consensus now among Scripture scholars, have held that "the law" usually means the law of Moses or the old covenant law. When Paul, then, says we are not *under the law* (Gal 3:23; 4:5; 5:18), he is not saying that Christians are above law, especially moral requirements, and do not need to be law-abiding. Rather, he is saying that Christians, simply because they are Christians, are not obligated to keep all of *the law of Moses*. It is this understanding of the phrase "the law" that will be followed here.

At the same time, the New Testament relates to the Old Testament law as authoritative. Paul says that his faith in Christ does not nullify the law,

Do we then overthrow the law by this faith? By no means!
On the contrary, we uphold the law. (Rom 3:31)

In First Timothy, the principle is laid down,

Now we know that the law is good, if any one uses it lawfully
... (1 Tim 1:8)

Christ himself said, referring probably to the *torah* or Pentateuch,

> "Think not that I have come to abolish the law and the
> prophets; I have come not to abolish them but to fulfil
> them." (Mt 5:17)

Paul as well spoke of the importance of fulfilling the law (Gal 5:14;
Rom 8:4; 13:8).

The question, then, is how new covenant people can use the law
lawfully. Perhaps the best way to put the question, using the term
both Christ and Paul use, is how can new covenant people *fulfill*
the law? The word "fulfill" in this context probably indicates that
when new covenant people fulfill the law, they live according to the
purpose for which it is given. That includes doing those things in
it that are intended for all human beings to do and treating those
things in it that are covenant-dependent—that is, only intended for
the old covenant and the people of the old covenant—in the appropriate way.[6]

The key to understanding how Christians should approach the
old covenant law is to understand that its primary purpose was to
bring into existence the old covenant people, Israel. Israel was to
be a community, a people, who would know the one true God, who
would worship him, and who would live a moral life—more fully at
least than human beings who lived in paganism and therefore were
under the dominating influence of false teaching and of demons.
This community was also to be a people who would somehow bring
the blessing of Abraham to all the nations on earth.

---

[6] The issue being discussed here is the question of how new covenant people do (or do
not do) what the old covenant law says. It is not the question of how people get into
the new covenant and so receive salvation, which has to do with their appropriating the
results of the work of Christ. As the introduction to the first part of the book says (see p.
11), this kind of concern is treated in *Redeemer* and not in this book. Important as this is
as an ecumenical concern, it is now possible to rely on the work of the *Joint Declaration
on the Doctrine of Justification* to establish a certain level of theological convergence in
this area, while recognizing that Lutherans are not going to give up their emphasis on
law and gospel and the theology of the cross while Catholics are not going to give up
their emphasis on the seven sacraments and the importance of penance.

The New Testament understands the new covenant people of God, the Christians, to be the successors of the old covenant people of God; a people who, like the old covenant people, worship the one true God, live a moral life, and bring the blessing of Abraham to all the nations on earth. They are not successors in the sense that Israel and its law are repudiated as not being of God (Rom 11:2). They are not successors in the sense that now that the new covenant has come, old covenant people are no longer in a relationship with God at all, although some Christian teachers have taken and some even now take that view. They are successors in the sense that God has taken what he has already given the old covenant people and transformed it by sending his Son and his Spirit and so provided a life that is more spiritually effective and a fuller version of his will for the human race. They are the fulfillment of Christ's prediction, *Therefore I tell you, the kingdom of God will be taken away from you and given to a nation producing the fruits of it* (Mt 21:43).

This change did not imply a lack of all continuity between the old covenant people of God and the new covenant people of God, as if God had decided to reject the people of Israel and choose a Gentile people in their place. The new covenant and the new covenant people were built on the old covenant and the old covenant people. The old covenant, like the covenant with Abraham and the covenant with Noah, was an "everlasting covenant" (Gen 9:16; 17:7). A man born under the law, a Jew, Jesus Christ, was the cornerstone on which the new covenant people were built (Mt 21:42). A body of old covenant people (the Apostles, the disciples) were the first new covenant people and the leaders of the new covenant community or Church. The first new covenant people of God were a remnant in Israel who believed the Gospel about Christ and also believed in "the law," the Pentateuch (Rom 11:1–6).

The New Testament sees the new covenant people of God as the *Israel of God* (Gal 6:16), *the Israel according to the Spirit* (1 Cor 10:18; Gal 4:29) and the *true circumcision* (Phil 3:3; Eph 2:11). Moreover, many New Testament and early Christian writers (e.g., 1

Pet 1:1–2:10) apply passages about the old covenant people directly to the new covenant people. The new covenant people of God are not a rejection of the old covenant people of God, much less a rejection of the old covenant. They are a continuation of it, but in a new stage of God's working with his people.

The new covenant people, the Christian church, at first included only Jews, but Jews who had been "spiritualized" by receiving the gift of the Holy Spirit as a result of belief in Christ. They soon also included non-Jews, people from the other nations, who also had been given the gift of the Spirit. When God, through the work of Peter, a Jewish apostle, poured out the Spirit upon the Gentiles of the house of Cornelius without requiring them to first become Jewish proselytes he *visited the Gentiles to take out of them a people for his name*, as James said in Acts 15:14.

God's work of creating the new covenant people of God is summarized in a passage in the Letter to the Ephesians:

> Therefore remember that at one time you Gentiles in the flesh, called the uncircumcision by what is called the circumcision, which is made in the flesh by hands—remember that you were at that time separated from Christ, alienated from the commonwealth of Israel, and strangers to the covenants of promise, having no hope and without God in the world. But now in Christ Jesus you who once were far off have been brought near in the blood of Christ. . . . So then you are no longer strangers and sojourners, but you are fellow citizens with the saints and members of the household of God, built upon the foundation of the apostles and prophets, Christ Jesus himself being the cornerstone, in whom the whole structure is joined together and grows into a holy temple in the Lord; in whom you also are built into it for a dwelling place of God in the Spirit. (Eph 2:11–22)

A little further, the letter says that,

the Gentiles are fellow heirs, members of the same body, and partakers of the promise in Christ Jesus through the gospel. (Eph 3:6)

When the above passage talks about the saints and members of the household of God, it is speaking about Jewish Christians. Gentiles, non-Jews, were added to them through belief in Christ and the outpouring of the Holy Spirit. Both together now are heirs, recipients of the blessing promised to Abraham for all the nations. Both together form the new covenant church, the one body of Christ.

We tend to call the new covenant people of God "the Church." When we do, we use a term that many think only applies to new covenant people. But when people read the Greek Bible, they discover that the Greek word in the New Testament for church was already used to describe the Israelites in the Old Testament. The RSV and other translations use the word "congregation" to translate it, or sometimes the word "assembly" (e.g., Num 16:3; cf. Acts 7:38). We could retranslate it to be closer to the Greek Bible and speak of the Church of Israel as well as the Church of Christ. When the first Jews became believers in Christ, and when the first non-Jews joined them, together they formed one Church of God, the Church of God made "new."[7]

Sometimes when people speak of "the Church," the accent is on the Church as a structured body and often as a body governed in a certain way. To be sure, the community of Christians in the New Testament times had a structure. That structure was based on the structure of old covenant Israel; although the way in which it is related is a complex question with ecumenical issues beyond the scope of what can be treated here. Nonetheless, the Christian Church is primarily a community of people who are alive in Christ with the new covenant life of the Spirit—Jews and non-Jews alike.

The new covenant people of God, then, are built upon the old covenant people of God and take the fulfillment of God's purpose

---

[7] For a further development of the meaning of "new" in this context, see "The Old and the New" in chap. 10.

for the human race to a new stage. That means that they fulfill the old covenant law and do not abolish it (Mt 5:17). That also means, however, that they do not have to observe the provisions of the law that were intended for particular historical circumstances, nor do they have to observe the provisions of the law that were old covenant-dependent if they themselves are not Jews.

The old covenant law was given to form the sons of Israel into a people and therefore to give them a way of life. The new covenant people are built on the old covenant people but have been transformed to include more than old covenant people. They therefore have a way of life built on the old covenant law, but also transformed to include people who do not need to keep the whole old covenant law. We therefore now need to look at the way in which the new covenant people follow the old covenant law.

Fulfilling the Law

What parts of the law of Moses, then, do Christians have to obey and do, and what parts do they not have to do? This is a complex issue, especially because the New Testament writers seem to have believed that Jewish Christians and non-Jewish Christians should approach it differently. There is evidence that New Testament Christians thought that Jewish Christians should observe the provisions of the old covenant law (see the special exegetical discussion on "Jewish Christians and the Law" at the end of this chapter). Non-Jewish Christians were, however, spiritually part of God's people and so no longer truly part of "the nations," yet they were not Jews and for the most part had not been circumcised.[8] They were therefore not obligated to the whole law of Moses (Gal 5:3). We will focus in this section on how all Christians approach the law of Moses, prescinding from the question of how Jewish Christians should approach it.

---

[8] There is a technical note beginning on p. 426 on the term "the Gentiles," which is a translation of "the nations."

Orthodox Christian teachers would say that Christians may not do certain things like murder, steal, or commit adultery. And most of them would cite the old covenant, which contains the Ten Commandments, as a definitive authority for what we may not do. On the other hand, orthodox Christian teachers would also say that all Christians do not have to circumcise their children or abstain from eating pork, much less offer animal sacrifices in the temple in Jerusalem, although these things are also prescribed in the old covenant law. How then are Christian teachers able to tell the difference?

First, Christians are simply expected to do what the moral law in the old covenant teaches. They are not supposed to kill, commit adultery, steal, and so on, because these are part of the moral law. There are many questions connected to the definition of murder or adultery or stealing, but there is no question that many things simply need to be avoided. Christians cannot kill other human beings who have done nothing to deserve the death penalty simply because they do not like them and would rather they were dead. Christians cannot engage in promiscuous sex. These things are simply wrong.

As Paul teaches (e.g., Rom 2:12), these things are not wrong because the old covenant law teaches they are wrong, as if it had been fine for people to do them until the old covenant law came along. Rather, the old covenant law forbids them because they are intrinsically wrong. Those who know the old covenant law, therefore, old and new covenant people alike, need to follow what the law says about these things.

Second, Christians do not need to (and in some cases should not) follow the interpretations of some of the Jewish teachers, including some interpretations that are now authoritative in rabbinic Judaism. They especially should not automatically follow the teachers that Christ referred to as *the scribes and Pharisees* (e.g., Mt 5:20) or those that follow *the tradition of the elders* (Mt 15:2; Mk 7:5; probably the same people), or the Sadducees (Mt 16:11–12). Here there is a mistake that is commonly made; namely, that because Christ opposed various teachings of the Jewish teachers that they held to be based on the law, does not mean that he was against the law or was trying to abolish it. There is no place where it can be shown that he abolished a teaching of the law. In fact, as we have seen, he said,

> "Whoever then relaxes one of the least of these commandments and teaches men so, shall be called least in the kingdom of heaven; but he who does them and teaches them shall be called great in the kingdom of heaven." (Mt 5:19)

Third, Christians are not more lenient or lax in the way they follow the moral instruction of the law than old covenant people. In fact, Christ was often concerned with the leniency of the scribes and the Pharisees rather than their strictness. To be more precise, Christ objected to their being strict in some areas and lenient in other areas. The Pharisees were very strict, for instance, in observing purity laws and special interpretations of the law, but some were lax in observing what Christ considered to be true righteousness and the will of God (Mt 23:23). Christ objected to the Pharisees and the scribes as "legalists" because they often missed the purpose or significance of the law, not because they tried to obey the law.

Christ even stated that his disciples should uphold a higher standard of conduct than the scribes and Pharisees, when he said, *For I tell you, unless your righteousness exceeds that of the scribes and Pharisees, you will never enter the kingdom of heaven* (Mt 5:20). As the Christian Father Irenaeus of Lyons put it, he "extended or enlarged" the application of the moral provisions of the old covenant law.[9] As a result, the obedience and therefore the lives of his disciples would more completely fulfill what God was looking for when he gave the moral provisions of the old covenant law.

Christ also put a greater focus on what some have called the interiorization of the law. Not only were his disciples not to murder, they were also not to be hostile to one another or live unreconciled with them (Mt 5:21–26). Not only were they not to commit adul-

---

[9] Irenaeus of Lyons, *Against Heresies*, 4:13.

tery, they were to guard their inner thoughts from looking lustfully (Mt 5:27–30). While Christ could make legal decisions (*halakhic* decisions) about morality, he mainly gave what some have called wisdom instruction about how to live, what we might call moral exhortations. The Sermon on the Mount (Mt 5–7) provides a compendium of his instruction with only the section on divorce (Mt 5:31–32) perhaps counting as a legal decision.

The same is true with the Apostles. The book of James is an extended moral exhortation. Most of Paul's teaching about how to live consists in moral exhortations, although he too could give legal decisions (e.g., in 1 Cor 7:1–16; 10:23–30, but not in most of the letter). First Timothy 1:8–11 gives perhaps the best summary of upholding the moral provisions of the old covenant law while putting the priority elsewhere in normal teaching:

> Now we know that the law is good, if any one uses it lawfully, understanding this, that the law is not laid down for the just but for the lawless and disobedient, for the ungodly and sinners, for the unholy and profane, for murderers of fathers and murderers of mothers, for manslayers, immoral persons, sodomites, kidnapers, liars, perjurers, and whatever else is contrary to sound doctrine, in accordance with the glorious gospel of the blessed God with which I have been entrusted.

In other words, the moral commandments rule out those things that are out of bounds and rule in those things that are obligatory. They are not, however, the main focus of Christian instruction. Legal matter plays a larger role in Rabbinic Judaism, perhaps partly because the Mishnah and Talmud are mainly law books, but Rabbinic Judaism never lost the tradition of moral exhortation that it also inherited from the wisdom literature of the Old Testament and the synagogue preaching, as can be seen in the midrashic literature and the Targums.

The main question, however, has to do with the ceremonial

provisions of the Mosaic law. The ceremonial provisions of the law deal with the old covenant ceremonies connected originally to the tabernacle and then to the Jerusalem temple and its system of worship. How does the new covenant, and therefore new covenant people, Christians, fulfill these aspects of the law? Clearly they do not fulfill them literally, in the sense in which those to whom the law was originally given fulfilled them. The first Christians, even the first Jewish Christians, did not fulfill them by building a new temple in Jerusalem, finding believing descendants of Levi and Aaron, making them their priests, and offering sheep and goats as sacrifices.

The observance of the ceremonial provisions of the law by new covenant people was described in First Peter:

> Come to him, to that living stone, rejected by men but in God's sight chosen and precious; and like living stones be yourselves built into a spiritual house, to be a holy priesthood, to offer spiritual sacrifices acceptable to God through Jesus Christ. (1 Pet 2:4–5)

Some early Christian writers summarized this by saying that all the new covenant people fulfill the old covenant ceremonial law "spiritually."

To begin with, both Jewish Christians and non-Jewish Christians fulfill the law by being joined to Christ. He has made it possible for them to be in the kind of relationship with God that constitutes the new covenant relationship. As Paul put it in Ephesians 2:18, *through him we both have access in one Spirit to the Father*. Both Jews and Gentiles are put into a new spiritual relationship with God the Father through the work of Christ and by receiving the gift of the Spirit of God.

One result of their new covenant relationship with God is that Christians become *a spiritual house*. "House" in the Scripture was often used as another word for "temple." The temple in Jerusalem was "God's house" (e.g., in 1 Chron 6:48). To say that they are a *spiritual* house either means that they are not a material building or that they are made into a temple by the indwelling of the Spirit in them (Eph 2:21; 1 Pet 2:5; 1 Cor 3:9, 16–17; 2 Cor 6:16; 1 Tim 5:4) or very likely both. To say that they are *a holy priesthood* means that they have been consecrated or appointed as ministers of God to have direct access to him and offer him worship and sacrifice (Eph 1:4; Heb 10:19–22; 1 Pet 2:5, 9; Rev 1:6; 5:10; 20:6).

Finally, to say that they were *to offer spiritual sacrifices* means that their prayers (Acts 10:4, 30–31; Heb 13:15; Rev 5:8; 8:3–5), almsgiving (Rev 5:8; 8:3; Heb 13:15; Phil 4:18; 2 Cor 9:1, 5, 12), other good deeds (Heb 13:16), and also their lives as a whole (Phil 2:17; Rom 15:16; Eph 5:2; Rom 12:1) are to be an offering of worship to honor God. Although these are also part of Jewish life and pleasing to God when Jews perform them, for new covenant people these will be accepted because of the work of Christ. Christ's offering of himself as a sacrifice (1 Cor 5:7; Eph 5:2; Heb 9:26; 10:10, 12) has put them into a relationship with God that allows them to make offerings to him and have those offerings accepted.

There are two other main kinds of ceremonial provisions that are not mentioned explicitly in the passage we have been looking at in First Peter: the laws about ceremonial impurity and purification and the festal cycle. In the new covenant, the various forms of ceremonial impurity are understood as types of the true impurity; namely, sin. Christians are initially purified by faith and Baptism (Acts 15:8–9), and they maintain themselves in a state of purity by avoiding sin or repenting when they have not done so (1 Jn 1:9; 2 Tim 2:21–22; 1 Pet 1:22; 2 Cor 7:1; Jas 4:8; Tit 2:14).

Most early Christians saw the pattern of old covenant prayer to be a model that was instructive for them as well, although not legally binding. They were to pray daily and observe a weekly celebration of God's redemption. This they did by observing the Lord's Day on the first day of the week in honor of the Resurrection (Rev 1:10; Acts 20:7; 1 Cor 16:2). To give one example, Ignatius of Antioch, writing within twenty years of the death of the apostle John, said in his letter to the Magnesians (section 9):

Let every friend of Christ keep the Lord's Day as a festival, the resurrection day, the queen and chief of all days of the week and the day on which our life sprang up again and victory over death was obtained in Christ.

They also seem to have observed a yearly festal cycle, although initially it only included Passover and Pentecost. "Passover" is the standard Christian name (e.g., *páscha* in Greek, *pascha* in Latin, *pascua* in Spanish, *pâque* in French, etc.) for what English-speakers call "Easter," and is the celebration of the death and Resurrection of Christ by which new covenant people are redeemed from bondage and raised to new life.

Pentecost—which the Jews in the time of Christ celebrated as the end of the season beginning with Passover, the fiftieth day after Passover (cf. Lev 23:16), and the time of the giving of the law on Mount Sinai—is the celebration of the gift of the Spirit, by which the law is written in the hearts of new covenant people (2 Cor 3:3). The New Testament Pentecost, as we have seen, completed the redeeming work of Christ in a similar way that the giving of the law completed the Exodus. The early Christians spoke of Pentecost (literally, the "fiftieth" day) as the last day of the season of the Fifty Days.

Early Christians did not, however, celebrate Tabernacles (Booths), the third pilgrim feast, and that was for an important reason. Tabernacles was the completion of the old covenant festal cycle. It was the feast of the final ingathering of the harvest each year, but also the time when the temple in Jerusalem had been completed and dedicated. It also was understood to be the feast of the kingship of God, when he ruled over his people directly, as he did in the wilderness when he was bringing them to Sinai and then to the promised land. Moreover, in the prophecy of Zechariah 14, commonly taken as a prophecy of the age to come, Tabernacles would be the feast that would be celebrated not just by Jews but also by the nations (see especially verses 9 and 16). The early Christians saw Tabernacles as the feast that would not be fulfilled until after the Second Coming of Christ, so they did not celebrate it but looked forward to celebrating it after the Second Coming.[10]

The observance of the ceremonial *provisions* of the law, then, was changed for non-Jewish Christians. It was changed because the new spiritual order instituted in Christ opened up membership in the holy people (the "saints") to Christians from the Gentiles and gave them access to God without needing to become old covenant people. The physical system of old covenant temple worship was replaced by worship in the Holy Spirit. This became the case first when the Holy Spirit was given on the day of Pentecost and definitively the case, even for Jewish Christians, when the Roman armies destroyed the temple in Jerusalem after the Jewish revolt in AD 70, and took away the land of Palestine or Israel from the rule of Jewish leaders. We will consider the difference the new covenant made more fully in chapter 10.

Just because the new covenant does not require the literal observance of the ceremonial provisions of the old covenant law for all Christians, this does not mean that the Old Testament has become obsolete and purely of historical interest for new covenant people, or even only applicable to Jewish Christians. If it were not for the Old Testament, we would not be able to understand the instruction in First Peter 2:10 that we just looked at, because we would not know what a temple, priests, and sacrifices were, and consequently we would have an impoverished understanding of Christian teaching. Once again, the Old Testament was *written for our instruction.*

Christ himself fulfilled the law in all the ways his disciples did, especially by obeying it according to the intention of the lawgiver, his heavenly Father and so living a sinless life. He also, however, fulfilled it in an equally significant way; namely, by fulfilling the prophecies contained in it. And he came to do what the old covenant law predicted: to be the prophet like Moses and the king like David, and subsequently become the heavenly high priest.

To describe Christ's fulfillment of the law in such a way is still

---

[10] Daniélou, *The Bible and the Liturgy,* chap. 20.

too external. He came to embody in himself the new spiritual order. He also came to pass that new order on to those who would believe in him, turn to him, and let themselves be joined to him spiritually. Finally, he will come again to give the fullness of spiritual life to those who believe when he destroys the power of sin and Satan and establishes the new creation. In short, he not only fulfilled the law in the sense of carrying out or obeying the provisions that were applicable to him, he accomplished in his own person the intended purpose or goal of the giving of the law. We will discuss this more fully in chapters 10 and 11.[11]

Concluding comment. The old covenant began with Abraham and the promises and covenant God gave to him. He was the first person in the human race to have a special covenant relationship with God, one he passed on to his descendants. The old covenant then moved on to a second stage (or sub-stage) with the Exodus of the people of Israel and their winning of the promised land. By the conclusion of that stage they had become a people in covenant relationship with God, a people that lived a way of life that expressed his own character. In the next chapter we will look at the third stage of the old covenant, the establishment of the kingdom of Israel.

The old covenant did not complete the process of restoring the human race to what God created it to be. The Fall was only partially reversed. The sinfulness of the human race was still active enough that the old covenant law was both a source of blessing and a restraint on the sinfulness of the old covenant people. As Paul put it, the law functioned as a guardian to keep the old covenant people out of trouble, especially the trouble they would encounter by approaching God in a wrong way (Gal 3:22–23).

The second stage of the old covenant built on the first one. At the beginning of the Exodus there was a recognizable group of descendants of Abraham, Isaac, and Jacob who knew who God was. At the end of it, this collection of tribes and clans had become a people

---

[11] For the further question of what sense it makes for Jewish Christians to keep the old covenant ceremonial law, see the special discussion below on p. 308.

with a common worship and a common way of life. Now it was a particular people who would be central to moving forward God's purpose for the restoration of the human race. In the next stage we will see how that people was developed so that they would be ready to receive the messiah, the Christ, and become the launching pad for bringing the blessing of Abraham to all nations.

CEREMONIAL TYPOLOGY

The earliest Christians were familiar with the ceremonial provisions of the old covenant and the use of them for Christian instruction. The most significant interpretations are as follows, and they provide a good summary of the Christian understanding of the ceremonial law.

The Place of God's Presence on Earth

The tabernacle/temple: The building in which God dwelt, a type of Christ's body and the Church

The ark of the covenant: The base of God's throne, his footstool on earth

The holy of holies, the holy place, the courts of the Lord: the parts of the temple with the closest access to God's presence, the holiest places on earth, types of God's heavenly throne room

The altars of sacrifice and incense: The tables on which offerings were placed when given to God, a type of the heavenly altar (Rev 6:9–10; 8:3–5)

The menorah: The seven-branched candlestick in the holy place, a type of Christian churches now (Rev 1:20) and also of Christ in the new Jerusalem (Rev 21:23)

The land: The place where God's people dwelt, with God enthroned in their midst, the type of life in Christ and the blessing of the Holy Spirit, and also of "heaven;" that is, the new heaven and earth in the age to come

The Ceremonies

Priests: Men established to come near to God and make offerings to him, types of Christ and of Christians

The high priest's garments, the jewels: The special clothing, covered with jewels, that priests had to wear when drawing near to God, types of righteousness and virtues, good character needed to draw near to God

Sacrifice, offering, gift: Gifts given to God in worship to acknowledge him as God and thank him for his blessings, types of Christ's death and Resurrection, the life of Christians, and special actions of service to God

Incense: Sweet-smelling smoke, a type of prayer

Ceremonies of consecration: Ceremonies that ordained people and things for the service of God, involving purification, anointing, bestowal of special clothing, and offerings (all types of becoming a Christian). In some traditions consecration ceremonies are used for establishing ministers and places of worship

Anointing: Anointing with oil, signifying consecration to the service of God, a type of the giving of the Holy Spirit to Christ ("the anointed one") and to Christians

The sabbath and feasts: Old covenant days set aside to honor God, types of new covenant days set aside to honor God

The Moral Life

Clothing: A symbol of character, both bad character and good character

Impurity: Various physical conditions that disqualified people from coming into the presence of God, a type of sin

Blemishes: Various bodily defects, a type of sin

Leprosies etc.: Various corrupting diseases, a type of sin

Ceremonies of purification/cleansing: Ceremonies that took away impurity, a type of repentance and receiving forgiveness

Sprinkling: A rite of applying sacrifices for purification, a type of receiving the benefit of the sacrifice of Christ

Initiation

Circumcision: A ceremony of initiation into the old covenant, a type of Christian conversion and interior renewal through the gift of the Spirit

Proselyte baptism: A ceremony of initiation into the old covenant, a type of Christian Baptism

Degrees of Holiness

The Old Testament teaches the basic truth that the closer people come to the presence of God, the holier is the place and the more careful they need to be about how they act and about their own condition. Some later Jewish writings presented that truth by speaking of the ten degrees of holiness. Upon the earth, the closer one came to the special location of God's presence, the holier was the place. The following chart contains a diagram of the temple at the time of Christ and a list of the ten degrees of holiness, drawn from the *Mishnah* (*Kelim* 1:6–9), which presents the idea of the ten degrees of holiness. Noteworthy is the fact that the land of Israel was a holy place.

THE DEGREES OF HOLINESS

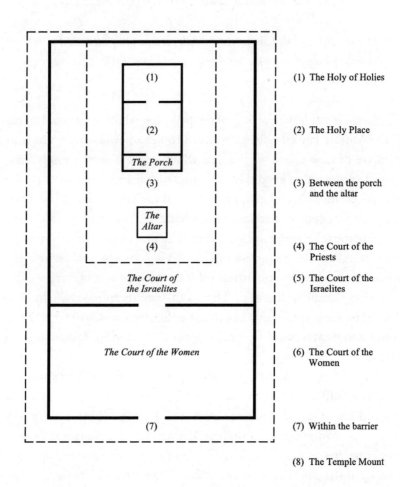

(1) The Holy of Holies

(2) The Holy Place

(3) Between the porch and the altar

(4) The Court of the Priests

(5) The Court of the Israelites

(6) The Court of the Women

(7) Within the barrier

(8) The Temple Mount

(9) Jerusalem

(10) The land of Israel

Special Exegetical Discussion:
Moral, Ceremonial, and Civil Commandments

The traditional division into moral, ceremonial, and civil gives
us a very helpful tool for sorting out the issues related to keeping
the old covenant law.

There is a traditional way of determining which commandments
of the Mosaic law all Christians need to keep because they are con-
stitutive of new covenant life and which ones at least some Christians do not need to keep.[12] It was based on a distinction between the
moral, ceremonial, and civil provisions of the old covenant law. Each
category was approached in a somewhat different way.

The moral provisions are those that have to do with basic human morality, the requirements for living an acceptable or righteous human life. People often refer to these in a summary way as
"the Ten Commandments." The "Ten Commandments," though,
cannot be seen as the only ten items obligatory on Christians. Each
commandment should be understood as a heading for an area of
morality.

For instance, one of the Ten Commandments is "You shall not
kill." It would be better translated "You shall not murder," because
the old covenant law is not against all killing. Some killing was
fine, even commendable, such as killing in self-defense or to save
someone being attacked—not to mention swatting mosquitoes
and uprooting weeds. On the other hand, the old covenant law
is strongly against the taking of innocent human life, and that is
murder.

There are also provisions in the law that say in effect, "You shall
not wound an innocent human being" (e.g., Ex 21:15–27). The latter
provision is understood to be a specification or application or der-
ivation of the commandment against murder. If people are not sup-

---

[12] For example, *Summa Theologiae*, I-II, q. 99 (New York: Benziger Brothers, 1947); *The Westminster Confession of Faith*, chap. XIX (New York: *The Constitution, Presbyterian Church (U.S.A.), Part I, The Book of Confessions*, 1983).

posed to take away someone's life, they should also not be allowed to damage someone's life, especially someone's ability to function normally. That is common sense and comes from understanding the purpose behind the commandment forbidding murder; namely, understanding the value it is intended to preserve, the life of innocent human beings. Damaging that life is a step toward taking it away completely.

There are a number of provisions of the old covenant law that deal with certain circumstances that are now rare or non-existent. For instance, Exodus 21:28–32 contains provisions for what to do if someone's ox gores someone else to death. Nowadays, few people have oxen, because they do not belong to an iron age agricultural society—or any traditional agricultural society, for that matter. For those in a technologically-based society, the law is in a certain sense obsolete. But it can and should be applied in an analogous way, for instance, to being harmed by a vicious dog.

The Ten Commandments and the other provisions of the moral law that come under the heading of the Ten Commandments are obligatory for all new covenant people. They are fundamentally a development of the Noahide commandments or the natural law and are a statement of how God wants people to live to be in his image and likeness. There are various views of how they relate to the Noahide commandments and the natural law.[13] It is, however, enough at this point to see that there are parts of the old covenant law that need to be followed by new covenant people, and these can be summarized by referring to "the Ten Commandments."

The ceremonial provisions of "the law" have to do with the old covenant ceremonies connected to the temple and its worship. There are some commandments about the worship of God that have to do with the moral law. For instance, both the Noahide com-

---

[13] The sabbath is a special case, and there are ecumenical differences about how it is to be observed—i.e., on Saturday (the seventh day of the week) or on Sunday—as the Lord's Day. Those who hold to the latter usually distinguish between the aspect of the sabbath laws that is covenant-dependent and the aspect that is of natural law. In such an understanding, setting aside a regular time (day) to worship God fulfills the natural law, but the sabbath does not have to be observed on Saturday.

mandments and the Ten Commandments forbid idolatry, that is, worship of false gods. This is a moral commandment, not a ceremonial commandment.

On the other hand, the commandments to build a tabernacle of a certain size and design, the commandments for establishing a priesthood of the descendants of Aaron and Levi and for how they should function, the commandments to offer certain sacrifices, the commandments to keep certain rules of purity and impurity, and the commandments to celebrate the yearly cycle of feasts are all to be classified as ceremonial commandments. They are not classified as ceremonial commandments because all commandments having to do with worship are ceremonial in this sense. They are not classified as ceremonial because ceremonies of any kind are optional or even to be avoided, as we saw when we looked at some of the New Testament understanding of the ceremony of Baptism. Rather, calling them "ceremonial" is a shorthand way of indicating that they are provisions required for the temple worship of the old covenant, not commandments of natural morality.

The ceremonial commandments of the old covenant are not obligatory for all new covenant people. For perspective, it is helpful to note that not all of them were understood to be obligatory at the time of Christ and the Apostles even for all Jews. Jewish teachers distinguished between the parts of the old covenant law that were obligatory for Jews living in the land of Palestine and those that were obligatory for those who were not.

For instance, the laws that commanded that all male Jews of a certain age (and health) should go up to Jerusalem three times a year to celebrate the feasts of Passover, Pentecost, and Tabernacles were not considered obligatory for diaspora Jews because most of them could not do that while living a significant distance from Palestine. On the other hand, the fast for the Day of Atonement was considered obligatory, because Jews did not have to go to Jerusalem to do that. In addition, after the destruction of the temple in AD 70, the laws connected to worship in the temple were no longer obligatory for any Jew.

To say that the ceremonial commandments are not obligatory for new covenant people does not mean that these commandments have nothing to do with new covenant life and are unimportant for new covenant people. It also does not mean that new covenant people should skip reading the book of Leviticus, which is largely about the ceremonial commandments. More to our point, however, the ceremonial laws in Leviticus and other parts of the Pentateuch are important for new covenant people because the ceremonial laws were also written down *for our instruction*, as Paul said (1 Cor 10:11) and as we have considered in the section of this chapter on "Fulfilling the Law."

The third category of old covenant laws is the civil laws. These have to do with the way the corporate life, including the government of Israel, is to be carried out. They include provisions for criminal and civil trials, for penalties for wrongdoing, for taxation, for a judicial system, for a king, an army, and many other governmental positions and institutions. The way new covenant people approach them is more complex than the other kind of laws and their applicability is less easy to interpret.

To give a quick summary, few of the civil laws are simply applicable, as they stand, to new covenant people. New covenant people do not have to have a king and army, for instance, nor do they have to impose the death penalty on Christians who commit certain serious sins, nor take up arms against the enemies of God's people (persecutors, as in Mt 5:43–48). Like the provisions of the ceremonial law, civil laws do not have to be followed literally by new covenant people.

On the other hand, the principles involved in setting up the civil life of the people of Israel in the land of Israel have traditionally been held by the Christian churches to be applicable to their corporate life, and that of any well-run civil society as well. Here we could point to such examples as the rule of law, the principle that people are innocent until proven guilty, the establishment of a court system and a system of fair trials, and other such features of the old covenant civil law. The civil laws of the people of Israel have had a great impact in establishing what we would consider just, civilized government in many nations of the world.

Some of the particular old covenant civil laws are applicable to Christian corporate life, or Church life, by what could be called spiritual or typological transposition. For instance, the Apostle Paul in First Corinthians 5 dealt with the case of a man living in incestuous adultery. According to the law of Moses, such a man was to be put to death. In the new covenant, however, he was to be put out of the community and avoided until he repented.

In the old covenant, Israel was a nation living on a land of its own, and in order to keep Israelite life pure, certain criminals had to be put to death. In the new covenant, the Christians live together in a community and live the new life in the Holy Spirit in that community in the midst of a non-Christian society. To put someone out of that community and the protection of its way of life was to deliver them to Satan (1 Cor 5:5) in order to keep the community pure for the indwelling presence and worship of God (1 Cor 5:6–8). It was also hopefully a measure that would obtain the guilty person's salvation.[14]

The distinction made here between moral, ceremonial, and civil laws does not make it possible to understand how every single provision of the old covenant law should be approached by new covenant people. The law that says *you shall not boil a kid in its mother's milk* (Ex 23:19) could be understood as a provision of humaneness (perhaps symbolic humaneness) to be followed by everyone, or it could be understood as a ceremonial provision (whose purpose we probably no longer understand), and therefore does not need to be followed. Or to use more important examples, among Christian teachers there has been a controversy over whether the laws about the sabbath and those about tithing are moral or ceremonial laws.[15] Nonetheless, the distinction gives us a broad understanding as to the way new covenant people can regard the old covenant law as

---

[14] For more background here, see "The Sociological Stages of God's People," p. 334.

[15] For the issues connected with tithing, see Stephen Clark, *Christian Tithing* (East Lansing, MI: Tabor House, 2006). This contains a more extensive discussion of the normative nature of the old covenant law for Christians.

authoritative and yet still not believe that every provision must be obeyed by them.[16]

Contemporary scholars sometimes object to the practice of using the distinction between the moral, ceremonial, and civil laws as a basis for an approach to the old covenant law. They mainly tend to object to it on the basis that it cannot be found to be explicitly stated in the Old Testament and, even more, that the three kinds of law can be found indiscriminately put together in many legal texts in the Pentateuch as if there were no distinction between them. Both observations are true, but to draw the conclusion such scholars do is based on a misunderstanding.

The distinction between the three kinds of law does not come from the literary way the Old Testament authors presented "the law." They were simply dealing with God's teaching for old covenant people who lived in the land of Palestine in the first millennium BC and wrote down various provisions in the way they judged would be helpful for their audience. Once the circumstances changed and once the stage of God's plan changed, it became necessary to sort out how to approach the various legal provisions of the Pentateuch, as rabbinic scholars did. It especially became necessary for Christians once the new covenant came.

Sorting out what approach to take requires doing what most legal scholars do when asking about the authority of various laws in any body of laws; namely, asking what the purpose (the reason for the legal provision) was. As in the interpretation of any body of law, there may have been various reasons for a given provision in the Pentateuch or for how it is stated. It may have been given to deal with some situation, whether to deal with a particular circumstance that may no longer be the same, or perhaps to deal with a past set of historical circumstances. Or it may have been given to uphold the approach of a particular stage of God's plan or to uphold good human life in general (i.e., enjoining basic morality). While sometimes we cannot determine which of those it is in regard to particular pro-

---

[16] For the special case of the "Apostolic Decree" in Acts 15:29, see the references in footnote 18.

visions, for the most part we can. That allows us to make the traditional useful distinction between moral, ceremonial, and civil law, and to use it to interpret the old covenant law without distorting the original revelation or meaning of the text.[17]

In the old covenant stage of God's plan, God was concerned with forming a people for himself and making them a nation among nations in a land of their own. He was also originally helping them to live in a bronze and iron age world, a pre-industrial society of a certain sort that was dominated by polytheism. He then allowed them to be scattered among the other nations, where they might influence those nations, hopefully for the good. Finally, he was looking forward to sending his Son and Spirit to this people so that they could move into a stage of his plan that would more fully realize his purpose and will for human life, namely, the new covenant stage. He even knew that future generations of those people would live in a technologically advanced society.

God was, in short, establishing a way of life for the people of Israel that was adapted both to the circumstances they were in and to the stage of his plan they were in. It therefore contained both covenant dependent elements and universal elements. The universal elements carried over into the new covenant stage for all new covenant people and need to be followed in a way adapted to various new circumstances in which new covenant people might live.

Special Exegetical Discussion:
Jewish Christians and the Law

Jewish Christians originally kept the ceremonial law. The Messianic Jews of today try to do so as well.

---

[17] Jonathan Klawans in *Impurity and Sin in Ancient Israel* (Oxford: Oxford University Press, 2000), 22, not only makes use of the distinction between "ritual" (viz. ceremonial) and "moral" as foundational for understanding matters of impurity in the Hebrew Bible, but also defends the necessity of using terms that are not used in the biblical texts for our own clarity of communication.

When we read the Acts of the Apostles, we find a complicating fact. The first Christians did keep the ceremonial provisions of the old covenant law. They attended the temple. They observed the purity laws in the Old Testament and probably kept kosher. How can that be if new covenant people do not observe the ceremonial provisions of the law?

There are a number of views on this. One view, predominant among many Christian teachers until the last century, is that this was a leftover practice. The Jewish Christians followed the ceremonial provisions of the law because they had always done so. It took a while for them to draw the full implications of what Christ had done (and taught) and drop these things.

The second view is that the Jewish Christians did not need to observe the ceremonial provisions of the law, but they did so for missionary reasons. They knew that if the Jews of their time saw them as not keeping the whole law, they would be scandalized and not be open to becoming Christians (Acts 6:14). Many Jews who have become Christians nowadays elect to keep the law the way the Jews around them do so that they can have more success in evangelism among non-Christian Jews.

The third view is that the early Christians, especially the Apostles who laid the authoritative foundation of the Christian church, made a distinction between Jewish Christians and non-Jewish Christians. The non-Jewish Christians did not have to keep the whole law, but only the parts that were not covenant-dependent. The Jewish Christians did need to keep the whole law, at least those parts applicable to people in their circumstances.[18] This seems to be the likely understanding of Paul's approach, which he summarized by saying,

---

[18] For a contemporary presentation (defense) of this view, see Richard Bauckham, "James and the Jerusalem Church," in *Jewish Believers in Jesus: The Early Centuries,* ed. Oskar Skarsaune and Reidar Hvalvik (Peabody, MA: Hendrickson, 2007), 55–95, especially section 2 "The Community Life and Practice"; and more broadly Bauckham, "James and the Jerusalem Church," in *The Book of Acts in Its First Century Setting: Palestinian Setting,* ed. Richard Bauckham, (Grand Rapids, MI: Eerdmans, 1995), 415–480.

I testify again to every man who receives circumcision that he is bound to keep the whole law. (Gal 5:3)

This also seems to be the position of the Council of Jerusalem described in Acts 15, which presupposes that the Jewish Christians observed the whole law, but decided that the converts to Christianity who were not Jews (who were from "the nations") did not need to. Why, after all, would they bother discussing whether Gentile converts needed to observe the whole law if they themselves did not do so and did not think they needed to? Such a view also seems clearly expressed in Acts 21, where Paul goes through a temple ceremony to show that he himself keeps the whole law (Acts 21:24, 26) and asserts that he has not offended against the Jewish law (Acts 25:8; 28:17). It also seems to be supported by the fact that the Jewish Christians in Jerusalem were zealous for observing the ceremonial law (Acts 21:21; RSV: the customs).

This explains a fact that can be exegetically disorienting. The earliest Church was a body of Jews, new covenant Jews because they believed in the Gospel and had received the Holy Spirit. They were understood to be the holy remnant of Israel, the true Israel that was the foundation upon which the broader church of Christ that included those that came from the Gentiles could be built (Rom 9:1–7; 11:1–6; Eph 2:11–22).

It is for this reason that many believers in Christ who wish to remain Jews (keeping the old covenant law) often describe themselves as messianic Jews (and by preference not "Christians," although they see themselves as believers in and followers of Jesus Christ, the messiah). They do so in order to make clear that they are Jews and think they should remain Jews. We could say that the Apostles and the rest of the first Christians were messianic Jews, although for a while there were no other Christians to distinguish them from.

The discussion of these three views, and the evidence for them, is quite complicated, and at the moment there is nothing like a uniform consensus of Christian teachers. Some objections to the third view recede if we keep in mind that the early Christians (and Jewish teachers of the time) probably distinguished between how the Jews kept the law in the land of Israel and how they kept it in the diaspora. As we have seen there were many provisions of the law of Moses that did not apply in the diaspora, such as the legal provisions for tithing.

If we also keep in mind that the early Christians did not accept all the interpretations that rabbinic "orthodoxy" later made, even more objections fade away. Moreover, even now Jewish teachers are not united on how to keep the provisions of the law, with some designated as "Orthodox," some as "Conservative," and some as "Reformed." Nonetheless, it does seem clear that the early Jewish Christians believed that they should follow all the ceremonial provisions that were applicable to them.

The main objection to the third position is probably the question as to what sense it makes for the Jewish Christians to observe all the provisions of the old covenant law. A statement that Paul makes three times focuses this question: *neither circumcision nor uncircumcision counts for anything* or *is of any avail* (1 Cor 7:19; Gal 5:6; 6:15). The crucial question for a sound interpretation is "avails for what" or "counts for what?" The answer is probably avails for receiving the blessing of Abraham, the relationship with God given by the new life in the Spirit. Both Jewish Christians who observe the ceremonial provisions of the law of Moses and non-Jewish Christians who do not have received that.

Many Christian teachers have interpreted such statements by Paul as meaning that no Christian has to observe the law of Moses and possibly even should not do so. First Corinthians 7:19, however, says that *neither circumcision counts for anything nor uncircumcision, but keeping the commandments of God. Keeping the commandments of God* counts for both Jewish Christians and non-Jewish Christians, and Jewish Christians in the early church seemed to understand that they had to keep more of the Mosaic law than non-Jewish Christians did in order to keep God's commandments. Moreover, not being circumcised does not count for anything either. Not keeping the ceremonial commandments does not make one a better Christian.

If, however, the non-Jewish Christians could have just as good a relationship with God as the Jewish ones, and if they, too, could be (spiritual) descendants of Abraham and full or righteous members of God's people—and if the old covenant law is *a yoke . . . which neither our fathers nor we have been able to bear*, as Peter put it in Acts 15:10 or *a yoke of servanthood*, as Paul put it in Galatians 5:1—why would the Jewish Christians bother to keep the whole law? Or, why might God want them to?

There are various answers given to this. Some say Jewish Christians should keep the whole law simply out of obedience or covenant faithfulness. Some say they should do so to be and remain Jewish, because to live a Jewish way of life is part of Jewishness. Some develop this view by saying it is important to do so to reach many Jews with the Gospel message. Some add to that the ecumenical intention that Jewish Christians can contribute to healing the relationship between the Christian churches and the Jewish people. Some say that there is still a purpose in God's plan for the Jews as a priestly people, to testify to the holiness of God. Some finally say that keeping the whole law is a privilege and a blessing (cf. Rom 9:4–5; 11:29).[19]

At this point, it is enough for us to observe that the founding Apostles did not require the Christians who came "from the nations" to be circumcised and keep the whole law, although they did seem to expect that Jewish Christians would. Therefore, many of the provisions of the law of Moses are covenant-dependent. Although they are important for all Christian instruction, they do not have to be kept literally by all Christians to belong to the new covenant people of God in a righteous way, a way that is pleasing to God.

---

[19] For a discussion of messianic Judaism and the issues connected to it, see Mark S. Kinzer, *Postmissionary Messianic Judaism: Redefining Christian Engagement with the Jewish People* (Grand Rapids, MI: Brazos, 2005) and *Israel's Messiah and the People of God: A Vision for Messianic Jewish Covenant Fidelity* (Eugene, OR: Cascade Books, 2011). For an important argument for Jewish Christians keeping the whole Mosaic law, see the Jewish theologian Michael Wyschogrod, "A Letter to a Friend" in *Modern Theology* 11:2 (April 1995): 165–171.

CHAPTER NINE

SAMUEL, KINGS, AND CHRONICLES: DAVID THE KING

TEXT: FIRST CHRONICLES 10–20; SECOND CHRONICLES 1–9

Stages	Founders	Events	People	Covenants	Inheritance
V **Kingdom of** **Israel** **(Exile)**	David (Solomon)	Anointing of David Building the Temple	Jerusalem Zion	Covenant of Kingship	Full Kingdom

ISRAEL ASKS FOR A KING

Introduction to the chapter. Much happened between the completion of the work of Joshua, narrated at the end of the book named for him, and the establishment of the kingdom of Israel. For something like two hundred years, the Israelites lived in their land, and they experienced a mixed success. Although they possessed much of the promised land, they did not inhabit or rule all of it. In addition, they had many enemies who attacked them effectively (1 Sam 7:10–11). When they turned to the Lord, he delivered them, often by sending his Spirit upon individuals called judges (Judg 3:10; 6:34; 11:29; 13:25).

The people of Israel also had experienced many disgraceful incidents. The beginning of the book of Judges, the account of this period, says,

> Whenever the LORD raised up judges for them, the LORD was with the judge, and he saved them from the hand of their enemies all the days of the judge; for the LORD was moved to pity by their groaning because of those who afflicted and oppressed them. But whenever the judge died, they turned back and behaved worse than their fathers, going after other gods, serving them and bowing down to them; they did not drop any of their practices or their stubborn ways. (Judg 2:18–19)

The end of the book of Judges summarizes the period by saying,

> In those days there was no king in Israel; every man did what was right in his own eyes. (Judg 21:25)

It was a time of moral and political anarchy in Israel as a whole—and that was connected to the lack of a king.

In this chapter we will look at the establishment of the kingdom of Israel. The key figure in this establishment is David the King, and, in a supportive role, his son and successor, Solomon the King. In doing so, we will look at the beginning of a new stage of God's plan, the third stage of the old covenant. With the establishing of the kingdom of Israel and the building of the temple, the old covenant order was completed.

The completion of the old covenant order does not mean that the old covenant completely succeeded in what God had intended for it. It was also a mixed blessing, as the previous stages of God's plan had been, and so looked forward to a further stage. With the establishment of the kingdom, with the law and the land and the tabernacle/temple inherited from the Exodus, the old covenant people of God were in a position to receive their true king, the Son of God himself, who would bring his people into the life of the age to come.

When we speak of a kingdom, we might be referring to a territory, the land over which a given king rules, or a body of people, the people over which a given king rules. However, we are always speaking about a king, the leader who rules the people and the land. And we are speaking of the fact that he reigns or rules, that is, governs the people and the land, determining how things go, or at least how many things go. The Gospel message speaks of the kingdom of God, the time when God will fully reign over the earth and all things will be done on earth as they are in heaven. The establishment of the kingdom of Israel was a step toward the full kingdom of God.

Israel asks for a king. First Samuel takes up where Judges leaves off. In the fourth chapter, we find that the Philistines, neighbors of Israel on the Mediterranean coast, defeated an Israelite army, captured the ark of the covenant, and destroyed the temple at Shiloh, the main Israelite sanctuary. They then held hegemony over Israel. At that point, the Lord raised up the last judge of Israel, the prophet Samuel, who provided a respite for the Israelites from the domination of the Philistines and "judged the people" righteously.

Toward the end of Samuel's life, a momentous incident occurred. He received a delegation of the elders of Israel, the leaders of the various tribes and clans. Their message was unwelcome to him:

> Then all the elders of Israel gathered together and came to Samuel at Ramah, and said to him, "Behold, you are old and your sons do not walk in your ways; now appoint for us a king to govern us like all the nations." But the thing displeased Samuel when they said, "Give us a king to govern us." (1 Sam 8:4–5)

Samuel then turned to the Lord for direction.

> . . . And the LORD said to Samuel, "Hearken to the voice of the people in all that they say to you; for they have not rejected you, but they have rejected me from being king over them. According to all the deeds which they have done to me, from the day I brought them up out of Egypt even to this day, forsaking me and serving other gods, so they are

also doing to you. Now then, hearken to their voice; only, you shall solemnly warn them, and show them the ways of the king who shall reign over them." (1 Sam 8:6–9)

So Samuel took these words to the people.

> He said, "These will be the ways of the king who will reign over you: he will take your sons and appoint them to his chariots and to be his horsemen, and to run before his char- iots . . . He will take your daughters to be perfumers and cooks and bakers. He will take the best of your fields and vineyards and olive orchards and give them to his servants . . . And in that day you will cry out because of your king, whom you have chosen for yourselves; but the LORD will not answer you in that day."
>
> But the people refused to listen to the voice of Samuel; and they said, "No! but we will have a king over us, that we also may be like all the nations and that our king may govern us and go out before us and fight our battles." And when Samuel had heard all the words of the people, he repeated them in the ears of the LORD. And the LORD said to Sam- uel, "Hearken to their voice, and make them a king." (1 Sam 8:11–22)

As a consequence of the petition of the elders, the Lord had Samuel anoint Saul as king.

The exchange above is high drama, but it is easy for readers nowadays to fail to understand it. We have an interchange between three parties: Samuel, the acknowledged leader of all Israel; a dele- gation of the leaders of Israel, often referred to in the account as "the people"; and the Lord. Samuel is the most difficult to understand.

Samuel was a prophet and God's servant. He had, however, set up his two sons as his successors, seemingly creating what would be a de facto (prophetic) dynasty, but his sons were not handling themselves in a commendable way, and the Israelite people saw that.

Although the leaders of Israel said they continued to think highly of Samuel, they had a complaint, and we are informed that it was a justified complaint. Samuel, however, did not deal with the complaint about his sons any more than his predecessor, Eli, had dealt with a similar situation. Samuel even seemed to deliberately ignore it (1 Sam 12:2).

The delegation of the leaders of Israel had a solution. They were tired of how badly things had been going. They wanted a king—like the nations around them. We might say that they wanted to "modernize" their nation, moving from a tribal society depending on a charismatic leader, or a "judge," in emergencies or difficulties to an organized nation with an ongoing judicial system and a standing military capacity. We might sympathize with their request. Samuel, however, did not. In effect they were telling him that they did not want to continue in the way he had been handling things.

Samuel then took his problem to the Lord. The Lord's response is also difficult for us to understand. On the one hand, he sympathized with Samuel (cf. 1 Sam 3:30). The Lord had been leading his people, making use of charismatic leaders. If his people simply relied on him and his provision, he would make things work well (cf. Judg 2:18–19 above). They, however, did not, so he let them suffer the consequences of their lack of good relationship with him time and time again.

He gave Samuel an answer to make. Surprisingly to many readers, the answer was not: you are rejecting me and I will condemn you in asking for a king. His answer, in fact, was: you may have a king, and I will appoint one for you. He had to tell Samuel more than once to do what the people asked. On the other hand, his answer was not simply positive. He told Samuel to warn them that the kingship would require an expenditure they were not prepared for, and he perhaps implied that a king could easily become a tyrant and replace his rule over his people with a problematic government. Both these things were true. And he told Samuel, his loyal servant, not to take their desire for a king personally. Whether Samuel was at all consoled or not we are not told, but we would guess not.

One common interpretation of this interchange is to sympathize with Samuel and hold that the kingship was a mistake. The people were simply rejecting God by wanting a king, and they should have continued to rely on God and continued in "the good old ways." This view can easily be influenced by modern antinomianism and rebellion against authority. At least those who express it do not always take into account the fact that "the good old days" were not presented in the Scripture as good, and that Samuel in fact was not about to leave the Israelites in a very good condition, with his successor sons not following in his own good ways, and probably with the Philistines still dominant.

Such a view does not take into account something else; namely, that the Lord then proceeded to guarantee the kingship. He appointed Saul, and then he appointed David. Through both of them, but David especially, he liberated his people from the Philistines—in fact from all of their enemies—and established one of the most successful states of the time. Moreover, he made the kingship a divine institution, establishing it in the law (Deut 17:14–17). In fact, when rabbis later taught about the prerogatives of the king, they used Samuel's presentation in 1 Samuel 8 as a description of how the king should function, not as a description of a tyranny (e.g., Maimonides, *Mishneh Torah*, V, 4). In this they were following 1 Samuel 10:25 that says, after Saul was established as king,

> Samuel told the people the rights and duties of the kingship; and he wrote them in a book and laid it up before the LORD.

Those who follow a model of scriptural criticism that distinguishes different sources—sources often at odds with one another but put together without full integration—sometimes hold that we are here seeing two different views of kingship, one positive and one negative. They hold that these come from two different sources, each with its own view of kingship, that have been stitched together. Rather, as many now hold, we are simply looking at a narrative style that is different than our own. The Lord's attitude toward the kingship has to be understood by the way he actually deals with it.[1]

To be sure, the Lord does sympathize with Samuel's reaction— to a certain extent. There is something problematic about God's people simply wanting to run their own affairs "like all the nations" around them. There is also something problematic about their coming "in a complaining spirit" (Maimonides, *Mishneh Torah*, V, 1) to a prophet God had chosen. Moreover, the Lord upholds a servant of his who has been faithful to him.

But such considerations did not mean that kingship was all wrong, as the book of Deuteronomy makes very clear. The Lord wanted Israel to be a kingdom, with a stable authority that could claim the people's obedience. In fact, the Lord did not side with Samuel, but with the leaders who wanted a change. Even Samuel himself later conceded that as long as the people and their king feared and obeyed the Lord, "it will be well" (1 Sam 12:14).

Nevertheless, the Lord's decision that Israel should be a kingdom did not mean that kingship was not problematic at all. A question raised by the account is: how could the kingship be approached so that it was not a rejection of God himself as the true king of his people and so that the potential for corruption could be avoided? To see the answer, we need to look at the accounts of the first two kings of Israel, Saul and David, and then to the new covenant fulfillment of the kingship.

The failure of the first king. Chapters 8–12 of First Samuel describe the choice of Saul as king, and chapter 13 begins the description of Saul's reign. Saul's main challenge was to free Israel from the Philistines and the other hostile tribes in the area. The Israelites had been beaten down for a while, but Saul slowly put together a standing army and began to reverse the Philistine domination. In other words, he did what a king is supposed to do for the people. But not

---

[1] Baruch Halpern, *The First Historians: The Hebrew Bible and History* (University Park, PA: Pennsylvania State University Press, 1996), 184 supports this view by saying, "Chapter 8 and 10:17–27 are not antimonarchic. Kingship was approved, if reluctantly, by Yhwh; Yhwh himself elected this king (cf. Deut. 17:14f)."

all went well. He failed to act in a way that was pleasing to God.

The event that most clearly demonstrated the failure of Saul is described in chapter 15 (cf. also 1 Sam 28:18). Saul was sent a solemn command from God through a prophetic word by Samuel to "utterly destroy" [RSV] the Amalekites. This he only partly did, and so disobeyed. After this act of disobedience Samuel said to him,

> "Has the LORD as great delight in burnt offerings and sac-
>   rifices,
>   as in obeying the voice of the LORD?
> Behold, to obey is better than sacrifice,
>   and to hearken than the fat of rams.
> For rebellion is as the sin of divination,
>   and stubbornness is as iniquity and idolatry.
> Because you have rejected the word of the LORD,
>   he has also rejected you from being king." (1 Sam
>   15:22–23)

Saul was the first king. He was not a bad man, nor was he simply disloyal to the Lord. He did, however, act in a way that was only partially obedient. The reason is that he was not *a man after [the Lord's] own heart* (1 Sam 13:14). Because our culture tends to understand the heart as the seat of the emotions or affections, we easily can misunderstand what is being said about Saul. "Heart," however, is the Hebrew word that is most commonly used to speak about the mind or the inner intentions. Saul, then, is a man whose thoughts and plans do not line up with the Lord's. The key is that he does not always do what the Lord tells him to do, at least not consistently, and that shortcoming seems to be rooted in a slackness in his desire to obey God.

We can see this in the way that Saul dealt with God's direction about the Amalekites (1 Sam 15). Although Saul destroyed much of the Amalekites' possessions, as he was told to do, he allowed some of them to be kept, which he was forbidden to do. He excused this by saying that they were saved to offer sacrifice to the Lord. But as

Samuel makes clear, sacrifice is not a substitute for obedience. First and foremost, the Lord was looking for a king who would obey him and who wanted to obey him as his servant.

The command to destroy the Amalekites is a special case in the history of the Israelite monarchy and has occasioned much discussion. A full discussion of this matter goes beyond the scope of this book, but the incident is probably a matter of spiritual warfare, warfare with Satanic forces, not just the human warfare that we have considered in discussing the challenge of the Canaanites in the land. The Amalekites were a people who tried to destroy God's people while they were being redeemed by God and were being provided for by him in the wilderness (Ex 17:8–16; Deut 25:17–19). Their attack was therefore more directly on God himself than most later attacks and was perhaps the paradigm example of other nations attacking God by attacking his people. For a similar but lesser example, see the Moabite attack on some of the Israelites mentioned previously in chapter 7.

The Amalekites could be considered as typological of those who seek to wipe out God's people and God's rule in the world, and God's response was typological of his commitment to destroy the kingdom of Satan. God's command for how to deal with the matter was likely in many respects beyond the comprehension of his servants, but therefore all the more needed to be strictly obeyed.

Samuel had pronounced that the second king of Israel, Saul's successor, David, would be a man after God's own heart (1 Sam 13:14). Although, as we shall see, he was not perfect himself, he had the key qualification for a king. He put the honor of God first and was determined to obey him—and repent when he did not. If the king obeys God and leads the people in obeying God, the nation will do what God wants. God will reign over his people through the king.

The book of Deuteronomy gives the instructions for the good king, the king who functions the way God wants him to:

> And when he sits on the throne of his kingdom, he shall write
> for himself in a book a copy of this law, from that which is in

the charge of the Levitical priests; and it shall be with him, and he shall read in it all the days of his life, that he may learn to fear the LORD his God, by keeping all the words of this law and these statutes, and doing them; that his heart may not be lifted up above his brethren, and that he may not turn aside from the commandment, either to the right hand or to the left; so that he may continue long in his kingdom, he and his children, in Israel. (Deut 17:18–20).

DAVID, THE MODEL KING

The sources for the life of David. We now need to look at David and his reign as the king of Israel. Although Saul is the first king of Israel and began the process of establishing Israel as a kingdom, David is the one who established what kingship in Israel should be and what it means for God's people to be a kingdom. As a result, David the King is crucial for understanding the New Testament and especially for understanding who Christ, the son of David and the anointed King of Israel, is.

The chief sources for the life of David are First Samuel 16 to First Kings 2 and most of First Chronicles. The accounts of David in the books of Samuel are one of the most engaging narratives in Scripture. They are, in addition, one of the best and in certain respects the earliest narrative historical works that allow us concretely to see events from three millennia ago. And the story they narrate contains the kind of dramatic events that grab the imagination.

First Chronicles, however, is a very different work. It omits the stories that attract our greatest interest: the conflict between David and Saul, the adultery of David, and the revolt of Absalom. Instead it presents a picture of David as the ideal ruler, the one who established the foundation of the life of the people of Israel throughout the centuries—especially the worship of Israel, that which united Israel even after the loss of the territorial empire. First Chronicles is the book that concentrates on the chief long-term accomplishments of David and provides the understanding of David that marks Jewish history and that determines how the New Testament approaches him as well.

We are once again presented with two accounts that cover the same events. There are those who see them as in contradiction with one another, as some see the two accounts at the beginning of Genesis. They are, however, not in contradiction with one another, although there are some discrepancies between them. There are others who see Chronicles as an attempt to "sanitize" David, leaving out all the discreditable features. This does not hold up completely well, partly because some of David's failures are presented (notably the affair of the census in 1 Chron 23), and because Samuel and Kings could also be charged with sanitizing David (2 Sam 23:1–5). In addition, many scholars think some of the material in Chronicles is drawn from Samuel and Kings, or possibly both drew on some of the same sources, and Chronicles did not intend to simply replace them, much less refute them.

The more likely historical hypothesis is that the writer of Chronicles expected the reader to be familiar with other Israelite historical writings, including the books of Samuel and Kings, and decided to write a different kind of account of the important elements of Israel's history—one that highlighted certain abidingly significant events. The dominant interest it shows is in David's role in establishing the worship of Israel. This is perhaps because at the time of the Chronicler, there was no Davidic king, and it was the worship of Israel that bound the people together, both in the land of Israel and the diaspora.[2] At any rate, we will pass over the passages of greatest human interest in the books of Samuel and Kings and instead look at David as First Chronicles teaches about his significance, with occasional supplements from Samuel and Kings.

David's achievements: the "empire" and its capital. David, first of all, was very successful as a king, from the time when he began to

---

[2]   For a development of this view, see Patrick Henry Reardon, *Chronicles of History and Worship: Orthodox Christian Reflections on the Books of Chronicles* (Ben Lomond, CA: Conciliar Press, 2006).

take responsibility for the affairs of Israel as a servant of Saul to the end of his reign, even after the rebellion of his son Absalom. If we look for the primary reason behind the insistence of the elders of Israel to have a king, it does not seem to be failures in the administration of justice they were seeking to correct, although that was a factor. Rather, it was what we might call national defense—the security of a people surrounded by enemies, especially the Philistines—that was their concern. Like Israel, there were many other tribal groups at the time, but those who survived the best, at least in the agricultural lands, were the ones organized as kingdoms.

A king was a military leader. He either commanded the army personally, or he oversaw a commander-in-chief that he appointed. In order for the people to have an effective standing army, they needed a certain level of internal organization. This a king could provide because of his authority. As, however, Samuel emphasized to the elders when they demanded a king, there would be a cost. A king with a standing army needed resources, and so they would have to provide those resources, paying a price they were not accustomed to pay. Although perhaps they did not fully know what having a king meant, the Israelites had experienced enough of the domination of the Philistines to want a change.

Saul provided a rudimentary form of kingship, and in so doing improved the ability of the Israelites to defend themselves against the Philistines. David, however, was what we might call a leading statesman of his time. He was a great military leader and organizer. As Second Samuel 8:6 and 8:14 put it, "The LORD gave victory to David wherever he went." In so doing, David not only freed Israel from the domination of the Philistines for all time, but he established a hegemony over Israel's neighbors, so that modern scholars often describe the result as "the empire" of David and his son Solomon.

The consequence of David's work was that Israel finally had the full inheritance God promised to it, that is, the promised land. Enclaves of foreign people inside the land were eliminated or subdued; the borders were made secure. He took the organization of the kingdom to a new level (1 Chron 18:14–17; 2 Sam 15–18). He "administered justice and equity to all his people" (1 Chron 18:14; 2 Sam 8:15). A greater prosperity for all the people seems to have gone along with his military and governmental successes. David's personal ability and the fact that the Lord was with him resulted in God's promised blessing being fulfilled.

One of the very first things David did was to conquer the city of Jerusalem and make it his capital, as we can read in First Chronicles 11. From the human point of view, this was a strategic step. The kingdom of Saul had been predominantly made up of mountain settlements in Judah; the central tribal areas of Benjamin, Ephraim, and Manasseh; Galilee; and the western Transjordan. They were, however, separated from one another by Canaanite possessions in the lowlands, and Judah was partially separated from Benjamin by the Jebusite city of Jerusalem.

David's initial conquest of the city, even before his definitive defeat of the Philistines, meant that the two areas that would provide his greatest strength were now united geographically. There was, however, an even more significant result. David was from Judah, the tribe that most clearly supported him as one of their own. Saul and his family had been from Benjamin and northern Israel. David had been chosen as king of Judah first and then subsequently the tribes of Israel gave up on the house of Saul and chose David as their king as well. Jerusalem was on the boundary between these two groups and became the tribally neutral place from which David could govern the whole country.

Capitals are very important to the success of a people, but the capital of a people like Israel was even more important. Not only were the new inhabitants of Jerusalem inter-tribal, with servants of the king from all the tribes living there, but it was the place of the temple, with many Levites and priests (a tribe scattered through all Israel) either living there or staying there for lengthy periods of time. As the site of the temple, the place where all Israel gathered three times a year to live together and celebrate the goodness of the Lord, Jerusalem became not only the secular capital of Israel, but also the acknowledged home, the dwelling place, of all godly Israel-ites (cf. Ps 122).

Jerusalem was not just the dwelling place of the old covenant Israelites as a nation. It has become the city of the new covenant people of God as well (Gal 4:26). Moreover, at the end of the book of Revelation the new Jerusalem will come down from heaven as the eternal dwelling place of all the redeemed. Jerusalem is the city of God through all ages, the type of God's people, and it was King David who established Jerusalem as the city of God.

David's achievements: the worship. David's next greatest accom-plishment was closely related to the establishment of the city of Jeru-salem. He also established the worship of Israel. There was certainly a worship of God on the part of the Israelites before David came along. We read about altars and temples, including the central sanc-tuary at Shiloh that was destroyed by the Philistines (1 Sam 4–6). We read about priests and sacrifices and rites of purification. But it was the worship of a tribal society. It seems to have been broadly the same among all the tribes, but it was not unified, at least not after the fall of Shiloh.

David had the vision for a unified worship in Jerusalem. He de-cided that he would build a temple in Jerusalem for all Israel. The Lord, however, did not approve, as Nathan the prophet told him (1 Chron 17; cf. 2 Sam 7). David was the man of war who was to es-tablish the secure position of the people of Israel. His work was to be completed by his son and successor Solomon, the man of peace, who would actually build the temple, the source of peace with God and with one another in the capital of Israel.

The fact that he was not allowed to build the temple did not prevent David from being the establisher of the unified worship of Israel. One of the very first steps he took was to bring the ark of the covenant, the earthly equivalent of the throne of God, to Jeru-salem and set it up in a tent on the site of the future temple. He also brought the altar of burnt sacrifice there.

According to First Chronicles, David was the one who ordained the building of the temple. David did not actually build the temple building, for that task was reserved for his son Solomon. Yet in First Chronicles 22:1, David was the one who said, "Here shall be the house of the LORD God and here the altar of burnt offering for Israel." Furthermore, it was David who gathered together all the workers and materials; it was David who charged Solomon to build the temple; it was David who made all the preparations so that Solomon could build it. Psalm 132 celebrates David's role in building the temple in Jerusalem.

Sirach 47:9–10 says that David also took a concern for the orderly worship of God. First Chronicles describes this as setting up the order of worship of the Lord that would eventually be carried out in the temple. His work for the establishment of the central worship in Israel is described in some fullness in First Chronicles, chapters 15, 16, and 23–26. As a result of David's work, Israel, as well as the Christian people, has been a nation unified by their worship together of the one true God—even when they did not have a physical land and a physical capital city.

David's relationship with God. Key to David's achievements was his own relationship with God. Not only did King David establish the worship of God in Jerusalem, he also wrote many of the hymns and songs (the psalms) used in the worship of God. In fact, the book of Psalms, the hymnal or songbook of God's people, was attributed to him as the principal or perhaps originating author. He did not write all the contents, but he seems to have been a notable psalm writer (2 Sam 23:2), much like Romanus the Melodist or Charles Wesley were notable in Christian history for writing hymns.

This gives us a further understanding of why David was a man after God's own heart. He sought to be obedient and keep God's commandments, but in addition, he was personally devoted to the Lord. As the book of Psalms instructs us, he saw the Lord as *a shield about [him], [his] glory, and the lifter of [his] head* (Ps 3:3). Sirach 47:8, summarizing what had been passed down, said, *In all that he did he gave thanks to the Holy One, the Most High, with ascriptions of*

glory; he sang praise with all his heart, and he loved his maker. His obedience to God in action was motived by his personal love of God.

There is another important basis for David being a man after
God's own heart. He was a spiritual (charismatic) man. This goes
back to God's choice of him. When Samuel anointed David to be the
king of Israel to succeed Saul, the Spirit of the Lord came upon him.
In First Samuel 16:13 it says,

> Then Samuel took the horn of oil, and anointed him in the
> midst of his brothers; and the Spirit of the LORD came
> mightily upon David from that day forward.

The Spirit of the Lord and spiritual power departed from Saul, but
went with David, with results that all could see.

Perhaps connected to this anointing, perhaps coming even earlier, the Spirit of the Lord made David a prophet, one who could speak
by inspiration of God and the things of God even in his psalms. The
"last words of David" state this clearly:

> Now these are the last words of David:
>   The oracle of David, the son of Jesse,
>   The oracle of the man who was raised on high,
>   the anointed of the God of Jacob,
>   the sweet psalmist of Israel:
> "The Spirit of the LORD speaks by me,
>   his word is upon my tongue.
> The God of Israel has spoken,
>   the Rock of Israel has said to me . . ."
>   (2 Sam 23:1–3)

In the New Testament, David is considered to be one of the main
prophets because of the prophetic nature of the book of Psalms (cf.
Acts 2:30). Many of us miss this point because our tendency is not
to see the psalms as prophetic but to see them as just Israelite devotional literature in various literary forms. But for the New Testament

the Psalms were a book of prophecy (for example, Mt 20:43; Acts 1:16; 2:25; 4:25). In Luke 24:44 we read how the risen Lord Jesus used the law, the prophets, and the psalms to outline all the things that were said about him. In other words, he himself said that the psalms speak prophetically about him.[3]

The work of King David. Like Moses, David had a successor who furthered and completed his work, namely his son Solomon. As we have seen, it was Solomon who actually built the temple. He also developed the organization of the kingdom. His reign, at least most of his reign, was a time of strength and prosperity. The zenith of the history of the kingdom of Israel likely occurred under Solomon, who surpassed David's kingdom by building upon David's work (2 Chron 9:22–28; 1 Kings 4:20–21; 10:23–27).

Solomon also made his own important contribution to the people of Israel. He was a man of wisdom. We might say that he was a broadly educated man, somewhat familiar with the learning of other nations. This included practical wisdom in how to prosper, both personally and as king. Under Solomon there was a cultural flowering in Israel, much of it finding its way into the Scriptures as we have them. The book of Proverbs, the originating classic of Israel's wisdom literature, was attributed to Solomon (Prov 1:1), much as the book of Psalms was attributed to David. Solomon's reign, at least the greatest part of it, was the completion of David's work, and, despite problems, left strong foundations for old covenant life.

Nonetheless, it was David who was the main founder of the new stage of God's people. He gave the people of Israel security and success, established the city of God and the worship of Israel, and served as an important prophet of the messiah and the new covenant to come. But first and foremost, imperfect as he was, David was the ideal king, the King of Israel who ruled God's way with God working through him to establish the kingdom.

---

[3] A similar understanding, from before the writing of the New Testament, can be found in the Dead Sea Scroll 11QPsa in Geza Vermes, *The Complete Dead Sea Scrolls in English* (London: Penguin, 2011), 313.

DAVID AND HIS DESCENDANT(S)

The anointed king. As we have seen, David was the one who fully established the people of Israel as a kingdom. His kingdom did not just exist while he was alive, but it continued with his descendants reigning as kings after him. He began a kingdom, but also a dynasty to rule that kingdom, and that dynasty continued ruling for centuries. In fact, it was one of the longest lasting ruling dynasties in earthly history. However, God intended more to come out of the work of David than David's contemporaries would have understood. This has to do with David's anointing.

Second Samuel 23 begins, "The oracle of David, the son of Jesse, the oracle of the man who was raised on high, the anointed of the God of Jacob . . ." David was the anointed one. The Greek work for "the anointed one" is "*ho christós*" or, anglicized, "the christ." The Hebrew word, anglicized, is "the messiah." David was a messiah or christ. Anointing in the time of David was the way someone could be appointed to or established in office, especially when there was an unclear succession. Through Samuel, David was anointed by God to be the King of Israel.

There were anointed kings, but there were also anointed prophets and anointed priests in the history of Israel. The word "anointed" or "messiah" does not automatically refer to an "anointed king," but we use the Hebrew term "messiah" almost exclusively to mean an anointed king. When the question is raised in the New Testament, "Is this the Messiah (the christ)?" the question being asked is, for reasons we will soon see, "Is this the anointed king?" not the anointed prophet or the anointed priest, or any other kind of anointed one.

The house of David. The future of David's house or dynasty was at least partly established by an important old covenant prophecy; one we can read about in First Chronicles 17 or Second Samuel 7. David had decided to build the temple for the Lord. Nathan, apparently the chief prophet at the time, when he heard about it said the equivalent of, "Oh yes, splendid idea, go ahead and do it." But then he was forced by God to go back and give a prophecy saying the opposite.

Nathan's prophecy began by telling David that he should not build the temple. It then says some important things about how God worked with David himself:

> "I took you from the pasture, from following the sheep, that you should be prince over my people Israel; and I have been with you wherever you went, and have cut off all your enemies from before you; and I will make for you a name, like the name of the great ones of the earth. And I will appoint a place for my people Israel, and will plant them, that they may dwell in their own place, and be disturbed no more; and violent men shall waste them no more, as formerly, from the time that I appointed judges over my people Israel; and I will subdue all your enemies." (1 Chron 17:7–10)

The prophecy then continues on to speak about David's descendants and how the Lord will work with them:

> "Moreover I declare to you that the LORD will build you a house. When your days are fulfilled to go to be with your fathers, I will raise up your offspring after you, one of your own sons, and I will establish his kingdom. He shall build a house for me, and I will establish his throne forever. I will be his father, and he shall be my son; I will not take my steadfast love from him, as I took it from him who was before you, but I will confirm him in my house and in my kingdom for ever and his throne shall be established for ever." (1 Chron 17:10–14)

The prophecy most immediately concerns Solomon, the son of David who was David's successor, the first fulfillment of the prophecy. He is the one who would build the house (the temple for God). But the Lord would use him to continue David's house (his dynasty), and so God would build a house for David instead of David building one for God. The house of David was to be a key piece in God's plan henceforth.

The prophecy also says, "I will be his father and he will be my son." There is a special father-son relationship between God and the king, so the king is the "son of God" in an important way. As we will see, this is a significant truth about the messiah. The version of the prophecy we read in 2 Samuel 7:14–15 adds,

> "When he commits iniquity, I will chasten him with the rod
> of men, with the stripes of the sons of men; but I will not take
> my steadfast love from him, as I took it from Saul, whom I
> put away from before you."

Solomon did commit iniquity and was punished with successful rebellions against his rule and other troubles. In this his history was similar to that of his father David, who, despite being a man after God's own heart, had sinned seriously by committing adultery and murder and who also had been punished with rebellion and trouble in his house. In this he was also like Moses and Aaron. All fail at important points and create difficulties for God and the people with whom he is working—a consistent Old Testament pattern as we have seen.

Nonetheless, the prophecy adds a very important further point. Not only will Solomon himself not be rejected as king (as David was not), but,

> "'And your house and your kingdom shall be made sure for
> ever before me; your throne shall be established for ever.'"
> (2 Sam 7:16)

God, in other words, was entering into a covenant commitment with the line of David, a commitment that he would be faithful to forever, as he was faithful to the commitments he made with Abraham and with the people of Israel at Sinai. He would be a good father to them, blessing them when they did well and punishing them when they did badly so they would get back on track (cf. Prov 3:11–12). In choosing David and Solomon, God was entering into a special father-son relationship with the royal descendants of David, one that in an unforeseeable way would restore his father-son relationship with the human race.

Solomon, the one immediately mentioned in the prophecy, did not live on earth forever and continue to reign over Israel. Nor did any of his contemporaries who heard this prophecy expect that to happen. But his house and his kingdom and throne were prophesied to last forever. No doubt for the first centuries of the kingdom of Israel and Judah, people understood the prophecy in a literalistic way and expected the Davidic dynasty to last forever. This did not, however, happen because of the iniquity of the people and their kings, and the kingdom of Israel was destroyed as an earthly monarchy. The only way it would then be possible for the prophecy to be fulfilled would be for a new anointed king, a messiah from the descendants of David and Solomon, to be raised up.

The Messiah to come. The prophecy of Nathan was an important prophetic message from the Lord about the house of David. It is referred to in various places in the Old Testament. It is repeated and elaborated in Psalm 89. Other psalms say some similar things. Psalm 2, often quoted in the New Testament, speaks about how God's anointed king will defeat all of his people's enemies and says:

> I will tell of the decree of the LORD:
> He said to me, "You are my son,
>   today I have begotten you.
> Ask of me, and I will make the nations your heritage,
>   and the ends of the earth your possession.
> You shall break them with a rod of iron,
>   and dash them in pieces like a potter's vessel."
>   (Ps 2:7–9)

Another equally important psalm in the New Testament is Psalm 110, which contains the following stanza:

> The LORD says to my lord:
>   "Sit at my right hand,
> till I make your enemies your footstool." (Ps 110:1)

New Testament writings consider these psalms messianic prophecies, and there are many other messianic prophecies in the Old Testament. A messianic prophecy is one that comes in a time of trouble and that promises a messiah, an anointed king, who will come and rescue his people. The book of the prophet Isaiah contains a number of them. One of the most important and well-known ones is in Isaiah 9:6–7:

> For to us a child is born,
>   to us a son is given;
> and the government will be upon his shoulder,
>   and his name will be called
> "Wonderful Counselor, Mighty God,
>   Everlasting Father, Prince of Peace."
> Of the increase of his government and of peace
>   there will be no end,
> upon the throne of David, and over his kingdom,
>   to establish it, and to uphold it.

The prophecy in Isaiah 11:1–5 adds some unexpected facts about this anointed king:

> There shall come forth a shoot from the stump of Jesse,
>   and a branch shall grow out of his roots.
> And the Spirit of the LORD shall rest upon him,
>   the spirit of wisdom and understanding,
>   the spirit of counsel and might,

the spirit of knowledge and the fear of the LORD.
And his delight shall be in the fear of the LORD.

He shall not judge by what his eyes see,
    or decide by what his ears hear;
but with righteousness he shall judge the poor,
    and decide with equity for the meek of the earth;
and he shall smite the earth with the rod of his mouth,
    and with the breath of his lips he shall slay the wicked.
Righteousness shall be the belt of his waist,
    and faithfulness the belt of his loins.

See also Isaiah 61 for a similar prophecy. This descendant of David who is to come will be known for the anointing of the Spirit upon him. He will rule the earth, and he will do so by the power of his word, not the power of his sword.

For a while the kingdom of Israel lasted as an independent nation in the promised land. There were ups and downs, not unconnected to their unfaithfulness to God. The kingdom of Solomon split into two nations, the northern kingdom called the kingdom of Israel and the southern kingdom called the kingdom of Judah. Then the northern kingdom fell to the power of the empire of Assyria in 721 BC and the southern kingdom to the power of the empire of Babylonia in 586 BC. The people were taken captive and a large part of them brought into exile in the land of Babylon, in the shadow of the temple that was the successor to the tower of Babel (Babylon). The Scriptures, both Old Testament and New, are agreed that this was due to their unfaithfulness to the covenant with God.

The Persian Empire conquered the Babylonian Empire and succeeded to its dominance over the remnant of the Israelite people— by the hand of God for the sake of the plan of God (Is 45:1–7). The Persian kings allowed the people, now usually called the Judahites or the Jews, to return to the land of Judah. Many did, although many stayed in Babylonia. The Persian king also underwrote the construction of the second temple. The Jews slowly prospered and recovered. Eventually Alexander the Great conquered the Persians and the Hellenistic empires replaced Persian power. They, in turn, were for the most part conquered by the Romans, whose empire included the promised land.

During this time the Jews scattered farther. While there was a strong and growing settlement in the promised land, the diaspora had begun. The word diaspora means "scattering," and the Jews were scattered over much of the known world. For a brief period of time, Jews in the promised land revolted from the power of the Hellenistic monarch of Syria and established an independent kingdom under the Hasmonean rulers. The Davidic monarchy, however, was not re-established, and the Jewish kingdom soon fell under the domination of the Romans. The full old covenant order, presided over by a king from the house of David, was never restored.

Something new, however, came to birth in this period. The exile, as a discipline inflicted by God, worked to the good in an unexpected way. Many, perhaps most, of the Jews in exile in Babylonia turned back to the Lord. They had no temple, sacrifice, or officiating priests (Dan 3:15 LXX). They did, however, have the law, and they gathered in synagogues (assembly halls), with scholars of the law—the scribes, later referred to as the rabbis—teaching them how to live as faithful old covenant people outside of the promised land. Those who returned to the land rebuilt the temple and its worship, but they also brought with them the law, the synagogue meetings, and the scribal teachers. This strengthened their life as old covenant people.

Some have said that God had the Jews "build an ark in Mesopotamia," possibly the land where Noah built the first ark. They built the ark of "Judaism," a further ordering of the life of the old covenant people, one that would allow them to maintain their covenant relationship with God outside the land of Israel. This served to preserve them in the diaspora, and it has preserved them to this day, after they were again exiled from the land of Israel in AD 70 and AD 132. Judaism is not the focus of this book, but out of Judaism with its Scriptures, especially the law, the synagogue worship, and the teaching scholars, came the forms of life that later on allowed the Christian people to prosper. The ark of the church of Christ was built out of the materials provided by diaspora Judaism after the exile. But that gets ahead of our story.

Nonetheless, the promise to David about his house remained. The messianic prophecies remained, never totally fulfilled. The people of Israel restored their life in various ways at various times, but they never had a Davidic king, even though they knew who the descendants of David were. Nor did God raise up a Davidic king for over five hundred years.

JESUS THE MESSIAH, THE SON OF DAVID AND OF GOD

The Son of David. The Gospel of Matthew begins with a genealogy that has an unusual feature. It is structured in groups of fourteen: *the generations from Abraham to David . . . the generations from David to the deportation to Babylon . . . and from the deportation to Babylon to the Christ,* [the messiah] (Mt 1:17). Almost certainly that does not mean that there are exactly fourteen generations from Abraham to David and from David to the deportation to Babylon and from the deportation to Christ. There are other genealogies in the Old Testament that Matthew certainly knew and that give a different number for some of these generations (see, for instance, First Chronicles 3:11–12).

While scriptural genealogies are not fictional, they are usually selective to make a point.[4] We saw that the beginning of the book of Genesis, narrating the beginnings of the human race, structured the stages by generations of ten (Adam to Noah and Noah to Abraham). So why does this genealogy center on fourteen?

Many think the number fourteen was chosen because that was the number of David's name. Hebrew, like Greek, used letters for

---

[4] For more background, see the technical note on genealogies (p. 406).

numbers. Aleph (Alpha) the first letter was number 1; Beth (Beta) was number 2; and so on. David was spelled in Hebrew with three letters, and when those letters were added together, they gave the number fourteen, which was the number of his name (cf. Rev 13:17–18 for a similar approach). That probably means that the genealogy was coded to emphasize that Christ was the descendant of David.

Abraham was the man chosen by God to enter into a covenant relationship with God, and that covenant contained a promised blessing. David was chosen by God to be the descendant of Abraham who established the kingdom of Israel in such a way that the promise given to Abraham was fulfilled in its old covenant form. Then the deportation to Babylon, much like the Flood, destroyed the old order with its unfaithfulness, and prepared for a new creation of the people of God.

The deportation to Babylon brought to an end the rule of the house of David in its old covenant earthly form without cancelling God's promise to David. Those who believed in the prophecies of the Old Testament expected that there should come a messiah from the line of David who would restore Jerusalem and the kingdom of Israel (Lk 2:25, 38). But nothing happened until the time was right (Gal 4:4). Then, the messiah appeared, filled with the Spirit. That messiah, a son of David, was Jesus Christ.

When in Hebrew people wanted to say "descendant of," they said "son of." Christ, then, was a descendant of David, and it was publicly known who was of the house of David. Often when Jews were speaking of the anointed king, the messiah, that they were looking for, they would say "*the* son of David," referring to that son of David who would be the restored king of Israel. Many referred to Christ that way. We can see that in the genealogy in Matthew, but also in certain Gospel passages. For instance, in Matthew 12:22 it says,

> Then a blind and dumb demoniac was brought to him, and he healed him, so that the dumb man spoke and saw. And all the people were amazed, and said, "Can this be the Son of David?"

Or at Christ's entry into Jerusalem on Palm Sunday, the crowd in acclaiming him said,

> And the crowds that went before him and that followed him shouted, "Hosanna to the Son of David! Blessed is he who comes in the name of the Lord! Hosanna in the highest!" (Mt 21:9)

In predicting the birth of Jesus to Mary, the Angel Gabriel said,

> "He will be great, and will be called *the Son of the Most High*;
> and the Lord God will give to him the throne of *his father David*,
> and he will reign over the house of Jacob *forever*;
> and of his kingdom there will be no end."
> (Lk 1:32–33, emphasis added)

Jesus Christ, then, was the son of David, but also the Son of God in a greater way than David was. That we now need to consider.

The Son of God. People in the time of Christ said something more about this son of David. As Gabriel predicted, they said he was the Son of God. We can see this in Peter's confession in Matthew 16:16. Following Jesus' question, "But who do you say I am?" Peter replies,

> "You are the Christ, the Son of the living God."

In saying that, Peter was saying, "You are the anointed king, the Messiah, who is God's son."

We need to see Peter's response in the light of the messianic prophecies. As we have seen, in Nathan's prophecy in First Chronicles 17 and Second Samuel 7, God says of the descendant of David who would be the king of Israel, *I will be his father, and he shall be my son*. There is, then, an important connection between being messiah and being Son of God.

"Son of God" can be used in several different senses. Adam was described as the son of God. His descendants, individually and corporately, were supposed to be sons of God. Adam, of course, lost his good relationship with God, and Christ came to restore it. As a result of the work of Christ, we can be sons (and daughters) of God. That means that we belong to the restored human race that is in good relationship with God and serves to advance his kingdom. We, like Adam and many of his descendants, can say, "I am a son of God"—but we cannot say, I am *the* Son of God.

As the messiah, Christ could say he was *the* Son of God. This is probably what Peter was asserting about him. There is thus a special sense of "Son of God." First of all, it was a sense that could be applied to those who were the kings of Israel, like Solomon. They were sons of God in a special way, one that indicated a special relationship with God by which he sought to work through them.

Christ, however, did not apply the term to himself in the same way Solomon might have. We can see why in an interchange he had with some Jewish teachers (Mk 12:35–37):

And as Jesus taught in the temple, he said, "How can the scribes say that the Christ is the son of David? David himself, inspired by the Holy Spirit, declared,

'The Lord said to my Lord,
Sit at my right hand,
till I put your enemies under your feet.'

David himself calls him Lord; so how is he his son?" And the great throng heard him gladly.

Christ is here quoting Psalm 110, the psalm of David that was a messianic prophecy. David, the speaker identified in the title of the psalm, calls the one who would be his son his "Lord." In so doing he was indicating that the messiah to come would be greater than he (David) himself was. Christ, then, acknowledged by many as the son of David, was implying that there was something yet more important about his relationship with God than David's, and that implies that he was more than just a more successful version of anointed king than David was.

This brings us to a third sense of "Son of God," namely, the divine Son of God. Here, the line in the prophecy that says "sit at my right hand" is especially significant. Christ, after his Resurrection, ascended to heaven and there was seated at the right hand of God.

When we think of installations of kings, we think almost exclusively of coronations ("crowning" ceremonies). The crown is a token of authority, and putting it on the new king is a way of expressing that he is now king. But even in contemporary installations of a king, part of the installation ceremony is for the new king to sit on the royal throne. No one else is or was allowed to do that. When Christ was seated at the right hand of God, he shared God's own throne, the throne from which God ruled his creation (Rev 22:3). Christ then was installed, not just as King of Israel but as King of the Universe—but he did not sit on God's throne in an idolatrous way, claiming that which no one but God could claim.

In sharing God's throne, Christ did not replace God, but he reigned together with God. He was able to take this role because of his obedience to God his Father, but also because he was *born before all ages* (the Nicene Creed) as the divine Son of God, *the unique, only one of a kind,* [RSV: *only*] *Son of God* (Jn 1:14), Son in a way no other son of God could be. It was to his divine Son, and could only be to a divine Son, not even to the highest angel, that God said, "sit at my right hand" (Heb 1:13).

Christ had a certain equality with God as the sharer of his throne and therefore of his kingship. That equality was the equality of a son, who, like all legitimate sons, shared the nature and rank of his father, the one from whom he derived his being, although still under and obedient to him (cf. Jn 4:34; 5:30; 6:38; 8:55; 14:10, etc.). As a result, he was the Son of God in a way no previous king of Israel had been, David himself included. He was still the human Son of God who was the King of Israel, but he also, as divine Son of God, was king of the universe, fulfilling the messianic prophecies in a way that previous generations would not have imagined.

As the son of David, Christ did what David did. He gave the people of Israel their full inheritance. He gave them safety from their enemies. He built their city, the new Jerusalem. He established the worship of God his Father that would be pleasing to him. He also did what Solomon, the son of David, did. He built their temple, the new covenant temple. He established peace throughout the city. He brought prosperity. He brought together teaching that would allow God's people to live well. In addition, he embarked upon the responsibility of ruling the nations, like both David and Solomon, until God his father would definitively put all his enemies under his feet, as Psalm 110:1 prophesied.

The kingdom of God. Christ put to rest the question about the challenge of human kingship that Samuel had raised. David was a king after God's own heart. But he did not succeed in fully bringing God's kingship to the people of Israel. No king, prophet, or priest did. Many strove to reach the ideal, but the Old Testament contains stories of their only partial success along with many failures.

The solution to this problem is found in the New Testament. In Jesus Christ, we have a king who is a man, but who is also the Son of God in such a way that when this king reigns God reigns. He is perfectly united with his Father, sharing his being or nature so that when he acts, his Father acts. The divine Word, who, as derivative from the divine speaker of that Word, God the Father, was therefore also the divine Son, *begotten but not made* (the Nicene Creed), came to earth and was born of a human woman, the Virgin Mary, the wife of Joseph of the house of David. He became a human being, Jesus of Nazareth, the son of David, to reign over his people so that they had a king who was a human being and an Israelite, but at the same time they also had God himself as a king.

As the human Son of God, Christ was in God's image and likeness. As the divine Son of God, he was his image (Col 1:15; 2 Cor 4:4). As Hebrews 1:3 (NIV) puts it,

> The son is the radiance of God's glory
> and the exact representation of his being,
> sustaining all things by his powerful word.

To say that he is *the radiance of God's glory* is to say that he is like a ray of light, derived from the originating light, God's glory, and at the same time of the same nature as that light. To say that he is *the exact representation of his being* (or *nature*) is likewise to say that he comes from God the Father, but also is the true image of God and so the same in nature as God. In other words, though a human being, divinity was in him and was his.

The divine Son existed before creation itself. He was therefore able to be the agent of God the Father's creation and governance of the world (Heb 1:2; Col 1:16–17) in a fuller way than any charismatic king like David that God worked through could have. When he became incarnate, died, rose, and ascended, he who was fully the image of God, the full expression of his nature and therefore his character, began to reign over all of creation with a divine and therefore fully righteous and just reign.

But there were not two sons, a human son and a divine Son, joined together by unity of purpose or will. Christ was both human and divine and could act in a human way and a divine way, but he was only one existing being. He was the human and divine Son at the same time, not two sons but one and the same Son. When he acted, the human King of Israel and the divine King of the Universe acted as one person.[5] This is not to say that his divinity absorbed his humanity in such a way that he no longer acted with a fully human mind and will. He was complete in his humanity and complete in his divinity. It is, however, to say that his humanity and divinity were united in how they worked so that his human nature did not act in a way incompatible with his divine nature or with the will of his divine Father.

---

[5] For a fuller presentation of the relationship of the divine Father and his only Son and also of the divine and human in Christ, see *Redeemer,* chap. 6. Neither this book nor *Redeemer* contains a full presentation of the doctrines of the Trinity and Incarnation.

As a result, Christ was the head of the human race, and could only be the head of the human race if he was himself human and acted as a human being. He, however, also acted with divine power and with the fullness of divine character. This means that his human action was an expression of his divine nature. Moreover, he began to share this divine power and character with those Israelites and those human beings from the other nations who chose to follow him—but without making them fully divine. In so doing, he brought humanity, the human race, into a new stage of its relationship with God, as we will see.

Christ did not simply do what David did, or what David would have done if he had more power, that is, bring rest from the enemies of God's people and establish an acceptable worship of God. He also did not simply do what Solomon, the first royal son of David did, that is, bring peace, prosperity, and wisdom about how to live well. He did not, in short, simply establish a well-working old covenant kingdom. He brought a new kingdom, a new rest from enemies, a new blessing, a new wisdom, a new Jerusalem, a new temple, because he brought a new relationship with God, a new covenant. In doing so, he brought into greater effectiveness the kingdom of God, the kingdom God intended from *the foundation of the world* (Mt 25:34), and he will fight until God's will is done—on earth and in us—as it is in heaven.

The difference between the new covenant and the old covenant will be the subject of the next chapter and the nature of the completed kingdom of God will be the subject of the following chapter.

KINGDOM TYPOLOGY

The typology of the first Christians included a kingdom framework, especially for the work of the messiah.

The Kingdom (of Israel and of God): The reign or rule of God over the people of Israel, a type of the Church of Christ in the

new covenant and of the kingdom of God over all creation at
the end of time

The King of Israel: The ruler of the people of Israel, a type of
Christ

The Messiah: The anointed king, a title of Christ

Jerusalem: The capital city of the kingdom of Israel and the
place of assembly of the people of Israel, a type of the Church
of Christ after the first coming and **the new Jerusalem** after
the Second Coming

Mount Zion: The highest point of the city of Jerusalem where
the temple was placed, a type of the place of God's presence in
the new covenant, especially after the Second Coming

The land: The full extent of the old covenant land of Israel,
which included the promised land and territories inhabited by
many of the nations, a type of the new covenant "land of the
living"—Christ and the Holy Spirit

CHAPTER TEN

CHRIST AND THE
NEW COVENANT

**TEXT: SECOND CORINTHIANS 3:1–4:6;
HEBREWS 12:18–29**

Stages	Founders	Events	People	Covenants	Inheritance
VI **Dispensation** **of the** **Spirit**	Jesus Christ (His Apostles)	Crucifixion & Resurrection Pentecost	Church of Christ	New Covenant	Life of the Spirit

Introduction to the chapter. So far we have been reading passages from books of the Old Testament and seeing how they present the stages of God's plan. We have been reading them in the light of the New Testament, seeing what New Testament writers have said about Old Testament texts. That has given us insight into those stages from the perspective of what they have led to and will lead to, and of the significance new covenant spiritual teachers have seen to be already present in them.

Now we will look at what the New Testament says about the new covenant itself. In a certain way, the whole New Testament is about the new covenant. This is, however, not a book about all of Christianity but about how to read the Old Testament in the light of the New. Therefore, we mainly want to look at New Testament passages that tell us how New Testament writers see the new covenant in its relationship to the old. The chief of these are the texts cited above: 2 Corinthians 3:1–4:6 and Hebrews 12:18–29.

The coming of the Christ. The beginning of the first century AD was a troubled time for the Jewish people. The Romans had supported the kingdom of Herod the Great as a Jewish client kingdom. When Herod died, the Romans took over the rule of Judaea, and consequently much of the promised land, the city of Jerusalem, and the temple came directly under the power of a Gentile nation. The kingdom of Israel had clearly not been restored. For some this was a clear turn for the worse, a return to the domination of the Gentiles. For others, this was just a further manifestation that the exile that began after the fall of Jerusalem to the Babylonians in 586 BC had not yet ended by the restoration of the Davidic (messianic) kingdom, much less the prophesied establishment of the full messianic kingdom with the hegemony of Israel over the nations.

In this environment, John the Baptist appeared and began to preach repentance. He saw the current situation as due to the unfaithfulness of the Jewish people. He told them that physical descent from Abraham was not enough to make them sons of Abraham and that they therefore could not inherit the blessing of Abraham in their current condition. He pointed out the one who would bring the solution, who would baptize in the Holy Spirit. He himself was just the forerunner, but the expected one was present in the person of Jesus of Nazareth.

Jesus Christ then began to preach the same message of repentance. He was, moreover, a very great miracle worker. He healed people, he cast out demons, he had prophetic knowledge, and he even could command the wind and the waves if need be. People flocked to him and recognized him as a man who was spiritually more powerful than any Israelite who had yet appeared. He himself acknowledged that he was greater than Solomon, the immediate subject of Nathan's prophecy (Mt 12:42), greater than David himself, who called him Lord (Mt 22:41–46), and greater even than the temple (Mt 12:6), the dwelling place of God.

Many of the Jewish people, including the disciples who would be his Apostles, accepted him as the messiah, the one who would restore the kingdom to Israel. When Christ asked his disciples who they thought he was, Peter replied, *the Christ, the Son of the living God* (Mt 16:16). His disciples seemed to expect him to march on Jerusalem, raise his standard as the true king of Israel, and drive out the Romans. Christ, however, then told them that he would be put to death and rise again, and said that if they were to be his disciples and follow him, they would have to be prepared for the same fate. This announcement met with resistance in them, probably because they thought he might be predicting his (and their) defeat. A true messiah was not supposed to be defeated.

But it had to be (Lk 24:26).

The Transfiguration. In all three synoptic Gospels we then have an account of a striking event, one that is usually referred to as "the Transfiguration."[1] The account in Matthew is as follows:

> And after six days Jesus took with him Peter and James and John his brother, and led them up a high mountain apart. And he was transfigured before them, and his face shone like the sun, and his garments became white as light. And behold, there appeared to them Moses and Elijah, talking with him. And Peter said to Jesus, "Lord, it is well that we are here; if you wish, I will make three booths here, one for you and one for Moses and one for Elijah." He was still speaking, when lo, a bright cloud overshadowed them, and a voice from the cloud said, "This is my beloved Son, with whom I am well pleased; listen to him." When the disciples heard this, they fell on their faces, and were filled with awe. But Jesus came and touched them, saying, "Rise, and have no fear." And when they lifted up their eyes, they saw no one but Jesus only. (Mt 17:1–8)

---

[1] For a discussion of some of the different treatments of the Transfiguration in later Christian teachers, see Raniero Cantalamessa, O.F.M. Cap., *The Mystery of the Transfiguration* (Cincinnati: St. Anthony Messenger Press, 2008), chap. 1.

Christ had taken three of his disciples, Peter included, up onto a mountain, one traditionally identified with Mount Tabor on the southern edge of Galilee. There, before their eyes, he was changed and began to appear strikingly different. It says in the Gospel text,

> And he was transfigured before them, and his face shone like the sun, and his garments became white as light.

The word *transfigured* translates a Greek word that could be translated into English as *transformed*, but also transliterated as *metamorphosed*. That is the word we would use to describe what happens when a caterpillar becomes a butterfly. When he was transfigured, Christ's nature remained the same, but he was changed in such a dramatic way that it almost seemed that he had become a different being.

Many of the Fathers understood the Transfiguration to be something that happened inside the disciples. The disciples saw *the glory of God in the face of Christ* (2 Cor 4:6); that is, they recognized his divinity. Other Fathers understood the Transfiguration to mean that Christ was changed into his glorified body. The glory that he had within him transformed him physically and appeared externally (cf. Mt 28:3). He took on for a short time the body he would have after his Resurrection.

Either way, Christ was transfigured and manifested who he was so his disciples could look past the upcoming humiliation and death of his crucifixion and see where it was leading—to the Resurrection and a glorified humanity. He also did this so they would see what they themselves would become. The Transfiguration was a preview of the future of redeemed humanity.

We will return to the Resurrection and glorification. At this point, however, the next thing that happened is of immediate significance for us. The disciples saw two men speaking with the Lord, and they were also glorified. The two men were Moses and Elijah. Moses stands for the law. Elijah stands for the prophets. The two main representatives of the old covenant were talking to the one whom they had predicted.

Moses and Elijah were also the two men who, to seek God, had gone to Mount Sinai, the mountain apart that was the mountain of God and that had been replaced by Mount Zion and its temple as the dwelling place of God. They were not with Christ on Mount Tabor to indicate that this was the place where another and better temple building would be built. Rather they were there to acknowledge the one who would in his own person replace the temple, and Sinai before that, as the dwelling place of God's presence on earth.

In the account of the Transfiguration in the Gospel of Luke, it says they *spoke of his departure* [more literally: *exodus*], *which he was to accomplish at Jerusalem*. They did not just speak of his coming death, but of his *exodus* from this fallen world to *enter into his glory* (Lk 24:26). They were not revealing to him what would happen. That he already knew. They were probably confirming what he had said and they had predicted. Probably they were also instructing his disciples, using the special authority of their positions. Perhaps they were also seeing for the first time the fulfillment of that which they had said would come to pass. Then *a bright cloud*, the manifestation of the divine presence, *overshadowed them and a voice from the cloud* proclaimed that he was *the* Son of God, and that he was the one who would fully reveal the plan of God, foreshadowed and witnessed to by the old covenant law and prophets.

The old covenant, as we have already seen, points to the new covenant and is fulfilled in the new covenant, because the new covenant contains the Son of God manifested to the world. He is the one who fulfills all the types of the Old Testament—not just the type of the anointed king, the messiah—about the coming one who will bring salvation to his people. He is the one who will lead the human race into the fulfillment of God's plan, the purpose for which God created it, the full realization of the kingdom in the age to come. In fact, as we will see, he embodies in his own person the fulfillment of God's plan now after his Resurrection, and he is already communicating participation in it to those who come to believe in him, though not yet in its fullness.

The Transfiguration occurred at the turning point of Christ's earthly ministry. From then on, forces, human and spiritual, began to move to put him death. He at the same time increasingly began to instruct his disciples that this had to be. He was establishing a kingdom, the kingdom of God, but it would not be by beginning a military uprising against the Romans. He had first to *give his life as a ransom for many* (Mk 10:45). As the book of Hebrews puts it, he had to *put away sin by the sacrifice of himself* (Heb 9:27). He then would rise and pour out the Holy Spirit upon his disciples. They in turn would take the message of his death and Resurrection into the whole world and establish the new covenant people of God. This would mean a new step in God's plan, the stage of the new covenant.

THE OLD AND THE NEW

The beginning of the new covenant. The new covenant is explicitly spoken about in a number of places in the New Testament. The first is in the Gospel of Luke, during the Last Supper. There the Lord speaks of the contents of the cup poured out for and given to the disciples as *the new covenant in [his] blood* (Lk 22:20; 1 Cor 11:25). We might say that he was in the process of establishing the new covenant by letting his body be broken and his blood be poured out. And his words and actions at the Last Supper were communicating the significance of his upcoming sacrificial death. Christ's death was an essential step, because it would make possible and bring about the new covenant.

This truth has an unexpected consequence. If Christ was establishing the new covenant in his blood, that is, by his death (and Resurrection), then most of the Gospels are not describing new covenant times. We tend to think that they are, because they are part of the New Testament and are describing Christ's ministry. But Christ was *born under the law, to redeem those who were under the law, so that we might receive adoption as sons* (Gal 4:4) as Paul put it. He was born an old covenant man, an Israelite. He entered this world as part of the old covenant, so he could bring old covenant people into the new covenant.

Yet, it was not a merely old covenant man who was born into the world. It was the Son of God, the Word of God, who entered into the world and took on human nature. As we have seen, inside him was something divine, and he acted with a power and wisdom that was not merely human, a power and wisdom that no mere human being, even the most powerful and prophetically endowed charismatic human being, could equal. Yet he still had something of the human nature of Adam, subject to weakness and death. The seed of the new covenant was in him, but still under the human conditions of the old covenant.

The new covenant begins with Christ's death and Resurrection, and with the outpouring of the Spirit at Pentecost. It was with his Resurrection that he entered upon the glorious life that *swallowed up ... what [was] mortal* in him (2 Cor 5:4). It was then that the new covenant life was made available to other human beings, to those who belonged to the old covenant and to those who did not. It is this new covenant life that we will look at in this and the next chapter.

Second Corinthians 3:1–4:6. There is a lengthy passage in which the Apostle Paul discusses the nature of the new covenant and its relationship to the old—Second Corinthians 3:1–4:6. This is the fullest text on the difference between the old and new covenants. In the current chapter, we will primarily look at this passage, and then secondarily the next most important passage on the topic, Hebrews 12:18–29.

The Second Corinthians passage comes in the context of Paul defending himself and his ministry from certain criticisms. He claims that the Corinthian Church, or community, which he founded, constitutes a letter of recommendation of himself as an Apostle, a letter written by Christ because it indicates that Paul was successful in his work as an Apostle and so knew what he was doing.

The way Paul describes the community gives us a first contrast between the old covenant and the new:

> You yourselves are our letter of recommendation, written on
> your hearts, to be known and read by all men; and you show
> that you are a letter from Christ delivered by us, written not
> with ink but with the Spirit of the living God, not on tab-
> lets of stone but on tablets of hearts of flesh [RSV: human
> hearts]. (2 Cor 3:2–3)

Paul is referring to the giving of the law, the Ten Commandments,
by God to Moses. They were written by Moses on *tables* or *tablets* of
stone, a first table or tablet containing the commandments of love
of God and a second one containing the commandments of love of
neighbor (Ex 34:28; 31:18). They were written down so that people
could read them or hear them read and do them.

At the same time Paul is not just referring to the giving of the
law. He is also drawing a contrast between the stone tablets of the
old covenant law and the living letter that is the Christian community. The Corinthian Christians have the commandments written
inside of them by the Spirit of God. The living God gave them his
Spirit, and the Spirit within gives them *hearts of flesh* (a more literal
translation of *human hearts*) and writes God's law on those hearts.

Paul here is alluding to two prophecies from the Old Testament
which predict that Jews, exiled for their unfaithfulness to God,
would be restored by the making of a new covenant in which God
would *write* [*his law*] *on their hearts* (Jer 31:33). This would be done
by taking away their *heart of stone*, their hard, un-submissive heart,
and replacing it with *a heart of flesh*, and *putting his Spirit in them*,
which would cause them to keep the law (Ezek 36:26–27). Stone is
hard and only its surface can be written on when letters are carved
or engraved on it. Flesh is more malleable, and capable of receiving
many things internally, in this case receiving and being formed by
the law of God.

Paul is saying, then, that the Christian community, the new covenant people of God, was the fulfillment of prophecies in the Old Testament. It was particularly the fulfillment of prophecies of the restoration of God's people as a people faithful to the commandments of

God. This came about because of the gift of the Holy Spirit that was put inside of them and enabled them to know and keep the law. The new covenant community, the Church, as a body of people who have the law written on their hearts by the Spirit of the living God, is the *Israel of God* (Gal 6:16), *the Israel according to the Spirit* (1 Cor 10:18; Gal 4:29) or the *true circumcision who worship God in the Spirit and glory in Christ Jesus* (Phil 3:3; Eph 2:11), as we have seen in chapter 8.

The key, then, to the advantage that the new covenant brings is the gift of the Holy Spirit. In the new covenant, the Spirit is poured out upon human beings. This does not mean that he flows over them externally, but that he enters into them or fills them. Nor does it mean that he enters into them and just sits there to be adored. Rather he enters into them the way wine might enter into the blood-stream (Eph 5:18) and influences the way they live and act. Nor does it mean that he just came into them to work through them charismatically as he did with many old covenant figures. Rather, he changes new covenant people themselves and so allows them to change the way they live. He is the *life-giving* Spirit, giving them new life, forming people into the image of God and enabling them to keep the commandments.

The gift of the Spirit is the specific *newness* of the new covenant. It is the element of the new covenant that makes the greatest differ-ence in the way God's people live their lives. In the old covenant, the Spirit was present and at work, probably working *through* various godly men to bring about important results. In the new covenant, however, he is present *in* those who believe in Christ, giving them new life from the inside, as well as working through them to advance the kingdom.

This new covenant community is not a repudiation of the old covenant community, but a transformation of it through the Holy Spirit. To speak of the new covenant as "new" does not imply a put-ting away of the old covenant, but rather a renewal of it. By the Gos-pel and the gift of the Spirit, the life of the old covenant is made new, "for the Jew first" and then extended to "the Greek" (Rom 1:16), the first of the Gentiles.

Nor does the work of the Spirit replace all mediation of God's life in this world. The new covenant people of God can renew their life in him through word and sacrament, physical signs in this world through which God communicates his truth and life. That interaction, however, does not substitute for his direct spiritual presence in them, but strengthens it. The ongoing presence of the Spirit in the Christian community turns the godly community life of the old covenant into the spiritual community life of the new covenant.

In Second Corinthians 3, Paul goes on to give us another contrast between the old covenant and the new. He is talking about how he has managed to bring about the existence of a Christian community, a body of people with the law written on their hearts. His explanation is that God allowed him to be a minister or servant of a certain sort:

> Such is the confidence that we have through Christ toward God. Not that we are competent of ourselves to claim anything as coming from us; our competence is from God, who has made us competent to be ministers of a new covenant, not in a written code but in the Spirit; for the written code kills, but the Spirit gives life. (2 Cor 3:4–6)

God had granted Paul the competency to serve people by making them part of a new covenant. Paul did not do this by giving them a new *written code,* as the old covenant was given at Sinai, but by dispensing *the Spirit.* Through the giving out or serving up of the Spirit, the new covenant was begun on the day of Pentecost and then spread by the Apostles. As we will see, the way the Apostle Paul dispensed the Spirit was primarily by preaching the Gospel to them.

After speaking about his competency, Paul adds a word of explanation, *for the written code kills, but the Spirit gives life.* This sounds very negative on the old covenant, but as is clear from the rest of the passage Paul did not take a mainly negative view of the old covenant. Here, however, he is making a particular point about it in a condensed way.

The law of Moses, the written code, gave instructions about how to live and death penalties for not living accordingly. However, it lacked something; namely, a provision for giving the people an adequate forgiveness of sins they had committed and the ability then to keep the commandments and live the law. Those shortcomings were made up by the atoning death of Christ and the gift of the Spirit of God, as prophesied in Jeremiah and Ezekiel. Christ's death (and Resurrection) takes sin away effectively and gives life, life that involves the capacity to live the way God wants us to.

Paul then goes on to make another contrast between the old covenant and the new covenant:

> Now if the dispensation of death, carved in letters on stone, came with such glory that the Israelites could not look at Moses' face because of its glory, fading as this was, will not the dispensation of the Spirit be attended with greater glory? For if there was glory in the dispensation of condemnation, the dispensation of righteousness must far exceed it in glory. Indeed, in this case, what once had glory has come to have no glory at all, because of the glory that surpasses it. For if what faded away came with glory, what is permanent must have much more glory. (2 Cor 3:7–11)

In order to understand what Paul is saying here, it helps to first understand something about his vocabulary. The words "splendor" and "brightness" in the RSV are translations of the Greek word for "glory," and "glory" has been substituted for them in the above quotation. As we have seen, "glory" is a word that means "greatness" or "power," but power that is manifest or shines out. Speaking Bible language, we could say that a bolt of lightning is glorious. It shines, but it shines because it is power, electric energy flashing through the sky and capable of causing very significant effects.

Paul, then, is comparing the old covenant, the covenant that dispenses or serves up condemnation and death, and the new covenant, the covenant that dispenses or serves up righteousness, a good relationship with God. The old covenant definitely was glorious or splendid, because God was in it and at work. This became visible in the way Moses' face was transfigured or glorified when he spoke to God and received the old covenant law. The old covenant, however, was simply a step in God's plan. The new covenant is what God was aiming at and is the covenant that will endure. It is far more glorious.

There is a familiar image that illustrates what Paul is saying here. If we are in a dark room and light a candle, the candle will light up the room and look quite bright. If, however, the sun then shines into the room, the candle will not look bright at all. In fact, its light will be lost in the brightness of the sunlight. In a similar way, the old covenant had glory but that glory was much less than the glory of the covenant that was to come, and its light is now hardly visible because of the light of the new covenant.

The new covenant, then, has *more glory* [RSV: *splendor*] than the old. That means in this context that it has more of God's presence and action in it. It therefore is more spiritually effective for making human beings what they were created to be. To use the simple word the book of Hebrews often uses, it is *better* (e.g., Heb 8:6).

There is another important contrast Paul is making between the old covenant and the new covenant, and that is the way the new covenant allows us to see the glory of the Son of God and in doing so, be ourselves transformed. To make his point about the old covenant having God's glory in it, Paul referred to what happened after Moses came down from Sinai with the tablets that had the law written on them. His face shone with the glory that had come from being in the presence of God (Ex 34:29–35). For the Israelites, this was too much to take, probably because they had just committed the sin of the golden calf and now were afraid to get too close to God's presence.

Moses then put a veil on his face so that the Israelites did not see that glory any more. Paul then describes the long-term effect of that veil:

Since we have such a hope, we are very bold, not like Moses, who put a veil over his face so that the Israelites might not see the end of the fading splendor. But their minds were hardened; for to this day, when they read the old covenant, that same veil remains unlifted, because only through Christ is it taken away. Yes, to this day whenever Moses is read a veil lies over their minds; but when a man turns to the Lord the veil is removed. (2 Cor 3:12–16)

The veil Moses put on at Sinai has an important typological significance, based on the fact that "Moses" refers not only to the man Moses who mediated the law, but also often in Scripture stands for the law he mediated. When Jews who have not entered into the new covenant through faith in Christ hear the law of Moses, the Pentateuch, read in the synagogue, they are in effect looking at Moses who received the old covenant revelation. They, however, cannot see something that is really in it and was shining from him when he came down from Sinai. They cannot perceive the full glory of God revealed in the Old Testament text. It is veiled from them. But conversion to Christ takes that veil away.

Paul then goes on to explain why it is that the Jews cannot see the full glory of God in the old covenant writings, but Christians can:

Now the Lord gives [RSV: is] the Spirit, and where the Spirit of the Lord is, there is freedom. And we all, with unveiled face, beholding the glory of the Lord, are being changed into his image [RSV: likeness] from one degree of glory to another; for this comes from the Lord who gives [RSV: is] the Spirit. (2 Cor 3:17–18)

This is a difficult passage, and there is especially much controversy over the meaning of the first and last clauses, *the Lord is the Spirit.*

The simplest explanation of this phrase, one that has a certain probability, is that it means, "the Lord gives the Spirit" (cf. 1 Cor 15:45). Another, perhaps better, explanation was given by the Church Father Basil of Caesarea who said, "As the Father makes himself visible in the Son, so the Son makes himself present in the

Spirit" (*On the Holy Spirit* 26.64). Whether we understand the verb "is" here as "gives" or "is present in," *the Lord* here is Christ, the Son of God. He is the one we turned to when we believed the Gospel (2 Cor 3:16). He is the one who is the image of God (2 Cor 4:4) and into whose image we are changed (2 Cor 3:18).

Christ gives the Holy Spirit to those who turn to him. The Holy Spirit allows us to see his glory, which is the glory of God. That then has an effect on us. By looking with faith at Christ, revealed to us in the preaching of the Gospel, and being given the gift of the Holy Spirit, we are being transfigured or transformed into the image of Christ and so are becoming more glorious (spiritually alive and effective). We are like Moses who beheld the glory of God on Mount Sinai and in so doing became more glorious.

This is sometimes said in a different way in later Christian teaching by speaking of our deification or divinization (*théosis* to use the Greek word). This does not mean that we simply become gods, omnipotent, omniscient, omnipresent. Rather, it means that we share more fully in the divine nature, becoming more like God in our capability to express his character. To use the phrase in 2 Peter 1:4, we become *partakers of the divine nature* or sharers in the divine life. This goes back to what we have seen about Christ as the divine Son of God who has the glory of God in him.[2]

There is likely an analogy here with a mirror. If we hold a mirror up to a light, the mirror looks at (beholds) the light, but it also reflects the light it beholds. It is transformed from something dark to something light-filled. Looking at the Lord's glory, then, changes us. We are being changed by the Spirit, who gives us light and life, changed into people who have the law written on their hearts and who are having the image of God restored in them. *From glory to glory* refers to change in us as a result of participating in the life of Christ, whether it is referring to the change from being in the old covenant to being in the new or to the change in us as we grow spiritually in the new covenant life, or perhaps to both.

---

[2] For a fuller understanding of deification in Christian teaching, see Daniel A. Keating, *Deification and Grace* (Naples, FL: Sapientia Press, 2007).

If we understand in this way what Paul is saying, then it implies something we have already seen. If, when we turn to the Lord without a veil over our face, we see the glory of Christ the Son of God; and if our turning to the Lord is like what happened to Moses, then Moses was talking to the Son of God, and it was his glory that was glorifying Moses' face. This, then, is another passage that says Christ was at work in the old covenant. Even though in Moses' time he had not yet become incarnate, he was the one who appeared to Moses and gave him the law.

There is a further important implication, and it has to do with the word *image*. The RSV in this passage translates the Greek word for image by "likeness." Such a translation makes it harder to see certain connections between this and other scriptural texts. Paul is actually saying that Christ *is* the image of God, and in the new covenant we are being transformed into the image that he is. "Image" as we have already seen does not have to mean a merely external picture of something, in this case God, but commonly means something that also participates in the reality itself (cf. Heb 10:1). This implies that when the first human beings were created in the image and likeness of God, they were being created "in" Christ, the Son of God, who is the true image of God (Col 1:15–17; 2 Cor 4:4). New covenant people are having that image restored in them (Col 3:10).

Paul then goes on in the same passage to further defend himself by saying that he does not need to use human cunning or dubious scriptural interpretations to get people to believe in Christ. The preaching of the Gospel has its own power. For those who believe, the Gospel is light shining in the darkness as the uncreated light of God shone into the darkness of nothingness and chaos on the first day of creation:

Therefore, having this ministry by the mercy of God, we do not lose heart. We have renounced disgraceful, underhanded ways; we refuse to practice cunning or to tamper with God's word, but by the open statement of the truth we would commend ourselves to every man's conscience in the sight of God. And even if our gospel is veiled, it is veiled only to those who are perishing. In their case the god of this world has blinded the minds of the unbelievers, to keep them from seeing the light of the gospel of the glory of Christ, who is the image [RSV: likeness] of God. For what we preach is not ourselves, but Jesus Christ as Lord, with ourselves as your servants for Jesus' sake. For it is the God who said, "Let light shine out of darkness," [Gen 1:3] who has shone in our hearts to give the light of the knowledge of the glory of God in the face of Christ. (2 Cor 4:1–6)

In other words, the light of the Gospel reveals who Christ is, the Lord of all and the divine Son of God. If we accept the Gospel with faith, we can see Christ, proclaimed in the Gospel for who he is, and so see the glory of God in the face of Christ. We can come to see through faith what the Apostles were able to see on the Mount of Transfiguration. Seeing him, knowing who he really is, will allow him to transform us through the working of the Spirit in us and through his own glory transfiguring us, so that we can become more and more like him.

This, too, can be illustrated by a common experience. We might go into a dark room, hoping to find out the time and wondering how to get enough light to see the clock. Then we look at a digital clock, and there shining before us is the time. The clock has the electric power inside that allows it to produce a light that shines of itself and so to communicate the time to those who otherwise would not know it. In a similar way, the Gospel, when it is preached to us, has spiritual power inside that lets us see the truth of the glory of Christ. Just as God created the world by having light shine out into the darkness, so he re-creates the world now by shining out into the darkness through the preaching of the Gospel. The new covenant is the new creation begun in Christ, the new Adam.

One difference, then, between the old covenant and the new is the way the Son of God and the Spirit of God are present and active in the new covenant. The new covenant creates a body of people who have the law written on their hearts and so keep the commandments of God. They can do so because the Spirit of God has been put inside of them as a result of their faith in the preached Gospel, and thereby they see the glory of the Son of God in the face of Jesus Christ. They themselves are transformed in him. They themselves have become spiritualized and glorified—through the work of Christ and of the Spirit.

THE ALREADY AND THE NOT YET

The new covenant was not completely established with the earthly work of Christ, nor with the outpouring of the Holy Spirit on the day of Pentecost, nor even with the death of the last Apostle. It will not be completely established until Christ comes again in glory. Moreover, Christians do not yet experience the ancestral curse fully lifted. They are still subject to sickness and other weakness, to corruption and death. The Christian people are also not fully successful in living out the commandments of God. Many even seem more like old covenant people in the way they relate to God than like what Paul indicates new covenant people should be.

Paul experienced these various difficulties in his own work as an Apostle, and he goes on in chapter 4 of Second Corinthians to speak about that. He was afflicted, perplexed, persecuted, and struck down, but not crushed, driven to despair, forsaken, or destroyed. He lived and worked in an in-between state, not yet experiencing the completion of all we can hope for, but still experiencing the power of God working in and through him.

Paul describes his situation at the end of chapter 4, where he affirms the hope that gives him a foundation for a difficult service:

So we do not lose heart. Though our outer human being [RSV: nature] is wasting away, our inner human being [RSV: nature] is being renewed every day. For this slight momen-

tary affliction is preparing for us an eternal weight of glory
beyond all comparison, because we look not to the things
that are seen but to the things that are unseen; for the things
that are seen are transient, but the things that are unseen are
eternal. (2 Cor 4:16–18)

As a persecuted and opposed Christian Apostle, Paul underwent a
great deal of physical suffering, but there was something inside of
him that renewed his strength, especially by letting his endurance
through trials renew his hope.

The RSV translation above might give the impression that he
was looking forward to being crushed by the heaviness of the upcoming glory. Other translations, like that in NIV, give a clearer
sense: Paul was looking forward to *an eternal glory that far outweighs*
his light momentary afflictions here and now. The image behind the
statement is that of an ancient scale, which was a balance, commonly
used in the ancient world in buying and selling. In such a scale the
more valuable outweighed the less valuable. Paul, then, was looking forward to a glorious future, a future in which he and the world
around him would be glorified, a future that would outweigh, and so
more than make up for, his current suffering.

Paul goes on to describe something more of his current state
and what he can hope for:

For while we are still in this tent, we sigh with anxiety; not
that we would be unclothed, but that we would be further
clothed, so that what is mortal may be swallowed up by life.
He who has prepared us for this very thing is God, who has
given us the Spirit as a guarantee. (2 Cor 5:4–5)

According to Paul we should not be anxious that we might simply
go out of existence after this life, or perhaps that we might be left
as mere spirits without bodies. Rather, we should be anxious to get
to the point where *this tent*, that is, our current bodies, will be made
immortal with a fuller life, because they will be glorified. In other

words, we should be eager to experience the full life that God has already prepared for us.

Paul ends this passage with a phrase that sums up the relationship of this stage of the new covenant to the one to come. God *has given us the Spirit as a guarantee*. In Ephesians 1:13–14, the same thing is said:

> In him you also, who have heard the word of truth, the gospel of your salvation, and have believed in him, were sealed with the promised Holy Spirit, which is the guarantee of our inheritance until we acquire possession of it, to the praise of his glory.

The word "guarantee" refers to the first installment of a payment yet to be fully made. In the context of Second Corinthians 5:5 we might understand it as the down payment on a house. The initial payment is part of what the original owner is to be given, but at the same time it functions as a guarantee or pledge of what is to come. The buyer gives enough of what he owes in order to assure the seller that what has already been paid is great enough that the agreement will not be abandoned. God has guaranteed the future that Paul hopes in by giving Paul and other Christians a first installment of what is to come.

In Second Corinthians 5:5, Paul is speaking primarily of what will happen to Christians individually. In Romans 8:18–25, he puts into a broader context the gift of the Spirit as a guarantee of what is to come:

> I consider that the sufferings of this present time are not worth comparing with the glory that is to be revealed to us. For the creation waits with eager longing for the revealing of the sons of God; for the creation was subjected to futility, not of its own will but by the will of him who subjected it in hope; because the creation itself will be set free from its bondage to decay and obtain the glorious liberty of the

children of God. We know that the whole creation has been groaning in travail together until now; and not only the creation, but we ourselves, who have the first fruits of the Spirit, groan inwardly as we wait for adoption as sons, the redemption of our bodies. For in this hope we were saved. Now hope that is seen is not hope. For who hopes for what he sees? But if we hope for what we do not see, we wait for it with patience.

Christians will experience a fuller, glorified life, because creation as a whole will be glorified. It will be set free from the slavery or bondage that comes from the decay and mortality that is the consequence of fallenness and will be freed to be the way the Lord fully wants his creation to be. We will then experience our full adoption as sons, our fuller redemption, not just of the inner person but of the outer person, the body, as well.

In the case of the new covenant life, the assurance is the gift of the Holy Spirit, the *first fruits of the Spirit*. Because he lives inside of us, we already begin to experience something of that glorified life that God has in store for us. But we do not experience it in its completion. We do not experience the full harvest, which is still on its way. To use a common phrase, we have it "already and not yet." We already have it in part, but we do not yet have it completely. The transforming glory of God is already in us, but it has not yet transformed our physical natures—because we have not yet entered into the glory of the age to come.

We Have Come to the Heavenly Jerusalem

The new covenant in the Book of Hebrews. There is another important presentation of the "already and not yet" of the new covenant realities, and that is found in the Letter to the Hebrews. Many hold that Hebrews was addressed to a group of Jewish Christians who were suffering persecution. They therefore were facing a temptation to spurn Christ, his atoning death, and the gift of the Spirit (Heb 10:29) and return to a merely old covenant life.

The focus of Hebrews is on the superiority of the new covenant to the old, based on the superiority of what Christ, the Son of God and the great high priest, can do in contrast to what the ministers and ritual of the law can do. Chapter 8 presents this fact in verse 6:

> Christ has obtained a ministry which is as much more excellent than the old as the covenant he mediates is better, since it is enacted on better promises.

The chapter then goes on to quote the prophecy of Jeremiah that promises the new covenant to come (Jer 31:31–34) and contrasts it with the covenant on Sinai:

> For he finds fault with them when he says:
> "The days will come, says the Lord,
> when I will establish a new covenant with the house of Israel
> and with the house of Judah;
> not like the covenant that I made with their fathers
> on the day when I took them by the hand
> to lead them out of the land of Egypt;
> for they did not continue in my covenant,
> and so I paid no heed to them, says the Lord.
> This is the covenant that I will make with the house of Israel
> after those days, says the Lord:
> I will put my laws into their minds,
> and write them on their hearts,
> and I will be their God,
> and they shall be my people." (Heb 8:8–10)

Hebrews 12:18–29. Hebrews then proceeds to explain how the work of Christ, *the high priest of the good things that have come,* made possible the blessing of the new covenant. The section we will be looking at more fully is further on in the letter and is part of the concluding exhortation of the main exposition of the letter. It is a section that gives a description of the new covenant life. It begins with a contrast:

> For you have not come to what may be touched, a blazing fire, and darkness, and gloom, and a tempest, and the sound of a trumpet, and a voice whose words made the hearers entreat that no further messages be spoken to them. For they could not endure the order that was given, "If even a beast touches the mountain, it shall be stoned." Indeed, so terrifying was the sight that Moses said, "I tremble with fear." (Heb 12:18–21)

This passage is a description of the giving of the law on Sinai. *What may be touched* is a way of speaking about the inauguration of the old covenant. It indicates that old covenant realities are fundamentally realities of this earth, material things that we can sense and so relatively easily understand. This description serves the same purpose as the one Paul sometimes gives when he describes old covenant life as a life *in the flesh* (e.g., Phil 3:2–6) in contrast to life in the Spirit; that is, it points toward the way the old covenant was inferior to the new covenant.

Old covenant people are people who have come to Mount Sinai. As we have seen, God appeared there in a way that must have seemed something like a volcanic eruption. The description can be found in Exodus 19–20 and Deuteronomy 4–5. There was fire, a dark cloud, a mighty wind, and a great noise. There was also a loud voice, when God *declared to you his covenant, which he commanded you to perform, that is, the ten commandments* (Deut 4:13). Before that there had been a command to put a boundary around the mountain, and that if any man or animal crossed the boundary, it should be stoned (Ex 19:12–13), a grim warning of the danger of coming too close to the living God. The whole experience was designed, as Moses said afterwards, *to put the fear of [God] before your eyes, that you may not sin* (Ex 20:20).

The book of Hebrews then turns to what new covenant people have come to, namely heavenly realities:

> But you have come to Mount Zion and to the city of the living God, the heavenly Jerusalem, and to innumerable angels in festal gathering, and to the assembly of the first-born who are enrolled in heaven, and to a judge who is God of all, and to the spirits of just men made perfect, and to Jesus, the mediator of a new covenant, and to the sprinkled blood that speaks more graciously than the blood of Abel. (Heb 12:22–24)

New covenant people have come to the heavenly *Mount Zion*, the temple mount, in *the heavenly Jerusalem, the city of the living God*. They have not come to the Mount Zion and Jerusalem that are in the land of Palestine, but they have come to heaven itself, the true Mount Zion and Jerusalem, where the redeemed people of God are gathered to worship God.

In heaven, there are *innumerable angels in festal gathering*. Heaven is the place where those who belong to God gather to celebrate God's victory and goodness. With those angels are *the assembly* [Church] *of the first-born who are enrolled in heaven*. These are probably the faithful Christians, who are the first-born because they are in the first-born Son of God (Col 1:15). With these angels and new covenant saints, there are also old covenant people, the righteous ones of the old covenant who have now been *completed* (RSV: *made perfect*) and glorified in Christ. It is commonly held by Christian teachers that, because of their faith in the prophesied messiah and their faithfulness to the law of God as they understood it, the righteous or just people of the old covenant had already participated enough in the grace of God that they too had a place in the heavenly Jerusalem to come (Heb 11:13–16).

This gives us a further perspective on the Christian community, the Church. The Church does not just include those who are alive now. It includes Christians who are no longer alive, as well as saints of the old covenant, and saints like Abel, Enoch and Noah, who were neither Christians nor Israelites. It also includes the holy angels of God. We are spiritually united with all who are, who have been, and who will be God's.

Finally, in the midst of the festal participants we come to a judge who is God of all, that is, God the Father. Along with him we come to Jesus, the mediator of a new covenant and to the sprinkled blood [of Christ] that speaks more graciously than the blood of Abel. Both the saints of the old covenant and earlier eras and those of the new covenant are only there because of the sacrifice that Christ, the great high priest (Heb. 4:14), has offered and which has made the new covenant possible. As Hebrews said earlier,

> Christ has entered, not into a sanctuary made with hands, a copy of the true one, but into heaven itself, now to appear in the presence of God on our behalf. Nor was it to offer himself repeatedly, as the high priest enters the Holy Place yearly with blood not his own; for then he would have had to suffer repeatedly since the foundation of the world. But as it is, he has appeared once for all at the end of the age to put away sin by the sacrifice of himself. (Heb 9:24–27)

In other words, it is because Christ is the eternal Son of God and the great high priest and has offered the effective sacrifice for sins that he has been able to bring those who believe in him, including those who lived before him, to the heavenly Jerusalem with the heavenly sanctuary.

We have not come to what may be touched, the old covenant order, but to what cannot be touched, heaven itself. There is Christ and those who belong to God in Christ. But the Letter to the Hebrews is speaking in the past tense. This is not a promise of going to heaven in the future. We are already there. Those who are in the new covenant are participating in heaven and the heavenly worship. Hebrews is saying what Paul said, but saying it in a different way. Because we belong to Christ, we are *already* in heaven—but we are *not yet* fully there.

The passage we have been reading, an emphatic statement of the spiritual superiority of the new covenant now, concludes with an exhortation to make sure we fully receive the kingdom of God. The Letter to the Hebrews clearly recognizes that there is more to come:

> See that you do not refuse him who is speaking. For if they did not escape when they refused him who warned them on earth, much less shall we escape if we reject him who warns from heaven. His voice then shook the earth; but now he has promised, "Yet once more I will shake not only the earth but also the heaven" [Hag. 2:6]. This phrase, "Yet once more," indicates the removal of what is shaken, as of what has been made, in order that what cannot be shaken may remain. Therefore let us be grateful for receiving a kingdom that cannot be shaken, and thus let us offer to God acceptable worship, with reverence and awe; for our God is a consuming fire [Deut. 4:24]. (Heb 12:25–29)

This is a warning. We have received participation in the heavenly kingdom. We have received something that will endure through the final cosmic shaking and bring us through it as well. But we cannot turn away from that and return to a merely old covenant life or we will lose our heavenly inheritance.

Some say that the old covenant is a religion of fear, but the new covenant is a religion of love. It would be more accurate to say, in accordance with the exhortation in Hebrews, that the old covenant is a religion of fear, but the new covenant is a religion of greater fear.

The new covenant fear should certainly be based in a fear that can look at the results of disobedience to God in the Old Testament narrative and be very eager not to let the same thing happen to us. But it should be a fear that goes along with a confidence that we can avoid that condemnation. The Letter of John makes clear that a life of love of God and love of neighbor should *cast out* such a *fear* (1 Jn 4:18).

The greater new covenant fear is the *reverence and awe* that comes from perceiving the greatness of God's gift and the greatness of the God who has given it. It is the fear of God that moves us to give him *acceptable worship*, recognizing that he is the same God as the God of the old covenant, a *fire* that can *consume* those who do not approach him in an *acceptable* way, but also a God of the new covenant with a great high priest who intercedes effectively for those who belong to him.

The Eucharist. The passage we just looked at in Hebrews 12 ends with an exhortation: *and thus let us offer to God acceptable worship, with reverence and awe.* If we have received a kingdom that cannot be shaken and a participation in heavenly worship (vv. 22–23: a *festal gathering and . . . assembly*), then we too should express that reality and our response by worshipping God in an *acceptable* way, the way he wants.

As with most things in the new covenant, our new covenant worship is based on old covenant worship, in this case the worship service (or "the liturgy" to use the anglicized Greek word for worship service) that we take part in when we assemble as a people. This means not only do we praise God with psalms and hymns and spiritual songs (Col 3:16) like those in the book of Psalms and elsewhere in the Old Testament. This means not only do we listen to and respond to God's word in the Scripture, as Jews and Christians have done throughout the ages. It also means we should participate in a ceremony that expresses the truths of our relationship with God. These include the foundational truths that we have been considering since the first chapter of this book, but especially the truths we have been considering in this chapter, the truths of the new covenant life in the Spirit.

This ceremony is spoken about in the New Testament,[3] and by

---

[3] The Last Supper: Matthew 26:20–30; Mark 14:17–26; Luke 22:14–23; 1 Corinthians 11:23–26; *and possibly* John 6:51b. Instructions on the Eucharist: John 6:25–71 (more specifically vv. 51–59); 1 Corinthians 10:14–22; 11:17–34; *and possibly* Hebrews 13:9–16. The "breaking of bread" as a reference to the Eucharist: *probably*

subsequent Christians has often been called the Eucharist (a word which means "the thanksgiving"), the Lord's Supper (1 Cor 11:20), the Divine Liturgy, or the Mass. This ceremony was formed upon the worship services in the old covenant, in particular the communion offering [RSV: peace offering] in the temple, including the Passover sacrifice, which was a special communion offering. The communion offering always included a sacrificial meal of what was offered to God as a way of sharing in the benefits of the sacrifice. The ceremony of the communion offering strengthened the union between God and the worshippers.

We have already seen the Eucharist mentioned in the New Testament in First Corinthians 10:3–4 (see p. 93 in the chapter on typology). There the Eucharist is not understood so much as an offering, but as an instance of spiritual feeding, the spiritual feeding that unites people with God and strengthens them as God's people. The manna in the wilderness and the drinking of water from the rock are types of the spiritual food and drink in the Eucharist.

The Christian Eucharistic ceremony, by some referred to as the Eucharistic celebration, is the ceremony by which the Christian people express and renew their participation in the new covenant when they assemble together. There are many theological issues connected to understanding the Eucharist. Discussing them is beyond the scope of this book, which is focused on the stages of God's plan. Here we simply want to see the Eucharist in relation to the new covenant and why it expresses and renews our new covenant relationship with God and Christ.[4]

Acts 2:42, 46–7; 20:7–12; *and possibly* Luke 24:13–43 (cf. also Acts 27:35).

[4] The presentation of the Eucharist in the above text mainly treats the significance of the Eucharist ceremony, especially its significance as a covenant renewal ceremony, in this case the renewal of the new covenant relationship with God. It is beyond the scope of a book like this to treat the special theological questions concerning the Eucharist such as the nature of the Eucharist as a sacrificial action and the relationship of the Eucharistic elements to the presence of Christ. Those who believe, for instance, in a real presence, whether understood as transubstantiation, consubstantiation or virtual presence, and those who believe in a symbolic presence, can normally agree on the significance of the ceremony. The theological differences have been treated extensively in the ecumenical dialogues of the last number of years, resulting in a sig-

First of all, the Eucharist involves the breaking of bread and the blessing of a cup of wine. This action involves the offering of the bread and wine to God in thanksgiving for what he has provided and then distributing it to the participants in the ceremony. These things are done in a sacrificial meal as well as in other meals (cf. 1 Tim 4:3–5). These blessings normally express the purpose of the offering.[5]

The people of Israel ate the sacrifices prescribed for the old covenant people and so became *sharers [RSV: partners] in the altar* (1 Cor 10:18), sharers in the benefits that came from the offering to God. Likewise, the Christian people in the Eucharistic ceremony also become sharers in the benefits that come from the new covenant sacrifice. This does not mean that in a sacrificial meal what is offered is sacrificed in the sense of killed or poured out over again. That occurred on the altar in the temple for the people of Israel. Rather, they partook of what had been offered and so shared in the offering. In a similar way, the Christian people in the Eucharistic ceremony partake of what has already been sacrificed and now is being re-presented: the Body and Blood of Christ (1 Cor 10:16–17; 11:27; Jn 6:54).

In the Eucharist the Body and Blood of the Lord are separated from one another. This represents the death of the Lord when the body and blood of the Lord were separate, the body broken and the blood poured out. The Eucharist, then, is a calling to mind or com-

---

nificant measure of convergence. Nonetheless, theological differences remain. These differences, however, do not necessarily touch the understanding of the significance of the Eucharistic ceremony—although normal teachings about the Eucharist vary considerably in the fullness of their treatment of the significance of the ceremony. For a summary of the meaning of the Eucharist see the multilateral ecumenical dialogue paper: *Baptism, Eucharist and Ministry*, Faith and Order Paper #111 (Geneva: World Council of Churches, 1982), 10–17, which also flags the points where there is no clear convergence. For a survey of the ecumenical dialogues that concern the Eucharist, see Stephen B. Clark, *Catholics and the Eucharist: A Scriptural Introduction* (Ann Arbor, MI: Servant, 2000), 235–237.

[5] For a fuller treatment of the Eucharist as a covenant renewal ceremony and also of the meaning of the blessing prayers at the Eucharist, see chapter 4 of *Catholics and the Eucharist* (pp. 103–123).

memoration of the death of the Lord on the Cross, the time when he made the once for all sacrifice of himself to put away sin (Heb 10:26).

The Eucharistic prayer that we pray *in remembrance of [Christ]* (1 Cor 10:24–25) is a calling to our minds of that on which our new covenant life is based. But more importantly it is a calling to the mind of God what Christ did. It is the kind of "remembering" that many prayers in the Scripture ask God to do, for instance, in Psalm 20:2–3 addressed to the king of Israel:

> May he send you help from the sanctuary,
>   and give you support from Zion!
> May he remember all your offerings,
>   and regard with favor your burnt sacrifices!

God is not absentminded, needing to be reminded of things he has overlooked. Rather, we are calling something to his attention and using that as the basis of what we are asking him to do. In this case we are calling to mind the sacrifice of Christ on the Cross so God will allow us to share in the benefits of that sacrifice by partaking of the Body and Blood of the Lord.

It is not an accident that the word Eucharist means thanksgiving. It is a thanksgiving offering (cf. Lev 7:11–15) for what God has done in Christ. When the Christian people partake of the Body and Blood of the Lord they are fed spiritually, renewed in the new covenant life that Christ has won for us. The Body and Blood of Christ are spiritual food and drink (1 Cor 10:3–4), because partaking of them strengthens our union with Christ and so strengthens our sharing in his life, the life that comes from the gift of the Spirit. This, then, is a new covenant communion (peace) offering, which strengthens our relationship with God as we offer it in thanksgiving for what he has done in Christ to enable our new covenant relationship with God to happen.

Christ, however, is not still dead, even though we are representing his death on the Cross symbolically in the Eucharist. He has risen from the dead and entered the heavenly holy of holies. This is portrayed in Revelation 4–5 where he stands before his father in heaven, probably on the place of the heavenly altar (Rev 5:6), presents what he has done to redeem the human race, and intercedes for his disciples. In so doing, he was enabled to open the scroll of God's plan and consequently—through the work of the Holy Spirit and of his people who preach the Gospel and rescue people from the power of Satan—bring about the fulfillment of the purpose of God for creation. This he will complete when he comes again and unites his people fully to himself.

As we have seen in considering Hebrews 12, we have come to heaven and are participating in heavenly worship. Just as the new covenant is not simply earthly but also heavenly and our worship is not simply earthly but also heavenly, the Eucharistic ceremony is not simply earthly but also heavenly. We are renewing our new covenant relationship with God by being brought by the Holy Spirit of God to his heavenly throne room where Christ is seated at his right hand but also present in his Eucharistic Body and Blood on earth that he might feed us with the spiritual life that is embodied in him and that he came to bring to us.

The Eucharist, then, is worship. It is a commemoration and re-presentation of the sacrifice of Christ by which we are saved and a renewed participation in and strengthening of the benefits of that sacrifice by partaking of his Body and Blood. It is furthermore a participation in the worship that is even now going on in heaven, thanking God for what Christ has already done and interceding for the completion of what has not yet fully happened. It is an expression of the whole new covenant by the new covenant people and a renewal of that covenant relationship through the power of the Holy Spirit.

New Covenant Blessings

The Letter to the Ephesians begins with a prayer blessing God that summarizes the teaching we have been looking at in this chapter.

> Blessed be the God and Father of our Lord Jesus Christ,
> who has blessed us in Christ with every spiritual blessing in
> the heavenly places ... (Eph 1:3)

In this prayer, what God has done for us in Christ is described with the phrase *every spiritual blessing in the heavenly places.* Christ brings us the fullness of such blessing, although that blessing was foreshadowed, predicted, and prepared for in the old covenant.

The blessings of the covenant of Sinai are, to all appearances, blessings of this world. The people of Israel were given a physical land to live in. They farmed that land which was *flowing with milk and honey,* and it provided them with good things to eat and drink. As they lived in that land, they increased and multiplied, becoming numerous and strong. Enemies, pagan nations who worshipped false gods, surrounded them, but God protected them from those nations, gave them victory in battle, and freed them from enemy oppression. They went up regularly to the temple in Jerusalem, where God was present, and worshipped him, acknowledging him as their king, receiving instruction in his law, and thanking him for the blessings he gave them. As long as they were faithful to his covenant and kept his commandments, these blessings were theirs.

The blessings of the people of Israel were real and worthwhile, but they are not well described as *every spiritual blessing in the heavenly places.* They prefigured and foreshadowed those spiritual blessings, but they were earthly, not heavenly blessings, natural or physical, not spiritual (1 Cor 15:46–47). The blessings in Christ are different.

The prayer in Ephesians 1:3 describes the blessings given through Christ as "spiritual." "Spiritual" here as in other places does not mean "immaterial," but "of or in the Spirit." The blessings in Christ are given to us by the agency of the Holy Spirit. They do not make us or our lives immaterial or non-human. Rather, they spiritualize us and our lives, filling us with the power and presence of God, allowing us to live in a higher, godlier way.

The prayer also describes these blessings as being given *in heavenly places.* First Corinthians 15:47–49 says the blessing given to us makes or will make us "of heaven" rather than "of earth." The heavenly character of our call or blessing does not mean that we leave the earth or cease to function on earth. Rather, it means that we come into a new relationship with God with a freer access to his presence which is "in heaven," his throne room. With such blessings, our life is lived more for God and more from his presence and his power, even while we are still living this present life on earth.

The spiritual, heavenly blessing Christ gives us is a new life in God, the life of the kingdom of God, the life of the Spirit. The primary content of this blessing is a better relationship with God—our sins are forgiven, the Holy Spirit is poured out upon us, we are allowed into the presence of God in a new way, we have the relationship of sonship with God, he dwells inside of us. To live in such a relationship is a higher life, a spiritual or heavenly one.

At the same time we are changed. The gift of the Spirit gives us new power to live the new life; the character of God is formed in us; we are freed from the oppression of evil spirits; we experience charismatic gifts working through us. This is life on earth "spiritualized" and made "heavenly."

Finally, we also have a share in the kingdom to come. When the kingdom comes fully or when we ourselves "go to heaven," we will experience the blessing of God in a full way, including the blessing of having all our material needs and desires satisfied. As a result, we look forward to the time when God will fully reign and we will live with him "face to face." This future orientation likewise makes our life heavenly.

We will look at the full coming of the kingdom in the next chapter.

Special Exegetical Discussion:
The Sociological Stages of God's People

A major issue that regularly surfaces is how various provisions in the Scripture are to be applied in the life of the Christian people, especially in relationship to those outside the Christian community, but also often in relationship to Christians who belong to other Churches and Christian communities. The discussion is often very confused, in large part because of the failure to make distinctions between the various sociological situations in which the Christians have found themselves. The discussion that follows here makes the main distinctions.

For instance, we can read discussions about Christian engagement in warfare in the early church. They note that Christians did not very often seem to participate in the Roman army at first but later the Roman armies were made up mainly of Christians and commanded by Christians. Various reasons are given, but often the discussions omit the fundamental fact that, with the conversion of much of the Roman Empire, the Christian people had moved from a diaspora situation to being a nation among nations.

It is one thing, for instance, to think Christians should not engage in warfare when they lived in the pagan Roman Empire, whose legions protected them and their neighbors reasonably well. It is another thing to think that Christians who lived in a Christian Roman Empire should let the Huns pillage, plunder, and rape, burning churches and monasteries, and not fight to ward them off. They had to handle a new and different situation.

We have already observed that the sociological situation comes into play as well in understanding the differences in the stages of God's plan. The Israelites had their own system of administering judgment and sometimes executed wrongdoers. The diaspora Jews and the Christians in the Roman Empire before the conversion of the Empire could not do that. They took a different approach, as we have seen in the earlier discussion in chapter 8 on the civil commandments.

Below is an empirical description (sociological) of the stages of the development of God's people. The focus is on the relation of God's people to others around them, and does not attempt to present all the important aspects of their development. Starting with stage 6, it is a sketch of the development of the Christian people/culture.

The Major Kinds of Relationship to Others

1. *A nation among nations:* God's people governing themselves, living in their own territory, and subject to no other human government except perhaps in a tributary way.
2. *A subject nation:* God's people governing themselves, living in their own territory, but under the active government of another nation or empire.
3. *A diaspora:* God's people living in another nation's (or other nations') territory as resident aliens, with a limited government of their own, and subject to the government of the territory they are part of.
4. *A nomad tribe:* God's people living as a nation without their own land, sometimes living in lands unclaimed by any other nation, and sometimes living as resident aliens in the territory of another nation but on a temporary basis.
5. *A sect:* a grouping of God's people living within a larger grouping of God's people, partly identifying with and participating with the larger grouping, but partly living a separate way of life, with a separate corporate identity under a separate government.
6. *Secularized (partly assimilated) Christians:* Christians living in a secularized society, unable to maintain the integrity of their way of life or a clear corporate identity.

The Major "Stages"

Old Covenant
1. The patriarchs (a nomad tribe)
   a. A wandering tribe, sometimes in the desert, sometimes resident aliens
   b. Resident aliens in Egypt

2. The kingdom of Israel (a nation among nations)

a. Under the judges (a tribal confederacy)
b. Under the kings of Israel (a nation)
c. Under the kings of Israel and Judah (two nations)

3. The exiles: (a diaspora scattered/dispersed among several nations)

4. The Jews in Palestine: a subject nation
   – co-exists with stage 3
   a. Under the high priest
   b. Interlude: Maccabean/Herodian independence (a nation among nations)
   c. Under the Romans until AD 70: governed by procurators and client kings

5. The "sects/parties," the Essenes, Pharisees, et al. (sects in Judaism)
   – co-exists with stages 3 and 4

New Covenant

6. The "saints" in Jerusalem (a sect in Judaism)
   – the Christian version of stage 5

7. The early church in the New Testament (a diaspora)
   – the Christian version of stage 3; co-exists with stage 6

8. The early church in the beginning of the patristic period (a diaspora)
   – a continuation of stage 7; in some places continuing to modern times (e.g. in South India)

9. Christendom (a nation among nations)
   – a Christian version of stage 2

   a. After 313: the united Christian Roman Empire and other Christian nations (e.g., Armenia, Nubia)

   b. After 800: the Byzantine Empire, the Latin Christian commonwealth[6], and other Christian nations

   c. After 1453 in the East: the Orthodox Russian Empire and Orthodox nations

   d. After 1803 in the West: Latin Catholic nations, Latin Protestant nations, and others

   e. Throughout this stage in most parts of the Christian world: some Christian sects (e.g., Waldensians, Anabaptists) functioning as diasporas

   f. After 1688? British Empire and USA (1776): Christian nations with many churches

10. The dhimma:[7] a diaspora and/or subject nation of Christians in Muslim countries
   – co-exists with stage 9

11. Secularized Christians (overlap with the later stages of 9 and 10)

   a. Gradually secularizing society overall (beginning about 1750)

   – rally and rout from nation to nation

   b. Predominant secularization: Christianity privatized

   c. Predominant secularization: Christianity persecuted (e.g., Communist countries)

---

[6] The Latin Christian nations gave the Byzantine emperor a certain precedence until the coronation of Charlemagne (AD 800). From then on there was a Western emperor. After the breakup of the Carolingian Empire, the Latin Christian nations gave the (German) Holy Roman Emperor a certain precedence as the chief lay ruler of Western Christendom until the abolition of the Holy Roman Empire in 1803. The years AD 800 and 1803 can be taken as convenient dates for the start and end of the commonwealth of Western or Latin Christendom, although secularization began before 1803.

[7] *Dhimma* is a Quranic word for diaspora groups and subject nations in a Muslim society. They were given a special status in Islamic law. The Turks in the Ottoman Empire used the word *millet*.

    d. "Christian communities": churches and communities that resist secularization and live like diaspora groupings in society and secularized churches

12. The new Jerusalem

CHAPTER ELEVEN

THE COMPLETION OF THE NEW COVENANT

TEXT: 1 CORINTHIANS 15:20–58; REVELATION 21–22

Stages	Founders	Events	People	Covenants	Inheritance
VII Glory	Jesus Christ	Second Coming Completion of All Things	New Jerusalem	New Covenant	New Earth (Heaven on Earth)

Introduction to the chapter. With the death, Resurrection and Ascension of Christ and his outpouring of the Holy Spirit on the day of Pentecost, the new covenant stage began. At that point it began to co-exist both with the old covenant stage and with the stage of the sons of Noah, the stage of fallen humanity. Now there are pagans, Jews, and Christians (including Jewish Christians): people living in unredeemed, fallen humanity, people in the old covenant, and people in the new covenant.

That is not where God intends to leave his creation. We live at a transitional time when different human beings live in more than one stage or era of God's working with the human race. But the purpose of God is to bring the whole human race to a final stage. That stage will be inaugurated when Christ comes again. That stage, however, will not be a further covenant but the final stage of the new covenant.

In this chapter we will mainly look at the two Scripture passages cited above that will let us see something of the nature of the age to come.

The Second Coming. Before he was crucified, the Lord was brought to trial before the Sanhedrin, the governing council of the nation of Israel. The high priest and most of the council were seeking to put him to death. They knew he was dangerous and they believed he was making a claim about himself that they did not accept. They sought witnesses against him, but they could not find two witnesses who agreed with one another and who presented evidence for a charge against him with enough substance to lead to the death penalty.

At last they found two who both claimed that Jesus had said that he could destroy the temple and raise it up in three days. The high priest demanded that he answer the charges, but Christ would say nothing. Then the high priest, probably exasperated, said,

> "I adjure you by the living God, tell us if you are the Christ, the Son of God." (Mt 26:63)

In saying this, the high priest solemnly put Jesus under oath, not to answer the charge of the two witnesses, which was only indirectly damaging, but to respond to the underlying question. Did Jesus believe he was the Christ, the Son of God, the anointed king of Israel, the messiah, who was come to rule over Israel and establish its pre-eminence in the world? The high priest feared that as a false messiah, Jesus would fail and provoke the Romans to bloody retaliation (Jn 11:47–48). To this Jesus responded, showing respect for the solemn oath of the high priest, even though seeking to fulfill the prophetic word about the sacrificial lamb who "opened not his mouth" (Is 53:7),

> "You have said so." (Mt 26:64)

In other words, "you are the one who said it, not me (although it is true)." And then he finally spoke out:

> "But I tell you, hereafter you will see the Son of man seated at the right hand of Power, and coming on the clouds of heaven." (Mt 26:64)

He was saying, "You have said I am the Messiah, yet you do not realize what kind of messiah I am and how I will establish my kingdom. You may put me to death, but I will appear again, and when I do I will be seated at the right hand of God and will come on the clouds of heaven to establish the kingdom of God. I am a heavenly king with divine power, and I will change human history when I come."

In saying this, Jesus was referring to two passages in the Old Testament, passages the high priest and the Sanhedrin would be very familiar with. The first we have already seen when we looked at Psalm 110:

> The LORD says to my lord:
>   "Sit at my right hand,
> till I make your enemies
>   your footstool." (Ps 110:1)

In other words, the son of David, the messiah, would sit on the throne of God, sharing his authority, while God's kingdom was being fully established.

The second passage came from an important prophecy in the seventh chapter of Daniel. It was in the context of the judgment by God when the kingdoms of the earth that had set themselves up against God would be put down. The prophecy is in the form of a vision reported by Daniel. It begins:

> As I looked,
>   thrones were placed
>   and one that was ancient of days took his seat;

his raiment was white as snow,
    and the hair of his head like pure wool;
his throne was fiery flames,
    its wheels were burning fire.
A stream of fire issued
    and came forth from before him;
a thousand thousands served him,
    and ten thousand times ten thousand stood before
        him;
the court sat in judgment,
    and the books were opened. (Dan 7:9–10)

Daniel, in other words, saw God seated on his throne, surrounded by angels in heaven. He was manifest in glory and power. And he was holding court.

As Daniel watched, the main beast representing the anti-Christ and his kingdom was destroyed. Then Daniel had another vision:

I saw in the night visions,
    and behold, with the clouds of heaven
        there came one like a son of man,
    and he came to the Ancient of Days
        and was presented before him.
And to him was given dominion
    and glory and kingdom,
that all peoples, nations, and languages
    should serve him;
his dominion is an everlasting dominion,
    which shall not pass away,
and his kingdom one
    that shall not be destroyed. (Dan 7:13–14)

In other words, a son of man, a human figure, came to God and was given the authority of king over all the earth in an eternal rule. When this prophecy was referred to, as Christ did in speaking to the high priest, this figure would be described as *the* son of man.

This son of man would ascend to heaven. He would come up to God on his throne to receive his commission. Then he would sit at the right hand of God the Almighty, sharing his authority over all the earth and the power to implement God's judgment. He would then come from heaven to judge the living and the dead and establish the new creation. When he would come, he would represent and be accompanied by *the people of the saints of the Most High* (v. 27)—another example of the link between a royal individual and his people. This son of man, this king to come, was he himself, the Lord Jesus Christ, and when he would come, he would be accompanied by his people who would be given in him *an everlasting kingdom* and with him *reign for ever and ever* (Rev 22:5).

Christ's first coming and his earthly mission was an important first step. It would lead to the outpouring of the Holy Spirit, and he would begin to establish his kingdom through the work of the Apostles and through those who preached the Gospel of the kingdom with and after them. But even more important would be his Second Coming, when he would bring the full kingdom of God and the completion of God's plan for the human race and all creation. This he proclaimed as he was about to be condemned to death and die for the sins of the world.

THE NEW WORLD

First Corinthians 15:20–58. There are two comings of Christ to establish the new covenant. Both comings could be described as the coming of the redeemer to raise up the human race from where it has fallen. As the book of Hebrews says, Christ came the first time "at the end of the age to put away sin." Some day he will come again "to save those who are eagerly waiting for him" (Heb 9:26–28). Each of his comings is a salvation and a redemption, a freeing from bondage and oppression. Each of his comings is a raising up of the human race and a giving of life.

What Christians will be given after the Second Coming is the same reality that they have after the first coming: justification, union with God, holiness, victory, and freedom. The pardon or freedom from condemnation we receive now is the same one we will have at the last day. We will be found "in him" with a righteousness or justification that comes through faith in him (Phil 3:9). The new life we have now is the same life we will have at the last day. "When Christ who is our life appears, then you also will appear with him in glory" (Col 3:4). "We know that when he appears, we shall be like him" (1 Jn 3:2).

Yet, as we have also seen, the life we will have after Christ's Second Coming will not be simply the same as before. We already have the new covenant life, but we do not yet have it in its full extent. Here, due to fallenness and spiritual warfare, we toil and suffer for the kingdom. But at the Second Coming, everything will be different. The fullest New Testament presentation of the difference is in First Corinthians 15.

In that text, Paul is dealing with an opinion of some in the Corinthian church. They said there was no resurrection of the dead—such a thing was impossible. Paul's response was that of course there is a resurrection of the dead. We know that Christ has been raised from the dead. That is central to the Gospel message that we have received. Many in fact have seen the risen Christ and talked with him. If Christ, who died for us, has been raised, there has to be a resurrection from the dead. Dead human beings can be raised to life, as we have seen happen with Christ.

Paul concludes his discussion of Christ's Resurrection by saying to the Corinthian believers,

> If for this life only we have hoped in Christ, we are of all men most to be pitied. (1 Cor 15:19)

He was speaking about the Apostles, who had staked everything on the Resurrection of Christ, but what he says also applies to all Christians. As good as the Christian life here and now is, there is something much better to come, and those who have suffered for Christ and his work, especially those persecuted and martyred, will receive a blessing that will make up for all the earthly suffering.

Paul then goes on to give an overall picture of God's plan and how the resurrection of the dead fits into that:

> . . . first fruits of those who have fallen asleep. For as by a man came death, by a man has come also the resurrection of the dead. For as in Adam all die, so also in Christ shall all be made alive. But each in his own order: Christ the first fruits, then at his coming those who belong to Christ. Then comes the end, when he delivers the kingdom to God the Father after destroying every rule and every authority and power. For he must reign until he has put all his enemies under his feet [Ps 110:1]. The last enemy to be destroyed is death. . . . When all things are subjected to him, then the Son himself will also be subjected to him who put all things under him, that God may be everything to every one. (2 Cor 15:20–28)

As we have seen, the first human being, Adam, failed the test of obedience to God, and the result was death, the mortality of the whole human race. But Christ, the Son of God, became a human being, suffered, died, and rose in obedience to his Father, so that all those who believe in him might have eternal life. He is the *first fruits* of the redeemed human race given as an offering to God, like the first sheaf, the beginning of the grain harvest at the feast of Pentecost. The full harvest, all the redeemed, will be given when he comes again.

What Christ made possible by his death and Resurrection and the establishment of the new covenant will be brought to completion after he comes again. At the end, Christ will destroy *every rule and every authority and power*, that is, the kingdom of Satan and his spiritual armies. When this fallen world accepts Christ's authority, he will be able to deliver his kingdom to God the Father, with all rebellion and disobedience put away. God will then rule completely, being *everything to every one.*

Paul then responds to the underlying question: How are the dead raised? What kind of body will they have? He begins by using an analogy. We are familiar with seeds—hard, dry, and for all practical purposes dead, unable to move. A seed is buried like a dead body, but at a certain point something affects it, and it begins to grow into a plant. The plant does not look like the seed at all, but it is nonetheless the same being. Paul could have given the example of the caterpillar and the butterfly. The caterpillar goes into a cocoon and is inert, for all practical purposes dead. Then at a certain point it comes out and when it does, its body is dramatically different from the one it had before, yet it is the same being.

Paul's conclusion is that there are various kinds of bodies and some are greater than others in "glory," that is, ability to function and act effectively. Therefore, there can be a resurrected body that is immortal, and consequently different from the one we now have. But furthermore, a body that seems dead has within it the ability to change, to metamorphose, into another kind of body. Just because human beings are now dead, unable to move or change, does not mean they have to remain that way forever. Paul then moves on to say,

> So is it with the resurrection of the dead. What is sown is perishable, what is raised is imperishable. It is sown in dishonor, it is raised in glory. It is sown in weakness, it is raised in power. It is sown a physical body, it is raised a spiritual body. If there is a physical body, there is also a spiritual body. Thus it is written, "The first man Adam became a living being"; the last Adam became a life-giving spirit. But it is not the spiritual which is first but the physical, and then the spiritual. The first man was from the earth, a man of dust; the second man is from heaven. As was the man of dust, so are those who are of the dust; and as is the man of heaven, so are those who are of heaven. Just as we have borne the image

THE COMPLETION OF THE NEW COVENANT 349

of the man of dust, we shall also bear the image of the man of heaven. I tell you this, brethren: flesh and blood cannot inherit the kingdom of God, nor does the perishable inherit the imperishable. (1 Cor 15:42–50)

The analogy of the seed allows us to see what happens in the resurrection of the dead. Dead human beings do not just get brought back to life or resuscitated. Rather they are transformed or metamorphosed into human beings with a different sort of body. It is a body that is imperishable, more glorious, more powerful, and more spiritualized. As a result, they can live forever.

But how does this come about? Paul's account goes back to the situation at the beginning of the human race. As we saw, we are the descendants of Adam, and we inherited from him a human nature that was mortal and had to die. We also saw that Christ is the new Adam, *the last Adam*, or, as we might restate it, the Adam for the last times or the Adam who is in himself the completion or final version of the human race. Christians are joined to him, are incorporated into him, and so take on his nature or image. We have already to some extent taken on his image as a result of becoming a Christian and entering the new covenant. Now the change that was produced in the inner human being will reach to our body, the outer human being (2 Cor 4:16; RSV: inner and outer nature). Just as he is now glorified in body, so will we be.

Our bodies will become spiritualized, not in the sense that we will become immaterial. There are no such things as immaterial bodies. Rather, the Spirit of God who now dwells in new covenant people will renew their bodies as well, so that they can function in a more spiritually capable way. As Paul puts it in Romans 8:11:

If the Spirit of him who raised Jesus from the dead dwells in you, he who raised Christ Jesus from the dead will give life to your mortal bodies also through his Spirit which dwells in you.

We now have bodies that are merely *physical*. They are put togeth-er in the way the bodies of all the descendants of Adam are. In the resurrection of the dead, the Spirit who is already in those who be-long to Christ will transform them and give them a new life. The resurrected Christ *became a life-giving spirit* and has already given us spiritual life, but then he will extend that life so it transforms our bodies as well.

There are some Christian teachers who take the view that the work of Christ restores us to the condition of Adam and Eve when they were created—human beings as God meant human beings to be. Paul, however, seems to be saying the work of Christ does that and more. It brings us to a more glorious, spiritual state than Adam and Eve had attained before the Fall, the state to which God had in-tended to bring the human race even from the very beginning.

Paul then gives another principle: *flesh and blood cannot inherit the kingdom of God, nor does the perishable inherit the imperishable.* By *flesh and blood* he probably is not referring to our human nature, but to our human nature as we now are in this fallen world. In our current state we could not survive in the full kingdom of God, the glorious heavenly kingdom. We need to be given an *imperishable* na-ture before we can be in such a glorious environment and survive.

Behind this is a truth we are all familiar with. If we take a seed from a cherry tree and plant it in Florida instead of Michigan, it may sprout but it will soon die. But how can this be when there is so much more warmth and light in Florida? The answer is simply that the cherry tree is not fitted for that climate any more than orange trees are fitted for Michigan. The cherry tree cannot take the Florida climate. In a similar way, our current bodies cannot take the climate of heaven. To live "in heaven," we need to be metamorphosed or transfigured as Christ was so that we have glorified or spiritualized bodies.

Paul then concludes his presentation of the resurrection of the dead by describing the moment of great change:

Lo! I tell you a mystery. We shall not all sleep, but we shall all be changed, in a moment, in the twinkling of an eye, at the last trumpet. For the trumpet will sound, and the dead will be raised imperishable, and we shall be changed. For this perishable nature must put on the imperishable, and this mortal nature must put on immortality. When the perishable puts on the imperishable, and the mortal puts on immortality, then shall come to pass the saying that is written:

"Death is swallowed up in victory" [Isa. 25:8].
"O death, where is your victory?
O death, where is your sting?" [Hos. 13:14].

The sting of death is sin, and the power of sin is the law. But thanks be to God, who gives us the victory through our Lord Jesus Christ. (1 Cor 15:51–57)

At the end of human history as we know it, the last trumpet will sound. This is the trumpet that announces the final judgment of God, the action by which he will change the human race for the better. He will do this by abolishing death, the death that was the lawful sentence on the human race because of the sin of Adam, repeated by his descendants, the human sin that stung and still stings human beings to death. Some new covenant people will not have died to this earthly life, but all of them, dead and living alike, will be transformed. They will be given a transformed human nature, one that can endure the climate of heaven, and that will allow them to live eternally.

The Second Coming of Christ, then, will begin *the age to come*, a new era, the last stage of God's plan. It will inaugurate a new world, a world that will function in a very different way from the one we now experience. This we will now look at.

THE VISION OF THE COMPLETION

The book of Revelation is the last book of the New Testament. It is the end of the New Testament just as the book of Matthew is the beginning. But it is also the end in another sense. It is the book that presents the completion of the new covenant taught about in the New Testament, the end or goal toward which the new covenant and God's entire plan are leading.

The majority of the book of Revelation is a series of visions and explanations of those visions. The very last vision in the final two chapters, Revelation 21 and 22, is a vision of the completed plan of God, the human race as God wanted it to be from the beginning and will bring it to be in the end. It is this that we will focus on.

The wedding (marriage) of the Lamb. Just before the final vision, there are two preparatory visions. The first is the vision of the whore of Babylon, the city that represents the worldly, idolatrous society and civilization that stands opposed to God's plan for the human race and persecutes the saints of God. Its ruler is ultimately Satan, the dragon, the prince of this world. The second is the vision of the Word of God, our Lord Jesus Christ, come down from heaven in his Second Coming. He engages in the last battle when he destroys the kingdom of Satan on earth.

Before Christ comes down, however, there is an anticipatory celebration of what he will accomplish:

> Then I heard what seemed to be the voice of a great multitude, like the sound of many waters and like the sound of mighty thunderpeals, crying,
>
> > "Hallelujah! For the Lord our God the Almighty reigns.
> > Let us rejoice and exult and give him the glory,
> > for the marriage of the Lamb has come,
> > and his Bride has made herself ready;

it was granted her to be clothed with fine linen, bright
    and pure"—
for the fine linen is the righteous deeds of the saints.

And the angel said to me, "Write this: Blessed are those
who are invited to the marriage supper of the Lamb." (Rev
19:6–9)

The result of the Second Coming will be the marriage of the Lamb,
Jesus Christ.

We use the word "marriage" to speak of two different but related
things. We use it to speak of the relationship of husband and wife,
which endures, hopefully, throughout life. We also use it to speak of
the process that begins or institutes their marriage relationship. In
the latter sense, the chief step is the wedding, which is often simply
called the marriage. We say, "My friend invited me to his marriage,"
meaning to be present when he got married.

In the process of getting married among Jews at the time of
Christ, there were two chief steps. The first was "betrothal," the
solemn agreement or contract that the man and woman would be
husband and wife. At this point, the two were married. Mary, for
instance, was Joseph's betrothed, but therefore his wife, his woman, and they could not be separated without a divorce, even though
the marriage had not been consummated (Mt 1:18–25). The Jewish
betrothal was not the same as our engagement, which is simply the
promise to enter into marriage.

The second step occurred when the man "took" his woman, his
bride, and they began to live together. This was described as the
wedding or the marriage. The bride was supposed to be ceremonially purified beforehand and fittingly clothed; there was a feast to celebrate the event; and they became "one flesh" in sexual intercourse.
The equivalent of betrothal in modern Western marriage occurs
during the marriage ceremony when the couple commit themselves
to one another, and the equivalent of the Jewish wedding occurs in

the same ceremony when the bridegroom takes the bride from her family so he can bring her to his house where they then live together. The Jewish marriage in scriptural times contained only the second element of the modern Western marriage.

In the Old Testament, marriage was used as an analogical description or image to speak about the relationship of God and his people (e.g., Is 54, 62, Jer 3, 31, Ezek 16, 23) and, in the new covenant, of the Son of God and his people. The Church was betrothed to Christ after his First Coming and so married to him in the sense of being covenanted or committed to him (e.g., 2 Cor 11:2). But then, when he comes again to "take" his bride, there will be a marriage feast, and they will be fully united. It is this that the last chapters of Revelation describe.

The marriage of Christ was an analogical description or image, then, of Christ being united with his people. The bride was a corporate people, even at the point of betrothal (cf. 2 Cor 11:2). It is true that individual Christians need to convert and be baptized and at that point they too are united with Christ, but this happens in becoming part of his people. Almost always in Scripture, maybe always, the bride or the wife of God or Christ is a corporate body, not an individual—the people of Israel or the Christian church. This continues to be true in Revelation. The bride is the new Jerusalem, a city.

For contemporary readers, there is a more serious challenge to understanding the meaning of the marriage of Christ in the book of Revelation. Here it is clearly an image and is sometimes misinterpreted or over-interpreted. We live in a time when Christianity is being heavily influenced by a romantic and erotic culture. As a result, the marriage imagery is romanticized and often eroticized by many Christians. God (Jesus), they say referring to this image, is so much in love with people that he longs to unite each individual to himself.

But such an interpretation does not fit with the marriage image in Revelation. The bride of Christ in Revelation is a city, not an attractive young woman, or even an individual Christian. The bride is a city—men, women, and children, young and old alike, living together in the same place, surrounded by walls and gates (that is, bristling with fortifications) and clothed in righteous deeds (Rev 19: 8)—and now united to Christ. The special exegetical discussion that follows here discusses the marriage analogy more fully.

There is also a very important point about the use of the marriage analogy in Revelation that is often missed in the romantic interpretation of the image. The marriage of the lamb is yet to come and is an image of Christ bringing his people into a full relationship with himself. True, he had a relationship with them before, a covenant relationship. But the full relationship, the one that everything before was aiming at, will come when he takes his bride at the Second Coming. Then he will be fully united to his people. The meaning of this relationship is unfolded in the vision that follows the proclamation in Revelation 21:1–5.

The New Jerusalem. The last vision begins with an annunciation of what John, the author of Revelation, was seeing:

> Then I saw a new heaven and a new earth; for the first heaven and the first earth had passed away, and the sea was no more. And I saw the holy city, new Jerusalem, coming down out of heaven from God, prepared as a bride adorned for her husband; and I heard a loud voice from the throne saying, "Behold, the dwelling of God is with men. He will dwell with them, and they shall be his people, and God himself will be with them; he will wipe away every tear from their eyes, and death shall be no more, neither shall there be mourning nor crying nor pain any more, for the former things have passed away.
>
> And he who sat upon the throne said, "Behold, I make all things new." Also he said, "Write this, for these words are trustworthy and true." (Rev 21:1–5)

The vision is a vision of the *new heaven* and *new earth*, prophesied in Isaiah 65:17–25. At the end, God is not just going to rescue the human race and "bring them to heaven." He is going to re-create everything, including the earth, the place where human beings live, so that it will be the way he wants it to be. As a result, the effects of fallenness, the *mourning* and *crying* and *pain* and especially *death* will be gone. Everything will be *on earth as it is in heaven* (Mt 6:10). Heaven will be joined to earth in a new way.

The vision is also a vision of a city, *the new Jerusalem*, the restored Jerusalem prophesied in Isaiah 65:17–25, now brought into existence as part of the creation of the new heaven and earth. This city stands in contrast to the whore of Babylon, and is presented as a virgin *bride*, a people faithful to their covenanted Lord and not having adulterous intercourse with idols and false gods. The bride is *adorned for her husband*, that is, clothed in *the righteous deeds of the saints* (Rev 19:8).

This city is *coming down out of heaven*. It is not built up by human hands, a city and tower of Babel or Babylon, reaching up to heaven, claiming equality with God. It is constituted by a relationship with God, coming from God himself and offered to the human race, to establish it as a people of God, a community in Christ. It is, as *a loud voice from the throne* of God proclaims, both a temple, a place where God *will dwell with* human beings, and a covenant relationship uniting God and human beings so that he will be their God and *they shall be his people*.

The final vision in Revelation begins with another proclamation from God the Father, the one who sat upon the throne:

And he who sat upon the throne . . . said to me, "It is done! I am the Alpha and the Omega, the beginning and the end. To the thirsty I will give from the fountain of the water of life without payment. He who conquers shall have this heritage, and I will be his God and he shall be my son. But as for the cowardly, the faithless, the polluted, as for murderers, fornicators, sorcerers, idolaters, and all liars, their lot shall be in the lake that burns with fire and sulphur, which is the second death." (Rev. 21:5–8)

God proclaims that *it is done!* This is the true completion of *all the work which God had done in his creation* (Gen 2:3). The proclamation is a promise to those who hear—a promise of the gift of the Holy Spirit, *the fountain of the water of life* and the *heritage* or *inheritance* of the relationship of sonship with God, the full blessing of Abraham spoken about in Galatians 3:14. Those who thirsted in their earthly life for God and his life will have this. Those who lived in wickedness and immorality cannot have this, but will experience *the second death.*

Then an angel from heaven comes to John and summons him to a fuller view of the new Jerusalem. Like all the visions in the book of Revelation, it is a composite picture, in this case, a picture of the things that have been prophesied about the completion or consummation of all things.

> Then came one of the seven angels who had the seven bowls full of the seven last plagues, and spoke to me, saying, "Come, I will show you the Bride, the wife of the Lamb."
>
> And in the Spirit he carried me away to a great, high mountain, and showed me the holy city Jerusalem coming down out of heaven from God, having the glory of God, its radiance like a most rare jewel, like a jasper, clear as crystal. It had a great, high wall, with twelve gates, and at the gates twelve angels, and on the gates the names of the twelve tribes of the sons of Israel were inscribed; on the east three gates, on the north three gates, on the south three gates, and on the west three gates. And the wall of the city had twelve foundations, and on them the twelve names of the twelve apostles of the Lamb.
>
> And he who talked to me had a measuring rod of gold to measure the city and its gates and walls. The city lies foursquare, its length the same as its breadth; and he measured the city with his rod, twelve thousand stadia; its length and breadth and height are equal. He also measured its wall, a hundred and forty-four cubits by a man's measure, that is,

an angel's. The wall was built of jasper, while the city was pure gold, clear as glass. The foundations of the wall of the city were adorned with every jewel; the first was jasper, the second sapphire, the third agate, the fourth emerald, the fifth onyx, the sixth carnelian, the seventh chrysolite, the eighth beryl, the ninth topaz, the tenth chrysoprase, the eleventh jacinth, the twelfth amethyst. And the twelve gates were twelve pearls, each of the gates made of a single pearl, and the street of the city was pure gold, transparent as glass. (Rev 21:9–21)

John was taken up to *a great high mountain*, like the mountain that Ezekiel was taken to so he could see the new Jerusalem (Ezek 40:2). The city was a cube, a holy of holies like the holy of holies on earth (also a cube), and was coming down onto that mountain. The city had a wall with *twelve gates* and *twelve foundations*. The gates had the names of the *twelve tribes of the sons of Israel,* the twelve patriarchs who were the sons of Jacob, the ancestors of the old covenant people of God. The foundations had the names of *the twelve apostles of the Lamb,* the "patriarchs" of the new covenant. Together they made up the twenty-four elders (Rev 4:4), who functioned as a wall to protect the city of God. The city was a new covenant city built upon the Apostles who established the new Israel out of the twelve tribes of the old covenant Israel.

The city was adorned with twelve stones, like the robe of the high priest when he officiated in the temple (Ex 28:17–20) and like the robe of Adam in paradise (Ezek 28:13). It was built of *pure gold,* itself like *a most rare jewel.* But first and foremost, it *had the glory of God.* The city was a temple and was arrayed in priestly adornments, because God dwelt in it. But God's presence had so filled this temple, his glory was so fully entered into a material medium, that the city was like *clear glass, radiant* with or glowing with God's glory. John saw a city, but at the same time he saw the manifest presence of God on earth.

Having viewed the city from the outside, John was then enabled to view the city from the inside:

> And I saw no temple in the city, for its temple is the Lord
> God the Almighty and the Lamb. And the city has no need
> of sun or moon to shine upon it, for the glory of God is its
> light, and its lamp is the Lamb. By its light shall the nations
> walk; and the kings of the earth shall bring their glory into
> it, and its gates shall never be shut by day—and there shall
> be no night there; they shall bring into it the glory and the
> honor of the nations. But nothing unclean shall enter it,
> nor any one who practices abomination or falsehood, but
> only those who are written in the Lamb's book of life. (Rev
> 21:22–27)

John saw no temple building in the city. The city itself was a holy of
holies. The temple for this city was simply the indwelling presence
in it of *the Lord God the Almighty and the Lamb,* which no longer
needed to be distanced and so veiled from the people by an inter-
vening material form.

Moreover, *the glory of God is its light and its lamp is the Lamb. The
Lamb* is the lamp or the lampstand or the candlestick, depending on
how the word is translated. He is the incarnate one, a material being
within this world, but he contains the glory of God, which is light,
and he is so transparent that that light is a light for the whole city of
God. Paul saw *the glory of God in the face of Christ* (2 Cor 4:6). John
now sees Christ, the lamb of God himself, and from him the glory of
God shines and fills the city. The whole city becomes a holy of holies because the glorified Christ is present in it with his divine glory
fully manifested or unveiled and reaching everything.

To this city that is a temple the nations, the Gentiles, will have
full access and will come through its open gates as prophesied (Is
60:11). They will bring all the wealth they have to make offerings
to God, *glory* here probably meaning, as it often does, "wealth." This
city is the new Jerusalem. Jerusalem was and is the city of David, the
city of the anointed king, the messiah. It is the capital of the land the
Lord gave his people and the place of government of those people.
It is also the place where the Lord God's people come up to keep

festival. It was prophesied that at the end all the nations would come up and celebrate the feast of Tabernacles with the Jewish people in Jerusalem (Zech 14:16–21), and that is being described here.

All the nations will come up to the new Jerusalem, but not every individual. Only those *written in the Lamb's book of life*, only those who belong to Christ, will come. They come because they have submitted to Christ, their king and Lord, and now bring the gifts that express that submission. As in the initial proclamation, the human race has been sorted out. Those who have been committed to and practiced immorality and uncleanness will be banished. Those who belong to the Lamb and are clothed in the righteous deeds of the saints will enter.

The vision continues. Now John sees the life of those who live in the city keeping festival:

> Then he showed me the river of the water of life, bright as crystal, flowing from the throne of God and of the Lamb through the middle of the street of the city; also, on either side of the river, the tree of life with its twelve kinds of fruit, yielding its fruit each month; and the leaves of the tree were for the healing of the nations. There shall no more be anything accursed, but the throne of God and of the Lamb shall be in it, and his servants shall worship him; they shall see his face, and his name shall be on their foreheads. And night shall be no more; they need no light of lamp or sun, for the Lord God will be their light, and they shall reign for ever and ever. (Rev 22:1–5)

The *water of life*, as we have already seen, is the Holy Spirit. That water flows from the throne of God and the Lamb in the temple, as in the prophecy of Ezekiel 47. It gives life to the city. This expresses the old truth from the beginning that God's creation only finds life and blessing in God's kingdom. It is only when God rules and when rational creatures submit to that rule that they have true life.

The water of life allows *the tree of life* to grow in the city of God. Paradise, the Garden of Eden, is restored in the city. The tree of life has become twelve trees, providing food for each month of the year and for each tribe of the people of God, which now includes all *the nations* of the earth. They come to the city of God and find *healing* and life in it. The wounds of sin and fallenness are gone, and the wholeness of new life prevails.

All that is accursed is now gone from the city and therefore from the restored human race. Such things cannot exist in the presence of God and cannot exist where his rule is effective. The *throne of God and the Lamb* are in the city, and that which is accursed has been destroyed. Only the holy can stand God's presence.

The inhabitants of the city of God are his *servants*, a priestly people. They are keeping festival there, *worshipping him*. The image is not one of an overlong liturgy, sure to tire everyone out. It is an image of a liturgical celebration, including a banquet, a celebrative meal, with much singing and dancing and dramatic events. It is the image of people rejoicing in what God has done.

The source of that joy is God himself. This is the beatific vision. That phrase means a sight that by itself is enough to make people blessed or happy. The sight is the sight of God. Now his servants can *see his face*. They do not see him as in a dark mirror where they can barely make out who he is (1 Cor 13:12), as they did in the first stage of the new covenant where they walked *by faith and not by sight* (2 Cor 5:6). They see him *face to face*. They can see him this way, and they can have confidence that they will always remain there, because *his name is on their forehead*, as it was on the crown of the old covenant high priest (Ex 28:36; 39:30). They belong to him and will belong to him for all eternity in his everlasting covenant.

Night will be no more. The old sources of light, *sun* by day and *lamp* by night, are no longer needed (Is 60:19). As this description began (in verses 21:22–23), so it ends. God is the light of the city of God. His presence, like the presence of the sun in the material world, brings the warmth and light that allows human beings to stay alive and to function as human beings. Life flows from the throne. The glory of God in the kingdom of God fills the city of God with life and blessing.

God's servants shall *reign forever and ever*. They keep festival, but they also care for God's material creation, bringing it to the purpose for which God made it. The whole of creation, tended by the hands of the new human beings, becomes a perfect material reflection of the immaterial glory of God.

THE BEGINNING AND THE END

We see in the vision at the end of the New Testament a vision with many elements brought together, indeed fused together. The plan of God has reached its end, attained its goal, accomplished its purpose. All the prophecies are fulfilled. All the types and symbols find full realization. Everything is now brought to completion.

It is first of all the establishment of the human race as God has intended it to be. Redeemed human beings constitute the new Jerusalem, the city where all those who belong to Christ the Son of God enter and keep festival, celebrating the goodness of the work of God. They are in full covenant relationship with God. He is their God and they are his people. They are his sons and daughters and his heirs. They have received the full inheritance, the blessed life that is a share in his own blessedness.

The whole earth, the whole of material creation, is now renewed, brought to life and fully manifesting the goodness and greatness of its Creator, fully deified. It is gold, refined from any admixture and purified from any uncleanness, shining with the glory of God. And it belongs to the sons and daughters of God. They reign over it, tending the new paradise, rejoicing in its goodness, no longer needing to guard it from evil.

The glorified sons and daughters of God experience the fullness of his presence. They are filled with him, fully spiritualized in his Holy Spirit, formed fully into his image in his Son. In seeing him face to face, not only do they see him as he is, but they see all of creation in the light of him, coming from him and going toward him.

They have his law fully written in their hearts by the glory of God within. Sin no longer dwells within them and the curse is gone. His glory has entered into them in such a way that their obedience to him is an expression of the fact that they fully want what he wants. They and all creation with them have entered into the full *freedom of glory of the sons and daughters of God* (Rom 8:21).

In this vision, we can see all the stages of God's plan brought to consummation. Paradise is restored. The blessing of Abraham is given to all the nations. The old covenant is completed in the new. God's people have reached the end of their exodus journey and been given their true inheritance, the land of the living. The kingdom of God is on earth as it is in heaven. Every spiritual blessing is given in the heavenly places. Heaven has come to earth.

We can, however, see something more. To see that, we have to look at some of the details of the vision. The sun and moon are gone. So is the sea. So is the night. To understand why, we have to return to the first chapter of Genesis.

In order to create the world, the light had to shine into the darkness on the first day (Gen 1:3–5; 2 Cor 4:6). This darkness covered everything and perhaps symbolized nothingness, the nothingness that would give birth to corruption and death, the nothingness that surrounded the light and threatened to extinguish it. The light was uncreated light, the light of God's presence in the midst of the darkness, and from that light God began his work of creation. He divided off the light from the darkness and then he separated the waters of the abyss so that there was a clear space, heaven. In that space he formed material creation, the earth, covered with vegetation.

He then populated his creation. He put the lesser lights in the sky (sun, moon, stars) to rule the day and night. He put birds in the air, fish in the sea, and animals on the earth. Then he established the human race, his son, made in his image and likeness, to bring the material creation to its purpose, made male and female to share the nature of the animals and so to reproduce and to develop into a race that could make the earth into a garden of delight, a paradise.

Now, after the Fall, after the dominion of darkness (Col 1:13–14), the rule of the dragon, Satan, has been destroyed (Eph 6:12; Rev 12; 20:1–3, 7–10). The darkness has failed to overcome the light (Jn 1:5). The prince of this world has been cast down and cast into the lake of fire (Jn 12:31; Rev 12:9; 20:10). The human race has been brought into the kingdom of God and reigns with God over all of his creation. That which was opposed to his purpose, seeking to establish a world different than what God wanted, is defeated.

The final vision in Revelation seems to tell us that all that is more than defeated. It is gone. The waters of the sea that once overwhelmed much of the earth in the Flood, and have threatened to do so again, are gone. The sun and moon are no longer needed because the light of God's glory fills all of his material creation completely. They too are gone. Night and darkness have vanished.

Strictly speaking, darkness has never existed. It is the absence of light. Strictly speaking pure formlessness has never existed. It is the absence of that which makes every definite thing possible. Strictly speaking nothingness has never existed. It is the absence of positive being. But we are looking at a book filled with images, where the incomprehensible is expressed in the form of material pictures and analogical descriptions. And we are looking at a history in which God has been resisted by the dominion of darkness, but now we are foreseeing his absolute victory.

If light has replaced darkness, if form and order have replaced formlessness, if being has replaced nothingness, that can only mean that God's work of creation is now fully established and complete. It is no longer threatened by lapsing into non-being. It is no longer endangered by nihilistic forces opposed to God and his plan. That which could destroy has been banished, made to be without force, made to be of no effect, made to be no longer a threat.

Creation has been brought to completion and will now unfold its full power and beauty, not static, but moving harmoniously to tell the glory of God (Ps 19:1). Some Christian teachers hold that when the new Jerusalem is established on earth, creation will have reached its final form. Others have held that at that point, creation has gotten through its birth pangs and will begin to develop to more and more glorious forms. Either way, the creative or beginning work of God is finished, and God can enter his rest, the eternal sabbath, which is the age to come, whose glories can only be expressed to us dimly and weakly, but which are of surpassing excellence.

All this is the work of the Spirit of God who moved over the waters in the beginning, who was at work in the kings, and priests, and prophets of the old covenant, who was poured out on God's sons and daughters on the day of Pentecost, and who will bring about the new heaven and earth. All this is the work of the Word of God through whom all things were created, in whose image the human race was formed, who entered his creation as a human being to save it and to reopen paradise, and who will come a second time to bring it to completion. All this is the work of him who sits upon the throne and whose complete will and good pleasure will be brought to pass by the ways of his incomparable and inscrutable wisdom. *He spoke and it came to be. He commanded and it stood forth* (Ps 33:9).

> And he said to me, "These words are trustworthy and true. And the Lord, the God of the spirits of the prophets, has sent his angel to show his servants what must soon take place. And behold, I am coming soon."
>
> Blessed is he who keeps the words of the prophecy of this book. (Rev 22:6–7)
>
> Amen. Come, Lord Jesus! (Rev 22:20)

Special Exegetical Discussion:
The Marriage of Christ and the Church

The consummation of the marriage of Christ and the Church is an image of the fulfillment of the covenant commitment, not of romantic or erotic ecstasy.

Marriage is used as an analogical description or image of the relationship of God to his people in both the Old Testament and the New Testament. Because we live in a romanticized and eroticized culture, this image is frequently over-emphasized. Some teachers even say that "the Scriptures use this image more than any other" for God's relationship with humanity,[1] although this is manifestly inaccurate. The image of the king and his subjects (see for example Rev 4–5; 21:5; 22:1), and the image of father and son (see for example Gal 3:26; Rev 21:7) are both much more common than husband and wife. All three images—a king and his subjects, a husband and his wife, a father and his son—are of a God who loves human beings (Tit 3:4), even though contemporary people with a prejudice against monarchy cannot easily conceive of a king who loves, that is, cares for, his people out of dedication, and are losing the experience of fathers and sons who love one another throughout all of their lives.

To round out the picture, the image of the warrior who slaughters the enemy is even more common than the image of husband and wife. It is not accidental that Christ is portrayed at the end of the book of Revelation both as a warrior rescuing his people and as a bridegroom taking his wife (both are to be found juxtaposed in chapter 19). This is now even more foreign to our culture, although history gives us many examples of fighters who have given their lives to destroy enemies, thereby saving others from oppression—and our own time does as well.

In the Scriptures the analogical description or image of marriage is probably always used for the relationship of God to a body of people, not to an individual. Of course, the two are connected. If Christ unites himself to his Church and shares his life with his Church, he also thereby unites himself to the individual members of his Church and shares his life with them. Likewise, if individuals join the Church, a body of people united with Christ, they too are thereby united to Christ. Nonetheless, marriage is used in Scripture

---

[1] Christopher West, *The Theology of the Body Explained: A Commentary on John Paul II's "Gospel of the Body"* (Boston: Pauline Books & Media, 2003), 12.

for the relationship of Christ to a body of people, the Church, and when the New Testament speaks of the relationship of God to an individual, the analogical description of sonship, often adoption, is primarily used.

But more important, the marriage image is often misunderstood in modern Christian teaching. Images are applied in an analogical manner. Marriage as we know it is between two human individuals, a man and a woman. The marriage of Christ and the Church is applied to the glorified Son of God and a body of people, his followers. It is applied because there is some similarity between the two analogues, but we need to be able to see the point of similarity in order to interpret it well and not read something into it that is not there.

The image of marriage in regard to the relationship of Christ and the Church is not used in Scripture as the image of a romantic relationship, but as an image of covenant and covenant commitment. It was probably first used as an image of God and Israel in Hosea, where Hosea was told by God to marry a prostitute—not someone he married because of romantic attraction—and predictably she committed adultery. The marriage relationship in Hosea is the image of human breaking of the covenant with God and of God's unfailing commitment to the people he is in a covenant relationship with. It is a commitment expressed in severe judgment (not just tender wooing) but then in restoration. It was used in a similar way in other prophets (Is 54, 62; Jer 3, 31; Ezek 16, 23). Paul used the image in a similar way as well in Second Corinthians 11:2 to warn the Galatians that they were betrothed to Christ and now needed to be faithful to him.

The image of the marriage of Christ and the Church was used in the book of Revelation to refer to the Second Coming. The bride had already been betrothed to him. She then was "taken" to him in the marriage. As a result, she lived with him and received every spiritual blessing from him—*the Lord God will be their light, they shall see his face, and his name will be on their foreheads* (Rev 22:4–5). The image is still not of romantic love but of covenant relationship and commitment. The commitment has already been made. Christ can be relied on to come to fulfill that commitment by establishing the full union of living together, and we will not be able to sue him for breach of promise. The Jewish marriage process provides an apt image for a two-step process of entering into a union based on a covenant relationship.

Ephesians 5:31–32. One of the more important passages that sees the New Testament as a fulfillment of the Old Testament and is based on the marriage analogy is Ephesians 5:31–32.[2] It bears on the discussion of the marriage of the Lamb in the book of Revelation. The full passage reads as follows:

> Wives, be subject to your husbands, as to the Lord. For the husband is the head of the wife as Christ is the head of the Church, his body, and is himself its Savior. As the church is subject to Christ, so let wives also be subject in everything to their husbands. Husbands, love your wives, as Christ loved the Church and gave himself up for her, that he might sanctify her, having cleansed her by the washing of water with the word, that he might present the Church to himself in splendor, without spot or wrinkle or any such thing, that she might be holy and without blemish. Even so husbands should love their wives as their own bodies. He who loves his wife loves himself. For no man ever hates his own flesh, but nourishes and cherishes it, as Christ does the Church, because we are members of his body. "For this reason a man shall leave his father and mother and be joined to his wife, and the two shall become one flesh." This mystery is a profound one, and I am saying that it refers to Christ and the Church; however, let each one of you love his wife as himself, and let the wife see that she respects her husband. (Eph 5:22–33)

---

[2]   For a fuller exegesis of Ephesians 5:31–32, see Clark, *MWC*, 72–87.

Three things are helpful to note as we examine the passage. First of all, it is not primarily about Christ and the Church, but about husbands and wives and how they should relate to one another. Wives should be subordinate to their husbands, and husbands should care for their wives. Christ and the Church are given as a model for husbands and wives to imitate, and therefore the passage does not attempt to provide a complete view of the relationship of Christ and the Church.

Second, the husband is exhorted to love his wife, but he is not exhorted to love her in a romantic, emotional way, as some interpret the passage. The two, of course, can be combined, but the question here is what is being presented in the text. The husband is exhorted to care for his wife, even at personal cost. This is especially clear with the second example, the way a man loves his own body. Hopefully he does not love his own body in a romantic or erotic way, but he always cares for it well if he can. The passage is not speaking against a man loving his wife in a romantic way, but the passage is not written to encourage romantic love but faithful care.

Third, each time the passage mentions the relationship of Christ and the Church, it says something about the relationship, but sometimes what is said does not apply to the husband and wife relationship. Probably this happens because the relationship of Christ and the Church is the main subject of the Letter to the Ephesians. In other words, the passage is using Christ and the Church as a model for the husband-wife relationship, but it also provides an opportunity to say something more about Christ and the Church at the same time.

The first development of the Christ-Church analogy is that Christ is the savior of the Church and gave himself up for her in his death on the Cross that he might make her holy by purifying her from sins. Most scholars think that *washing of water with the word* is a reference to Baptism, which is possibly here seen as an analogy of the purifying bath a wife undergoes in the Jewish marriage ceremony. The fact that Christ saves the Church indicates that Paul is not thinking that the husband should care for his wife just the way Christ cares for the Church. The husband is not the wife's savior, and he does not cleanse her from her sins, much less baptize her into himself. Rather, Paul is using what Christ does for the Church as a model of service love.

We can see the same truth expressed in First John 3:16 where it says, *By this we know love, that he laid down his life for us; and we ought to lay down our lives for the brethren.* The text then goes on to explicate the kind of love it has in mind by warning against *having the world's goods and seeing his brother in need, yet closing his heart against him.* In other words, the love that Christians are being exhorted to when they imitate the Lord in *laying down his life* is providing for the needs of their fellow Christians. The Lord himself said, *love one another as I have loved you* (Jn 15:12), and went on to refer to his death on the Cross as an example. In a similar way, the husband's love for his wife is to be a love that provides for her.

This raises the question of how what Ephesians says about Christ and the Church relates to what Revelation says about the marriage of the Lamb. In particular, when does Christ *present the Church to himself in splendor* (possibly: *in glory*)? Two answers are given. One is that he does so in the first stage of the new covenant. This would fit well with the possible reference to Baptism and to what Paul says in Second Corinthians 11:6. The other answer is that he purifies the Church from sin here and now so that she will be *clothed with . . . the righteous deeds of the saints* (Rev 19:8) and so be prepared for the Second Coming when he can present her to himself and take her as his wife. This fits better with the picture of the Church as a pure bride in the second step of the Jewish marriage ceremony.

It is the second development of the Christ-Church analogy in the passage that is of most significance to the New Testament interpretation of the Old Testament. In verse 31, Ephesians says, "*For this reason a man shall leave his father and mother and be joined to his wife, and the two shall become one flesh,*" quoting Genesis 2:24 after the creation of Eve. The Ephesians passage then goes on to say, *This mystery is a profound one, and I am saying that it refers to Christ and the Church.* In other words, the account of Adam and Eve in Genesis 2 has something to do with Christ and the Church.

Mystery in Pauline writings often has the meaning of something that was hidden and now has become known (e.g., Eph 3:8–10; Col 1:26). So to say that the phrase about the joining of man and woman (in this case Adam and Eve) in Genesis is a mystery is probably to say it has a meaning no one could see before the coming of Christ, because it is only revealed in him. Adam and Eve prefigured Christ and the Church. Just as Adam needed to have a wife to bring into existence the human race, so the new Adam, Christ, needed to have a wife, the Church, to bring into existence the new human race. He needed, as Ephesians 5:30 put it, members for his body.

Over the centuries, Christian teachers have developed this typological understanding of the Church. The Church was created out of Christ's side, so she shares his nature, but as his partner (Gen 2:21–22). She is his helper (Gen 2:18). He is the savior who offered himself in sacrifice that his people might be cleansed of their sins, but she, the Church, is the mother of all living (Gen 3:20), who, along with him, brings to birth the truly living. She is united with him even now and will be fully united with him in the age to come. In other words, the end brings the beginning to completion. What Adam and Eve began but failed to accomplish well, Christ and the Church will bring to full completion at the end.

CHAPTER TWELVE

The Stages of God's Plan: Development

Introduction to the chapter. We have been looking at the various stages of God's plan and have seen how human history, indeed creation itself, has changed. Now it is time to review the unfolding of the plan as a whole. We want to see it as a development through historical time. In each stage, God is about the same thing he has been about from before time began, and that he will be about after human history as we know it will be over—while in each stage he is about it in a different way.

In the beginning of the twelfth chapter of the book of Revelation, there is "a war in heaven," probably after the Resurrection and Ascension of Christ. As a result of the war, Satan and his angels are defeated, cast down from their heavenly position of power. Then there is a proclamation:

> And I heard a loud voice in heaven, saying, "Now the salvation and the power and the kingdom of our God and the rule [RSV: authority] of his Christ have come . . ." (Rev 12:10)

In one way the proclamation is strange. The kingdom of God has always been in place, and the rule of his Christ has been in place at least since his baptism and in a certain way since the light shone into the darkness on the first day of creation. But at this point in the book of Revelation the last battle is about to come when both *the kingdom of our God and the rule of his Christ* will finally triumph and usher in the final stage of God's plan.

The proclamation may be strange, but it is not false. It is a proclamation that could be made at the beginning of every stage of God's plan, in fact at the beginning of every action of God to advance his plan. It is a cry of triumph. It is an announcement of a new stage of God's advance. And yet, it is true in a different way for each stage of God's plan. The coming of God's kingdom is steady, stage-by-stage, but at each stage it is a different coming. God is coming to reign with and through his Christ in different ways in each stage.

THE DEVELOPMENT OF GOD'S PLAN

On the next page is a chart that reviews the stages of God's plan. It picks out the constant feature of God's purpose, but at the same time it indicates the change in the way that purpose is realized as God moves his plan forward. It summarizes truths we have already looked at, but puts them together in a way that allows us more easily to see the progress in the way his plan develops.

THE STAGES OF GOD'S PLAN: THE DEVELOPMENT

Stages	Presence	Communion	Wisdom	Life	Salvation
	---- *Constant purpose* ▽ *Changes in mode*	---- *Constant purpose* ▽ *Changes in mode*	---- *Constant purpose* ▽ *Changes in mode*	---- *Constant purpose* ▽ *Changes in mode*	---- *Constant purpose* ▽ *Changes in mode*
I **Sons of Adam**	Walking	Freedom	Command	Abundance	Security
Fallen	Exile	Primitive Worship	Law by Nature	Essential Provision	Some Protection
II **Sons of Noah**	Same	Same	Noahide Command-ments	Same	Primitive Justice
III **Patriarchs**	God's Visits	Same	Promise to Abraham	Prosperity of the Chosen Ones	Protection of "God's Anointed"
IV **Dispensation of Sinai**	In the Tent	Ceremony of the Law	Law of Moses	Covenant Prosperity	A Nation among Nations & War with Nations
V **Kingdom of Israel** **(Exile)**	In the Temple	Temple Worship	Same & Wisdom Teaching	Same	Same
VI **Dispensation of the Spirit**	Holy Spirit in Us	In Spirit and Truth	Teaching of Christ & the Apostles	Every Spiritual Blessing & Life of the Spirit	Diaspora Evangelism & Spiritual Warfare
VII **Glory**	God's Glory in All	Face to Face	Vision of God	Glorification	Reigning with Christ

Explanation of the Development Chart

We have already looked at the first part of the chart of the stages of God's plan (p. 133). It laid out the elements of each stage. This second part of the chart focuses on the development from stage to stage. It lists aspects of the relationship between God and man in which God's purpose is constant, but which change in the way God realizes that purpose as his plan unfolds. It therefore picks out different areas in which God relates to the human race in a somewhat different way as human history moves on, and it indicates the changes these areas undergo. The main areas are:

Presence: God is present to people in various ways through history, and the form of his presence makes different kinds of access to him possible.

Communion: God allows people to commune (interact) with him and respond to him to establish a good relationship (union) with him. This column lists the ways he allows people to draw near to him.

Wisdom: God teaches people, gives them insight about what he is like and wisdom and understanding about what he will do for them (his promises) and how they are to live (his commandments). His teaching becomes fuller and more developed as he moves human history on, and people's obedience to him can fulfill more of his purpose for how a human being should live.

Life: God gives people life by creating them and providing for them and then by re-creating them through the gift of the Spirit and bringing them to glory. The more they share in the life he gives, the more effectively they can live for him.

Salvation: God protects people from dangers and enemies in the course of history by helping them but also by fighting with them when they confront their enemies. Increasingly he allows them to advance his kingdom and put down the enemy.

"Salvation" is used by some more broadly to mean receiving the full blessing.

FROM STAGE TO STAGE

The Blessing. On the above chart, there are five columns. They pick out five aspects of the way God deals with human beings. He is present to humans to establish relationship with them. He allows them to interact with him to strengthen and grow in that relationship with him. He imparts his wisdom to them so that they can know him and understand how to live. He gives them life so that they prosper. He saves them and protects them from their enemies so that they can increasingly fulfill his call to them and bring creation to the glory he has for it. We could pick out other ways of describing God's work, but these five allow us to see the main features of its development.

In each area, God's work of fulfilling his purpose and providing life for those in relationship with him is constant, because his aim for human beings remains the same throughout all of history and he is at work to progressively bring it to pass. Yet in each area the form his work takes, the way he accomplishes his purpose, and the grace he gives does change.

God is always with us, and he rules over and provides for us and the rest of creation all of the time. If he did not, we would go out of existence. He is not only the Creator in the sense that he brought everything into existence; he is the Creator in the sense that he keeps on sustaining his creatures in existence. Moreover, he does not just keep creation in existence and leave it to its own devices. Rather, he guides it as it unfolds and develops. Its development is shot through with false starts and dead ends because of the independence he allows for it and the opposition he faces from the work of Satan, but in the end the whole of creation will arrive at the place God intends for it.

The critical path lies through the human race. God did not only create an inanimate universe to arrange in a stunningly beautiful pattern; he did not only create animate beings to evolve into a profusion of different designs; he also created beings who, like himself, could know the truth, choose the good, and cooperate in making a world of beauty. He created them as personal agents so that they would be in personal relationship with him as his sons and daughters and be his partners in developing creation. The human race was created to bring creation, at least material creation, to the full excellence that God intended for it.

The stages of the blessing. In the first stage of God's plan, God "walks" in paradise and enters into conversation with Adam and Eve. The image of his walking in the garden conveys a sense of immediate access to him on the part of the first human pair, although with a certain distance because he is not always with them. Perhaps when he walked in the garden he even adopted a physical form and was present to the first human beings as if he were a human being. He at least had a means to talk with them and interact with them on the earth and did so with paternal familiarity and regularity.

He had placed them in a garden of abundance, paradise, the garden of delights. They lacked for nothing. He had also given them a command, one that restricted their access to the tree that was the source of better life until they had attained the wisdom to use its power well, and by implication he was gradually instructing them in how to live. The account seems to describe the newly created human beings as child-like, without the mature human and spiritual development that was to come, but already with the potential for it.

The first human beings dwelt in complete security—until the serpent arrived. Despite the goodness of God's creation in which they lived, there was more to the universe than they realized, some of it not in good relationship with God. By their disobedience, they lost their protection. The result was a break in their relationship with God leading to exile and progressive distance from him. Created without any admixture of evil, they now had come to a fallen state.

With Noah and the Flood and the restoration after the Flood, God's relationship with the human race changed somewhat. God intervened to contain the fallenness of the human race. He clarified and enlarged their knowledge of the law by nature. He insisted that they establish some means of justice to restrain murder and other wrongdoing, protecting them in a basic way from one another. But they still ended up living in exile, without much if any communion with God and without very good relationships with one another.

During the first two stages—the era many human beings now live in—the story has been mixed. The human race has been able to continue. For the most part human beings have been able to find the essential provision they need to stay alive and reproduce. They have been able to protect themselves from the normal dangers of a disordered material creation with some degree of success. They have known basic morality, the law by nature, and if they followed it, they were protected from the worst of human and spiritual danger. If they did not, they were open to control by the kingdom of darkness and to judgment by God.

Some fallen human beings also knew enough to worship God, offering him sacrifice for what he had freely given them. That does not mean they were monotheists, but many at least seemed to recognize a high god. Most, however, in addition worshipped idols that were the work of their hands and the demons that were behind them. In general, they were distanced from God and his presence.

With the old covenant, God set out to rescue the human race from the condition it was in. He began by relating to a small group, the patriarchs: Abraham, Isaac, and Jacob, and their descendants. For the most part the conditions of their life were the same as those of the sons of Adam and Noah. But he began to intervene in a new way, promising a blessing to those he called to be part of his people.

God spoke to the patriarchs, but he also appeared to them in some kind of human form. He directed them more specifically in what he wanted them to do, and guided them, often without their knowing it. He made a covenant with them and their descendants, promising a good future. As a result of their relationship with him, they were especially protected from the worst danger, and they prospered in striking ways, increasing and multiplying even in the bondage of Egypt. In short, they lived the life of the rest of the human race in many respects, but something new had begun.

When the time came, God called Moses, and through him Aaron and others, to undertake the work of establishing a developed old covenant people of God. He gave them a law, the law of Moses, that taught them a way of life as a people that would allow them to live with him and to treat one another well. If they followed that law, they would prosper and be secure from their enemies.

God now began to dwell in the midst of his people in an ongoing and manifest way. This began with the pillar of cloud and fire that led them out of Egypt and through the wilderness to his mountain, Sinai. Then he instructed them to build a tabernacle modeled on his own throne room in heaven, and he was present in that tabernacle. From then on, he did not just speak to people from time to time or appear to them from time to time. He dwelt in their midst, and he allowed them a means to have regular access to him—although with some distance, due to their propensity to disobedience rooted in their sinfulness.

The completion of this stage of God's plan was the entry into the land of Canaan, led by Joshua. The people of Israel had become an army. They established a hegemony over the land and began the full possession of it. No longer did the pillar of cloud and fire appear, but they had the ark of the covenant in their midst. No longer did they need a special provision, food and drink from God. From now on they could live from the produce of the land.

The final stage of the old covenant, the establishment of the kingdom under David, was a development of the previous stage. The people of Israel moved from being a tribal confederation to being an organized kingdom. In so doing they were not only able to defend themselves more effectively from their enemies, but also to rule over them under David and Solomon. They also were enabled to develop a higher culture, a godly culture, passed on through the teaching of wisdom, especially practical wisdom.

More significant, David and Solomon built a temple on Mount Zion in the city of David to replace the old tabernacle. Now the presence of God could be found in a stable way in one location. He dwelt in the temple. His people could come to him there and find access to his presence, and he would teach them, answer their prayers, and help them.

With the fall of Jerusalem to the Babylonians, with the destruction of the temple, with the captivity of the Davidic king, and with the exile of the people from the land, a major change occurred. No longer was the old covenant order as we find it in the Pentateuch intact. The diaspora had begun.

In the diaspora, the law and study of the Scriptures became central, and the people gathered together in synagogues to worship God. There were various restorations in the land of Israel, including a rebuilding of the temple and the establishment of a kingdom—although not under a descendant of David. The restorations were incomplete in various ways, and the memory was carefully guarded that this was not the old covenant ideal. Nonetheless a new form of life for the covenant people of God was already in existence in its main lines.

About a thousand years after the third stage of the old covenant began, as the old covenant people became accustomed to living with God, both receiving his blessing and enduring the bad consequences of disobedience, the new covenant came into existence. God sent his only-begotten Son into the world who became a human being, Jesus of Nazareth. Through "becoming flesh," what Christian teachers later described as the hypostatic union, he dwelt in a human nature so fully that God lived on earth to bring people into union with himself. He then sent his Spirit to dwell in them in an ongoing way. His Apostles continued and developed his work, passing on this new life to those who believed in the Gospel.

With the redemption won by Christ and the gift of the Spirit, those who follow Christ have a new relationship with God. He dwells in them as in the temple. They do not need to go to the mountain in Jerusalem to worship him. In any place and at any time, they can enter into God's presence spiritually (Jn 4:23–24). They are able to enter into the true holy of holies, heaven itself, through the Spirit dwelling in them, and relate to God with a spiritual freedom and directness. As the Church of Christ, they have become a kingdom of priests and a holy nation who can offer spiritual sacrifices to him through Christ.

When people build a house, they instruct the architect about what they want the house to be like. He investigates the proposed building site and the circumstances where the house will be built, and then he builds a model. In one way the model is not like the house itself. It is just an assemblage of cardboard and wood or whatever material or medium is at hand. In another way it is like the house. From it you can see what the house will be like when it is done—making allowance for the change in medium. The relationship between the old covenant order and the new covenant order is something like that.

The medium for the new covenant is the Holy Spirit and life in him. The pattern or design of the two covenants is recognizably the same. We can learn from the old covenant what God is about. The material out of which the building is built, however, is different. As a consequence, we can relate to God through the new covenant order in a different way. In the new covenant, we now can live a truly spiritual life, enabled to relate to God with a new directness and freedom of access and enabled to live in the world with a greater power to live a life pleasing to him and to advance his kingdom.

In the last stage, when the Lord comes again, the way God is present to the human race will again change. It will be the same covenant, the new covenant. It will be the same Holy Spirit, still dwelling in people. The Lord himself will be the same, still glorified in his humanity and seated at the right hand of his Father on the heavenly throne, but the wraps will be taken off.

Sometimes we go into a garage to see a car that has been wrecked but not destroyed. If we arrive just before the body is repaired, the most important mechanisms may have been restored, so the car can be driven, but the car still does not look great. But then various body parts are replaced and the various protective coverings used in the repair are taken away, and what was there already is now visible so that it might even look like a brand new car. Something similar will be the case when the Lord comes again and reveals the work he has already done with the human race.

Instead of his presence being hidden, God's glory will shine forth and permeate all of creation. It will not only be in the inner nature of people, those who have experienced his redeeming grace, but it will transform and glorify their bodies. It will not only be in people, but it will be in all of creation, now fully united to him and fully expressing his will. All barrier, all resistance, will be gone and, as far as their created limitations allow, his sons and daughters will have full access to him. They will see him face to face, with no veil or distance. His glory will enter into them, and they will be able to share his reign over creation, bringing it to its full splendor.

READING THE OLD TESTAMENT HERE AND NOW

We are not yet in the age to come. We live in hope, but we wait for it in patience (Rom 8:24). Nor, if we are Christians, are we simply in the old covenant stage of God's plan, even if we are Jewish believers. We still read the writings of the old covenant, the Old Testament, but we read them as new covenant people.

As we have seen, many Christians do not read the Old Testament, and if they do, do not get much out of it. Many have learned to read it, but they read it for simply historical knowledge. Worse, many have learned to apply it to their lives as if they were old covenant people. In fact, many, even though they believe Christian doctrine, relate to God as if they were old covenant people.

A Christian is supposed to read the Old Testament in the light of the New. Most basically that means that we should read the Old Testament in the perspective of the further set of facts that the New Testament tells us about and the further understanding of the spiritual realities behind those facts. The New Testament tells us that God sent his Son into the world to become human, to die, to rise again, and to ascend to heaven. He came to pour the Spirit of God out upon those who believe in the good news of the coming of the kingdom through his work of redemption and who form part of his Church, the new covenant people of God. The New Testament also tells us that his Son will return again to judge the living and dead, to finally destroy the rule of Satan, and to bring a new heaven and a new earth.

We can understand the meaning of what is described in the Old Testament in a new way once we understand what it was leading to in God's plan. Abraham was not just an early nomad who handled himself with courage and perseverance in circumstances very different from those we live in. He was the father of those who believe, the man who received the promise of the blessing we now enjoy and who gives us an example of the faith that we needed to receive it and even now need to keep on living in it.

The Exodus from Egypt, the giving of the law on Mount Sinai, and the entry into of the land of Canaan was not just the story of a primitive set of tribes who escaped from oppression by the action of God, who were organized into a people, and who were enabled to lay claim to a land to live in. It is also the first version of our life as a new covenant people of God, and a pattern of how we need to live that life.

The story of David is not just the "rags to riches" story of a shepherd boy, then military chieftain, at the beginning of the first millennium BC who rose to become the head of a prosperous and strong empire in the Near East. He was the first king after God's own heart, who established the kingdom that Christ was able to transform into the beginning of the spiritual kingdom of God on earth. He was the inaugurator of the dynasty that our king, the Lord Jesus, belongs to.

There are many more examples to cite. The Old Testament leads to the new covenant both in its first and second stages. The more we read it in that light, the more value we can draw from it.

It also goes the other way—from the Old Testament to the New—and perhaps that is more important for our instruction. We cannot really understand, for instance, what it means that the

Church is the temple of the Holy Spirit if we do not understand what a temple is, and that we learn by reading the Old Testament. We cannot understand why it is important that Christ's death and Resurrection is an atoning sacrifice if we do not understand what an atoning sacrifice is, and that too we learn by reading the Old Testament. We cannot understand what a covenant is or a messiah, or what many of the things we encounter in the New Testament are without the Old Testament.

We may need to study to understand what is going on in the book of Leviticus or in much of the Pentateuch, not to mention the writings of the prophets. But once we do, we can reach a fuller understanding of the New Testament itself and what it teaches. Even more, we can read the New Testament itself more spiritually if we see it within the whole purpose and plan of God.

We can also read the Old Testament for personal spiritual growth, for prayer, and for entering more and more into the blessing of God. This applies especially to the parts of the Old Testament like the prayers in the book of Psalms and other places in the Old Testament or wisdom literature like the book of Proverbs or the prophecies that potentially apply to us personally. The tendency of modern Christians in reading such parts of the Old Testament is often to play first millennium Israelite—what would it have been like to have lived back then and have experienced life happening the way the early Israelites did. The result is usually that they then do not know how to apply very well what is said.

The key here is to understand the Old Testament typologically. When we read or pray a passage about the temple—for instance, an exhortation to go up to the temple or a desire to abide in the temple—we should not think mainly of the temple in Jerusalem that no longer exists, but rather of the Church and the assemblies of the Church or of heaven itself. When we read about the king and how he protects us or how his work might be thwarted, we should think mainly about Christ. We should do the same with all the other Old Testament realities that are no longer part of our life as new covenant people, but foreshadowed our life.

Modern Christians can especially have trouble when they encounter passages that seem to present earthly values that do not simply map onto Christian values. To apply them well, we need to understand such realities as types of New Testament realities, as they have been transposed into the kingdom of God and spiritualized. To do that we need to understand that:

- The life that God offers us is not just a long life before our earthly death, but eternal spiritual life in Christ.
- Our inheritance is not just a portion of the earth (the land of Canaan) that we possess and live from, but it is a portion of the kingdom of God.
- The enemies whose oppression we are freed from are not just pagan nations or personal enemies, but they are spirits and angelic forces from the kingdom of darkness.
- Our redemption and salvation are not just redemption and salvation from physical dangers and earthly enemies, but from sin and Satan.
- Access to the presence of God is not just in the temple in Jerusalem, but within us, through the indwelling of the Holy Spirit who brings us into the heavenly temple itself, and some day it will be even fuller when we see God "face to face."

If we look carefully at how the New Testament speaks about Old Testament realities like life, inheritance, enemies, redemption, salvation, and access, we find that they are most commonly understood in such a "spiritual" way, except when the New Testament is speaking about old covenant circumstances. A spiritual interpretation of Old Testament prayers, then, interprets their meaning the same way that the New Testament does—namely, as fulfilled in Christ.

Already—not yet. In our Christian experience of life, we find ourselves in two ages. In the Holy Spirit we have the first installment of our inheritance. We can already live the life of the age to come and experience the powers of the kingdom to come (Heb 6:5). We experience a better life here and now precisely because we have a more spiritual life but also because our heavenly Father provides for the earthly needs of the disciples of his Son (Mt 6:32–33).

Yet, at the same time, we still wait for the deliverance of our bodies and of all creation when we will possess the full inheritance and the earth will be fully transformed in the kingdom of God. Our earthly, material lives are now changed by the power of the Holy Spirit, but we are not fully transformed and therefore not fully able to enter into the kingdom of God (1 Cor 15:50).

Consequently, we experience lacks and needs due to the unredeemed state of the world around us, the incomplete state of our bodily transformation, and the fact that this unchanged earth is not our real home. We, in fact, sometimes experience even worse tribulation than we would otherwise because of the enmity of the kingdom of darkness against the true disciples of Christ (Jn 15:18–20). In short, we are only partway to the full blessing that is the complete fulfillment of God's promises.

Yet, if we read the Scripture spiritually, if we read the whole Bible and grasp the process of the stages of God's plan, we will see our lives in a life-giving perspective. We will be able to say with Paul,

> I consider that the sufferings of this present time are not worth comparing with the glory that is to be revealed to us. . . . For I am sure that neither death, nor life, nor angels, nor principalities, nor things present, nor things to come, nor powers, nor height, nor depth, nor anything else in all creation, will be able to separate us from the love of God in Christ Jesus our Lord. (Rom 8:18, 38–39)

And we will eagerly say with the concluding words of all the Scriptures,

> Amen. Come Lord Jesus! (Rev 22:20)

Glossaries of
Technical Terms

Some Terms for the Nature of the Scriptures

Scriptures An English word for "writings." "*The* Scriptures" is short for "the *sacred* Scriptures" or "the *holy* Scriptures," that is, the writings that come from God.

The Bible This word comes from a late Latin form (singular) of a Greek word meaning "the books" or "scrolls." The Bible, then, is The Book or perhaps The Book of Books, the most important book ever written. It is the writings in this book that are the word of God.

The word of God This phrase is a literal translation of a Hebrew phrase meaning "message from God" or "communication from God." In English we usually use "word" to mean a single word. The Hebrew equivalent could be used for a single word, a statement, or a lengthy discourse. The phrase "the word of God" therefore means a communication from God, and, applied to the Scriptures, means they are a communication from God.

Revelation Knowledge we have by a communication from God can be described as revelation. It is often contrasted with knowledge we have by "reason," in this sense the natural human ability to know and understand things. Scripture contains revelation, but not everything in it has been revealed.

Inspiration The Scriptures are described in Second Timothy 3:16–17 as "inspired" (RSV), literally "God-breathed." Words are sounds that we make by breathing, and to say that the Scriptures are inspired is to say that they are breathed out by God, that is, spoken by him. He is the source or author of them. There are other things inspired by God besides the Scriptures, for instance, all true prophecy.

Canon The books in the holy Scriptures make up the canon. "Canon" in Greek was the ruler or standard against which other things were measured, so the books in the Scriptures are the supreme standard for Christian teaching, against which everything else needs to be measured. Adjective form: **canonical**.

Apostolicity New Testament books have to be "apostolic"; that is, they either had to be written by an Apostle (like the letters of Paul) or written under his authority (like the Gospel of Luke) or at least somehow accepted as authoritatively from the Apostles by the early church. The canon of the New Testament has been closed since the death of the last Apostle (probably in the nineties of the first century), because Christ chose the Apostles to lay the foundations of the Church and so to establish how Christianity was to be handed on.

Interpretation Interpretation can be used simply to refer to translation from one language to another, but it also means helping someone to understand the meaning of what is said. If the text contains instructions for how to live or act, the process of interpretation is sometimes described as applying the text to our circumstances or as the **application** of the text.

Exegesis Clarifying or explaining what the text says, expounding the text.

Hermeneutics For some the principles or theory or method behind the exegesis; for some, exegesis tells us what the text meant *then*; hermeneutics tells us what the text means *now*, and therefore is about application, especially contemporary application. "Hermeneutics" comes from the Greek word for interpretation.

Sensus plenior This is the Latin term for the "fuller meaning"; that is, the meaning that is actually in the text, but which can only be grasped when the text is seen in relation to things that are not explicitly stated in the text.

Eisegesis Reading something into the text that is not there.

Tradition The handing on or transmission of teaching. In much of past times this usually was done orally, and so we often speak of **oral tradition**. We also use the word to describe the result of that transmission as we can discern it in various writings. In Christian theology it often refers to what was passed on by Christian teachers but is not explicitly written down in the New Testament.

Analogy of faith The principle that no true interpretation of a passage in the Scripture can be contrary to the overall expression of biblical faith.

The rule of faith The rule of faith is a confession of faith for public use, especially in baptismal preparation, and is a summary of basic Christian doctrine. It was expressed in textual form by the creeds (e.g., the Nicene Creed or the Apostolic Creed).

Some Terms for Parts or Versions of the Bible

The Torah A Hebrew word for the first five books of the Old Testament, sometimes called the Book(s) of Moses, often referred to as "the law" or "the teaching" because it contains the foundational instruction for the old covenant.

The Pentateuch The Anglicized Greek name for the first five books or scrolls of the Old Testament, because originally the Old Testament was written on scrolls, and lengthier books took up more than one scroll.

The Hexateuch The first six books of the Old Testament: the Pentateuch (or Torah) plus the book of Joshua.

Apocrypha The books that were not accepted into the Hebrew canon by the rabbis, but were part of the Septuagint and generally accepted as scriptural by the Christian Fathers. They are commonly referred to as the Apocrypha (of dubious or false canonicity) by many Protestant authors, while they are commonly referred to as **Deuterocanonical** (belonging to the second canon, the first canon being books in the Hebrew Bible) by Catholic and some Protestant authors.

The Septuagint The third to second century BC translation of the Old Testament into Greek, the version most commonly used by the first Greek-speaking Christians. The word means "seventy," the traditional number of the translators. It is commonly abbreviated by LXX, the Roman numeral for seventy.

The Vulgate The main Latin translation of the whole Bible, done primarily by Jerome in the fourth century. The word means the popularly used version. It is commonly abbreviated by Vg.

SOME TERMS FOR RABBINIC JEWISH WRITINGS

Rabbi A term of respect used for teachers (scribes). "The rabbis" (adjective form: **rabbinic** or **rabbinical**) is commonly used to refer to the Jewish teachers after the destruction of Jerusalem in AD 70, those who laid the foundations of subsequent Judaism and those who passed it on, although much of their teaching and approach existed earlier.

Tanakh A Hebrew acronym for what now might be more commonly called the Jewish or Hebrew Bible or, by Christians, the Old Testament. The letters stand for the **T**orah (the Pentateuch), the **N**ebiim (the prophets, and therefore the prophetic writings, including most of what we would call the historical books) and the **K**ethubim (the writings, mostly what we would call the wisdom literature).

Torah A word meaning "teaching" or "instruction," translated into Greek by *nómos*, a word commonly meaning "law"; as in the section above, a term for the first five books of the Bible, the Pentateuch; perhaps more importantly, the teaching contained in those books, the law (of Moses).

The Mishnah A legal codification of important practical matters treated in the law of Moses and interpreted (applied) by rabbinic scholars. It was compiled at the end of the second century (c. AD 200).

The Talmud A word meaning "learning," used to refer to a commentary on the Mishnah, adding further elaboration of the Jewish law. There were two Talmuds, the Babylonian Talmud, the primary one in use now, compiled by the end of the fourth century (c. 500 BC), and the Jerusalem or Palestinian Talmud, compiled in the third century (c. 375 BC).

The Gemara The commentary on the Mishnah found in the two Talmuds, so that the Talmuds contain the Mishnah and the Gemara.

Midrash A Rabbinic commentary on Old Testament books, either explaining the Old Testament text or explaining how to apply it to life.

Targum An Aramaic translation of the Bible (Old Testament), a loose translation or paraphrase, often involving explanation.

Some Literary Terms for Describing Biblical Style

Chiasmus Literally a crossing pattern, a literary device in which words or ideas are stated and then restated in inverted order, following an A-B-B-A pattern or an A-B-C-B-A pattern; alternate form: **chiasm**; adjective form: **chiastic**.

Palistrophe An extended chiasmus. The central element is the focus of the presentation. Most commonly the elements after the central element present developments in the corresponding elements that precede the central element. Adjective form: **palistrophic**.

Parataxis The linking together of clauses or phrases without conjunctions when those clauses or phrases are in an ordered relationship to one another. This is often done by simply using "and." "Parataxis" comes from the Greek and means, "placing next to one another." It can also be applied to larger units of text. Adjective form: **paratactic** or **paratactical**.

Hypotaxis The linking together of clauses or phrases by conjunctions that explicitly express their ordered relationship to one another (e.g., if . . . then, therefore, not only . . . but also, etc.).

"Hypotaxis" comes from the Greek and means, "to arrange under." Adjective form: **hypotactic** or **hypotactical**.

Inclusion The repetition at the end of a section of text of a sentence or phrase with which it began. We could say in English that the inclusion **frames** an account or a section of an account, indicating that it is to be read as a unit. Also referred to as **inclusio**, using the Latin term.

Parallelism When two or three lines are parallel, the second or third line restates the first line in different words or, more commonly, restates it in a way that develops its meaning or sometimes states a second thought that is to be seen as similar to or related to the first thought. Biblical poetry is written in parallelism.

Prolepsis The representation of a thing as existing before it actually does or did so, especially common in the Scripture when describing a future state God is working toward as if it were already present. Adjective form: **proleptic**.

A Note on Hebrew Style

The following is a selection from G. B. Caird, an English Scripture scholar who is describing biblical language and thought modes:[1]

> Hyperbole or overstatement is a figure of speech common to all languages. But among the Semitic peoples its frequent use arises out of a habitual cast of mind, which I have called absoluteness—a tendency to think in extremes without qualification, in black and white without intervening shades of grey. . . .
> Parataxis is 'the placing of propositions or clauses one

---

[1] G. B. Caird, *The Language and Imagery of the Bible* (Philadelphia: Westminster, 1980), 110, 117, 118, 121.

after another, without indicating by connecting words the relation between them' (OED). Its opposite is hypotaxis, the construction of a sentence with one main clause to which subsidiary ideas are linked in subordinate clauses introduced by conjunctions or prepositions which make the logical connections clear (relative, temporal, circumstantial, final, consecutive, causal, concessive, conditional, etc.). Classical Greek and Latin are severely hypotactical languages. Biblical Hebrew is paratactical. Even beginners cannot fail to be struck by this contrast. . . .

Just because parataxis happens to be a mark of colloquial speech in many languages, it does not follow that it is a proof of naiveté when we find it in literary Hebrew. It is simply not true that the Hebrew speaker was unable to express logical connections. What is true is that Hebrew idiom prefers the paratactical style in which such connections are implicit and taken for granted. . . .

Anyone who habitually employs parataxis in expression will be sure to think paratactically as well. He will set two ideas side by side and allow the one to qualify the other without bothering to spell out in detail the relation between them. . . .

Hyperbole and parataxis go readily in double harness. Like Lawrence's Arab, the ancient Hebrew "inherited superlatives by choice" and was "black and white not merely in clarity but in apposition."

Technical Notes

These comments are designed to provide background for the readers for whom some of the material in the book is new or for those who want to understand how certain topics are being approached.

Technical Note: Curses and Vengeance

The Bible is often translated with words that were used by earlier English translators, especially the King James Version translators, and still are in use in many translations. Many of those words, however, have gradually changed their meanings. As a result, when we read translations and also Christian writings that are drawn from the Bible, we may be reading "Bible language;" that is, language that is no longer commonly used in English except by those who read earlier translations of the Bible. This can lead to a wrong impression of what the Bible teaches about what God is like.

One area where this problem can be most serious is when God's actions are described by negative words, words that indicate God is acting in a way that human beings do not, or might not, want him to. "Curse" and "vengeance" are two "Bible language" words that can mislead us.

Curse. The Hebrew Scriptures often use words that are translated as "curse" in most English versions. The word "curse," however, has some wrong connotations for modern English speakers. To read the Scriptures, especially the Old Testament, we need to understand the word, although normally we would do better to not use the word ourselves unless it is clear that we are using it in a special (technical) sense.

"Curse" goes along with "bless" (e.g., Gen 12:3, Rom 12:14). Both are words that are only used in reference to God and his action in ways that can be disorienting to modern English speakers. God blesses. When he blesses, he does good things for people. People who receive the blessing of God prosper in some way (e.g., Gen 12:2; 17:6, 20). When human beings bless themselves, other human beings, or things, they ask God to act and bestow a blessing (Gen 27:4; 28:3; 32:26; 49:25; Ex 23:25). Or when they bless God himself, they thank him for the blessings he has bestowed (Judg 5:2; Ps 16:7; 34:1).

God also curses. When he curses, he does things that people do not want to have happen. People who are under a curse from God do not prosper in some way and often suffer (e.g., Gen 3:17; Deut 27:16, 19, etc.). When human beings curse other human beings or things, they ask God to act and bestow a curse—or remove a blessing—(e.g., 1 Sam 14:24; 26:19; Sir 4:5–6). When they curse God, they rebuke him for the ill he has done, or even wish him ill, as if that were possible (Job 2:5, 9).

In modern English, "curse" has the connotation of being an expression of hatred or malice. It is often even divorced from its connection with God, so when people curse someone or something, they often only intend to wish them ill. Perhaps the image that is called up most quickly in modern English-speakers when they hear the word "curse" is the image of a witch or sorcerer who curses someone out of malice (usually revenge) or for pay from someone who wants to injure someone else.

In Scripture, however, cursing does not necessarily come out of hatred or malice. When people "curse" in the right way they are asking God to inflict a just punishment or to deter people from some wrongdoing. An extensive example is in Deuteronomy 27:15–26, where the Israelite people curse those who do criminal actions, but the kind of actions that are often hidden and so cannot be handled by legitimate authorities. When they utter the curse, they are in effect petitioning God to punish crimes that are beyond human reach.

When God curses people or things, he does not do so because he ultimately wishes them harm. He does so to punish or discipline them. The curse often simply follows as the penal consequence of their actions, and usually he has warned them ahead of time of what would happen if they did such things. Often the curse is disciplinary, meant to lead to repentance and amendment of bad conduct. People persist in a bad condition only when they refuse to repent and turn to God.

Vengeance. We sometimes hear that the Old Testament God is a god of vengeance, and the New Testament God is a god of love. This is one of the sayings that make modern Christians inclined to drop the Old Testament, or at least pay little attention to it. It is, however, a false statement. God is the same in both Testaments, and the Old Testament proclaims throughout that God is a god of "steadfast love and faithfulness."

God is, however, also "a God of vengeance" (Ps 94:1). He is a god of vengeance from beginning to end. Even at the end of the New Testament book of Revelation we read about God's vengeance (Rev 19:2). He can be a god of steadfast love and faithfulness and a god of vengeance at the same time, not to mention patience, kindness, wrath, and other positive or negative character traits. How his character is described all depends on what he is dealing with.

To begin to understand the way in which God is a god of vengeance, we need to understand the meaning of "vengeance" in the Scripture. It is not the same as "revenge" in ordinary English, although those who write on the subject very often confuse the two. "Revenge" in English primarily refers to those actions by which a first person or group "gets back at" a second person or group for what they have done that the first person or group regards as injuring them or sometimes that simply angers them. It is rooted in a desire to hurt or put down other people as personal retribution. It may sometimes be justified: those suffering people's revenge may deserve to suffer the consequences of what they have done. It is, however, often unjustified, simply an expression of human selfishness or pride and desire for personal victory. When unjustified, it is considered a sin or sinful orientation by most Christian teachers.

Vengeance, in the scriptural sense, is different than revenge, although they could overlap in meaning.[2] We can see this most clearly by looking at some passages in the New Testament, where the Greek words that translate the Hebrew words most commonly translated by "vengeance" or "avenge" are used. First of all, "vengeance" is used to describe what human governmental authorities do when they punish wrongdoing. First Peter 2:4 holds that governors are sent by God to punish those who do wrong and to praise those who do right, and the word "punish" is an alternate translation for "vengeance." Romans 13:4 says something similar when it says rulers serve God by "avenging" (punishing) wrongdoing. "Vengeance" then is one of the biblical language words that describe the penalization of criminals (wrongdoers) by lawful authorities.

Sometimes when lawful authorities execute vengeance, they are upholding one party in a conflict and penalizing the other. Most commonly, the English biblical translations use the word "vindicate" to describe what an authority does in regard to the party upheld. We can see this in the parable of the unjust judge, where the poor widow asks the judge to "vindicate me against my adversary" (Lk 18:3). He

---

[2] "Vengeance and revenge are ideas that would appear to have no good ethical validity whether coming from God or man. But such is not the case when the use of this root is properly understood in its OT setting and NT application. . . . In terms of the presuppositions of some modern 'Christian' theologies, such a God of vengeance will be labeled unchristian and unethical. Understood in the full orb of biblical revelation, balanced as it is by the mercy of God, divine vengeance is seen to be a necessary aspect of the history of redemption." R. Laird Harris, Gleason L. Archer, Jr., Bruce K. Waltke, eds., "1413 Mqn (*naqam*)" in *The Theological Wordbook of the Old Testament*, 2 vols. (Chicago: Moody Press, 1980).

is described as unjust not because he failed to punish the widow, but because he failed to vindicate (literally: avenge) the widow against her adversary. "Vengeance" ("vindication"), then, can be a kind of deliverance of the innocent or oppressed.

The nature of vengeance as lawful penalization is found in the Old Testament as well. In Exodus 21:20, there is a law that lays down that "when a man strikes his slave, male or female, with a rod and the slave dies under his hand, he shall be punished [literally: have vengeance taken upon him]." Modern readers misunderstand this when they assume that slavery is simply oppression, and not an institution that provides some protection for the slave (worker), but we see here a law that some governmental authority should execute vengeance on the slave's master for mistreating his slave.

Vengeance is not always a matter of governmental authorities exercising their responsibility. We read in Acts 7:24 about Moses getting in trouble with the Egyptian authorities. It says, "And seeing one of them [a Hebrew] being wronged, he defended the oppressed man and avenged him by striking the Egyptian." This was not a case of taking personal revenge on the Egyptian. Moses judged that the Hebrew was being oppressed and he should avenge him (in this case killing the Egyptian and so saving the Hebrew from being a victim of wrongdoing).

We could raise the question of whether Moses was justified in "taking the law into his own hands." That would get us into a discussion that would take us far afield. But we can at least see that the Bible sometimes uses "vengeance" or "avenge" to describe an action that was not within the jurisdiction of a lawful governmental authority, but did concern a matter of right and wrong. The basis for such an action is indicated in Genesis 9:5–6, where the word group "vengeance (nqm)" is not used, but where God requires retribution for murder. In a primitive society without a legal system, this obligation could be fulfilled by anyone, but was primarily expected to be fulfilled by the next of kin (the "redeemer" or "avenger").

One of the more common uses of the words for vengeance in the Old Testament is for what a person or a nation does in regard to its enemies. When the nation of Israel, for instance, wins a battle or war against an enemy nation, they are described as executing vengeance on that nation (Num 31:2–3; Josh 10:13; Jer 50:15). They are, however, acting in a lawless situation, that is, a situation in which there is no authority over the two nations with which one party can initiate a legal action. In such a case, vengeance is a matter of defending oneself. There is also, of course, a tendency to assume that when we have won a fight, we were justified in the first place, and only righting a wrong. But often we actually were justified in our action, and we can see that God sometimes gave the victory because the cause was just.

Of course, the line between vengeance and revenge can be impossible to draw, as we see in our own society and culture. Sometimes governmental authorities claim that they are exercising vengeance (rightful penalization of wrongdoing) but are actually using their position to take revenge on those who have injured them. Sometimes, the two are not mutually exclusive. Governmental authorities may be rightfully exercising their authority, but also experiencing the satisfaction of revenge on their enemies at the same time. Mixed motives are a normal part of human life.

There is a further complication in understanding vengeance (punishment). At times authorities are responsible to uphold their own position and the respect due to it. If a child is disrespectful, a father is responsible to correct or punish the child. If he lets his own or his wife's authority be disrespected, he is harming the family and often performing a disservice to his child who needs to learn proper respect. A king or president is responsible to punish treason, both to uphold his own position and to uphold the good order of the country. A judge is responsible not to allow contempt of court. And God himself acts in such a way. When those in authority uphold their own authority and do not allow disrespect, it can seem to those who do not understand such matters that the authorities are acting out of personal interest, but in fact they are responsible to do so, whether they want to or not.

The Scriptures very often describe God as a god who executes vengeance (not a revengeful god). He is not a legitimate human authority, but something much greater. As the one who created and sustains all things, he is the rightful authority over human authority, in fact over the universe as a whole. The psalm that calls God a god of vengeance also describes him as *the judge of the whole earth* (Ps 94:2).

For most of human history and today as well, the sphere of legitimate authority is limited. Most people would see the father or the parents in a family as having legitimate authority. Where there is a nation with good order, there are legitimate authorities who have the legal right and responsibility to punish wrongdoing. But there are many times in the history of most nations when that order has broken down, and there has yet to be a time when there is effective legitimate human authority between nations. There is nonetheless a rightful authority over all human affairs, and that authority is God.

The Scriptures describe God acting to take vengeance. When we have enough information about the situations in which he is acting, it seems that he exercises, or should exercise, his authority in situations where the human authority has broken down or is not effective (1 Thess 4:6) or where there is no human authority, as between a governor or government and its subjects (1 Sam 24:12; Jer 11:20; Rom 12:19) or between nations. In such cases he acts to vindicate the innocent and punish the wrongdoer. He especially does this in cases when his people are oppressed or being persecuted (Jer 20:15, 28; Rev 19:2; Rom 19:12).

It is likely that God's action of taking vengeance in many Old Testament passages and a few New Testament passages is connected to his covenant relationship with his people. As a covenantal relative, he is responsible to redeem and avenge his people when they are being unjustly oppressed or when they have been attacked unjustly. This responsibility is behind the New Testament teaching that Christians are not supposed to fight back when persecuted but to rely on God to avenge his people (Rom 12:19; Rev 19:2; cf. Deut 32:35; Ps 79:10)—but who also judges, i.e., takes vengeance on or punishes, his own people when they break the covenant (Heb 10:30; 1 Thess 4:6; Lev 26:25).

We may not always be able to understand how God governs the universe in a right way. We may not be able to understand why the various things he is described as doing in the Scripture are justified. But many of us have had the experience of seeing our fathers punish a brother of ours and not seeing it as justified, but also seeing them fail to punish a brother of ours when we are sure he deserves it. Later on when we grow up and have more experience of life (especially when we have children of our own to keep in order and to raise well), we see that most often our fathers were more far-seeing than we were at the time.

In our culture in general, and in contemporary Christian culture specifically, we see a certain softness toward wrongdoers, perhaps a maternal softness. But we also see and experience a stubborn conviction that it is outrageous to leave serious, oppressive wrongdoing unpunished.[3] This is the conviction that comes to expression in Psalm 94, which appreciates the fact that God is a god of vengeance, and sees it as an expression of his love for those who are oppressed (verses 16–18). Many of us wonder why he holds off for so long when we see what is going on around us:

> O LORD, thou God of vengeance,
> > thou God of vengeance, shine forth!
> Rise up, O judge of the earth;
> > render to the proud their deserts!
> O LORD, how long shall the wicked,
> > how long shall the wicked exult?
> They pour out their arrogant words,
> > they boast, all the evildoers.
> They crush thy people, O LORD,
> > and afflict thy heritage.
> They slay the widow and the sojourner,
> > and murder the fatherless;

---

[3] On this see C. S. Lewis, "The Humanitarian Theory of Punishment" in *God in the Dock* (Grand Rapids, MI: Eerdmans, 1970).

and they say, "The LORD does not see;
  the God of Jacob does not perceive." (Ps 94:1–7)

Judicial terminology. We very often take the scriptural words connected to "curse" and "vengeance" the wrong way because they are
most commonly judicial terms, that is, terms that have to do with
the upholding of justice. We may see them as expressions of human
malice or negative emotion and therefore wrong, so when God curses and executes vengeance we think he is doing something wrong.
Behind that, however, is a truth about the Scriptures, both Old and
New Testaments, that makes us misread much of the Scriptures.
Many times in Scripture, personal relational matters are understood
in judicial terms, when we would consider them primarily in feeling
terms.

We could take the example of divorce. If two people get divorced
now, we primarily focus on their personal motivation. One or the
other or both found their partner incompatible, or perhaps they
were resentful about how they had been treated or neglected, or
perhaps they did not "love" one another anymore. In the Scripture,
however, marriage was understood as a covenant relationship, and
ending a marriage was ending a covenant commitment. The primary
question in regard to divorce was whether an obligation was being
kept or broken. It did not matter nearly as much whether one partner got no subjective satisfaction from the relationship as whether
the obligations of the commitment were upheld or not.

Vengeance in the scriptural sense, then, is primarily a legal matter. Taking vengeance could be justified or not justified. But it is
supposed to be justified or else refrained from. It is not in principle
the same thing as personal revenge, however much the two may be
mixed together or however difficult it may be to determine which is
in play. At least when God is the agent, we can rely on the fact that he
is about establishing justice, and he is above taking merely personal
revenge. He has the responsibility to uphold the good order of the
universe.

Anger and wrath. Much the same things could be said about these words that is said about vengeance. These are words that in English refer to emotions. To speak of God's emotions, however, is to speak analogously of a being who transcends human emotions. When the Scriptures speak about the anger of God or the wrath of God, they are most definitely not saying that he just lost his temper or that he was having a temper tantrum. They are rather speaking about God responding to human actions the way a human being might who was perfectly just, had judged that something had been done that was seriously wrong, and was acting to right the wrong, that is, to punish it and restore the good order of the universe.[4]

TECHNICAL NOTE: GENEALOGIES

A bane of new readers of the Bible in our day are the genealogies that are sprinkled throughout it. They usually contain lists of names that seem unpronounceable, and they go on and on without seeming to make a point. They represent a style of writing that ancient readers thought elevated a text, but that modern readers would be happy to compress into a quick-moving summary sentence or two. Nonetheless they fulfill some important functions.

Stylistically, genealogies are connectors. They connect narratives of human events, and they were especially used to indicate lengthy periods of human history. When we pay attention to them, we can usually see an important historical link. However, they present us with some challenges of interpretation.

First, genealogies do not intend to list every actual link in a chain of descent the way a modern genealogy would do. Each step in a scriptural genealogy says that so-and-so "fathered" ("begat" in King James English) someone else. We would naturally understand that he was the immediate father of the person or people listed afterwards. Often, however, we can see that is not the case. For in-

---

[4]   The questions connected to the way the Scriptures speak about God as if he were a human being are treated more fully in the section "5. Anthropomorphism" in part II.

stance, Genesis 46:16–18 speaks of the "children born to Jacob by Zilpah" and includes not just their sons, but their grandsons and great-grandsons as well. To use a New Testament example, the genealogy of Christ in Matthew 1 gives us fourteen generations from Abraham to David, fourteen from David to the exile, and fourteen from the exile to Christ. Other scriptural genealogies and other information give us more links in the record. Chronological considerations also lead us to believe that many of the genealogies have been shortened.

Second, the numbers in the genealogies often seem to be symbolic. Why did the three steps in the genealogy of Christ only have fourteen generations and exactly fourteen generations? We discussed the reason in chapter 9 (p. 269), but clearly the numbers are chosen to make a point. The same could be said about the genealogies in Genesis 5 (from Adam to Noah) and Genesis 11:12–26 (from Noah to Abraham), which both contain ten generations.

Something similar could be said about the genealogy in Genesis 10, the genealogy of the sons of Noah, a genealogy of all the nations on the earth, or, to be more precise, of the known earth at that time. The number of the nations is seventy, a figure in the Hebrew Scriptures that stands for a sizable and complete contingent. According to many scholars, the table of nations does not indicate biological or ethnic descent, but political or geographical relationship.[5] Seventy was understood to be the symbolic number of the Gentile nations in the world, all the descendants of Noah (and Adam).

To understand the genealogies in Genesis, we also have to look at their literary function. The major genealogies mark off one narrative unit from another. The genealogy in Genesis 5 marks off the creation and Fall from the judgment of the Flood, and indicates a transition from one stage of God's plan to another. The genealogy in Genesis 11 marks off the account of Noah and his sons from the account of Abraham and the patriarchs. These genealogies look forward and backward at the same time. The genealogy in Matthew

---

[5] See "Genealogy" in *The Dictionary for Theological Interpretation of the Bible*, ed. Kevin J. Vanhoozer (Grand Rapids, MI: Baker Academic, 2005), hereafter cited as *DTIB*.

functions in a similar way. It does not mark off different narrative units in the Gospel book, but situates the life of Christ in sequence with the preceding salvation history.[6]

In contrast, the minor genealogies in Genesis, that of Cain in Genesis 4, that of the descendants of Nahor in Genesis 22, that of Ishmael in Genesis 25, and that of the descendants of Esau in chapter 37, have a different function. They seem to wind up the presence of the lines of Cain, Nahor, Ishmael, and Esau in the account of establishing of the old covenant people of God. They no longer formed part of those who were the possessors of the promised blessing.

Something similar seems to be true of the table of nations in Genesis 10, which, along with the story of the tower of Babel, winds up the sections of Genesis that deal with the human race as a whole before bringing the narrative to Abraham, the father of the people of God. The result of the Genesis 10 genealogy, then, is a picture of the whole known human race, concluding the chapters on human history before focusing on the history of the chosen people.

In one way genealogies in Scripture are like the charts of dynasties in modern history books, which let us see how individual kings or queens are located in families. In another way they are very different. They are not written to let us read off the actual historical family relationships historical step by historical step. Rather they are written to show us significant links in the development of God's plan. We may have lost the key to understanding why various items

---

[6] Genesis 2:4a uses the Hebrew word for a genealogy (*toledoth*), in the RSV often translated "generations of" or sometimes "descendants of." As a consequence, many scholars see this verse as the beginning of Genesis 2, because most of the genealogies in Genesis are titled by "these are the generations of" (Noah, the sons of Noah, etc.) and then followed by the genealogy. However, such a view of Genesis 2:4a makes no sense in context. The verse is not followed by a list of the generations. It is followed by the story of Adam and Eve. Moreover, it is "the generations of the heavens and the earth when they were created," not "the generations of Adam," which is found in 5:1ff. The list of the elements of the creation of heaven and earth are found in Genesis 1, not in subsequent chapters. The use of the word "genealogy" in Genesis 2a, then, probably has the unique position of being a conclusion to a list, not a title beginning a list, and it makes Genesis 2:4 into a transitional verse concluding Genesis 1, introducing Genesis 2, and linking the two by a chiastic structure (cf. footnote 2, p. 19).

are the way they are. We usually, however, can understand the nature of the link they are representing.

TECHNICAL NOTE: "CHIASTIC" PATTERNS

The literary styles we find in the Hebrew Bible are often significantly different from the literary styles we now use, different enough that they can provide an obstacle for understanding what various writings in the Bible are trying to convey. Among the various literary devices we almost never use is the chiastic pattern. If we can recognize and understand it, we can see much more about many biblical texts.

We often use an outline form when we want to order a paragraph or text so that we clearly move from one point to another. An outline form that orders the material logically makes use of the following pattern, sometimes designated as an A-B-C pattern:

A. Point 1
1. Sub-point 1
2. Sub-point 2
B. Point 2
1. Sub-point 1
2. Sub-point 2
C. Point 3
Etc.

Narratives often follow a similar pattern, except that they follow a temporal sequence:

A. Event 1
1. Step 1
2. Step 2
B. Event 2
1. Step 1

2. Step 2
C. Event 3
Etc.

A **chiastic pattern,** by contrast, follows an A-B-C-B-A pattern, sometimes called an odd chiastic pattern (because of the odd number of elements—five in this case) or it follows an A-B-B-A pattern, sometimes called an even chiastic pattern (because of the even number of elements—four in this case). In a chiastic pattern, words or ideas are stated and then restated in inverted order. A text that follows this pattern can be referred to as containing a **chiasmus** or **chiasm**. In what follows, we will mainly look at the A-B-C-B-A pattern, although the A-B-B-A pattern is also common.

The account of Noah and the Flood illustrates the chiastic pattern. In this case, there are somewhat clear markers in the text of the existence of the chiastic pattern:

> 7 days of waiting for the Flood (7:4)
> > 7 days of waiting for the Flood (7:10)
> > > 40 days of Flood (7:17a)
> > > > 150 days of water triumphing (7:24)
> > > > 150 days of water waning (8:3)
> > > 40 days' wait (8:6)
> > 7 days' wait (8:10)
> 7 days' wait (8:12)

> The start in the 600th year (7:11–12)
> The end in the 601st year (8:13–14)

The way the chiastic pattern forms the text is sketched in the following box:

THE STRUCTURE OF GENESIS 6–9

The state of the human race (6:1–8)

1. Corruption and judgment (6:9–22)

    2. Entering the ark (7:1–10)

        3. The rising flood (7:11–24) – 7 and 40 and 150 days

            4. God remembered Noah (8:1)

        5. The receding flood (8:1–14) – 150 and 40 and 7 days

    6. Leaving the ark (8:15–19)

7. God's promise (8:20–22)

Re-population and covenant (9:1–19)
The curse on sexual disorder (9:20–28)

In Genesis 6–9, there are 7 units that are descriptive of the Flood, and they are framed by a description of the state of the human race and then by a description of the re-created human race. Some therefore would say there are 9 units. The units are put together in inverted order, so that the rising and receding Flood correspond to one another (each sub-unit also corresponding to one another); entering and leaving the ark correspond to one another; and judgment and promise correspond to one another. In this type of chiasm, there is a central unit: "God remembers Noah."

"Remember" here is a Hebraic idiom for "being conscious of and acting on the basis of." Noah is a blameless man that God has chosen to renew the human race. Because of his relationship to Noah, God acts in a certain way in regard to the judgment on human wickedness.

The chiastic pattern usually makes a point. The central unit in the ABCBA pattern indicates the event that allowed the first half of the pattern to be reversed: "God remembered Noah." We can see from the chart above that the Flood was a response to the state of the human race. We can also see that it was Noah and his obedience to God that allowed the human race to be rescued and renewed. In other words, Noah plays the chief role in undoing the judgment, step by step, so there could be a new beginning.

The chart also allows us to see that sometimes there is a further point appended to the chiasm. In this case, many hold that the curse on sexual disorder is a response to the first part of the chiasm (6:1–4). Others hold that the whole account is framed by the notices of the life of Noah in 5:32 and 9:28–29. The chart of the account of Noah and the Flood is enough to let us see the basic elements of a chiastic pattern, even if we might also see it as nested in further elements.

It is helpful here to also note that the account of the Flood is written in a **paratactic** style, like much of the rest of the Scriptures. A **parataxis** puts together clauses or phrases without conjunctions when those are in an ordered relationship, or, commonly, simply uses an "and" to link them. We are supposed to understand the relationship by noticing the juxtaposition.

For instance, Genesis 8:1 says, *but God remembered Noah and all the beasts and all the cattle that were with him in the ark. And God made a wind blow over the earth, and the waters subsided.* We should see right away that the subsiding of the waters is due to God's "remembrance" of Noah. Few modern people would write the account this way. They would be more likely to say, "God remembered Noah . . . therefore he made a wind blow." or "Because God remembered Noah . . . he made a wind blow." In so doing we explicitly state the nature of the relationship.

In addition, it is helpful to note that there are other markers in the text that show us the existence of the chiastic pattern. The chronological markers indicate a chiastic relationship among the elements—markers to those who are paying attention and expect indicators of time to have symbolic meaning, as the original audience no doubt would have.

The chiastic pattern is common in the Scriptures. Genesis 2–3 is most likely in a chiastic pattern, although it is not as explicitly indicated in the text as it is in Genesis 6–9. The center of the chiasm is the act of disobedience, the eating of the fruit that expressed the desire for some kind of equality with God. Beforehand, there is an account of the blessings that God gave to the human race. After, in inverted order, are the "curses," the spoiling of the blessings that God had given, because of human disobedience. The end of the account mirrors the beginning, with the loss of paradise and the tree of life mirroring their being given at the beginning.

It is helpful to note that Genesis 1 is not written in a chiastic pattern. The account of the first "week" of creation is sequential. The relationship of the elements is not inverted, and the chapter can be outlined using the form that we are most familiar with.

As we continue, we will note other instances of the chiastic pattern, especially when the pattern makes clear what the text is trying to convey but is not developing the meaning explicitly, in a way that allows modern readers to see it clearly.

TECHNICAL NOTE: THE FOUR SENSES OF SCRIPTURE

Christian writers in the Western or Latin theological tradition have often spoken of the "spiritual senses" or the "four senses" of Scripture.[7] The word "sense" here is the same as "meaning," so occasionally we come across the phrase "the spiritual meaning(s)" of Scripture. When we speak about a spiritual sense or meaning of Scripture we are considering the text of the Scripture as signifying spiritual realities or truths that go beyond something plainly intended by the original sense or meaning of the words. "Spiritual" is used this way in Revelation 11:17 (and probably in Rom 2:25–29).

If we want to read many traditional Christian writings on Scripture, we should be familiar with the four senses—the historical (often called the literal) and the further spiritual senses (allegorical, anagogical, and tropological). We should also be familiar with some of the synonyms of these words. However, since most of us also read modern scholarly works and Christian teaching, and since these works use a different terminology, we need as well to be familiar with the modern terminology and how it relates to the traditional terminology. As we have seen in chapter 3, when modern writers speak about the spiritual senses of Scripture, they commonly speak in terms of "types," "antitypes," and "typology." Typology covers much the same things as the spiritual senses in the traditional terminology.

First, the main contrast in the four senses is between "historical" or "literal" on the one hand and "spiritual" on the other. The historical sense is the meaning of a text that refers to something that happened or existed in the past, much as things around us exist. We can read about the man David or the temple in the city of Jerusalem in various Old and New Testament writings, and they have an historical sense. If we could go back in time, we could see David, the temple, and Jerusalem in a particular time and place.

---

[7]   For Origen's use of this approach, see Henri Crouzel, *Origen* (Edinburgh: T&T Clark, 1989), chap. 4. For an accessible summary of Henri de Lubac's influential approach to spiritual exegesis, see Marcellino D'Ambrosio, "De Lubac's Hermeneutics of Tradition," *Letter and Spirit* 1 (2005): 147–157.

The historical sense is also spoken about as the literal sense. For most modern authors to say that something should be understood literally is to say that it is not understood with a figurative meaning or a literary meaning.[8] Traditionally, however, it was also used to say that something is not to be understood "spiritually" or only spiritually. "Literal" is contrasted to "spiritual" by the Apostle Paul in Romans 2:29 when he is talking about circumcision in the flesh (the literal sense, that is, what the original writing refers to) and contrasting it to circumcision of the heart (the spiritual sense).

Although some modern writers would contrast the literal sense of words with an analogical usage of them, most would not. Using an analogical or extended sense is generally (and correctly) considered to be a literal usage. When the Scriptures say that God is "on high," they do not mean that he is spatially above everything in creation— since space is an aspect of material creation. Rather, they are using a scriptural idiom to speak about God's transcendence, a word that had not been invented when most of the Old Testament was written. For them an analogical use of language about physical height was one way they could literally speak about the nature of God's relation to the material world.

Patristic and Medieval writers commonly divided the spiritual sense into three classes. The first was the allegorical sense. This refers to the way in which old covenant realities prefigured new covenant realities. To say that the Church of Christ is a spiritual temple, a temple of the Holy Spirit (Eph 3:21–22), is to make an allegorical interpretation. Paul used the word "allegory" this way in Galatians 4:24.

As we saw in footnote 2, p. 90, the word "allegory" or "allegorical" is often used in a different and narrower sense by many modern authors. They simply understand it as referring to the kind of literary form we find in *Pilgrim's Progress* or similar works where the elements of the narrative are deliberately written by the author to

---

[8] The term "literal" is treated more fully in the methodological discussions "2. Scriptural Interpretation and Literary Genre" and "6. Analogical Discourse." For the difference between modern and patristic usages of "figurative," see especially footnote 1, p. 480.

represent entities like virtues or emotions. Ancient authors, on the other hand, used "allegory" in a very broad sense. Any time a word or sentence was used with a semantic meaning different than its standard or normal sense, that could be described as "allegorizing." Figurative meanings like metaphor or hyperbole could therefore be considered "allegorical" in meaning, in contrast to modern usage. When we refer to or think about the allegorical sense of the four senses, it functions as a technical term in relation to the other senses and therefore has a specified meaning, but one that is not the same as the modern use of "allegory."

The second spiritual sense was the anagogical sense. This refers to the way in which old covenant realities or even new covenant realities prefigured the realities of the age to come after the Second Coming. The temple in Jerusalem prefigured the New Jerusalem that will come down from heaven at the end of time. Chapters 21 and 22 of the book of Revelation contain many old covenant references applied in an anagogical sense.

The third spiritual sense was the tropological. This is sometimes described as the moral sense. This refers to the way that old covenant events can be used to instruct new covenant people in how to live. We have seen this sense being used in First Corinthians 10:1–13, where Paul instructs his Christian community about obedience to God by using the events of the Exodus (see the section on typology in chapter 3).

There are two other terms that are helpful to note if we read more traditional writings, namely "mystical" and "mysteries." Spiritual interpretations of Old Testament passages are sometimes described as mystical interpretations or as containing a mystery. The root of both words refers to something hidden or secret. If, in Greek, we want to tell someone to say a prayer so no one else hears it, we tell them to say it "*mustikôs*," i.e., quietly. To say that a spiritual interpretation is mystical, then, is not to say that you need a special spiritual experience to understand it but to say that its meaning was hidden until the time of Christ and the preaching of the Gospel. Also, if we want to refer to the hidden meaning of something, we can describe it as a mystery (probably the meaning in Eph 5:32, see p. 371). Both "mystery" and "mystical" have other uses in Christian theology, for the most part involving extended meanings.

Selection from John Cassian

John Cassian (died ~AD 430), a patristic writer from southern France (Gaul) who was trained in the monastic life in Palestine and Egypt, seems to have been the first one to refer to the four senses of Scripture in the form that became classical.[9] He drew what he said from earlier Fathers. The following selection is drawn from his *Conferences* XIV (Post Nicene Fathers translation):

> But to return to the explanation of the knowledge from which our discourse took its rise. Thus, as we said above, *practical* knowledge is distributed among many subjects and interests, but *theoretical* is divided into two parts, i.e., the historical interpretation and the spiritual sense. Whence also Solomon, when he had summed up the manifold grace of the Church, added: "for all who are with her are clothed with double garments."[10]
>
> But of *spiritual knowledge* there are three kinds, tropological, allegorical, anagogical, of which we read as follows in Proverbs: "But do you describe these things to yourself in three ways according to the largeness of your heart."[11]
>
> And so the *history* embraces the knowledge of things past and visible, as it is repeated in this way by the Apostle: "For it is written that Abraham had two sons, the one by a bondwoman, the other by a free: but he who was of the bondwoman was born after the flesh, but he who was of the free was by promise."
>
> But to the *allegory* belongs what follows, for what actu-

---

[9] Origen had a threefold division.

[10] Prov 31:21 (LXX).

[11] Prov 22:20 (LXX).

ally happened is said to have prefigured the form of some mystery: "For these," says he, "are the two covenants, the one from Mount Sinai, bearing children into bondage, which is Hagar. For Sinai is a mountain in Arabia, which is compared to Jerusalem which now is, and is in bondage with her children."

But the *anagogical* sense rises from spiritual mysteries even to still more sublime and sacred secrets of heaven, and is subjoined by the Apostle in these words: "But Jerusalem which is above is free, which is the mother of us. For it is written, Rejoice, barren one who bears not, break forth and cry, you that travails not, for many are the children of the desolate more than of her that hath an husband."[12]

The *tropological* sense is the moral explanation which has to do with improvement of life and practical teaching, as if we were to understand by these two covenants practical and theoretical instruction, or at any rate as if we were to want to take Jerusalem or Zion as the soul of man, according to this: "Praise the Lord, O Jerusalem; praise thy God, O Zion."[13]

And so these our previously mentioned figures coalesce, if we desire, in one subject, so that one and the same Jerusalem can be taken in four senses: historically, as the city of the Jews; allegorically as the Church of Christ; anagogically as the heavenly city of God "which is the mother of us all"; tropologically, as the soul of man, which is frequently subject to praise or blame from the Lord under this title.

---

[12] Gal 4:26–27.
[13] Ps 147:12.

Technical Note: Numerology, the Number Seven

Most readers of the Scriptures, even today, notice the special role of numbers in the various books—without always being able to see why they are significant. Creation happens in seven days, and feasts are celebrated for seven days. There are ten commandments, ten plagues and tithes of 10% (tenth-ing). There are twelve tribes of Israel and twelve Apostles. Other numbers recur regularly: forty, seventy, one hundred and forty-four and then, less often, four, five and eight. Some of the numbers are multiples of the original number, for example, forty is 4x10, seventy is 7x10, 144 is 12x12, 144 thousand is 12x12x100.[14]

It turns out that there are other numerical values that are not so obvious to us. If, for instance, we count the number of times the name of God is mentioned in Genesis 1 or the number of Hebrew words in Genesis 1:1, it turns out that they are multiples of seven. Could that be accidental? The same thing turns out to be true in the book of Revelation and in other places in the Scriptures. Presumably an educated scribe would be able to look for such things and notice them, although they normally pass us by.

Numbers in Scripture are often symbolical. This is one of the areas where there is a broad agreement among Scripture scholars, traditional and modern—at least when they take the area into account. The following are some of the main numbers with the meaning that most recognize:

7	the number of completion or perfection, especially spiritual completion
10	the number of divine order or of government, the instrument of order
12	the number of God's people

---

14 E. W. Bullinger, *Number in Scripture: Its Supernatural Design and Spiritual Significance* (Grand Rapids, MI: Kregel, 1967) provides an extensive compendium of the various numbers in Scripture.

Less commonly recognized is:

4	the number of the created universe or at least of the material universe
8	the number of superabundance or new beginnings
40	the number of trial (testing, punishment) and of re-establishing order

When we recognize a symbolic number, it is supposed to orient us to the significance of something. So, when we see the seven days of creation, it should tell us that we are seeing an account of the whole of divine creation. That, of course, raises the question of whether the symbolic nature of the number overrules the literal meaning. In other words, does the fact that creation happens in seven days mean that it happened in seven "literal" days, or is it a symbolic device that tells us we are reading an account of all of God's work of creation, or even something else. Here scholars part company.[15]

In what follows we are going to consider the number seven, what it means and where it occurs. It is perhaps the most common symbolic number in Scripture, and it clearly seems to mean a complete divine action of some sort. It is especially a number that appears in worship contexts. We will look at the following instances of it:

- Genesis 1: the creation
- Exodus 39–40: the building of the tabernacle
- Leviticus 23, Numbers 27–28: the festal cycle of Israel

---

[15] The patristic commentators also recognized the symbolic nature of the numbers in Scripture. They, however, along with some Jewish authors like Philo of Alexandria, often used a more Greco-Roman approach to the symbolic nature of the numbers, one based on mathematical relations. Philo gives an example of this in *A Treatise on the Account of the Creation of the World as Given by Moses*, XIII.13: "Of all numbers, six is, by the laws of nature, the most productive: for of all the numbers, from the unit upwards, it is the first perfect one, being made equal to its parts, and being made complete by them: the number three being half of it, and number two a third of it, and the unit a sixth of it." For a similar example, see Augustine's comments on the ages in footnote 12, p. 45. A discussion of Augustine's similar approach to numerology can be found in his *On Christian Teaching* [*De doctrina Christiana*], Book Two, XVI (25).

- Joshua 6: the fall of Jericho
- Revelation, the Book as a whole: the completion of all things.

The fact that these five texts use the number seven as prominently and as regularly as they do probably means that in some way the significance of these events is similar. To summarize: the creation was intended to be a temple and a festival, a place and time in which God dwells. The tabernacle and the worship cycle of Israel is an old covenant completion of the creation by providing an initial place and time in which God was especially present and his people could relate to him. To establish it, the forces of darkness had to be destroyed and the inheritance given to God's people. At the end of time, creation will become a temple and a festival, in which the work of creation and the work of the old covenant are fully brought to completion, and God has entered into the relationship with his creation that he originally intended.

The creation. We have already looked at this in the main text and discussed the significance of seven and especially the sabbath day. Footnote 13 (see p. 48) says, "There is also a pervasive numerology in [Genesis 1] that indicates we are being given a statement about the completeness (including likely the future completion) of the universe. In addition to the 7 days that structure the account as a whole, there are 7 Hebrew words in 1:1; 14 (7 x 2) in 1:2; 35 (7 x 5) in 2:1–3. In Gen 1:1–2:3, God is mentioned 35 times, earth 21 (7 x 3), heaven/firmament 21, and the phrases 'it was so,' 'it was good' 7 times. Seven is the number of completeness and probably also the number of divine action. . . . The coded numerology indicates that we are reading an account of the complete work of creation."

We should note that the number seven is prominent on the surface of the text of Genesis 1, with seven days of creation and the sabbath as the seventh (special) day. But there is also a numerical code under the surface that pervades the account and that tells us that the account was structured in a highly unified way to make a point.

The Tabernacle. In recent years scholars have increasingly noted the parallels between the creation of the universe and the building of the tabernacle.[16] This includes not only the building of the tabernacle itself and its consecration, but also the making of the priestly garments and the consecration of the priests.

Some of the numeric use of seven and the parallels with the creation account are on the surface of the text. Moses spends seven days on Sinai getting revelation especially for the sanctuary (Ex 24:15b–18). After the sanctuary is built, it says "Moses finished the work" in almost the same words as God finishing creation (Gen 2:1–2). Then God comes to rest in the sanctuary (Ex 40:34).

There is, however, also a less obvious numerical code that pervades the account. The initial instructions for building the sanctuary are given to Moses in a set of seven addresses that conclude with the instruction to observe the sabbath. The sevenfold description of the making of the priestly garments is also given with a conclusion: "as the Lord had commanded Moses" (Ex 39). The same is true of the construction of the sanctuary itself (Ex 40).

The distinctive difference between the two accounts is that the tabernacle was built within the pre-existing creation by a human being (Moses). This leads to the understanding that the tabernacle is in a certain way the old covenant completion of creation, making it possible for God's presence to be accessible to old covenant people.

The feasts of Israel. The festal calendar of the people of Israel is likewise built on the number seven. The calendar is primarily laid out in Leviticus 23 and Numbers 27–28:

- The main unit was the week of seven days, ending in the sabbath, the seventh day.
- There was also a monthly pattern. Every month began with the observance of the new moon. The major feasts of Pass-

---

[16] For a fuller presentation of this topic see Anderson, *The Genesis of Perfection*, 201–202, or Jon D. Levenson, *Creation and the Persistence of Evil: The Jewish Drama of Divine Omnipotence* (Princeton, NJ: Princeton University Press, 1988), chap. 7.

over and Pentecost began on the full moon, when the night was brightest.

- Passover (and Unleavened Bread) was celebrated in the first month on the full moon. It was celebrated for a week (seven days).
- Pentecost or the Feast of Weeks was celebrated on the fiftieth day after Passover. It was the conclusion of a week of weeks (49 days) plus one from Passover. "Pentecost," the Greek name for the feast, means "Fiftieth."
- The Feast of Trumpets was the first day of the seventh month. The seventh month was the last month of a week of months. The Feast of Trumpets inaugurated two weeks of preparation for Tabernacles.
- The year at first began in March (Abib or Nisan, depending on which names of the months were being used). Later on, the beginning of the seventh month, the Feast of Trumpets, was considered to be New Year's day (Rosh Hashanah).
- The Day of Atonement was the tenth day of the seventh month.
- Tabernacles began on the full moon of the month. It was celebrated for a week, followed by an eighth day, the great day, the conclusion of the festal cycle.
- Seven days in the year are the most festive, because in them no servile work was to be done: the first and seventh days of Unleavened Bread, Pentecost, Trumpets (Rosh Hashanah), the Day of Atonement, the first day of Tabernacles and its eighth day.
- There was also a sabbatical year that occurred every seven years (a week of years).
- Finally, there was a jubilee year, the fiftieth year of the cycle, the year after a week of sabbatical years, plus one.

Eight was a special number, indicating a greater conclusion, but also a new beginning. The eighth day was also the first day of a new week.

- The fiftieth day was the eighth day of the seventh week or the conclusion to a week of weeks.
- For early Christians, the eighth day was the day of Resurrection of Christ, the day after the conclusion of his work of redemption, the first day of the new creation.
- Eight was also the number of Christ's name "Jesus," who was the embodiment of the new creation.
- Fifty was the number of Pentecost, the conclusion of the Passover season and the day of the outpouring of the Holy Spirit, the beginning of the new covenant.

The fall of Jericho. The number seven is also pervasive in the description of the fall of Jericho. The fall was primarily accomplished by a march of the Israelite army with the ark of the covenant (the place of the Lord's presence) around the city. The march went for seven days, with seven priests bearing seven trumpets before the ark and blowing the trumpets. On the seventh day the march occurred seven times. Then the army shouted, the walls fell, and the army went up to take the city.

The fall of Jericho is, as we have seen, typological. In this case it is typological of the spiritual warfare involved in the Israelites taking the land that was their inheritance, the place where they were to live and worship the Lord. Jericho typologically represented the spiritual power that opposes God's plan. The taking of Jericho was typological of the Lord defeating the Enemy, but also of the armies that were God's people taking their inheritance.

The future completion (the book of Revelation). The number seven is pervasive in the whole book of Revelation.[17] The book begins with a symbolic description of the Christian people: seven churches represented by the seven lampstands (referring to the menorah in the holy place), with the seven angels of the churches (probably

---

[17] For a fuller presentation, see Richard Bauckham, *The Theology of the Book of Revelation* (Cambridge, UK: Cambridge University Press, 1993), *passim*, especially 16, 24–25, 40, 66–67, 109.

referring to the guardian angels of the churches, but possibly to the bishops), and Christ and the seven spirits of God (the Holy Spirit) in the midst of the churches and speaking to them. The image is of the Christian people (the seven individual churches representing the whole church of Christ) as the temple of God on earth.

The coming judgment (Rev 6–19) is described in three series of seven, with the last series preparing for the final battle and the coming of the new Jerusalem from heaven. The three series together were symbolic of God's defeat of the kingdom of Satan and the gods that stood against him, making it possible for his people to take their inheritance.

As in the creation account and the account of the building of the tabernacle, the number seven is not only used prominently on the surface of the text, but a less obvious numerical code pervades the book: the three divine titles (the Alpha and Omega, the first and last, the beginning and end; the Lord God the Almighty; and the one who sits upon the throne), are mentioned seven times; the name of Jesus is mentioned fourteen times (7x2); the name Christ is mentioned seven times; there are seven beatitudes; and Christ says seven times that he is coming soon.

The number 12, the number of God's people, is also prominent in the book. The new Jerusalem had twelve gates with twelve angels; its length and breadth and height were 12,000 stadia (12x1000); and its walls were 144 cubits. The number of the disciples of Christ on earth is 144,000 (12x12x1000), with each tribe being 12,000. The number of the elders enthroned in heaven is 24 (12x2). The tree of life yielded 12 kinds of fruit.

Seven is the number for divine completion, and it applies to God's full presence in space and time: tabernacle/temple and sabbath/feast. The account of creation, ending with the sabbath, the day of rest and festival, presents the completed material universe as a temple. The account of the building of the tabernacle, flanked by the sabbath command, presents the old covenant ceremonial as the place and times of God's dwelling on earth now. The fall of Jericho presents the action of God in destroying opposition to establishing his worship on earth. The description of the age to come in Revelation presents the new Jerusalem with the feast of Tabernacles as God's full future presence in the whole universe after the fall of the kingdom of Satan. The use of the number seven indicates that these five realities are linked in God's plan and typologically related.

Technical Note: "Gentiles"

The word "Gentiles" can easily be confusing, because it can refer to various groupings. Sometimes it refers to all the nations of the world. Sometimes it refers to all the nations other than Israel or the Jews. Sometimes it refers to everyone who was not Jewish or Christian. Sometimes it refers to Christians who were not Jews.

Translations can be additionally confusing. The word "nation(s)" is used to translate the Hebrew and Greek words for a nation, usually in the plural. In the RSV and other translations, the English word "Gentiles" is commonly but not always used to translate "nations." This is an anglicized version of the Latin word for the members of the nations, *gentiles*, drawn from the word for "nation," *gens*. Sometimes the word "heathen" is used as a translation; sometimes "pagan." Each of these could do with some explanation.

First of all, Gentiles can refer to all the nations of the world. The "table of the nations" in Genesis 10 refers to all nations, including the ancestors of the Israelites. In Genesis 12, the descendants of Abraham will be a great nation, probably meaning the Israelites. In the New Testament, the Jews are always referred to as a nation in the Gospel of John, and they are commonly referred to that way in the Lucan writings (the Gospel of Luke and the Acts of the Apostles).

On the other hand, it was more common to see "the nations" as the non-Jews. There was Israel and the nations, the nations being everyone other than the Israelites. Israel was more commonly referred to as "a people," or the Israelites were referred to as "the people."

The Christians could sometimes be referred as a nation, distinct from the nation they might have lived in (Mt 21:43; 1 Pet 2:9; and maybe Rom 10:19). When they were so referred to, they were probably understood to include Jewish Christians.

Often the Christians were explicitly contrasted with the Gentiles (the nations). So Christians can be seen as non-Gentiles, simply because they are Christians (e.g., Eph 3:6; Eph 4:17; 1 Pet 2:12; 1 Cor 5:1; 1 Cor 12:2; 1 Thess 4:5, etc.). Many Christians are not Jews, but they are not Gentiles either; that is, they are not heathens or pagans.

When non-Jewish Christians were referred to in a way that indicated they were not Jewish, they were sometimes designated as "from the Gentiles" (Acts 15:23; Rev 5:9; Rev 7:9, etc.), or Gentiles who have turned to God (Acts 15:17, 19; Acts 21:25, etc.) or even those who were Gentiles in the flesh (Eph 2:11). Non-Jewish Christians were, however, at times simply referred to as Gentiles, usually in the context of speaking about Gentiles who had become Christians (Rom 9:30; 11:11; etc.).

The result of these variations in usage is that it can be difficult at times in the New Testament to tell if a given passage refers to pagans or non-Jewish Christians. The context has to be the deciding factor. It is better to avoid speaking simply about a Gentile Church (one with no Jewish Christian members) or about Gentile Christianity because of the potential ambiguity.

PART II:
THEOLOGICAL EXEGESIS AND HISTORY

The discussions in this part provide the theoretical underpinning for the main body of the book, the exegetical principles behind the main exposition. Together the individual chapters make a presentation of some basic principles of Scripture exegesis, although each discussion can be read by itself.

The issues in this part have been chosen because they are the ones that came up most commonly in discussions when the material in this book was taught in courses. Because of the topic of this book, the discussions in this second part primarily concern issues of history writing and interpretations of narrative sections of the Scriptures. They focus on the question of why we should accept the view that God orders history by stages of his plan. They do not treat more directly theological issues, such as creation *ex nihilo*, grace and free will, the problem of evil, the nature of prophecy, and the like.

There is, then, one overriding concern to this part, namely the viability of theological synthesis, especially in regard to God's plan as a whole. Much modern scholarship presumes that because the various parts of the Scriptures differ from one another so much, synthesis is out of the question. That is not true, but to create a solid synthesis requires following certain principles.

SUMMARY OF THE
METHODOLOGICAL DISCUSSIONS

The Scriptures can be put together in an intelligible and historically responsible synthesis to show the unity of God's plan and so to give insight into the purposes of God in creation.

METHODOLOGICAL DISCUSSIONS IN PART I
(The Foundational Methodological Discussions)

Spiritual Interpretation
(chapter 3)

Spiritual interpretation gives us a fuller meaning of the text, partly by seeing the text in the light of what it was leading to in God's plan, but also in the light of what we now know about its subject. The authority of the text determines the result, but the subject matter determines the proceedings (we primarily compare the text to the other texts on the same subject, rather than to its literary or historical antecedents).

The Stages of God's Plan
(chapters 5 and 12)

To put together a large amount of data, we need a synthesis based on one or more ways of putting together the data. Different syntheses are not per se problematic, although the data has to determine the resulting assertions.

Methodological Discussions in Part II

1. Modern Scholarship and Reading the Old Testament

To use the Old Testament as a Christian book, we need to make use of theological exegesis, which corrects the problems caused by the use of exclusively secular-historical methods, especially the "historical-critical method" and the "post-modern" methods.

2. Scriptural Interpretation and Literary Genre

To interpret the Scriptures well, we need to be able to understand the literary genres in which they are written. We should not interpret all narrative sections "literally."

3. Presuppositions

To interpret the Scriptures well, we need to be able to distinguish what they are actually asserting as distinguished from what presuppositions they are relying on.

4. Source Criticism

The Scriptures present us with a collection of genres and texts, some of which probably came originally from a variety of sources, not just from the human author of the final text. We need to know how to put them together to understand the Scriptures in their unity. We recognize them primarily stylistically (not mainly by their communicative art but by their overall approach).

5. Anthropomorphism

The Scriptures commonly speak about God as if he were a human being. That allows us to understand him better without our being able to tell fully what he is like in himself.

6. Analogical Discourse

We naturally use words in an analogical way, and scriptural writers mainly spoke about spiritual realities that way. Only later did theologies develop in which the analogical statements of Scripture were turned into technical ("scientific") speech.

7. The Intent of the Author

A scriptural text is not simply to be interpreted by the conscious intent of the human author as discerned by historical method. It is also to be discerned by the intent of God as conveyed by spiritual interpretation.

8. Eisegesis and Ideological Exegesis

Ideological exegesis involves imposing a modern ideological position on texts where it is absent and often where the texts take an opposed position. It is eisegesis, whereas theological exegesis is not.

9. Historical Reliability

The parts of the Bible that are intended to describe historical events do so reliably for Christian purposes, i.e., with reasonable historical accuracy, although modern historical method does not allow us to resolve questions of how precisely.

10. Spiritual Transposition

When the old covenant order is changed to the new covenant order, the old covenant order is transposed to a spiritual medium, the medium of the Holy Spirit. The concrete elements of the old covenant order are transposed and the provisions of the law are modified (spiritualized) according to the transposition (interpreted differently because they are fulfilled).

CHAPTER THIRTEEN

MODERN SCHOLARSHIP AND READING THE OLD TESTAMENT

To use the Old Testament as a Christian book, we need to make use of theological exegesis, which corrects the problems caused by the use of exclusively secular-historical methods, especially the "historical-critical" method and the "post-modern" methods.

Biblical scholarship and the Christian use of the Old Testament. Among Christians in the last one hundred years or so, the use of the Old Testament has declined—among some to the vanishing point. This is partly due to the lack of biblical formation. It is, however, also due to the approach of much scriptural scholarship, which has used what could be called a secular-historical method. When such approaches have been employed, they have contributed to Christians being unable to find a Christian use for the Old Testament.

The term "secular-historical approach" here designates the way many who identify themselves as Christians do biblical exegesis. To be sure, the term could certainly cover the way in which non-Christian scholars study the New Testament, but the focus of concern here is on exegesis done by people identified as Christians. It is the dominant exegetical approach in academic theology today, both in departments of theology or religious studies in secular universities in the English-speaking world and in many faculties of theology in seminaries and theological schools. It would be possible to speak of a variety of secular-historical methods—the historical-critical method (including at least form criticism, source criticism, redaction criticism, and tradition criticism), the history of religions method, etc.—just as it might be possible to speak of a variety of theological methods, but for our purposes to describe it as one (overarching) approach will be accurate.

I have chosen the term "secular-historical" to accommodate both the fact of the prevalence now of ideological approaches to exegesis (e.g., Feminist exegesis, Marxist exegesis, etc., which are secular) and, in contrast, the new strength of what will be described below as the approach of theological exegesis. Perhaps the previous term would have been "historical-critical method," which its practitioners often simply equated with historical method and was normally considered to be secular.[1]

The term "secular-historical" indicates that the approach of a given author does not take the view that fundamental Christian doctrines are true. Some of the authors in question intend to dispute, for instance, the Christology in the Nicene Creed. More to the point of our discussion, many assume that Christian doctrinal stances are irrelevant to scriptural scholarship and can be evaluated when the properly historical work is done. Many, perhaps most, would not assume that God was directly involved in what happened

---

[1] This term is still used in Catholic documents, and there it does often seem to be equated with "scientific" historical method. For a treatment of the current official Catholic Church commendation of the "historical-critical method" and its attempt to give a "properly-oriented" direction to it, see Peter S. Williamson, *Catholic Principles for Interpreting Scripture: A Study of the Pontifical Biblical Commission's* The Interpretation of the Bible in the Church (Rome: Editrice Pontificio Istituto Biblico, 2001). Simply treating historical method and its use in exegesis, with some attention to the peculiarities of historical-critical approaches, would have been clearer and simpler than the Pontifical Biblical Commission's approach. Martin Hengel makes this point in *Acts and the History of Earliest Christianity* (London: SCM, 1979; Philadelphia: Fortress, 1980), 54.

It is helpful to note that Continental European writers and those who are influenced by them would freely use the term "scientific" (*scientifique, wissenschaftlich*) for subjects in the humanities that are an academically recognized discipline. Anglo-American writers normally restrict "science" to the natural sciences, although they often also use the word for the "social sciences," but rarely for the humanities, including history. In normal Anglo-American scholarly discourse, the historical-critical method would not be understood to be "scientific."

in the events described by the Scriptures that were attributed to him by the scriptural texts.

Many secular-historical teachers approach the Old Testament as originating in a more primitive stage of God's workings with human beings. They see it as a historically useful book, perhaps teaching some lessons about how God works with people, but containing an approach different from that found in the New Testament. Some would go so far as to say that the New Testament writers largely misunderstood the Old Testament, because they simply read their own views into it. Because of lack of historical understanding—the kind of understanding we have acquired since the nineteenth century—New Testament writers could not understand what the Old Testament meant in its own context.

Such a view results in seeing the Old Testament as a separate work from the New Testament. We can read it to understand the history and religious views of the Israelite people, but we cannot use it for understanding Christianity, except for understanding the historical background of how Christianity developed out of Israelite religion. The Old Testament gives us some historical background to the New Testament (as do writings from Greco-Roman culture), but Christians cannot rely on it for instruction. Moreover, as modern people they certainly cannot read it the way New Testament writers and early Christian writers did.

We are at a point when the older dominant scholarly approach to scriptural interpretation (often referred to as "the historical-critical method") is no longer hegemonic in biblical scholarship and simply accepted by most scholars. Few, in fact, would now consider it to be the archetype of historical method in ancient history or biblical studies, though few would simply reject it *in toto*.[2] The chief question

---

[2] For a helpful brief discussion of the historical-critical method and critique of its limitations see Martin Hengel, *Acts and the History*, 129–130, a book that is not solely about Acts but also about the relationship of scriptural exegesis and historical method. One of the most penetrating critiques of the historical-critical method in its earlier (post World War II) manifestations can be found in C. S. Lewis' essay "Fern-seed and Elephants" in *Christian Reflections* (Grand Rapids, MI: Eerdmans, 1967). The observations in it are still applicable to much contemporary exegesis.

now is how to practice good historical method and how to relate the results to theological affirmations, not how to grapple with the traditional historical-critical method.

The scholarship that followed the historical-critical method has produced some helpful insights (exegetically and hermeneutically). It has, however, not been sufficiently "critical" of its own approach. It has been somewhat weak on historical method, producing an unusual scholarly subculture in the way it approaches historical issues. More importantly, it has been for the most part innocent of the "philosophical" underpinnings of its own method. It has also been somewhat disdainful of its critics, who have often made insightful objections. The discussions here include essays that deal with some important issues about the historical-critical method in Scripture scholarship—without seeing its exponents' work as overall worthless and in fact seeing much of it as valuable—but without seeing it as *the* exemplar of good historical method.

The historical-critical method has at times had a curious result, what one writer described as the "spiritual trivialization" of the Scripture. There is an example in the account of the flood in a respected commentary on Genesis.[3] This commentary is filled with theories of how the text is a composite of many sources (badly put together, an outsider might think), theories of historical development, reflections on how other Near Eastern texts of the time may have influenced it, and attempts to correlate the text with archaeological results. Some of this is potentially useful—especially for those who want to write a history about the ancient Near East or the people of Israel, but also for those who simply want to understand the meaning of the text as we find it.

There is, however, little in the commentary on what the writers were trying to say, much less what significance that might have. The actual content is for the most part not the focus of the commentary, and the importance of the teaching is rarely the focus, except when it inaugurates or fosters an historical change. In short, the commen-

---

[3] *Jerome Biblical Commentary* (Englewood Cliffs, NJ: Prentice Hall, 1968), 15–16.

tary is of little worth for a Christian trying to understand the meaning of the Scriptures (as distinguished from how they fit into the history of their period)—despite the fact that it has been regularly given to seminarians to equip them to use the Old Testament. And, not surprisingly, it does not have much to say about how a Christian might use the book it is commenting on.

The example I have chosen is from almost fifty years ago. Since then there has been much change. Some of it is due to progress in archaeology and studies of Near Eastern textual material. More of it is due to new intellectual approaches, such as structuralism, reader-response theory, and ideological exegesis (Marxist, Feminist, Gay, Environmentalist, Post-colonial)—sometimes summarized under the heading of "post-modernism." The result has been a broader array of opinions deemed respectable, and a greater challenge in trying to predict where Scripture scholarship is going.

Theological exegesis. In the midst of all this, some positive changes are underway. More theologians and Scripture scholars have been holding the view that it is not enough to read the Scripture as an historical artifact, however useful it may be to understand its historical context.[4] Moreover, there is a new emphasis on reading the Scriptures as a whole. Many scholars have persuasively shown that the different books and sections of books were written as unified wholes—even when they may have incorporated earlier sources—and need to be interpreted that way, rather than be disassembled and used to reconstruct and interpret hypothetical writings, authors, or editors, or ancient communities.[5] Others have shown that

---

[4]   A helpful presentation of the current stage of theological practice can be found in John Webster, "Theology After Liberalism?" in John Webster and George P. Schner, ed., *Theology After Liberalism: A Reader* (Oxford: Blackwell Publishers, 2000), 52–61. He uses the phrase "postliberal theology" to characterize many of the new approaches, and in the course of his discussion highlights the development of what is called below "theological exegesis" without using that term. His focus is broader than questions of exegesis.

[5]   Robert Alter in *The Art of Biblical Narrative* (New York: Basic Books, Inc., 1981), a still valuable book, probably was the most influential exponent of this view, although many others have contributed. It has become common to describe this as the "synchronic"

all these books were put together into a canon to create a unified understanding of the history of God's working with the human race, and therefore need to be understood that way.[6]

In addition, there is a new emphasis on benefiting exegetically from both patristic Christian exegesis and rabbinic exegesis. Patristic Christian exegesis is contained in the writings of authoritative Christian teachers in the first Christian centuries (the Church Fathers).[7] Rabbinic exegesis is contained in the writings of the normative Jewish teachers from that same time.[8] Both contain understandings of the Old Testament that can be very useful, to some extent because they are culturally closer to the original sources.[9] The revival of patristic exegetical scholarship has also given us the *Ancient Christian Commentary on Scripture*, a running commentary on both the Old and New Testament in the form of a catena of selections from pa-

---

approach, as distinguished from the earlier "diachronic" approach that seeks to describe how a text developed over time and that has dominated the historical-critical method.

[6] The chief recent proponent of this approach is Brevard Childs, whose developed approach can be read in Brevard S. Childs, *Biblical Theology of the Old and New Testaments: Theological Reflection on the Christian Bible* (Minneapolis: Fortress Press, 2011). The unusual phrase "canonical criticism"—perhaps chosen to get a foothold for canonical considerations in the dominant historical-critical method, which operated in terms of "criticisms"—is often associated with Childs, although apparently it originated with J. P. Sanders (see James Barr, *The Concept of Biblical Theology* [Minneapolis: Fortress, 1999], 387). The phrase "canonical approach," and sometimes "canonical method," may be more common (and accurate) now to describe the approach Childs advocated. He himself rejected the title "canonical criticism" in "The Canonical Shape of the Prophetic Literature," *Interpretation* 32 (1978), 46–55. "Canonical approach" is the title of the helpful entry by Christopher Seitz in the *DTIB* that discusses Childs' (and others') approach.

[7] William S. Kurz, S.J., in "Patristic Interpretation of Scripture within God's Story of Creation and Redemption" *Letter & Spirit* 7 (2011), 35–50, gives a short overall view of the patristic approach to interpretation in relationship to the current secular-historical approaches. A more thorough presentation of the patristic approach to exegesis, which Kurz cites, can be found in O'Keefe and Reno, *Sanctified Vision*.

[8] For "Some Terms for Rabbinic Jewish Writings," see p. 393.

[9] For a treatment of the value of rabbinic exegesis for Christian exegesis, see The Pontifical Biblical Commission, *The Jewish People and Their Sacred Scriptures in the Christian Bible* (Vatican City: Libreria Editrice Vaticana, 2002), sect. 22. http://www.vatican.va/roman_curia/congregations/cfaith/pcb_documents/rc_con_cfaith_doc_20020212_popolo-ebraico_en.html

tristic authors, one that gives a usable, even if sometimes uneven, overview of patristic exegesis.

The best term for one of the results of these new emphases seems to be theological exegesis. "Theological exegesis" as used in this book refers to an approach to exegesis that is based upon the following three principles:

1. *There is a unity to Scripture*: all of Scripture is canonical and therefore a reliable (authoritative) source for Christian teaching, even though the Old Testament part of the Scripture must be interpreted in the light of the New. The unity stems from the fact that it is all given by God.[10]

2. *The Scriptures are harmonious*: when we want to interpret the meaning of a particular text, we read other texts in the Scripture on the same subject, and we interpret the first text in the light of those others and in a way that does not contradict them.

3. *Exegetes or teachers should compare their results with other accepted authorities and their views of the text or the subject in question, and adjust their conclusions if need be.* Accepted authorities include the Fathers, the church creeds or confessions, and a theological approach one is committed to, especially an ecclesiastically endorsed one.

The word "theological" here is used to indicate that the exegesis is concerned to reach revealed (Christian) truth, not to indicate any special systematic approach. Each of these principles raises a number of important questions, many of which will be treated in the pages that follow. Christian teachers who adopt at least these three principles (they normally will follow other principles as

---

[10] Two recent statements of theological exegesis stress the truth that Scripture is *primarily* revelation, that is, has God as its author and is not primarily a product of human history: Matthew Levering, *Participatory Biblical Exegesis: A Theology of Biblical Interpretation* (Notre Dame, IN: University of Notre Dame Press, 2008), and John Webster, *The Domain of the Word: Scripture and Theological Reason* (London: Bloomsbury, 2012).

well) can be considered practitioners of theological exegesis.[11]

The phrase "theological exegesis" is narrower than the more common phrase "theological interpretation." "Exegesis" is here understood to refer to the process of clarifying the meaning of the text itself, including the theological teaching it provides. "Interpretation" is here understood to refer to the whole process of how to respond to the text, including, and perhaps especially, how to apply it in modern circumstances.

Modern theological exegesis differs from the theological exegesis used by the recognized traditional teachers, including the Fathers, the medieval theologians, and the Reformation and Counter-reformation theologians, as well as the authoritative rabbinical writers. Those who practice modern theological exegesis almost always accept the use of the modern historical methods and tools and affirm them as being helpful for the study of the Scripture, while also maintaining the canonicity and authority of the whole of Scripture. As a result, they let modern historical method shape the results, but they also let the authority of the Scripture and Christian tradition as a whole—and not just the results of the use of the historical method—determine the final results of the exegesis. Perhaps one of the most beneficial results of theological exegesis is to renew the Christian use of the Old Testament.

Theological exegesis can be seen as a synthesis of the results of historical method and theological or doctrinal conviction—though in some writings ending up only a mixture. It often issues in biblical theologies. Sometimes these are written on the premise that the teaching of the Scripture can be synthesized in biblical theology

---

[11] The term "theological exegesis" is used in Pope Benedict XVI's Apostolic Exhortation *Verbum Domini*: "On the other hand, since Scripture must be interpreted in the same Spirit in which it was written, the Dogmatic Constitution indicates three fundamental criteria for an appreciation of the divine dimension of the Bible: 1) the text must be interpreted with attention to the unity of the whole of Scripture; nowadays this is called canonical exegesis; 2) account is to be taken of the living Tradition of the whole Church; and, finally, 3) respect must be shown for the analogy of faith. Only where both methodological levels, the historical-critical and the theological, are respected, can one speak of a theological exegesis, an exegesis worthy of this book." For the term "analogy of faith" see "Some Terms for the Nature of the Scriptures" (p. 389).

into a whole without distorting any of the texts, and that biblical theology can provide material for more complete theologies using other materials.[12] Sometimes these are written with the understanding that biblical theologies should relate the scriptural texts to later authoritative texts. Theological exegesis also issues in works that describe themselves as "theological commentaries."[13]

There are two main currents of the theological interpretation of Scripture.[14] One stems from canonical criticism or the canonical ap-

---

[12] Barr, *Concept of Biblical Theology*, contains the currently most extensive survey of biblical theologies, although his focus is on the concepts behind them. For a subsequent biblical theology, significantly different than most of the earlier ones, see G. K. Beale, *A New Testament Biblical Theology: The Unfolding of the Old Testament in the New* (Grand Rapids, MI: Baker Academic, 2011). This would be an example of theological exegesis.

[13] Brazos, *Catholic Commentary on Sacred Scripture*, Editors' Preface: "This series responds to that desire [to study Scripture well] by providing accessible yet substantive commentary on each book of the New Testament, drawn from the best of contemporary biblical scholarship as well as the rich treasure of the Church's tradition. These volumes seek to offer scholarship illumined by faith, in the conviction that the ultimate aim of biblical interpretation is to discover what God has revealed and is still speaking through the sacred text. Central to our approach are the principles taught by Vatican II: first, the use of historical and literary methods to discern what the biblical authors intended to express; second, prayerful theological reflection to understand the sacred text 'in accord with the same Spirit by whom it was written'—that is, in the light of the content and unity of the whole Scripture, the living tradition of the Church, and the analogy of faith (*Dei Verbum* 12)."

[14] Identification of theological interpretation and theological exegesis has been relatively recent. One of the earliest volumes to treat it was *The Theological Interpretation of Scripture*, Stephen E. Fowl, ed. (Oxford: Blackwell Publishers, 1997). Fowl defined it by saying, "I take the theological interpretation of scripture to be that practice whereby theological concerns and interests inform and are informed by a reading of Scripture" (xiii). He then included a set of contributors with a wide variety of "theological" convictions, not all of them recognizably orthodox. Putting the definition in terms of theological concern and interest or even theological context, as some who take a canonical approach do, however, leaves theological interpretation open to the kind of theological concern that has an avowedly theological interest but views that interest even as expressed in attacking the Bible (see p. 512 of this book for one instance). Now the more authoritative volume in defining theological interpretation seems to be the *DTIB*. In the introduction Kevin Vanhoozer says (p. 22), "The theological interpretation of the Bible is characterized by a *governing interest* in God, the word and works of God, and by a governing intention to engage in what we might call, 'theological criticism.'" The stated intention seems to be "coming to hear God's word and to know God better" (probably the meaning of "theological criticism"). It is the

proach to scriptural interpretation.[15] Here the emphasis is that the book we now call the Bible (in somewhat different canonical forms depending on the tradition) is what we need to treat. Therefore we need to do our exegesis, or at least the final stage of our exegesis, in the context of the canon and of the theology of those who have accepted the canon and use it in their Christian life. The second stems from traditional Christian and patristic theology, where the fundamental Christian confessions (the rule of faith and traditional Christian understanding of the Ten Commandments) are simply determinative of the final result.

The two approaches overlap and normally are mutually reinforcing, but are not always identical. Many who consider themselves canonical critics would be open to taking the view that the exegesis of what the Scripture asserts, even in New Testament teaching, could be at odds with and even contradictory to what the rule of faith (say, the Nicene Creed) asserts.[16] It is only the second approach, the exegesis

---

emphasis on "acknowledgment of the work and word of God in and through Scripture" that aligns such an approach to theological interpretation with the works cited in footnote 6, p. 440 and those of other orthodox scholars, although the DTIB has contributions from a broader set of scholars.

[15] For helpful discussions of the nature of the canonical approach, see R. W. L. Moberly, *The Theology of the Book of Genesis* (Cambridge, UK: Cambridge University Press, 2009), chap. 1, and R. W. L. Moberly, *Old Testament Theology: Reading the Hebrew Bible as Christian Scripture* (Grand Rapids, MI: Baker Academic, 2013). He makes explicit the process of understanding what the scriptural texts say (determined by historical method) in relationship to the canonical context (determined by later considerations). He distinguishes a simply harmonizing approach to exegesis from what he refers to as "a range of highly complex synthesizing moves" (*The Theology of the Book of Genesis*, 15). His chap. 4 of that book in which he critiques James Barr's approach to the Fall is especially helpful and illustrative.

[16] The commonly used term "the rule of faith" or sometimes "rule of truth" is first found in the second century patristic teacher Irenaeus of Lyon (AH 3.4.2), who asserted its importance for interpretation of Scripture. Those who used the phrase did not seem to be referring to a text, like the creeds, but to the content of the Christian faith as summarized in the creeds. In Latin theology, Augustine's emphasis on the rule of faith in *De doctrina Christiana* (especially Book One, IV, 10–12) but also his use of it as a first step after what we might call textual criticism to exclude wrong interpretation (e.g., Book Three, II, 33–34) was very influential in subsequent Western theology. The early Christian baptismal creeds are various expressions of the rule of faith. The rule of faith can already be found in the New Testament in less fully developed form as outlined in J. N. D. Kelly, *Early Christian Creeds* (London: Longman, 1960), chap. 1.

that considers Christian doctrine (orthodox theology) foundational, that this book has in view when it speaks of theological exegesis.

Concluding comments. There are many issues connected to what counts as the teaching of the Scripture, some of which are quite complex. There are further questions as to how what we discern as scriptural teaching relates to orthodox Christian theology, sometimes formulated in different terms. Chapter 3 of this book contains an overview of theological exegesis. The following sections of this part will treat many of the particular technical questions.

In general, the discussions in this part take the view that much scholarly discussion adopts conclusions that go beyond the available evidence. Moreover, the conflict between Liberal historical-critical exegesis and Fundamentalist (anti-Modernist) exegesis that touches on historical accuracy cannot be simply decided on the grounds of historical evidence. Much of it has to be decided on hermeneutical grounds. Perhaps more accurately, it has to be decided on epistemological grounds.[17]

Sanctified Vision by O'Keefe and Reno, on pages 24–26 and 114–128 makes a helpful analogy between patristic interpretation and modern scientific method. Modern scientific method does not just assemble disparate data and leave it at that, much less promote different versions of a given science as equally valid, but interprets the data in the light of accepted scientific theories. In a similar way, the patristic interpretation (and all theological exegesis) interprets the scriptural data in the light of accepted Christian doctrine. It seeks to see everything in the data (all the passages in the Scripture) in its relationship to that doctrine, much the way modern scientific method sees empirical data in the light of accepted (unified) scientific theory. Theological exegesis, then, is "scientific" in this aspect of its methodology.

[17] The essay by Thomas McCall "Religious Epistemology, Theological Interpretation of Scripture, and Critical Biblical Scholarship" in James K. Hoffmeier and Dennis R. Magary, *Do Historical Matters Matter to Faith: A Critical Appraisal of Modern and Postmodern Approaches to Scripture* (Wheaton, IL: Crossway, 2012), lays out some of these issues in terms of contemporary analytic epistemology. As Joseph Cardinal Ratzinger (subsequently Pope Benedict XVI) put it in "Biblical Interpretation in Conflict" in *Biblical Interpretation in Crisis*, ed. Richard J. Neuhaus (Grand Rapids, MI; Eerdmans, 1989), 19, "The debate about modern exegesis is not at its core a debate among historians, but among philosophers."

SCRIPTURAL INTERPRETATION AND LITERARY GENRE

---

*To interpret the Scriptures well, we need to be able to under-
stand the literary genres in which they are written. We should
not interpret all narrative sections "literally."*

Introduction to the chapter. In the previous chapter we considered
the approaches of modern scholarship to scriptural interpretation,
especially the changing approaches that characterize much of academic scholarship in this area. The purpose of the chapter was to
present background to the discussions in the rest of this part of the
book. With this chapter we begin on the set of topics that consider
the exegetical principles behind part I of the book.

We live in a time in which much scriptural interpretation is
significantly different than it was two or three hundred years ago.
This is primarily due to the existence of modern science, including
modern astronomy, geology, and biology, but especially of modern
history. Modern history derives its knowledge of the ancient world
from other materials besides the biblical texts, including from writings of other peoples and from archaeology. One fundamental issue this raises for us is how the writings in Genesis and subsequent
books relate to the other knowledge we now have, especially to historical data.

The discussion often focuses on the question of whether the
writings in the narrative sections of the scriptural books are his-

torically accurate or not. That is, did past events that are narrated in Genesis actually occur, and occur in the way they are described there? The discussion is sometimes presented as being over the traditional understanding of the historicity of Scripture in contrast to the modern understanding. Some would hold that the traditional understanding took the view that all the parts of Scripture that were narrative in form, or at least seemed like historical narrative rather than a story, had to be held to be historically accurate, or the Scripture could not be relied on. Others would see the traditional understanding as "pre-scientific" and therefore naïve in terms of historical method.

Describing the traditional understanding in such a way does not lack all truth. Traditional Christian writers tended to assume that scriptural narrative was historically accurate, and many even considered a book like Job to be an historical account. However, to describe the change from "traditional" to "modern" interpretation that way is to miss some important features of it. We need to understand the debate in the context of the "Fundamentalist controversy" of the early twentieth century, or at least of the discussions about the historical accuracy of the Scripture going back to the sixteenth and seventeenth centuries. We especially need to understand the question of *literary genre*, that is, the form or style in which a particular text was written.

Taking the Scripture literally. The term "Fundamentalist" has at worst become a term of abuse and at times a term to designate someone who takes traditional religious beliefs, including moral stands, seriously (e.g., those who nowadays consider that homosexual actions are immoral because of what the Scripture says about them are regularly described as Fundamentalists). This latter understanding is vague to the point of confusion, because it would include all orthodox Christians. When discussing scriptural interpretation, people most commonly characterize Fundamentalists as people who "take Scripture literally."[1] Such a view can likewise be misleading, but it does highlight the key underlying issue.

There were (and are) Fundamentalists, although some of their descendants prefer to be described as Evangelicals and to distinguish themselves from "the Fundamentalists." Originally, they were a group of conservative Evangelical Christians who reacted to the growing theological liberalism in their churches and asserted the truths of what they called the fundamentals of the faith. They got their name from a statement entitled "Five Points of Fundamentalism" issued in 1895 at the American Bible Conference and from four volumes of articles called *The Fundamentals*, published in 1917. Most of what they upheld was simple Christian orthodoxy (like the reality of Christ's Resurrection). Some of it was Evangelical in the sense of a Reformed theological understanding of certain truths (like a particular substitutionary atonement view of the work of Christ). Many of them were well-educated and intelligent thinkers, and many of their exegetical positions (hardly all) would be preferred by most Scripture scholars today over those of the people they were opposing.[2]

The Fundamentalists probably got their reputation for being literalists because of the way they approached the historical nature

---

[1] James Barr in *The Bible in the Modern World* (London: SCM, 1973), 168–169, and in *Fundamentalism* (London: SCM, 1977), 40, would endorse the view that most people understand Fundamentalists as those who take the Bible literally, but holds that such a view is inaccurate. The Fundamentalists in his analysis are not literalists, but inerrantists.

[2] A current volume by a range of conservative Evangelicals, including some who would be considered Fundamentalists, that addresses the scriptural interpretation issues with a high degree of sophistication and competence is Hoffmeier and Magary, *Do Historical Matters Matter to Faith*. It provides an illustration of how such scholars can deal with intellectual issues with a sophistication that matches or exceeds that of more liberal scholars.

One of the more hostile and simplistic presentations of the "Fundamentalists"—paradoxically at odds with how Catholic ecumenical teaching recommends approaching "separated brethren"—can be found in the Pontifical Biblical Commission document *The Interpretation of the Bible in the Church* (available on the Vatican website as *L'interprétation de la Bible dans l'Église* [April 15, 1993], but not translated into English). An English translation can be found at https://www.ewtn.com/library/ CURIA/PBCINTER.HTM.

of certain texts in Scripture. Perhaps the most noteworthy example was Genesis 1. Many of them—although by no means all—held that God created the world in six "literal" days, and that he made human beings on the sixth. Many also held that if you did not accept that, you could not uphold the authority of the Scripture as the Word of God, because you would be saying that the text was erroneous. Other orthodox Christians did not want to defend such a view, and it became common to describe such a position as "taking the Bible literally" or taking a particular part of the Bible literally.

The idea of taking the Bible literally is not very clear. It has at least three possible meanings. First of all, we do not take it literally when we recognize that some of the assertions in the Scripture are figurative, that is, not standard or normal or plain speech. When you read that Cain killed Abel and think it means that afterwards there was a dead body, you are reading the story literally. If you think it means that Cain told Abel a joke and afterwards Abel "died laughing," you are not taking it literally, because the literal meaning of the words "kill" or "die" have to do with the ending of life. That is the standard or normal or plain meaning of those words. To use them to describe laughing is to understand them in a figurative or metaphorical way. Of course the story of Cain and Abel is to be read literally and not figuratively. Any Scripture scholar would say that.

The second meaning of taking the Bible literally is somewhat similar. We do not take the Bible literally when we recognize that some text is speaking about an event in an extended or analogical sense. In Genesis 3:7 it says, "Then the eyes of both were opened, and they knew that they were naked." Human nakedness is something seen by human eyes, but the text is not speaking about the simple registering of a physical sensation. Rather it is speaking about knowing something about what is seen, in this case the recognition of the significance of being without clothes. Or in Genesis 6:8, it says, "But Noah found favor in the eyes of the LORD." Not only does the Lord not have eyes, but the reference is not to physical sighting but to personal approval.

If someone says, for instance, that he "sees" that a geometrical proof is true, he is speaking analogically. The normal or standard or plain meaning of the word "see" has to do with seeing by means of our physical eyes. When we see a chair is green, we are literally seeing that that is the case. When we "see" the truth of a geometric proof, we are not using our physical eyes but our minds (intellects), and we are inclined to describe that as "seeing," because in both instances we are recognizing the truth of something. Using our minds and using our eyes for the acquisition of knowledge are somewhat similar and therefore using the word "seeing" for understanding is an analogical usage. Many statements in Scripture are worded in an analogical way. We will discuss this more fully in the discussion "Analogical Discourse" (p. 479).

The third meaning of taking the Bible literally is more relevant to our topic here. We decide not to take something literally when we judge that the literary genre of some narrative is not intended to convey historical events. Suppose we say that Gollum (Sméagol) in Tolkien's novel *The Lord of the Rings* killed his relative Déagol. When you read it literally, as you should, you presume that afterwards Déagol was no longer alive and his dead body was in the ground. And you would be correct. But you do not think you could go back in time and observe it happening. It is only a story in a novel.

On the other hand, if you read that Marcus Junius Brutus was one of those who killed Julius Caesar, you can have a reasonable confidence that you could go back to 44 BC and observe it actually happening. You would be able to check to see that Brutus was one of the ones stabbing Caesar, and that Caesar was dead afterwards. The difference between the two situations is the literary status of the referents of the words. In one case you understand them as referring to an event in a fictional story, in another you understand them as referring to what we would call an historical fact, an event that actually occurred in the past the way it is described. We might also speak about this by saying that the referent refers to something real, not imaginary as in the murder of Déagol.

Scholars would describe the correct understanding of these accounts in regard to the historical facticity of what they describe as in large part a matter of literary form or genre. We know that the account of Déagol's death is not an historical fact, because it occurs in a novel or a "fantasy," a genre of writing that does not narrate historical events. We would not even consider entering it in Langer's *Encyclopedia*. Caesar's death, however, is there.

Literary genre and historicity. We can distinguish four main modern interpretive approaches to the literary genre or form in relation to the historical facticity of scriptural narrative accounts, including the account in Genesis 1:

1. The accounts are simply ancient myth and have no truth-value. They do not indicate any historical facts, and they do not have any other truth-value either. All that we read are pieces of primitive mythology that are just historical relics, probably originating with the Babylonians. The main use of reading through the first chapters of Genesis is to look at an example of ancient mythology.

2. The accounts in Genesis are a symbolic story, a story written to teach a point. They have truth-value but do not express historical fact. They have no historical referent, but were written for instruction, using a dramatic form. Virgil's *Aeneid* is like this—a story of the foundation of Rome that Virgil probably did not think happened this way but made use of to give an orientation to how to think about Rome.

3. The accounts are "straight history," much like any of the history books that we find referred to in a modern introductory history course. The accounts not only have overall truth-value, but also historical fact value. If we were able to go back to about 4000 B.C., we would find the garden of Eden somewhere in the Near East, and if we arrived on the right day we would see the serpent discussing with Eve the fruit of the tree of the knowledge of good and evil.

4. The accounts are an historical story in which there is some kind of historical reference. The stories are not completely

made up, but refer to things that have an historical basis. On the other hand, the accounts are not written in the way we would say an historical account should be written. Rather, they are written fairly freely, in a way designed to bring out a point rather than produce verbally something like a photographic or stenographic record of how the events happened.

The first approach is not a good Christian approach, at least if we accept the Scriptures as the Word of God, as orthodox Christians do. It is spiritually wrong. It also is most likely historically wrong as well. The beginning of Genesis has certain similarities to Babylonian mythology and probably has been influenced by it in some ways, but it is significantly different in nature. Trying to establish that or even treating the question of the influence of ancient Near Eastern mythology on scriptural writings, however, would get us into an unnecessary lengthy discussion.[3]

For many orthodox Christians, the challenging question is how someone might say that the beginning of Genesis is true in any sense and not simply an historical account in the modern sense.[4] To il-

---

[3] For some presentations that argue this point, see Stanley Jaki, *Genesis 1 Through the Ages* (London: Thomas More Press, 1992), 11–22; and John Lennox, *Seven Days that Divide the World* (Grand Rapids, MI: Zondervan, 2011), Appendix A.

[4] This is not solely a modern problem, and viewing the days of Genesis in a non-literal way is not simply a move to cope with modern science. In the time of the early church, teachers, both Jewish and Christian, raised concerns with the straight history view for exegetical reasons. Philo of Alexandria, the diaspora Jewish teacher who died about 50 AD, said in *A Treatise on the Account of the Creation of the World, as Given by Moses* XIII.13, "The world was made in six days, not because the Creator stood in need of a length of time (for it is natural that God should do everything at once, not merely by uttering a command, but by even thinking of it); but because the things created required arrangement; and number is akin to arrangement." Clement of Alexandria in *Stromateis* 6:16 held that creation could not happen in time at all, because "time was born along with things which exist." Augustine of Hippo in *The City of God* XI:6, held: "As for these days [in the Genesis account], it is difficult, perhaps impossible to think, let alone explain in words, what they mean." Those who think these questions are modern questions related to the difficulties of harmonizing Genesis with modern natural science should read Augustine's *On the Literal Meaning of Genesis* or Basil's *On the Hexaemeron*, or Ambrose's work of the same name, all of whom worked to put together the account in Genesis with the natural science of their day, which, of course, was different from the natural science of our day, but presented similar problems.

lustrate that, let us take another look at Genesis 1. At first sight, it seems to be describing seven 24-hour days that occurred a long time ago. This was accepted by many rabbis, as the current dates for the years in the Jewish calendar show (April 2015 = Nisan 5775). Creation in this view occurred in 3761 BC. It would be common to describe this as the "literal view."

However, as many have noted—from the Fathers on, including Augustine and many modern writers who could be described as Fundamentalists (including James Orr, the one who wrote the relevant article in *The Fundamentals*)—that to view the first "week" of creation as a literal week is probably not true in an unqualified sense, or perhaps not true at all. Since the sun does not seem to be created until the fourth day, and since we (and the Hebrews) usually use the word "day" to refer to a solar day, the first three days could not be literal days, at least not literal solar days. During what the text calls the third day, for instance, we would not be able to observe a sunrise or sunset.[5]

In addition, the account does not clearly seem to follow a sequence that we, or probably the ancient Hebrews, would recognize as a narrative of causal development. As we have seen in Genesis 1, the sun comes after the light and the plants even arrive before the sun, although Hebrews probably could see that plants did not grow in places without sun. They may have been naïve in certain respects, but to say they were so naïve that they did not know such things is very unlikely.

There is, however, another and more significant feature of the

---

[5]   Origen in *On First Principles* (Gloucester: Peter Smith, 1973), 288, held that "Now what man of intelligence will believe that the first, the second and the third day, and the evening and morning existed without the sun, moon and stars?" Augustine in *On the Literal Meaning of Genesis*, 1.9–11, puzzled how these verses made sense physically and held, "But at least we know that it [the Genesis day] is different from the ordinary day with which we are familiar." Moreover, the view already existed in the early church that the "days" of Genesis referred to ages, based on Psalm 90:4 and 2 Peter 3:8. Justin Martyr, *Dialogue with Trypho*, LXXXI (ANF, I, 239), used such an understanding, as did Irenaeus, AH, V (ANF, I, 118). Both applied this view to Genesis 2:17 holding that Adam did die in that "day" (Genesis 5:5 says his death happened 930 years after, still within the "day" of a 1000 years).

account. The seven-day narrative seems to many to be written not in a chronological way but in an ordered or systematic or didactic (theological) or logical way. In other words, although at first the literary form of the seven days seems to present a narrative of the steps in which the universe was put together, looking more carefully at the account might indicate that the narrative framework rather presents a set of relationships that exist between the elements of universe (or a catalog of the main elements of the universe as human beings experience it), and is intended especially to emphasize that all of them were created by God for the purposes he had. Moreover, all of them had different functions in his plan.

We often use the approach of describing something in an ordered sequence that is not a developmental sequence. A surgeon might describe his new hospital, focusing on his points of interest. He might say "we put the operating room on the third floor with the wards on the floors above and below it for convenience. Everything else—offices including my own and the car park—was put on the first (ground) floor or in the basement." He hardly means that the builder began by suspending the operating room in the air and then completed the building around it. Rather he is laying out the spatial relationships of his main points of interest.

Some have said that in Genesis 1 the creation is described in an analogous way. Following an image used elsewhere in Scripture, creation was described as if the Creator were setting up a tent and then putting in the furnishings (Ps 104:2). Some have said that it is describing creation as the formation of the cosmos as a temple, first creating the building (or tabernacle/tent in the account of the original temple), then putting in the "furnishings." Both could be true.

If creation is described on the analogy of a human being setting up a tent or tabernacle/temple, the key to the description is the function of the different parts—first the tent is erected (Days 1–3), then the needed furnishings are put in (Days 4–6), and finally the people who will live in and use or worship in the tent enter (Day 6b). That is quite a different approach than one that describes creation as first the "Big Bang," then the formation of the stars, then the formation of our galaxy, then our solar system, then the cooling of our planet, then the emergence of life, etc.

While such an approach makes sense, it does not of itself explain why the account seems to give a chronological order in terms of seven days of creation. Most commonly those who take this approach interpret the seven-day sequence as a framework. Perhaps this kind of framework was used as a vivid way to distinguish the various realms of nature, perhaps to express God's developmental approach to creation, perhaps to emphasize the importance of observing the Sabbath, perhaps to describe the creation with the number seven, an important number that indicates a completion, perhaps all these, or even for some other reason beyond our recovery.[6]

According to such views, it is a mistake to try to correlate the details of the account in Genesis with the developmental causal sequences presented by modern science—especially if such correlation insists that the Genesis account, in order to be true, has to be structured on the developmental sequences used by modern science. The literary forms have such different purposes and different interests that they cannot be put together in such a way, but that does not mean they are not both true and useful for the purposes that gave rise to them.

Genesis 1, in these views, does not have the literary form of an historical narrative or of a developmental causal sequence, and so we ought not to read it as if it did.[7] Those who take the approach that it has a different literary form commonly say that the main "historical" fact is the fact that God created everything, including all those things worshipped by polytheists, and he created the cosmos with an order and a purpose. The second main "historical" fact is that God created human beings in his image and likeness to order the material creation, not worship it or worship anything in it.

---

[6]   Claus Westermann in *The Genesis Accounts of Creation* (Philadelphia: Fortress, 1964), 10–11 provides an overall view of this approach.

[7]   Jaki, *Genesis 1 Through the Ages*, uses the word "concordism" to describe this approach and in his book provides a history and critique of it. "Concordism" has for some become broader so that it can, for instance, refer to establishing a concord between the scriptural account and other historical data.

We should emphasize that these are truths, but not try to develop a correlation between each step in the creation account and each phase of our current scientific theories about the formation of the universe.[8]

We could also add that the account of creation in Genesis 1 could not be historical in the normal sense of history anyway. We normally reserve the word "history" to speak about accounts based on written documents from the past that are intended to describe what happened in the past. We speak of "pre-historical" events, meaning events that occurred before there were documents written by humans. Creation occurred before human historical writing existed. There was only one "eyewitness" who could have described it—the Creator himself. Christians believe that he has communicated that knowledge to us, but by revelation, not by any human beings writing down what they observed. And the human author or authors wrote down that revelation in a literary genre that communicates the message God intends us to understand.

Some form of the non-literal understandings of the temporal as-

---

[8] John H. Walton in *The Lost World of Genesis 1: Ancient Cosmology and the Origins Debate* (Downers Grove, IL: InterVarsity Press, 2009) has written a book with a somewhat different approach that has attracted attention among Evangelical scholars. He holds that the Genesis account is like other cosmological accounts in the ancient world in that it makes use of a "functional ontology" to describe the work of creation in Genesis 1, not a "material ontology." His book is effectively critiqued by John C. Lennox, the Oxford professor of mathematics and of the philosophy of science, in *Seven Days That Divide the World*, 131–134, and in a different way by C. John Collins in his review of the book referenced in the Reformed Academic blog, http://reformedacademic.blogspot.com/2009/11/lost-world-of-genesis-one-book-review.html.

Even more serious than the critiques that these authors mention is the underlying incoherence of Walton's ontological views. Although we often recognize the nature of things by the way they function and although "creation" can refer to bringing something into existence so that it functions in a certain way—even something that already exists in a different way—functions do not exist on their own, but are functions of existing things (which have a variety of natures, some of which are material in our sense, and some are not). "Function" is simply not the same as "existence." A function is a function *of* an existing thing. If Walton's ontological categories are not clear, then his use of them to sort the scriptural data cannot be sound, and Lennox points out a number of problems with his sorting of the scriptural data that are due to the lack of clear ontological criteria for his judgments.

pect of the account in Genesis 1 is perhaps the mainline view at the moment among orthodox Christian teachers, including many if not most conservative Evangelicals.[9] It does not take the approach that Genesis 1 has to be interpreted as an historical sequence because it is written in narrative form. It does not see Genesis 1 as mythological or even as a symbolic story, but rather as a theological or logical presentation using a temporal seven-day framework to present creation.

There are, however, many orthodox Christian teachers who would not simply accept such an approach and would hold that Genesis 1 is fundamentally an historical account or at least written in a developmental sequence that is not incompatible with modern science or even corresponds to it. Their arguments are worth considering. Moreover, they would not agree with many of the above points, and would present alternative understandings.[10]

The above presentation, however, is intended to make the point that the issue between these positions is not necessarily one of faith in the historical accuracy of the Bible, but of the understanding of

---

[9] James Barr in *Fundamentalism,* 40–42, holds that most conservative Evangelicals do not follow a "literal" understanding of the days of Genesis 1 and gives a survey of conservative Evangelical views in Great Britain at the time when his book was published (1977). He does not take into account, however, those who can be described as "young earth creationists," that is, those who believe that the days of Genesis are twenty-four hour days of one earth week, and that the universe is young (created about six thousand years ago, rather than the almost 14 billion years ago that is commonly held by scientists). For the most part, however, conservative Evangelical scholars would not hold to a literal understanding of the days of Genesis 1.

[10] A helpful contemporary presentation of this position can be found in John C. Lennox, *Seven Days That Divide the World,* chap. 3. He upholds the basic historicity (or perhaps we should say physics) of Genesis 1 in the sense of the temporal sequence of Genesis 1 having a reference that in some way corresponds to modern scientific cosmology without holding to a "literal" six day creation. He suggests that each day of the creation week might refer to the particular day in which "God injected a new level of information and energy into the cosmos in order to advance creation to its next level of form and complexity" (p. 55). He also allows for the reasonableness of orthodox Christian teachers upholding a different view than his. A similar view can be found in C. John Collins, *Genesis 1–4: A Linguistic, Literary, and Theological Commentary* (Phillipsburg, NJ: P&R Publishing, 2006), 122–129; and Vern Sheridan Poythress, *Inerrancy and Worldview: Answering Modern Challenges to the Bible* (Wheaton, IL: Crossway, 2012), 40–42, more fully developed in his book *Redeeming Science: A God-centered Approach* (Wheaton, IL: Crossway, 2006).

the genre of Genesis 1. Many orthodox Christian teachers hold that the genre of Genesis 1 is not a literal presentation, at least not in the temporal aspects of the text (the one earth week of seven days).

There is still a different approach, one that does not directly engage the question of historical accuracy, namely, the "esoteric teaching" approach. By "esoteric teaching" is meant teaching that is not given out publicly to all the world (which would be "exoteric teaching"), but is reserved for those who are initiated into its existence and meaning. In such a view, Genesis 1 would be coded and structured in such a way that it not only conveyed a public meaning, but also at the same time an esoteric teaching. This might explain some of the seeming anomalies in the text, such as the creation of light and the lights (sun and moon) on two different days or vegetation coming before the sun or unexplained literary features such as the presence or absence of the definite article before the word "day" at the conclusion of each of the seven "days" of creation. These might be clues to the esoteric meaning.

One of the main reasons for considering such a view is the section in *Mishnah Hagigah* 2:1:

> The forbidden degrees may not be expounded before three persons, nor the Story of [Neusner: the works of] Creation before two, nor [the chapter of] the Chariot before one alone, unless he is a Sage that understands of his own knowledge. Whosoever gives his mind to four things it were better for him if he had not come into the world—what is above? what is beneath? what was before time? and what will be hereafter? [Danby translation].

There are various reasons for the restricted teaching of the forbidden degrees that are given and the matter does not seem to be germane to our topic. The Chariot (the *Merkabah*), on the other hand, refers to the vision of God on his chariot throne in Ezekiel 1 and the story of creation refers to Genesis 1 (and possibly also Genesis 2). Both concern the nature of God. According to this text, they therefore describe something that should not be fully expounded except to someone who already understands something about the subject, likely the transcendence of the divine nature (perhaps also: and so do not understand the details literally).

These precautions might be due to the desire to ward off false conceptions of the divine nature. They might, however, be intended to guard against the passing on of esoteric teaching without appropriate safeguards or to guard against the intrusion of the wrong kind of esoteric teaching (Gnostic, for instance). The passage at least seems to indicate the existence of some accepted understanding that did not appear on the surface of the texts and that needed to be dealt with carefully. If so, we may have lost an exposition of Genesis 1 that some rabbis once were familiar with, including possibly an early Christian teacher with rabbinic training like the apostle Paul who spoke about heavenly things that do not clearly appear in our texts (2 Cor 12:1–4).[11] If so, this might explain some difficult features of Genesis 1–2 although the way it might is probably beyond our confident retrieval.

The principle that some modern Scripture scholars use that the text was written to be understood may not be true. That does not mean the text cannot be understood at all. The basic message can be understood, although all the anomalies cannot be explained in

---

[11] Gershom Scholem, perhaps the leading scholar of Jewish "mysticism," held in *Major Trends in Jewish Mysticism* (Jerusalem: Schocken Books, 1941, republished with a foreword by Robert Alter in 1995), 40–43, that the first phase of Jewish mysticism existed already among the Pharisees and Essenes in the Second Temple period and was concerned with esoteric teaching, teaching that was an antecedent of the Kabbalah. He applies this view more directly in *Kabbalah* (Jerusalem: Keter, 1974), 10–14, to *Mishnah Hagigah* 2:1. He holds that the sentence forbidding giving one's mind to four things is directed against Gnosticism, although not all scholars agree. *Hagigah* 2:1 is, of course, discussed in the Gemara in both the Babylonian and Palestinian Talmuds, and they do not clearly indicate the presence of esoteric teaching as much as the difficulty of these passages. The article "Hagigah" in the *Jewish Encyclopedia* (Jerusalem: Keter, 1974) broadly supports Scholem's position, especially in regard to the Jerusalem Talmud and provides additional references. A similar presentation can be found in Smith, *Priestly Vision*, 82–85, who, however, suggests earlier sources for esoteric and mystical teaching, namely, teaching stemming from the priestly authors of Genesis 1 and those like them.

a certain and satisfactory way. Perhaps the true position is that it was written to be partially understood and to give clues that there is more to the matter than the text clearly presents.

Literary genre and Scripture. The Scriptures as a whole are not written in only one literary genre. Parts are "straight history." Parts are historical presentations that have a fundamentally historical reference, but focus on showing the meaning of the events rather than making sure every detail is historically accurate. Parts are stories without any or much historical reference and are included to make a point or teach a truth. Parts are prayers, meditations, celebrations of victories, and many other kinds of writing.

Often we have trouble identifying the literary genre of a particular writing or interpreting it well because ancient writers, especially the ancient Hebrew writers who wrote the Old Testament, used genres and styles that we are unfamiliar with, and often mixed them in the same composition in ways we would not. As a result, there are various opinions on how to interpret a writing like Genesis 1. Neither Scripture scholars nor orthodox Christian teachers agree on how to read this and many other scriptural texts.

Fortunately, we can usually understand the truth the text is presenting, the message God wants us to grasp, without being able to identify with certainty the literary genre and the best way to interpret it in regard to the historicity of the events in narrative sections. The Scriptures may not be perfectly clear to us, but they are clear enough to accomplish God's purpose in inspiring them. Even though many texts must have been clearer to the original audience than they are to us, we can still understand them, at least the main points of most of them. Genesis 1 is one of them and has had a major impact throughout the ages in forming the minds of those who seek God.[12]

In the discussion "Historical Reliability" in chapter 21 (p. 519), we will discuss more fully the question of whether the events nar-

---

[12] For a discussion of the clarity of Scripture, including patristic views, see John Yocum, "Scripture, Clarity of" in the *DTIB*.

rated in the Scriptures "actually happened." In the following sections "Presuppositions," "Anthropomorphism," and "Analogical Discourse" we will consider other features of our use of language that affect how we understand many statements in scriptural accounts.

CHAPTER FIFTEEN

PRESUPPOSITIONS

To interpret the Scriptures well, we need to be able to distinguish what they are actually asserting as distinguished from what presuppositions they are relying on.

There is another view that is sometimes given as a reason not to accept the truth-value of the account in Genesis 1 and other sections of the Scripture. According to this view, the Old Testament has a cosmology that we do not have and would not accept. Many writings of the Old Testament speak in terms of a "three story universe," that is, the heaven above, the earth in the middle, and the underworld below as a kind of basement to the universe. We now know that is not the case, so that indicates to us that we cannot accept anything in the Old Testament.[1]

Such a view has some serious problems with it. The first is that it assumes the Old Testament writers had a cosmology that is similar to our own, similar enough that the two can be viewed as two theories that can be compared to one another and judged in terms of accuracy. Increasingly that has been seen to be a mistake. The Old Testament shows little interest in cosmological theories, as we have seen, although it is very emphatic that the world as we know it was created by God and is ruled by him. Rather, the Old Testament

---

[1] Rudolf Bultmann, "The New Testament and Mythology" in *Kerygma and Myth* (New York: Harper & Row), 3–8 is the classic source for this.

writers commonly just described the world as they experienced it, often using images that seemed to fit well, such as the world as a kind of tent.

The experience of most human beings is of living on dry land with the sky above and a kind of basement into which they put bodies when they bury them and from which come various things like animals who live there and probably spirits of the dead. We usually think about our surroundings as we experience them, and go from there.

For instance, all of us, including our scientifically trained meteorologists, speak of sunrise and sunset. Our scientific cosmology tells us that the sun does not rise and set, but rather the earth rotates on its axis, allowing us to see the sun at certain times. But to speak of a time in the day when our part of the earth turns towards the sun and another time in the day when it turns away is so far from our experience that even the most professional scientists speak of sunrise and sunset. That is not, however, a reason for rejecting the truth-value of meteorological statements, but rather of recognizing that the way we speak about such things begins with the way we perceive our experience. What we experience is what we most want to explain or at least speak about.

We all have presuppositions when we are trying to speak about events in our experience. To use an example from modern philosophy, we might be at a party, and we want to tell a friend that a certain person present was a schoolmate of ours. We might say, "The woman over there with the glass of wine in her hand went to the same school I did." That might be enough to identify her. But suppose the woman was not holding a glass of wine but a glass of some other beverage. Does that make my statement false, because there was no woman holding a glass of wine? Of course not. I was presupposing something that was not strictly speaking factual but close enough to identify her, and in fact the woman I was speaking about did go to the same school I went to, my friend was able to pick out the person I was talking about, and I did convey a true fact to him.

When we talk to people, we rely on many presuppositions when we speak. Sometimes the presupposition is not true or at least not accurately stated. That does not keep us from communicating effectively. Sometimes we even know we need to use the presupposition to communicate effectively. We speak of sunrise and sunset because that is the way everyone speaks (and even the way everyone thinks, even though most modern people religiously believe otherwise), and if we spoke about the hour when our part of the earth turned towards the sun, the person we were speaking to might not even understand us, or at least would wonder why we were talking in such a strange way.

There is an important distinction between what we are asserting and what we are presupposing when we speak. Our assertion can be true, even though our presuppositions may not be. To return to the three-story universe example, many Old Testament writers presupposed that was a good way to speak. That was the way everyone spoke. That was the way that corresponded to their experience, much as sunrise and sunset does to most of us today. If, however, we look for a place in the Old Testament where it asserts that there is such a thing as a three-story universe, we will look in vain. But the Old Testament does assert that God created everything in heaven, on earth and under the earth, and so he did.[2]

---

[2] Richard Swinburne, *Revelation: From Metaphor to Analogy* (Oxford: Clarendon Press, 2007), 27–37. There is another use of the term presupposition in exegetical discussions, which focuses not on the presuppositions in ordinary communication but the presuppositions behind various approaches in scriptural interpretation or in theology. Such presuppositions can be described as the principles underlying a given discussion. For an example of the presuppositions which "underlie the NT writers' interpretation of the OT," see G. K. Beale, *Handbook on the New Testament Use of the Old Testament: Exegesis and Interpretation* (Grand Rapids, MI: Baker Academic, 2012), chap. 5. These "presuppositions" are all discussed in this book, but are referred to as underlying principles, following more traditional terminology.

CHAPTER SIXTEEN

GENESIS 1, GENESIS 2, AND SOURCE CRITICISM

The Scriptures present us with a collection of genres and texts, some of which probably originally came from a variety of sources, not just from the human author of the final text. We need to know how to put them together to understand the Scriptures in their unity. We recognize them primarily stylistically (not mainly by their communicative art but by their overall approach).

Introduction to the chapter. Almost all modern scholars and many traditional writers notice that a shift occurs with Genesis 2:4. There is an easily perceptible difference in style between Genesis 1:1–2:4a and Genesis 2:4b–25.[1] Two of these differences are important to note at the outset.

First, there is the difference in literary form: the two accounts read differently. Chapter 1 is ordered and highly structured, giving an overview of the whole material universe. Chapter 2 is dramatic and concrete, presenting the beginning of one significant incident that affected the history of the human race. It develops around the interaction between the characters (persons) in a drama—God,

---

[1] The textual point at which the division occurs is disputed, but the different views do not make a major difference to the relation of the two sections. Here the view is taken that Genesis 2:4 is a transitional verse, ending the previous section and beginning the new section, but expressing a unity to the two sections by the chiastic way the verse is constructed.

Adam, Eve, and the serpent, in the order of their appearance.

Second, God himself is presented as if he were a human being in Genesis 2. He molds the clay and makes Adam and then Eve; he talks with Adam and Eve; he walks in the garden, etc. Yet he is clearly all-powerful, creating and forming the earth and the first human pair, and determining their futures. Moreover, in his own nature he cannot have a physical voice or physically walk in a physical space, because he created such things. To use the technical term, Genesis 2 makes use of a more *anthropomorphic* presentation of God, that is, speaking about God as if he were like a human being.

Third, there are some differences in the content as well. Some of these we have noted in chapter 2. Those differences have, however, occasioned considerable discussion.

It is common to speak about there being two creation accounts. Broadly speaking that is correct, but it obscures an important relationship between the two. Genesis 1 is the account of the creation of heaven and earth, that is, of the world or the universe. It is a solemn prologue to the whole Bible, and describes the world and its creation in an orderly way. Genesis 2 is the beginning of a unit that extends to the end of Genesis 4. It is the introduction to the account of disobedience to God and exile from paradise. Genesis 2 is not an account of all of creation, but an account of the creation of the human race in "the day that the LORD God made the earth and the heavens" and, more to the point, the background to the exile from the life God made the human race for, the life of paradise. That exile was caused by an interaction between God and the first humans, an interaction that has been portrayed effectively in a narrative way.

A scholarly concern. A common modern scholarly interpretation of the differences between chapters 1 and 2, often described as "The Documentary Hypothesis," comes from source criticism. Some source critics have claimed that what we have here are creation stories from two different sources. The older source critics usually spoke of Genesis 1 as the Priestly source and Genesis 2–3 as the Yahwist one. Sometimes they just used the initials "P" and "J" (from the German spelling of "Yahwist"). When they went on to discuss the whole Pentateuch, they added "E" (the Elohist source) and "D" (the Deuteronomist source).

To note that there is a difference between the two chapters is helpful, and few scholars would dispute that. Some traditional commentators noted many of the differences, and discussed the relationship of the two accounts. The view that many sections of the Pentateuch, and specifically the different sections of Genesis 1–4, come originally from pre-existent sources that the final author (or redactor) made use of—or possibly ones he made use of and one that he himself wrote—is not very controversial. Many modern commentators, however, go on to assign each section of the Pentateuch, sometimes each individual verse, to a source, and then give us an account of that source and its author, and often how and when it was written.

The sources referred to in the documentary hypothesis do not exist, or, to grant the most favorable understanding, do not exist independently any more. There are no P or J or E or D documents in our manuscript collection, nor have any been discovered among the Dead Sea Scrolls, much less in the Cairo Genizah. They are scholarly, speculative reconstructions, many of them very complicated. Moreover, the various reconstructions scholars have offered us rarely agree, never in all details. In addition, the scholars have not seemed able to convince one another of the superiority of a given version. For reasons like this, the documentary hypothesis as a whole no longer commands general acceptance.[2]

---

[2] For a few examples of those who distance themselves from the Documentary Hypothesis, see Umberto Cassuto, *The Documentary Hypothesis and the Composition of the Pentateuch* (Jerusalem: Shalem Press, 2006); Rolf Rendtorff, *The Problem of the Process of Transmission in the Pentateuch, Journal for the Study of the Old Testament Supplement Series* (Sheffield, 1990), vol. 89; Isaac M. Kikawada and Arthur Quinn, *Before Abraham Was: The Unity of Genesis 1–11* (Nashville, TN: Abingdon, 1985); Gary A. Rendsburg, *The Redaction of Genesis* (Winona Lake, IN: Eisenbrauns, 1986), especially chap. VI; R. Norman Whybray, "The Making of the Pentateuch: A Methodological Study" *Journal for the Study of the Old Testament Supplement* 53 (1989); Robert Alter, *Genesis* (New York: Norton, 1996), xl–xliii. A recent survey of the state of the discussion can be found in Richard S. Briggs and Joel N. Lohr, ed., *A*

The same thing happened in New Testament scholarship as well. Similarities were noted between the Gospels. Common materials in the collections of sayings in the Gospels, primarily Matthew and Luke, were isolated. A source "Q" was postulated. Then we had books written on the theology of "Q", whose original composition we have failed to find and probably never will.[3] Or differences were noted in the "Johannine writings," and then scholars found they could write a history of "the community of the beloved disciple."[4]

Many reconstructions have been based on a high confidence in the ability of scholarship to go beyond what it is in a text and reconstruct the history behind it. Since the result has not been one clearly accepted theory of how all this worked, many scholars now would hold that many if not most efforts at reconstruction have gone beyond what the textual evidence actually allows and cannot yield successful results,[5] although some pieces of it have held up.

Theological Introduction to the Pentateuch: Interpreting the Torah as Christian Scripture, (Grand Rapids, MI: Baker Academic, 2012), 9–13, a presentation by two students of R. W. L. Moberly and representatives of canonical criticism. A recent history of the process of "calling the documentary hypothesis into question" be found in Ignacio Carbajosa, *Faith the Fount of Exegesis: The Interpretation of Scripture in the Light of the History of Research on the Old Testament* (San Francisco: Ignatius Press, 2013), 56–79.

[3] Johnson and Kurz, in *The Future of Catholic Biblical Scholarship*, 30, describe how this works, citing somewhat extreme but existing examples of the process:

> In the name of history, compositions have been chopped into sources. Sources, in turn, have been sliced into ever finer layers of redaction and placed on slides. Then, like some home laboratory experiment in cloning, these textual tissue samples are used to reconstruct the putative histories of hypothetical communities. Not only is there a hypothetical source named Q, but Q is sliced into the layers Q1 and Q2 and Q3, which then are thought to yield the history of the 'Q community.' To find the history of the Corinthian community, Paul's letters to that church are broken into as many as six sources. The course of the 'Philippian controversy' is thought to be traceable once Paul's letter to the Philippians is broken into three sources that can then be arranged in sequence. Small wonder if the casual reader of commentaries concludes that biblical studies have little to do with the actual Bible.

[4] Raymond Brown, *The Community of the Beloved Disciple* (Mahwah, NJ: Paulist Press, 1979).

[5] Peter Stuhlmacher—himself an advocate of use of the historical-critical version of the historical method in Scripture study—in his evaluation of the state of the art in *Historical Criticism and Theological Interpretation of Scripture* (Philadelphia: For-

That does not mean there is no consensus about the existence of sources and even in broadly distinguishing the existence of certain sources (or, as some now would put it, "tracing source material"). Nor does it mean that attention to possible source material is useless. It is in fact often helpful. It does, however, mean that we are not considering something that can simply be seen in the text, nor even that the hypothesized documents actually existed, and therefore most observations on sources are speculative.

In addition and more significant for our purposes, there has been a recent emphasis on the importance of interpreting the work we have (as distinguished from a speculatively reconstructed work) and interpreting it as a whole. Many literary critics hold that Genesis, in the state we have it, and even the whole Pentateuch, are one book. We do not have a library of the Priestly, the Yahwist, the Elohist, and the Deuteronomist sources (the four most commonly mentioned sources), but one work put together in a certain way. If we do not read it and interpret it as a whole, we are likely to miss what it is saying.[6]

*A **theological concern**.* There is a further concern with some approaches to source criticism, a Christian concern, or, as some would

---

tress, 1977), 86, called for new developments in regard to method because "only by scientific and theoretical apprehension of the way in which we handle the tradition can we master the continually astonishing and at times even horrifying experience that a historical exposition of texts seldom leads to really commonly recognized results, but as a rule yields quite disparate data." Much writing on the "scientific and theoretical apprehension of the way we handle the tradition" does not seem to have improved the situation since then, and perhaps might create even more horror. More recently, Johnson and Kurz in *The Future of Catholic Biblical Scholarship*, 14–15, said about the historical-critical method, primarily addressing its use in New Testament scholarship, "This model has promised more than it can offer . . . It has not in fact led to an agreed-upon historical reconstruction of ancient Israel, of the human mission of Jesus, or of the development of early Christianity. In fact, the opposite is true: the more scholars have pursued these questions, the more elusive such agreement appears. There are on offer today more versions of 'the historical Jesus' and of 'early Christianity' than are compatible with the perception of history as a scientific discipline." Similar views by other scholars could be cited.

6 Robert Alter, *Genesis*, xxxix–xlii.

say, a faith concern. The effort to reconstruct the text so we can ascertain what the original text was and what the original author said is not only speculative, but the result is not the Scripture. The Scripture is what we have printed in our Bibles, not a hypothetical reconstruction. The actual Scripture is what we need to understand if we are looking for God's word.

We might accept the view that Genesis 2 probably was first written or spoken by a different human author than Genesis 1, and they were put together into one work either by one of those authors or by a third author (the editor or redactor). We might also accept one of the reconstructions on offer as the most likely. All that is something a good Christian teacher might do—even given the uncertainty of the theories behind such an approach.

Many Scripture scholars and theologians and popular authors, however, go beyond that to do problematic things with such a view. Some hold that Genesis 1 (the Priestly source) and Genesis 2 (the Yahwist source) represent two different theologies and in certain respects are in conflict with one another. We therefore need to pick one of them, the one that seems to be in most conformity with the Gospel message (often meaning the theological or ideological view the author is trying to advocate). Another more subtle way of doing the same thing is to say that one account is more primitive; the other is more advanced. We need to take the one that is advancing or progressing more towards the goal of the Gospel (which turns out to be the theological or ideological view the author is advocating).

This is, for instance, what some have done with the two accounts when discussing men and women's roles (one example of which can be found in chapter 2). Some will say that Genesis 1 comes from the Priestly source, while Genesis 2 comes from the Yahwist source, and they contain two different ways of looking at men's and women's roles. In the Yahwist view there is a focus on the subordination of women (at least in Genesis 3:16, but also sometimes in the creation of woman after and from the creation of man), while in the Priestly source the focus is mainly on equality and on both being in the image of God. We should affirm the approach of Genesis 1, not that of Genesis 2. In other words, it has been somewhat common to use reasoning of this kind to dismiss certain things in Scripture by positing conflicts between different sources and then opting for one or the other source.[7]

If there was an editor or compiler who put these two accounts together, he most likely believed that these two were consistent with each other, even if they contrasted to one another in certain ways. He probably would not have put them together if he thought that the two were simply contradictory and so cancelled one another out in their main assertions. This might even be considered the common sense view of the matter. The interpreters who make the two accounts present contradictory views of human life that cannot be reconciled go far beyond what a sober source criticism can allow us to do.

Genesis 1 and 2, then, are not two differing accounts of the creation of the universe. They are one account that gives an overview of the whole creation and a second account that develops the first by describing the background to the Fall of the human race. They present two perspectives in differing literary forms, but they are both Scripture and go together. Therefore, they should be expected to be in harmony with one another in all that they are seeking to assert.

We have to deal with the Scripture as it is given to us. We do not want to base our view of God's eternal Word on the shifting sands of scholarly opinion, much less on ideological reconstructions. We want to base it on the canon of Scripture, the book of Scripture that has been passed down to us, and that is one book, not a collection of disparate sources that we are entitled to choose from.

---

[7] Popular examples of this approach can be found in Arlene Swidler, *Woman in a Man's Church* (Paramus, NJ: Paulist Press, 1972), 34f, and Virginia Mollenkott, "Women and the Bible," *Sojourners* (February 1976): 22.

CHAPTER SEVENTEEN

ANTHROPOMORPHISM

The Scriptures commonly speak about God as if he were a human being. That allows us to understand him better without our being able to tell fully what he is like in himself.

Most modern Christians can read through Genesis 1 without any great concern about the things in it that are said about God. Genesis 2 is another matter. There we find, for instance, God walking in the garden, possibly waiting like a man in the subtropics until the midday temperature cools off. If we pay attention, we find him looking at the animals he created, including the first human being, and discovering that his work was incomplete. He omitted creating a partner for Adam, and so he had to go back and make up the deficiency. Perhaps we might surmise that he did not realize this until Adam pointed it out to him.

If, however, we are alert enough, we could have the same problem with Genesis 1. God creates by speaking. But how can he speak if he does not have lips and a tongue and vocal cords? What does it mean to say that he does such a thing?

Intuitively we think we know. For him to create by speaking is like our telling a good workman to do something, and he does it. Or perhaps a modern example is even better. It is like instructing our computer to do something, and it does it. There is some similarity in all these things, although there is a great dissimilarity as well.

After all, whom or what did God instruct, since at least in Day 1, nothing had yet been created. Moreover, as we can tell by the way everything began, God had no need of a workman or computer or anything other than his own infinite power.

In fact, we do not know exactly what it means to say that God walks in the garden, or that he speaks and something is created. We do not know, because God is beyond our comprehension. We are fairly sure the Scripture is saying something true about God. We do not close the book out of sheer puzzlement and confusion. We have enough intuition to go on, and we think what it says makes sense. But God is God, and our mind cannot go so far as to understand him fully. We can be grateful that he is kind enough to tell us about himself in a way that we are not left fully in the dark. And if we have enough intelligent humility, we will respect our limitations.

But what do we do with a text that one scholar described as "wildly anthropomorphic"—the scene of God with Adam and the animals. It seems even a bit disrespectful to God, because he seems to have missed something obvious in his first attempt to create the human race. Approached literally, the account would be disrespectful. But we would have to admit that it makes a point in a way that we cannot miss. It expresses in a vividly dramatic way that it would make no sense to create a male human being, an animal of a certain sort, without creating a female. Both are important—necessary even.

The account is obviously written by someone who liked to write a story with some dramatic effect. Perhaps we might even suspect that the human author introduced a bit of humorous exaggeration into the story to make the point more vividly. This takes us back to the observation about style. God is written about in a variety of ways in the Scripture, and often he is written about as if he were a human being (commonly referred to as "anthropomorphism").

We cannot always tell exactly what anthropomorphic descriptions mean about God. There have been major debates in Christian teaching about various instances of anthropomorphic descriptions of God and what they are asserting about God. But at least we can say that such descriptions usually make it easier for us to "get the point" of the particular account and ultimately they make it easier for us to know God. These are the linguistic ways God has revealed himself to us.

Christian teachers have often described this process of God revealing himself in a human way as "accommodation" (sometimes: "condescension"). He accommodated himself to us so he could communicate to us in a way we could understand. His speaking this way is similar to the way many adults now would communicate to children, seeking to find a way of speaking that the children would understand.[1]

The Scriptures and Christian and Jewish tradition have at the same time insisted that God is not literally the way he is spoken about in Scripture.[2] As the Creator of everything, he is greater than any creature to which he may be compared. As the prophecy of Isaiah, speaking of the glory of the Lord, says,

> To whom then will you compare me,
>> that I should be like him?
>> says the Holy One.
> Lift up your eyes on high and see:
>> who created these?
> He who brings out their host by number,
>> calling them all by name;
> by the greatness of his might,
>> and because he is strong in power
>> not one is missing. (Is 40:25–26)

---

[1]   The idea of accommodation is treated extensively in Stephen D. Benin, *The Footprints of God: Divine Accommodation in Jewish and Christian Thought* (Albany, NY: State University of New York Press, 1993). Though it treats the question of anthropomorphism, the focus is more on the provisions of the Old Testament law and the reason the law was given.

[2]   For one patristic overview of the meaning of physical traits, including emotions, ascribed to God in Scripture, see John Damascene, *The Fountain of Knowledge, On the Exact Exposition of the Orthodox Faith*, 1.11, (PG 94.7894228). This can be found in Volume 37 in the Fathers of the Church Series (Washington, D.C.: Catholic University of America Press, 1958).

Every comparison with a creature falls short of the greatness of the Creator. And yet, it is the Creator himself who presented visions and comparisons by the prophets and inspired writers, so that we might come to know him and understand his will (Hos 12:10).

Christians take a further step, because they believe that at one point God the Son became a human being. *Although he was in the form of God . . .* he took *human form* (Phil 2:6–8). He did so primarily to enable a human being to redeem the human race by the power of God. The result, however, is that God himself translated his orientation and character into the medium of human nature with the result that we can understand better what he is like and what he is about in human history.

CHAPTER EIGHTEEN

ANALOGICAL DISCOURSE

We naturally use words in an analogical way, and scriptural writers mainly spoke about spiritual realities that way. Only later did theologies develop in which the analogical statements of Scripture were turned into technical ("scientific") speech.

Introduction to the chapter. In three of the previous methodological discussions, we have been considering the way the Scriptures were written in contrast to the way we normally write about Christian teaching. Some of the differences have had to do with semantics. "Semantics" is a term in modern linguistics that is used to indicate how language relates to reality, that is, the various ways in which what we say speaks about and is intended to indicate (signify) the way things are or have been or will be. It is commonly distinguished from syntactics, the way the words in a discourse structurally or grammatically relate to one another, and pragmatics, what we are trying to accomplish when we say something.

In the second methodological discussion, we looked at how literary genre shapes what we say. We especially looked at what it means to say or understand something literally, and we observed that a difference in literary approach can determine the ontological status of the intended referent (e.g., whether it is real or imaginary). In the third methodological discussion, we looked at the difference between what is being asserted and what presuppositions are being

used, and we observed that we need to grasp what is being asserted in any discourse to determine what is being said about the way
things are. We then considered the use of anthropomorphism in describing God, and observed that anthropomorphic language tells us
something about God, but not everything we might wish. These discussions are background to the present one, and each one touches
upon semantics.

We now will consider the analogical nature of much scriptural (and theological) discourse. From the beginning of Genesis, issues about the meaning of what is said constantly occur—acutely at
times if "the amount of ink spilled upon them" is any indication. Of
course, employing such a phrase does not mean that we look at most
copies of Scripture that have been used and see that the first two
chapters are covered with a great deal of an originally liquid but now
dried-out black substance (to illustrate one of the semantic issues).
We mean that our contemporaries, including Scripture scholars and
theologians, find it a challenge to understand how scriptural authors
use language, especially when they are trying to speak about spiritual realities—and many speak about that challenge at great length
and often unsuccessfully. The semantic questions raised by the Genesis text pervade the rest of Scripture, and they continue on in subsequent Christian teaching.

Analogous. When we speak in ways that are not simply the literal
sense we use words in an extended sense, and we do this most commonly by similarity ("analogously"). When something is similar it
is the same in some respects but also different in others. To say that
Socrates and Plato are human beings is to use "human being" in the
same way. To say that William I was the king of England and my
father was the king of the family is to use "king" in a similar but not
the same way. Both of them had the highest authority in a human
grouping, but their authority was only similar. William I could make
war, for instance, and my father could not.[1] From the point of view

---

[1]   In traditional semantic terminology, two words that are the same in meaning (the re-
    alities they refer to are the same) are characterized as *univocal* in meaning, and those

of the beginning of Genesis and in fact of most scriptural teaching, the scriptural authors use analogous speech to speak about much of life and especially about spiritual things.

For example, when we speak about God saying something, we are speaking analogously. We are using a word that means something human beings do with their breath, mouth, and vocal cords. God does not have those things. He made them. As we have noted, for God to speak and have the universe come to be is like our speaking and giving a command, but it must be very different as well. He apparently did not say, "let there be light" to anyone else, much less make a sound (which he had not yet created).

To give another example: when we speak about God living in heaven or reigning "on high" or when we look up when we pray to him, we do not think that if we just traveled upwards long enough we should find him, despite what Yuri Gagarin,[2] mentally crippled by his Communist education, thought. We are using analogical speech, in this case spatial speech, to talk about something that goes beyond what we can comprehend but that still makes some sense to us. Difference of location can be used analogously to speak about non-spatial differences in relationship to where we are, as when we speak of those in authority in relationship to us as "over" us. In this case we speak of God being "above" us to refer to the way God transcends our world.

The New Testament notably uses analogous speech in giving doctrinal teaching. We talk about the Church (the Christian people viewed corporately) as the body of Christ to indicate the unity between a group of people who believe in Christ with Christ himself, and thereby indicate that Christ functions in and through those people. We are not saying that the Church is a physical human body. We also talk about the Church as a temple of the Holy Spirit, not to

---

that are not the same at all are characterized as *equivocal* in meaning. Then two words that are similar in meaning (the realities they refer to are similar but not the same) are characterized as *analogous* in meaning.

[2] Yuri Gagarin was the Russian astronaut who, on returning from his space flight reported that God was nowhere to be seen, in contrast to the Apollo 8 astronauts, who on seeing earth from space read from the first chapter of Genesis.

indicate that it is a physical building (buildings and groups of human beings are quite different), but to indicate that the Holy Spirit is present in the group of people as God was in the temple. We talk about the Christian people as the children (sons and daughters) of God to indicate that God has established an ongoing relationship with them and given them a new kind of life, not that God sexually begot them.[3]

Moreover, we use all of these at the same time. To say that the Christian people (the Church) is the body of Christ, the temple of the Holy Spirit, and the sons and daughters of God is to make three different assertions about the Church. Each description taken literally is incompatible with the others. A body, a temple, and a son cannot be the same actually existing thing. But as applied in the New Testament these three descriptions are not incompatible assertions, because each phrase expresses a certain aspect of the relationship of the Church to God. They are not applied literally but analogously, that is, asserting that something similar is true about each of these things and the Church, but not that they and the Church have all the same characteristics.[4] To describe something typologically, as in this example, is to use analogous speech, saying that the referents are similar in their role or function in God's plan but not simply the same.

Sometimes this relationship is put together into a single description. The book of Revelation speaks about those who "washed their robes and made them white in the blood of the Lamb" (Rev

---

[3]   The fullest presentation of analogical descriptions of the Church in the New Testament can be found in Paul S. Minear, *Images of the Church in the New Testament* (Philadelphia: Westminster, 1975). He presents 96 images, although many are minor and some would not meet the definition of "analogical."

[4]   For a developed presentation of how a set of analogical descriptions go together to form an understanding of the same reality, see *Redeemer,* 88–90, 115–118, and 137–142. These sections treat the way three analogical descriptions of the reason for the effectiveness of Christ's sacrifice (payment for redemption, punishment instead of us, and giving as a sacrifice) come together into a fuller presentation. In addition, the results of Christ's work in us is described by three further analogical descriptions (judicial, ceremonial, and personal transformational) are discussed in the section on pages 284–289 of that book.

7:14). Anyone knows that washing clothing in blood will not make it white, but rather stain it red. But the phrase captures vividly and paradoxically that those who have been redeemed by the death of Christ ("in the blood of the lamb") have been transformed into people who live in some sense free from sin ("washed their robes and made them white").

Analogical speech is commonly contrasted to literal speech. There seem to be two main ways of defining the "literal meaning" of a word or phrase.[5] Perhaps the most common way is by saying that the literal meaning is what most people think is the normal or customary or standard meaning of a word or phrase,[6] or perhaps by saying the literal meaning is what the dictionary says it is.[7] This first way appeals to ordinary usage and to what most people recognize as the standard meaning.

This first way of defining "literal" has the drawback that people often differ on what is standard usage. Some might think, for instance, that "seeing" that one plus one equals two is literal speech, others not. In addition, dictionaries often differ. One might assign seeing that one plus one equals two to literal speech, and others not.

The second main way of defining "literal" is by saying that the literal meaning is the meaning that our physical senses and therefore our ordinary experiences provide for us.[8] "Seeing" refers to an operation of our eyes, not to our mind. Seeing that one plus one equals two is not literal speech according to this definition.

These two criteria of "literal" usage largely overlap. For the most

---

[5] Some prefer to use the term "lexical meaning." Peter Cotterell and Max Turner, *Linguistics and Biblical Interpretation* (London: SPCK, 1989), 140: "The lexical meaning is the range of senses of a word that may be counted on as being established in the public domain."

[6] *New Shorter Oxford English Dictionary*, (Oxford: Clarendon Press, 1993), (Hereafter *New SOED*) "Literal: Designating or pertaining to a sense or interpretation of a text, originally especially the Bible, obtained by taking words in the primary or customary meaning, and applying the ordinary rules of grammar, without mysticism, allegory, or metaphor; designating or pertaining to the etymological or primary sense of a word." The core of this definition goes back to Aristotle's *Poetics*, 21–22.

[7] Swinburne, *Revelation*, 13.

[8] See Aquinas, *ST,* I, q. 1, a. 9; I, q. 67, a. 1.

part, the meaning our physical senses provide for us is the commonly accepted meaning. In cases of disagreement, however, as in the example of seeing a mathematic truth, using the criterion of what our physical senses show us allows us to be more precise about what we mean by "literal." This is the definition of "literal" that we will use here.[9]

Analogical speech is extended speech. Extended meanings presuppose the literal meaning (the "primary" meaning) and apply it more broadly than its standard use allows. There are other ways of extending meanings besides analogical speech. When Genesis 49:10 says "The scepter shall not depart from Judah" to mean that the ruler of Israel will always be a member of the tribe of Judah, "scepter" stands for kingship not because it is similar to kingship, but because it is associated with kingship. Kings regularly use scepters as symbols of authority.[10]

"Literal" can be also used in a negative sense to refer to an inability to recognize figurative or analogous speech. We sometimes speak of people as having literal minds, meaning that they do not easily recognize metaphorical or humorous or ironical speech or are unimaginative in their thinking. More relevant to our subject, it is common for people studying Scripture to take a word or phrase in some text to be literal when it is actually metaphorical or analogical. In that case, we may say that they have taken the word "literalistically." They have misinterpreted it by understanding it to be literal.[11]

---

[9] For a further use of "literal" see the technical note on "The Four Senses of Scripture" on p. 414. This has a more restricted meaning than the one we are using here and functions as a technical term designating a certain kind of exegesis.

[10] It is common to describe this as extension by metonymy.

[11] There is yet another meaning of "literal," common in exegetical discussions, when it is used to describe translations. A translation is (more) literal when it attempts to represent the original language as closely as possible. It is contrasted to "idiomatic" when the translation attempts to render the text in phraseology that is normal usage in the language of the translation. Both can be literal in the sense being described in the above text.

Analogy and metaphor.[12] It is no doubt obvious that we have been speaking of descriptions of the Church that are not literal. As noted, the Church is not a physical body, a building, or a group of natural children. It would be common among Scripture scholars to describe these as metaphors or to describe this as metaphorical discourse. But such a response is misleading because it is ambiguous.

Metaphors, as understood by many, are figures of speech designed to adorn or enliven literary works.[13] While not simply literal descriptions or literal speech, the above-mentioned descriptions of the Church are more than figures of speech. They are not just ways that scriptural writers speak to present spiritual truths more vividly or elegantly or pleasingly. They tell us something about the nature of the Church and that seems to be the main reason to use them. In the Scriptures, they are not found only—or even mainly—in poetry but equally in prose teachings.

Alternatively, we might say that these descriptions are analogies or comparisons. That too, however, would be misleading. They are not just examples skillfully chosen to make a point clearer or easier to grasp.

There is a better way to describe these phrases than as metaphors (figures of speech) or analogies (simple comparisons), namely to describe them as analogical descriptions. They are employed to

---

[12] Swinburne, *Revelation*, chap. 3 provides an overview of much contemporary writing, especially in the Anglo-American philosophical tradition, on analogy and metaphor.

[13] A figure of speech is "a form of rhetorical expression which gives beauty, variety, force, etc. to a composition" (*New SOED*). The use of the word metaphor to speak about a kind of figure of speech goes back to Aristotle (*Poetics* 21–22). He also considered "analogy" a sub-category of metaphor (metaphor by proportion), and so established the usage that militated against using the word "analogy" for what we are terming "analogical discourse." Aristotle, however, indicated that metaphor was not just for poetic speech, but also for prose, and in prose it could be combined with the proper or standard (*to kúrion*) and appropriate (*tò oikeîon*) speech, that is, literal speech, to make clear assertions. He was, in other words, noting that what we are calling analogical discourse was ordinarily the standard way to talk about many realities. Aquinas made this point by contrasting the use of metaphor in poetry with its use in theology. Poetry makes use of "representations" to make writing more "pleasing," but theology does so because it is "both necessary and useful" in order to "raise [minds to which revelation has been made] to the knowledge of truths" (*ST*, I, q. 1, a. 9, ad 1 and ad 2).

convey content. They are ways the scriptural writers make their primary statements about the significance of the Church. We use them to think and teach about the Church.

This raises the question of the relationship of analogical descriptions to figurative speech in general and to metaphor in particular. There are two issues that come into play and the failure to distinguish them causes confusion. First, what is the way in which the words or phrases used in analogical descriptions speak about the realities they are referring to? This could be described as the semantic issue. The normal answer is that when we use analogical descriptions we are not speaking about two realities (e.g., temple and Church) in the same way but in a similar way (partly the same and partly different).

Second, why are we using analogical descriptions? Are we doing so to make our discourse more lively, interesting, or striking (see the definition in footnote 9, p. 484 above), or are we doing so because that is the best way to convey the content we want? This raises the literary issue, the question of the literary purpose of the use of the analogical description.

As already noted, it is common in scriptural exegesis to speak about analogical descriptions as metaphors. Metaphor is in fact an analogical usage. A metaphor is based in some similarity between that which is being referred to (the tenor, the target) and that which is being applied to it (the vehicle, the source domain). It is not, in other words, unreasonable to use the word "metaphor" for all analogical speech.

Analogical descriptions, moreover, are like metaphors in that they do not make sense if we take them literally.[14] To say that a set

---

[14] John R. Searle, "Metaphor" in Ortony ed., *Metaphor and Thought* (Cambridge, UK: Cambridge University Press), 114: "Suppose he hears the utterance, 'Sam is a pig.' He knows that cannot be literally true, that the utterance, if he tries to take it literally, is radically defective . . . The defects which cue the hearer may be obvious falsehood, semantic nonsense, violations of the rules of speech acts, or violations of conversational principles of communication." For a similar approach, but presented from the point of view of biblical diction with additional indicators, see Caird, *Language and Imagery*, 186–191.

of people is a temple, for instance, is nonsense. It is not; we know it is not; and we cannot even make any intelligible sense from such a statement taken literally. We therefore automatically, intuitively, do not take such a statement literally but take it as an analogical description.

At the same time, it is now the normal understanding that every kind of discourse that is not literal is figurative. And figurative usage is most often understood to be something employed for literary effect. Certainly the predominant understanding of a metaphor is that it is figurative and used for literary effect, even though often scholars understand it more broadly.[15] One consequence of this usage is that we find many writers holding that analogical descriptions are literal, even though they are normally not literal according to the definitions given above.[16]

We need a way of speaking about analogical speech when it is not used for literary effect but is primarily used to convey content. The term analogical description is a good way to do this. An analogical description is not literal speech, but it is not figurative in the

---

[15] In modern linguistic discussions, it is common to contrast "literal" with "figurative." The standard Greco-Roman understanding, however, would be to define words as used figuratively when they are used as one of the classical figures of speech, that is, the kinds of speech that make speech poetic or elevated. In such an understanding, metaphor and simile are both figures of speech that can assert the same predicate (characteristic) in different ways, although simile is literal and metaphor is non-literal.

[16] There has been a discussion about whether a phrase like "the Church is the body of Christ" is literal or figurative. E. L. Mascall, (Christ, the Christian and the Church: A Study of the Incarnation and Its Consequences [London: Longmans, Green, and Co., 1946], 112, 161) and J. A. T. Robinson (The Body: A Study in Pauline Theology [London: SCM Press, 1952], 51) held that it was literal. Mascall said, "While it contains of course a certain element of metaphor, the description of the Church as the Body of Christ is to be taken ontologically and realistically . . . It is not a mere metaphor, but the literal truth that the Church is the body of Christ." G. B. Caird (Language and Imagery, 131–133) disagreed, holding that metaphor could be used to talk about referents that were ontologically real. Mascall and Caird in fact probably agreed in the fundamental point (see Mascall's book Words and Images: A Study in Theological Discourse, [London: Darton, Longman & Todd, 1968], 94–101). Nonetheless the phrase is not used as a figure of speech in the sense of the SOED definition used in our text, but as a statement about a spiritual reality. The confusion in this dispute indicates the value of distinguishing metaphor as a figure of speech from an analogical description.

literary sense either. It is a mode of speech that allows us to speak in an extended sense and so provide true statements about reality, but statements that are not simply literally true. At the same time it is not normally used for literary effect, but because it is the best way, or at least a good way, to convey semantic content. While metaphor can convey true content as well (otherwise it would be useless), the reason it is employed is not primarily because it is the best way to state that content but for a literary effect.

We find analogical descriptions from the beginning of the Scripture to the end, especially when scriptural writers talk about spiritual things. This is not to say that there are no metaphors in Scripture, or even that we can always tell when a phrase asserting a similarity between two things is a metaphor (understood as a figure of speech) or an analogical description. For instance, when the Psalmist complains "I am a worm and no man" (Ps 22:6), we are sure he is not asserting that he went through a metamorphosis, but that the phrase is a metaphorical (vivid) way of saying he is "scorned by men and despised by the people" (the parallel phrase). Or when the Scripture says God is a dry wadi (Jer 15:18), a moth or a festering sore (Hos 5:12), a lion mauling its prey (Hos 5:14), or a nursing mother (Is 49:15), we can be confident that we are dealing with metaphors chosen for their vividness (and low correspondence). On the other hand, when God is spoken of as king, judge, or father, we know that he is not exactly like human kings, judges, or fathers, but we recognize that the way he functions in regard to us is similar and so we are dealing with analogically descriptive speech.

Technical discourse. The change that came with Greek philosophy was momentous in human thought, and the first systematic formulation of it was in Aristotle's *Organon*, although his approach was developed from that of Socrates and Plato and even some of the Sophists. It then was further developed in later Greek philosophy and in subsequent philosophy, including modern science (what was earlier called "natural philosophy"). We will speak about it as the development of technical or scientific discourse and thought.

"Technical thought" here means the approach to thinking and teaching that puts the priority on understanding the real world in such a way that we can clearly and precisely, and hopefully accurately, describe real things and how they function. It involves certain tools:

- The development of technical terms, words that pick out real entities or aspects of those entities and relations they are in in order to distinguish them from everything similar
- The development of statements, many of them laws, others of them theoretical principles, that formulate the relationship between the things expressed in the terms
- The development of intellectual disciplines, "sciences," organized bodies of knowledge of some area or reality in which ideally everything is explicitly related to everything else (systematized), especially noting what can be deduced from what

A technical term should be clearly and precisely defined, that is, defined in a way that allows us to distinguish its referent from everything similar. If it is part of a discipline that is put together in a modern way, it should be *the* way to refer to some reality. So if we are told that something is an amphetamine or a wolverine or a radius, we should accurately know what is being referred to and know some characteristics it has—as long as the word is being used in its technical sense. We also can be confident that the word is not being used in a figurative way, as long as the discourse that it is part of is technical in nature.

Here we find a key difference between technical and analogical thought. Analogical thought proceeds by similarity. Technical thought proceeds by distinguishing between similar things. Technical thought allows us to explicitly formulate relations of meaning, while analogical thought only allows us to see differences in meaning by context of use. Technical discourse and thought do the very thing that analogical discourse and thought normally do not do.

They explicitly distinguish similar realities or, to use a term some scholars use, they disambiguate words.[17]

Technical thought makes use of concepts. A concept in this sense is a technically understood grasp of the reality a technical term refers to. It is the mental representation that goes along with the technical expression, written or spoken. It grasps or understands the aspect of reality that the definition of the technical term specifies.

Technical thought is also for the most part abstract, not concrete.[18] It can, by using proper nouns, definite descriptions (e.g., *the* Queen of England), and other indexical words (e.g., demonstrative adjectives, pronouns like "I" or "you"), speak about or be applied to particular things. However, the terms and statements that make up a technical system or discipline are abstracted from concrete things that actually or possibly exist. The realities referred to by a technical term are considered in themselves (e.g., redness or size) rather than seen as an aspect of something that exists (e.g., something red or large).

Even when a technical term refers to something that exists, like a human being, it only refers to it in its essential nature, and it prescinds from all the other characteristics it may have. When we say, "Socrates was a human being," we are not referring to the fact that he was an Athenian, but merely to his humanity, one aspect of him (although the most fundamental). The goal of technical thought is to speak as exactly or precisely and objectively as possible about kinds of realities in the world and how they function, and it does so by making use of technical terms that are defined abstractly.

Analogical descriptions, in contrast, are concrete representations. They are used to pick out some characteristic as it inheres in things found in ordinary experience, the experience given to us by our senses as we live in this spatio-temporal world. Because an

---

[17] Alter, *Genesis*, xi ff.

[18] The definition used here is that an abstract word or statement speaks about a characteristic as separated from its presence in an individual thing. A concrete word or statement speaks about a characteristic as existing in an individual thing. It is common nowadays instead to understand abstract words or statements as speaking about characteristics that are immaterial or as referring to ideas.

analogical description is concrete, it potentially could refer to many other characteristics besides the one that is the point of comparison. We therefore need to understand in what respect it is similar to the thing we are describing by using it. We know many things about the temple in Jerusalem, but, as we have seen, most of its actual characteristics are not present in the temple of the Holy Spirit. We use the word temple to describe the Church because we understand both to be places where God dwells and in that respect are similar.

It is common to speak of analogical descriptions as images[19] and contrast them with concepts. Occasionally they are described as picture writing, because we can picture them as concrete existing realities, although at times they are an amalgam of different images that we cannot put together into one picture (e.g., Rev 7:14 as above or Rev 5:6). Speaking of all analogical descriptions as images has the difficulty that when the word "image" is used for analogical descriptions, it seems to lend itself to seeing them as metaphors or figures of speech, even though they are often sober statements intended to convey theological content, not phrases used to make scriptural writing more vivid or elegant or emotionally expressive.

It is more helpful to see images as only one kind of analogical speech. Especially in prophetic writings, like the Hebrew prophets or the book of Revelation, the Scriptures may speak about something analogically (e.g., God on his throne as ruling the universe, or his marriage with his people), but often do so in a dramatic context. God is a character in an event and is portrayed as sitting on his throne with people coming before him or marrying a woman who stands for a corporate body. In such instances we have a phrase that functions as an image or picture and it is the dramatic description as a whole that conveys the meaning of the passage, not just the analogical description being used as an image.

---

[19] Leland Ryken, Jim Wilhoit, and Tremper Longman III, eds., *The Dictionary of Biblical Imagery* (Downers Grove, IL: Intervarsity, 1998), xiii, give the definition of "image" as "any word that names a concrete thing (such as a tree or house) or action (such as running or threshing)," and hold that "The Bible is a book that images the truth as well as stating it in abstract propositions."

It is not the case, though, that every time these analogical descriptions are used, they are used as part of a dramatic portrayal and therefore as images. Sometime they are simply embodied in a phrase used in a prosaic discourse. When we read about the Church as the temple of the Holy Spirit, if we are familiar with the meaning of the phrase, most of us do not picture a building (and it is not helpful to do so). Rather we think of the Church as a body of people in whom the Holy Spirit dwells.

The development of scientific terminology illustrates another important feature of analogical descriptions. They can be turned into technical terms. Once they are clearly and precisely defined and used in an intellectual discipline, a science, they no longer function as analogical descriptions and for most of us do not call up images. They become the literal term or phrase to speak about something.

Paradoxically, scientific terms turn out very often to begin as images. "A black hole" does not seem to be literally a hole (in what stuff? what bounds it?), and an electromagnetic "field" is not at all an even piece of earth like a farmer's field. Moreover, we do not normally think of a literal field when we speak about an electromagnetic field, especially if we know much physics. We simply use the term in accord with its scientific definition, in other words, as a concept of a certain sort. Of course, we could go in the other direction and call the Mayor's desk a black hole, perhaps with perfect accuracy.

Owen Barfield in his book *Poetic Diction*[20] has made the important point that thinking analogically was not a special "poetic" mode of speech for earlier people like the writers of Scripture (or for many since then). To quote C. S. Lewis in summarizing Barfield's thesis,

> Mr. Barfield has shown, as regards the history of language, that words did not start by referring merely to physical objects and then get extended by metaphor to refer to emotions, mental states and the like. On the contrary, what we now call the "literal and metaphorical" meaning have both

---

[20] Owen Barfield, *Poetic Diction: A Study in Meaning* (London: Faber and Faber, 1952).

been disengaged by analysis from an ancient unity of meaning which was neither or both.[21] In the same way it is quite erroneous to think that man started with a "material" God or "Heaven" and gradually spiritualized them. He could not have started with something "material" for the "material", as we understand it, comes to be realized only by contrast to the "immaterial", and the two sides of the contrast grow at the same speed. He started with something that was neither and both. As long as we are trying to read back into that ancient unity either the one or the other of the two opposites which have since been analysed out of it, we shall misread all early literature and ignore many states of consciousness which we ourselves still from time to time experience. The point is crucial not only for the present discussion but for any sound literary criticism or philosophy.[22]

To put the same point differently, discourse cannot become metaphorical (discourse understood to be using extended or transferred meaning)—or recognized as being applied analogically, to use the term we have been using so far—until we have determined what the literal sense is or even that there is a literal sense.[23] Otherwise the two meanings are the same. Barfield attributed the distinction

---

[21] "Unity of meaning" would now be better phrased as "sameness of meaning." If in English we say two things are "one," we either mean that they are the same existing thing or the same kind of thing (having the same characteristic in common). The latter is no longer much used, so for most people now "unity" (the result of being one in some respect) indicates that two things (entities, parts) are united together, not that two things share the same characteristic. Lewis' and Barfield's point is that when words were used analogously, what we might now see as two different meanings (literal and analogous) were previously seen as the same meaning.

[22] C. S. Lewis, *Miracles: A Preliminary Study* (New York: MacMillan, 1947), 79. This important point, that we do not conceptualize something as distinct unless we have an analysis that contrasts it to something else, is developed more fully in chapters 10 and 16 of *Miracles*.

[23] Barfield's position is similar to that taken by the cognitive semanticists (George Lakoff, Mark Johnson, et al.), who hold that "metaphor" is a pervasive feature of ordinary language, and who go on to hold that there is no principled distinction between literal and metaphorical uses of language.

between literal and metaphorical to the fourth century BC Greeks, especially Aristotle.

Theology. This brings us to the question of theology. The word theology etymologically means thinking or speaking about God (and how created realities, especially people, relate to God). Genesis 1–3 is theology in this sense. However, as Greek philosophy influenced Jewish and Christian teaching, theology became shaped as a technical discipline. Terms became technical, doctrines became formulated, and theology books trying to cover all of Christian teaching in a systematized form were produced. Scriptural writings are not normally theology in this sense.

Technical theology has considerable advantages. It allows us to be clearer on what we believe and what we do not believe. On the other hand, it also creates a new kind of dispute, the theological or doctrinal disagreement (and anathema). That kind of dispute is often over the way analogical assertions can be correctly turned into clear and precise assertions. Christian theologians can collect all the statements in the Scriptures and the Fathers about the nature of the elements in the Christian Eucharist (most of them using analogical terms), but they then do not easily agree about what technical formulation is ontologically accurate.

The difficulty takes many forms. Theologians can discuss, for instance, whether the statements about moral matters (sin), being "defiling" are a technical formulation or an analogous usage.[24] Or we can read exegetical statements that Genesis 1:2 asserts the existence of pre-existent matter, despite the likelihood that the early ancient author probably did not think in such metaphysical terms or at least was not speaking in a metaphysical mode.

There is technical language in Scripture. Leviticus 11, for instance, is a chapter full of it. Some of it is biological (expressed in ancient scientific language). Some of it is ceremonial or ritual ("clean,"

---

[24] Jonathan Klawans in *Impurity and Sin in Ancient Judaism* (New York: Oxford University Press, 2000) presents a strong case for the latter, but documents that we are considering a persistent scholarly issue.

"unclean," "defile," "cleanse," and perhaps "abomination"). The ceremonial practice of the Jerusalem temple was technically developed in a precise way. Rabbinic teaching, especially in the legal area, was also very technical and systematically developed (e.g., most of the *Mishnah*). Patristic teaching was technical when it addressed certain issues, especially the ontological status of the Trinity and the Incarnation. But it is not until John Damascene's *Fount of Knowledge* in the eighth century that we have the first of what could be called systematic books of Christian doctrine. By the thirteenth century, we have full-scale systematical theological books like Maimonides' *Guide to the Perplexed*, and Aquinas' *Summa Theologiae*. Aquinas in fact begins by asking whether theology is a science and responds in the affirmative.

Nonetheless, most scriptural language, and patristic and rabbinic language as well, is analogical when it is not a description of something that can be experienced by our senses. As we have seen, analogical discourse is the normal mode of speech about spiritual matters, and when so used analogical descriptions are not figures of speech, poetic adornment, or rhetorical embellishment. Rather they are commonly elements of sober discourse that assert something about spiritual realities.

Models. There is another methodological concept that is a kind of analogical description and often used in contemporary theology and exegesis, namely, "model." A model is a complex of features in a recognizable concrete form or pattern. The term is used in scientific explanation heuristically or as a comparison. For instance in geometrical optics, light is understood as something traveling in a straight line and that model allows calculations of, for instance, how far a shadow is cast by something which presents an obstacle to the movement of light. Or physicists sometimes talk about the wave model of light and the particle model of light. Light, in other words, behaves in certain respects like a wave and in certain respects like a collection of particles. Both are true, although waves and particles do not behave the same way in all respects. "Model" as used in theology seems to be drawn from modern scientific method, although theological models do not allow confirmable predictions as scientific models do but can only be used to draw untestable hypotheses when used for inferences or used to represent some theory.

The term model is sometimes used by Scripture scholars to describe differences in the scriptural text. To return to Genesis 1, some scholars will talk about different models of creation that can be found in the Scriptures. They will say that Genesis 1 presents a model of creation by which God is a wise builder, while other texts present a model of creation by which God is a warrior who destroys chaos/disorder to establish an ordered universe.

This is not intrinsically a wrong way to speak about the scriptural texts, as long as we remember that "model" is a modern concept that we are using to understand the Scriptures and was not in the mind of the scriptural author or authors. Creation as building and creation as fighting are comparing creation to different realities, and one does not usually build and fight at the same time. The Scriptures do speak about creation in somewhat different ways.

There is, however, a perennial temptation for many contemporary Scripture scholars and theologians to see differences as somehow incompatible and therefore at odds with one another, and describing them as models makes that easier. They consequently have to be understood dialectically (in a Hegelian sense) or even as contradictions. It is easier to then see the Scriptures as a collection of disparate materials, not a unified revelation from God. It is also a short step to attribute one or the other model to an influence from outside Israel, perhaps from a Babylonian myth, or even to go so far as to label it as mythological. Once scholars forget or no longer advert to the fact that they are using a concept from outside the text and outside the thought of the scriptural authors, they can begin to construe what the scriptural authors were doing as if they were modern thinkers developing their own models or their own theologies at odds with that of others.

Instead of speaking about different models of creation, however, we can speak about different analogical descriptions. We can say that sometimes scriptural authors speak about creation as God building the universe, perhaps to be a temple; sometimes they speak about creation as God fighting or going to war to get the universe to turn out the way he wants it to in the face of opposition or the recalcitrance of his creation. The author may have simply used the analogical descriptions or images that conveyed what he wanted without setting them at odds with one another. And he may even have used phrases common in contemporary mythologies (e.g., Ps 74:13–15; 89:8–10; Is 51:9–11; Job 26:11–12, a rare usage in the Bible but sometimes cited as the example of a "model" of creation) the way we would use "cleansed the Augean stables," that is, without accepting the reality of the referents posited by Greek mythology.

To return to analogical descriptions of the Church, modern theologians sometimes talk about models of the Church or of other theological realities. Others are wary of doing so, because they suspect those who talk in such a way want to set the different models at odds with one another and hold that a choice needs to be made between models if we are going to have a Church. Here, however, the concern is a bit different than the concern about different scriptural ways of speaking about the creation, because modern theologians often do deliberately work with different models and do in fact come up with opposed ecclesiologies on that basis. The term model, then, fits better in the modern theological context and there the term analogical description sometimes does not capture the whole of what is going on.

We are past the point where we can simply return to the scriptural mode of speech. Nonetheless, if we are going to speak about what the Scriptures are asserting, we need to read them with the understanding that much of the Scripture is made up of analogical discourse. This is easier since we ourselves commonly use analogical discourse when we are not speaking "scientifically." It is still a normal mode of human speech, perhaps even the predominant one. Moreover, it is not an especially "poetic" way of speaking. It is the way we naturally think about similar realities, and it is the main way to speak about realities that transcend our everyday experience, especially the things of God.

CHAPTER NINETEEN

THE INTENT OF THE AUTHOR(S)

A scriptural text is not simply to be interpreted by the conscious intent of the human author as discerned by historical method. It is also to be discerned by the intent of God as conveyed by spiritual interpretation.

Introduction to the chapter. Typology is a principle of interpretation found in the New Testament that would almost never be used by a modern Scripture scholar. Few would approach any topic the way Paul does in 1 Corinthians 10. Many would explain that Paul's exegesis is typological, but none would give a typological exegesis on their own.

Perhaps the chief reason why modern Scripture scholars do not use the same approach to scriptural interpretation that the New Testament authors did has to do with their understanding of what they are engaged in. As we have seen in chapter 13, somewhere in the last two centuries, many Scripture scholars re-classified the study of Scripture from Christian teaching to history, in this case the study of historical forms of religion of the past. This likely occurred primarily because they were teaching at secular universities or other secular or secularized institutions. As a result, they accepted the view that the only methods they should use were those accepted by secular historians.[1]

---

[1] Bruce Vawter in *On Genesis: A New Reading* (Garden City, NY: Doubleday & Co., 1977), 33 provides a statement of the position: "The interpretation of Genesis for

Those who have asserted that Scripture should be interpreted solely in secular historical terms have often focused on the intent of the (human) authors. In this chapter we will look at the possible meanings of the intent of the author (and how to identify the author of a scriptural text). In the next chapter we will raise the question of eisegesis or what is actually "in" the text.

Two foundational principles. Two principles have characterized secular-historical exegesis—at least historical-critical exegesis—in its attempts to state the meaning of a text. First, "the intent of the author" is so fundamental that any understanding of a text other than that in accord with the intent of the author is seen as a later development or a reading into the text of something that is not there. Usually this means the *conscious* intent of the author.

This principle is sometimes re-stated by saying that a text must be understood only within the context in which it was produced, "context" meaning the historical time and place and the relationships to people, cultures, and institutions available to the author at that point. If a new meaning for a text appears a thousand years later than the writing of the text, then it is clearly not the meaning of the text, but is a later development or invention or a mistaken reading of the text.

Second, the way we get at the intent of the author is by historical method. There is a set of scholarly historical methods that yield the intent of the author, and from this we can glean the "real meaning" of the text. Consequently, if someone were to say that the real meaning of a particular text in the Old Testament had to do with Christ, it would be seen as an example of reading something alien into the

---

the Christian reader should be no different from its interpretation for anyone else. If Genesis is to appear as a relevant literature it can only do so when its original purposes are taken seriously and it is interpreted historically." Luke Timothy Johnson gives a reason for the change by speaking of "the sociological revolution in Scripture scholarship" that occurred in his lifetime, and says "There was a shift from seminaries to universities as the locus for Biblical scholarship, and conversation partners were other disciplines in the social sciences and the humanities" (Johnson and Kurz, *The Future of Catholic Biblical Scholarship*, 10–11).

text, because historical method makes clear that the authors could not have known anything about Christ since he had not been born on earth yet.

There is a view from a modern scholar that expresses this approach well. The scholar is addressing the passage in Genesis where God says, "Let us make man in our own image." Earlier we saw that many Fathers interpreted this passage by applying it to the Trinity, but this scholar rejects such a view.

> With whom does he take counsel and with whom does he share the idea of the divine image and likeness in which he contemplates the creation of man? These are celebrated questions to which no fully satisfactory answers have been given. We can probably dismiss a couple of the proposed answers out of hand. There is not, quite obviously, contrary to what some of the earlier Fathers of the church thought, any allusion to the Christian doctrine of the trinity of persons in the one Godhead. Only a thoroughgoing, unhistorical reading of the Bible could allow such an interpretation.[2]

In other words, if we follow the principles that the real meaning of the text is fully determined by the intent of the author and that the intent of the author is fully determined by the historical context in which he writes—which we understand through our knowledge of historical development—then the view that the text refers to the Trinity is unhistorical and should be dismissed out of hand. The Trinity was only revealed in the New Testament (or developed later), so the Old Testament writers could not have intended the text to refer to the Trinity.

If we accept this mentality we not only have to dismiss almost all Christian interpretation throughout the centuries, but we also have to dismiss much of the New Testament's interpretation of the Old Testament.[3] Nonetheless this scholar is correct in saying

---

[2] Vawter, *On Genesis*, 53.

[3] Josephine M. Ford, "Tongues-Leadership-Women," *Spiritual Life*, (Fall 1971) ex-

that from the point of view of much (though not all, as we will see) modern methodology the patristic interpretation of this passage is a "thoroughgoing, unhistorical interpretation." He draws from this fact a rejection of the view that the Old Testament should be read in the light of the New and considers it a self-evident conclusion.[4] As some have observed, this approach is no less dogmatic in its basis than Christian or Jewish theology, although it claims to be neutral and simply objective or "scientific."[5]

Texts and authors. As we observed in the first methodological discussion, there have been some changes in the approach of Scripture scholars, even secular ones, since the above quote was written. The principle that the meaning of the text is completely determined by the intent of the author is no longer accepted the way it once was. There is a recognition that, without distorting a text, it can often be read with further meaning, at least in the sense of new significance, in new contexts.

No one wants to hold that a text can be read in ways that are contradictory to its original meaning. Fewer, however, are now saying that the meaning is fully determined by what the author intended to say in the context of the historical moment when the text was written. Fewer still are saying there is only one possible legitimate meaning or use of the text, namely, the one consciously in the mind

---

presses this view clearly: "St. Paul's method of hermeneutics, that is, interpreting Scripture, is not a method which would be acceptable in the twentieth century. Indeed, to accept his method would be to fall into anti-intellectualism. One must always seek to integrate the best of human discoveries, such as contemporary scholarship, with our spiritual life. St. Paul takes what we might call a fundamentalist interpretation of the Genesis narrative."

[4] For a fuller discussion of the meaning of the "historical reliability" of the Scriptures, see the special discussion in chap. 9 (p. 519).

[5] For an insightful discussion of this approach and the problems associated with it see Jon D. Levenson, "Theological Consensus or Historicist Evasion?" in *The Hebrew Bible, the Old Testament, and Historical Criticism: Jews and Christians in Biblical Studies* (Louisville, KY: Westminster/John Knox Press, 1993), 82–105. See also the previously cited discussion of the historical-critical method by Martin Hengel (*Acts and the History*, 129–130), who describes the authors of the historical-critical method as commonly espousing a "dogmatic positivism."

of the author when he wrote the text—especially if we think this means we have to figure out what his conscious intention was rather than simply look at what the text seems to be saying in its context, much less ask what it means in a different context.[6] In recent years various approaches to literary texts, including the Scriptures, have grown up that allow for the legitimate possibility of other meanings to texts besides that of the original authors.[7]

Part of this change has come about because we often recognize that the conscious intent of any author does not completely form what he has written. We sometimes say, "that may have been what you meant to say, but that is not what you said." That is a recognition that a text often means a certain thing even if the author did not intend it to do so. The words have a meaning of their own that cannot be changed beyond a certain point, even by the original author.

More importantly, it can be possible to draw legitimate implications from texts that may not have occurred to the original author.[8]

---

[6] As J. P. Fokkelman put it in *Reading Biblical Poetry: An Introductory Guide* (Louisville, KY: Westminster/John Knox Press, 2001), 64, speaking of the time when the historical-critical method was dominant,

> Biblical texts were primarily studied diachronically: one hypothesis after the other was drawn up concerning the origin of the texts, their previous forms, the history of their transmission, and so forth. A valiant search also was conducted to discover 'the writer's intention,' as if it were even remotely possible to ascertain this if the text itself did not make it fully explicit. All this effort was based on the misguided conviction that a correct understanding of the text could not be achieved without first knowing how it originated, and that such a detour through the reconstruction of the text's history even constituted the principal access to its meaning.

[7] David C. Steinmetz, the professor of Church history at Duke University Divinity School, in "The Superiority of Pre-Critical Exegesis" in Stephen E. Fowl, ed., *The Theological Interpretation of Scripture*, 31, summarized his critique of the above position by saying, "The notion that Scripture has only one meaning is a fantastic idea and is certainly not advocated by the biblical writers themselves."

[8] R. W. L. Moberly in *Genesis*, 157, speaking of "the interplay between the biblical text and questions one brings to it," makes a similar point by saying, "On any reckoning it can often be a fine line between anachronistically imposing a mistaken sense on a biblical text in the light of later developments and being enabled by later developments to discern nuances and incipient tendencies in biblical texts that otherwise might have gone unnoticed." See Beale, *Handbook*, chap. 1 for a presentation of some of the ways this might work.

Once, for instance, we ask the question whether material creation began at a certain point in time or always existed, we are into a different consideration than the original author (perhaps a sixth century BC or earlier Hebrew) probably had. We can thank Aristotle or his immediate precursors who introduced ontological (metaphysical) thinking for the question.

Then we can draw the implication that Genesis 1 supports the Big Bang (or not). But given that this is a correct inference, we cannot go on to hold that our conclusion was in the conscious mind of the original author. We might have had to do a great deal of explaining before we could have gotten him to understand the issue, much less draw out of him what he thought the answer was. But that does not mean that the question as to the implication of the text is simply unreasonable on historical grounds.[9]

This does not mean the intent of the original author is irrelevant to our understanding of a text. To return to the example of the Trinity in Genesis 1, the original human author was speaking about the word and spirit *of God*. If, for instance, he had been speaking about the word of an angel or a teacher, the Christian Fathers could not have seen this as an instance of a reference to the Trinity. But the fact that he did not understand he was speaking about the Trinity does not automatically rule out the view that he was. To use a different kind of example, if the author did not intend to write history, but, say, a fable that would illustrate his point, we could not see the

---

[9] Levenson (*Hebrew Bible,* section I) applies this to the canon: "The fact of canon also challenges the most basic presupposition of historical criticism, that a book must be understood only within the context in which it was produced. The very existence of a canon testifies to the reality of recontextualization: an artifact may survive the circumstances that brought it into being, including the social and political sorts of circumstances to which so much attention is currently devoted. Indeed, it can outlive the culture in which it was produced." Moberly in *Old Testament Theology,* 155–162, the section entitled "Context, Recontextualization, and Canon" has a clarifying discussion about understanding scriptural texts in new contexts, with special attention to Levenson and Childs. The position of Levenson, Childs, and Moberly is, however, not yet theological exegesis. To be sure new contexts add new questions that were not in the conscious intention of the original author, and those can often be answered reasonably. But there is the additional conviction that we can understand the referents better than the original human author, and that gives rise to theological exegesis.

fable as history. But if he was writing some kind of history, we can reasonably ask about the nature of what he was writing about, that is, about the referent of his discussion, and perhaps come up with a good answer that he would not have realized (e.g., that his great fish were whales and could have provided good oil).

In addition, authors often write compositions that deliberately do not have one correct meaning, although some do. If we write that Napoleon lost the battle of Waterloo, readers are supposed to understand that there was a Frenchman named Napoleon who actually did lose an important battle in the early nineteenth century. The reader is not supposed to think that we are asserting that the Enlightenment suffered an important defeat at the hands of legitimate rulers, even though that could be an understanding someone might correctly draw from it. There is no doubt that seeing the fall of Jerusalem as an historical event that actually happened is the way we should initially read the account of it in Second Chronicles 36.

On the other hand, many scriptural and other writings are not that way. When an author writes a poem, perhaps a lament for someone's death like those in the Psalms, he likely does not primarily have in mind the death of a particular individual. Nor do we need to find out to whom he was referring in order to interpret and use the psalm well. It was probably deliberately written to be applied in many situations, or at least the final editor of the book of Psalms saw it that way.

As we have already noted, a typological reading of the destruction of Jerusalem by the Babylonians in 586 BC as referring in some way to Roman persecution of Christians (Rev 11:8) does not mean we think that the destruction never happened. We do. That is why the meaning of the author, what he thought he was writing about, is often called the "historical sense" (although the term "literal sense" is more commonly used). He did intend to refer to an historical event in 586 BC, although the author of the book of Revelation thought it had a broader (spiritual) application.

In short, understanding the intent of the human author of a section of Scripture insofar as we can discover it is an important part of good exegesis. It is normally the starting point. But it does not have to be approached as fully determinative of the meaning or meanings of a particular text.

The primary author. Only, however, if we believe there is something else going on in the writing and interpretation of scriptural texts that is not accessible to secular historical methodology can we put much credence in many of the ways the New Testament interprets the Old Testament. The spiritual principle of interpretation operates under the assumption that the text of Scripture and the events of Scripture are discerned spiritually, and are not adequately discerned by historical method alone.

To affirm spiritual interpretation does not mean we have to dismiss historical method, for it has important uses for Christian teachers and can help us in studying the Scripture. Nor do we have to see typology and historical method as antithetical to one another, as two methods that can in no way be combined. But to accept the validity of typological interpretation, we do have to say there is something more going on in the text than the modern secular-historical method can find.

To say this we do not have to take the view that the Old Testament author of Genesis 1–4 knew by revelation about Christ as the second Adam, although some Christian teachers have, or even that the author knew about it at all. Whatever view we take of how much the human author understood of the significance of what he wrote, we have to interpret the text not solely by the intent of the human author but also by the intent of the divine author. Because Genesis is the Word of God and so a document that in an important sense was written by God, not just by its human author, its fuller meaning is not simply accessible to the historical methodologies of the modern world, but may be accessible to us.

CHAPTER TWENTY

EISEGESIS AND IDEOLOGICAL EXEGESIS

Ideological exegesis involves imposing a modern ideological position on texts where it is absent, and often where the texts take an opposed position. It is eisegesis, whereas theological exegesis is not.

Introduction to the chapter. We are sometimes told that theological exegesis is eisegesis, that is, reading something into the text that is not there. To use the example in the previous discussion, if we see the Trinity in chapter 1 of Genesis, we are reading something into the text because it is not explicitly stated in the text and the human author probably did not know about it. Nonetheless theological exegesis is not eisegesis.

In addition, we find ourselves presented with a range of ideological approaches to exegesis: feminist exegesis, gay/lesbian (et al.) exegesis, liberation theology (Marxist) exegesis, environmentalist exegesis, etc. They come up with some regularity in this book, for instance in the section on "Disobedience" in chapter 2, which had to deal with feminist interpretations of Genesis 2–3. We find ideological exegesis where a modern ideological position is used to interpret the exegetical meaning of the text, so that the ideological position is found in the text when it is absent there or at least the text is held not to be in conflict with the exegetical position, even though it is.

These two matters are related. Therefore, in this discussion we will consider why ideological exegesis is eisegesis and theological exegesis is not.

Ideologies. By "ideology" is meant a deliberate theoretical approach to social structure and how contemporary society should be structured. "Ideology" in this sense is not found before the eighteenth century in Western society.[1] Ideologies seem to have first arisen in opposition to traditional class structure (against feudal or semi-feudal structures that privileged the aristocratic class). They became more developed with the socialist (especially Marxist) critique of bourgeois or capitalist society. Now they are more active in opposition to traditional approaches to sexual (gender) social roles and sexual morality.

Since the eighteenth century, the underlying principle of ideological development has been egalitarianism, with "liberty" (individual freedom of choice) a close second. In critiquing the social arrangements in one area or another, ideologies have advocated that the members of some group should be treated as equal to another, i.e., the same way as whatever group is considered to be privileged, and so have their freedom of choice expanded. The fact that scriptural writers have sat loosely to the existence of traditional social structures as long as they were not "oppressive" (e.g., Ps 72:14) or legally "partial" (e.g., Deut 16:19–20) has provoked Christians—including Christian Scripture scholars who are promoting different ideologies—to come up with special exegeses/hermeneutics that conform the scriptural texts to their ideological position or even reject texts that are not.

To discuss the different ideologies adequately is beyond the scope of this book. Their good points and their bad points are not

---

[1] See, Clark, *MWC*, chap. 19 for a fuller presentation of ideologies and their effects on Christian thought. *The Age of Ideology* by Henry D. Aiken (New York: Mentor, 1956) holds that ideological thinking characterizes a stage of human thought, especially nineteenth century philosophical thought, and he attempts to define ideology in chap. 1. This "stage," however, has continued among many beyond the nineteenth century.

easy to sort out without lengthy analysis. On the other hand, the ideological exegesis they give rise to raises a question that needs some discussion for the purpose of this book. If ideological exegesis is not acceptable because it reads something into the text that is not there (*eisegesis*), should not theological exegesis be rejected for the same reason?

Ideological interpretation. Eisegesis is a perennial problem for biblical study. Often a bad or poor interpretation that reads something into the text that is not there is simply a mistake, with no special motive behind it. There is, however, a standing temptation for students to see in an authoritative text what they want to see. There is, moreover, often a deliberate attempt on the part of interpreters to make the text say something it does not say, either to be able to use it as support or to neutralize the fact that it seems to be against something the interpreter holds to be true or important. Ideological exegesis is a form of eisegesis and can be produced in all these ways. Eisegesis has certainly flourished since scriptural books have been accepted as authoritative and therefore as in a position to arbitrate disputes, that is, since the scriptural canons were formed; but ideological exegesis in the sense defined above is new since the eighteenth century in Western society.

To illustrate ideological exegesis in action, we will look at instances of it that have come up in Genesis 2–3. This scriptural text describes a certain subordination of women to men, with the most prominent application in the scriptural canon being that the wife in a family should have a certain subordination to her husband as the head of the family, and the next most prominent being that the overall government of the Christian community (or the Jewish community or Israelite society) should be in the hands of men, at least in the absence of exceptional circumstances. Moreover, some New Testament texts (including 1 Tim 2:12–14; 1 Cor 11:8–9; and probably Eph 5:22–32) explicitly say that a certain subordination of women to men can be found in Genesis 2–3.[2]

---

[2]   For a discussion of these texts, see Clark, *MWC,* chaps. 1 and 2. For a discussion of

The subordination presented in Genesis 2–3 is primarily for the sake of unity, so that there can be one flesh, one family, one united community. This is not military subordination, slavery subordination, or mercenary subordination. This is also not the kind of subordination that is needed in task-oriented work together, as when a foreman directs a work crew or the leader of an army patrol directs his fighters. Rather it is the kind of subordination that is integral to good order in a relationship. The woman has her own role and her own responsibility as the man has his (1 Tim 5:14; Prov 31:10–31). She does not just do whatever he happens to want. Nonetheless there is an overall order in the family that secures its unity and, if working well, its harmony. In this it exemplifies the kind of order that we find in creation as a whole.

The term "feminist" by now has had a lengthy history, and there are many debates about what is truly feminism. We are in the middle of a societal development due to the development of technological society that means the traditional social roles for men and women are no longer viable the way they once were. As understood here, to advocate changes in the roles of men and women in society is not to be a feminist, nor is being interested in promoting the power of women.

On the other hand, an ideology has arisen, an offshoot of Marxism or at least influenced in its beginnings by Marxism, which can properly be called feminism. The feminist ideology is a strong form of egalitarianism, an egalitarianism that holds that there should not be any difference maintained between men and women (or among men or among women) other than on the basis of functional competence or personal preference, and is engaged in promoting women to positions of power to "equalize" their role with that of men. Feminists normally do not acknowledge the value of any special role for women (or men) and see any role differences as oppressive to women, and unjust.

Feminism has given rise to feminist interpretation, mainly pro-

---

Ephesians 5:22ff, see the "Special Exegetical Discussion: The Marriage of Christ and the Church" (p. 365); and for a fuller discussion, see Clark, *MWC*, chap. 4.

moted by women but also by many men.[3] Feminist interpretation
has held either that there is no support for any view of Genesis 2–3
that women should ever be subordinate to men simply because they
are women (as distinguished, say, from being an employee of someone who happens to be a man), or has held that the text can be dis-
regarded, or has held that such subordination came in with the Fall
and so is "lifted in Christ." If the text is read in the light of the relevant New Testament texts, it clearly presents some subordination of
women to men as due to creation and not to the Fall, and the husband's role as head of the family as one application of this teaching
that should be upheld. This is the straightforward position on the
interpretation of the Old Testament text—in itself and in the light
of New Testament interpretation.

Christian feminist interpreters have taken four different approaches to how to deal with Genesis 2–3, especially in combination
with the New Testament texts. First, some have taken the view that
these texts, at least some of them, do not mean what they seem to
say. To take a clear example, "wives subordinate yourselves to your
husbands" (Eph 5:22) is sometimes interpreted to mean that wives
should subordinate themselves to their husbands the same way husbands subordinate themselves to their wives (perhaps by seeking to
serve them or by being deferential to them). One extreme example
given is that wives should subordinate themselves to their husbands
by receiving their husbands' love. Such an approach is now found
primarily among Evangelical feminists, because most Evangelicals
uphold a strong form of biblical authority and need to find a way of
understanding biblical texts so that those texts either support their
ideological position or at least are not against it.[4]

---

[3]   See the section in Clark, *MWC* "Christian Liberationist Exegesis," 226–233, for a full-
      er description of the original Christian Feminist movement and its approach to ex-
      egesis. Elizabeth Schüssler Fiorenza's article, "Feminist Hermeneutics," *Anchor Bible
      Dictionary*, II:785, presents a more recent survey of the feminist approach to exegesis.
[4]   See Ronald W. Pierce and Rebecca Merrill Groothuis, ed., *Discovering Biblical Equal-
      ity: Complementarity Without Hierarchy* (Downers Grove, IL: InterVarsity Press,
      2005) for a full treatment of the stream of Evangelical feminism that seeks to uphold
      biblical authority. It contains many examples of ideological eisegesis.

Second, Christian feminists have taken the view that the texts that uphold any subordination of women to men are intended for a different social and cultural situation. The subordination of wives to husbands was the reigning approach in all of societies in the ancient world, and therefore Christians felt constrained to go along with the societal approach. Now modern society is different, and so we ought to conform to modern society, or at least we do not have to follow texts written for a different situation.

Third, Christian feminists have taken the view that we do not have to be "legalists" about following the Scriptures in regard to social arrangements. We can ignore them on certain points. This is probably the most common position among Christians nowadays who cannot be described as feminists, usually because they do not see how to deal with both the Scriptures and the culture together. When feminist interpreters take this approach, they often base it on the view that what is important for Christians is to follow the Gospel or the commands of love or the fruit of the Spirit, not the texts that advocate certain social "discriminatory" arrangements. Often they base it on the view that two texts, Galatians 3:28 and Ephesians 5:21, promote egalitarianism and so are the texts that should take precedence.

Fourth, Christian feminists of a more militant stripe have taken the view that they need to deliberately go against what many scriptural texts hold and especially the patriarchal presuppositions behind the Scriptures as a whole. Elizabeth Schüssler Fiorenza put it this way, "[Feminist hermeneutics] does not just aim at understanding biblical texts but also engages in theological critique, evaluation, and transformation of biblical traditions and interpretations from the vantage point of its particular sociopolitical religious location. Not to defend biblical authority but to articulate the theological authority of women is the main task of a critical feminist hermeneutics."[5] Her understanding of the theological authority of women is that "women's experience" (i.e., the "experience" of feminist women,

---

[5] Elizabeth Schüssler Fiorenza, "Feminist Hermeneutics," II:785.

or women who have had their "consciousness raised"—not all women, even though she ignores that qualification) indicates that any difference in social roles involving the authority of men over women is oppressive and needs to be attacked wherever it is found—including in the Bible.

Most feminist interpreters will make use of more than one of these approaches depending on the text they are dealing with. Some texts will call for (or be apt for) approach one, others for approach two, and others for approach three. Those who take the fourth approach often do not bother with the first three approaches.

The last three positions are not our concern here. They are primarily hermeneutical positions in the sense that they do not take their stand on exegesis of what the text says, but take it on principles about how to deal with texts that do not support the ideological position. They come from theories about how to relate to scriptural texts, especially those that seem to be instructing us what to do. Such texts are not to be followed (or "taken seriously"), because they are addressed to a different cultural situation, or because they differ from the more important things in the Scripture or because they teach oppression, and in fact should be opposed.

It is the first position—that the texts do not mean what they seem to say—that is the important one to consider here, because those who follow it read into the text a certain position that is held on grounds other than the Scriptures. It is this that we will refer to as feminist eisegesis (as distinguished from feminist hermeneutics). In short, we are not concerned with feminism as such, its pros and cons, a discussion that goes beyond the scope of this book, but simply feminist eisegesis. If feminist eisegesis or any other ideological eisegesis, is ruled out, how can it be acceptable to read into Old Testament texts positions held either on the basis of the New Testament or on the basis of later Christian theology?

Eisegesis. The question, then, is when is it acceptable to present an exegetical conclusion for a scriptural text that cannot be explicitly found in the text, whether as a result of ideological exegesis or as a result of theological exegesis.

We can begin with an approach that we have discussed in the methodological discussion on the relationship of Genesis 1 and 2, namely, source criticism. We are told—after the application of certain procedures like form criticism, redaction criticism, tradition criticism, etc.—that Genesis 1 and 2 come from two different sources put together by a later editor when Genesis or the Pentateuch was developed. We are also told, as we considered in chapter 4, that the account of the flood in Genesis 6–9 is a mosaic of texts from two sources that were sewn together by a later author.

Whether these scholarly opinions are true or insightful is not the question here. Here the question is whether these opinions are eisegesis. We have to begin by noticing that we do not have the postulated sources (and no one seems to expect we ever will find them). We then have to notice that they are not indicated in the text. We do not even find the sources indicated in the current division of the text into chapters. We certainly do not have the story of the flood nicely separated into two chapters, one from the first source and the second from the second source. We can find printed texts of Genesis in which the different sources are highlighted in different colors, but the highlighting is millennia later than the text we have.

We do find it difficult to say certainly how Genesis 1:1–2:4 and Genesis 2:4–3:24 go together. We also find it difficult to explain the seeming discrepancies in Genesis 6–7. If we have read these texts carefully, we might find it so helpful to hear that someone has given a coherent explanation of our difficulties that we will readily accept the Documentary Hypothesis, or at least a certain version of it. And we might be right to do so.

So, is the view that there are two sources, J and P, and maybe a third source, E, an instance of eisegesis? The answer should be no. They are not in the text, nor are they based on something obvious in the text, but the scholars who propose them do not usually claim that they are in the text. The claim that they existed is an historical hypothesis designed to explain what we find in the text, and it is based on certain indicators in the text that can perhaps convincing-ly, perhaps not, be arranged in certain patterns.

To use a different but analogous example, some scholars tell us that parts of Genesis are myth and other scholars that they have been produced by the influence of pagan myths from non-Israelite cultures. Of course, still other scholars have also told us that they were written to deliberately counter such myths.

Is the mythic status of certain sections *in* the text? Clearly not. Perhaps someday an ingenious scholar will publish a red-letter edition of the Scripture with the mythic sections in red to aid our ability to pick which parts are mythic and which not. Nonetheless, even if he or she does a brilliant job, the choice of which parts to redline cannot be claimed to be in the text (even though the parts are all there). Rather, the scholars come up with their views of the mythic nature of certain texts by seeing them in relationship to other texts outside the Scripture, finding certain similarities and differences, and, using some principles or theories of literary dependence, propose a helpful (or harmful, depending on one's viewpoint) classification for the texts.

Such an approach is no more eisegesis than the Documentary Hypothesis is. Rather it is a scholarly hypothesis designed to explain certain features of some scriptural texts in relation to extra-biblical mythological texts. Such relations are not *in* texts, but only appear when the texts are seen *in relation to* something they are being compared to or otherwise connected to.

Now let us look at some of the methods used in theological exegesis to exegete the Old Testament. The first is typology. According to the Apostle Paul, Adam is a type of Christ (Rom 5:14). Is that in the text in Genesis? The answer is no, but typology does not claim that there is an indication in the Genesis text about what is a type, much less what it is a type of. Rather, typology indicates a relationship between something that existed in the past (usually spoken about in the Old Testament) and something in the future (usually spoken about in the New Testament). It is the perception of a relationship and, like the previous two examples, is not *in* the text, but only appears when compared to something outside the text. What is outside the Old Testament text is usually in a New Testament text.

A second method used in theological exegesis is interpretation of prophecy, in this case Old Testament prophecy. For instance, does Isaiah 53 refer to Isaiah or Jesus Christ (Acts 8:34)? This raises a complex discussion, one that cannot be adequately handled in a book of this size.

Finally, theological exegesis makes use of a method of interpretation that provides a fuller meaning to the text that is different than typological interpretation and prophetic interpretation. We saw that in the discussion about seeing the Trinity in Genesis 1 (or using our knowledge of whales to understand what is being said about the "great fish" in Genesis 1 and other places). Supposing that it is correct to see the word and spirit of God in Genesis 1 to be a reference to the Trinity as many Christian Fathers thought, is that an example of eisegesis, reading something into the text that is not there?

Here too the answer is no. To be sure, it is not explicitly stated in the text that we are reading about the Trinity or that we are reading about sea-going mammals. However, something is being spoken about that is referred to in the text. There is a threefold working of God that is being spoken about there, or at least a spirit of God and a word (speech) of God that is being spoken about there. And there is a large animal that can be found in many oceans of the world even today that is being spoken about there.

What a text refers to or speaks about should be understood to be *in* the text. It is not necessarily in the text because that understanding is explicitly mentioned by the words of the text. But the referent of a text, at least when the text is speaking about something in the real world, is part of the meaning of the text. When we identify the referent and then use knowledge we have about that real object from other sources to understand what is being said, we are not reading something into the text. The whales really are in Genesis 1. The persons of the Trinity really are in Genesis 1. They are not being read into it. Our fuller understanding of those objects come from further knowledge we have about those objects, but the objects are really part of the meaning of the text.

Now we can look at ideological exegesis. Is that eisegesis? Most feminist scriptural interpretation is not exegesis as we have defined it but hermeneutical argumentation. Therefore it is not eisegesis. That applies to all but the first of the four feminist approaches mentioned above. That approach, however, is clearly eisegesis.

It is eisegesis because it involves wrong interpretations of the text. It regularly says that the text says something it does not say (e.g., that there is no subordination in Genesis 2–3). It also regularly denies something that other texts assert (e.g., that wives are in some sense under the authority of their husbands, as Ephesians 5:22ff asserts).

But why not simply say that the feminist exegetes make some mistakes, even perhaps many mistakes, even that they make so many mistakes they should not be considered qualified exegetes?[6] The answer is that what they read into the text is clearly an ideology they are promoting and that is the important point for this discussion. It does not take the hermeneutics of suspicion to see that. The ideology is right on the surface of the discourse the exegesis is found in. Their exegesis is ideologically motivated—as they usually admit. Perhaps they are convinced by their own exegesis or by the exegesis of another feminist, so they are sincere in what they

---

[6] A considerable amount of feminist exegesis is exegetically incompetent, despite the fact that the exegetes hold respectable academic positions. It is difficult to come up with an explanation for this apart from a view that ideological exegesis should be judged acceptable simply because of the importance of the ideological position it is upholding. John H. Elliott, in *I Peter: A New Translation with Introduction and Commentary*, AB 37B (New York: Doubleday, 2000), 596–598, and also in "Jesus Was Not an Egalitarian: A Critique of an Anachronistic and Idealist Theory," *Biblical Theology Bulletin* 32 (2002), 75–91, provides a convincing analysis of the exegetical incompetence of Schüssler Fiorenza's flagship book *In Memory of Her: A Feminist Theological Reconstruction of Christian Origins* (New York: Crossroad, 1992). Wayne Grudem, "The Meaning of κεφαλή ('Head'): An Evaluation of New Evidence, Real and Alleged" in Wayne Grudem, ed., *Biblical Foundations for Manhood and Womanhood* (Wheaton, IL: Crossway, 2002) does the same for Evangelical feminist Catherine Kroeger's article "Head" in *Dictionary of Paul and His Letters* (Downers Grove, IL: InterVarsity, 1993).

say. But objectively speaking, they read something into the text that is not there and substitute an ideologically motivated position for what is in the text.

We need to make two caveats. The first is that ideological eisegesis is not restricted to feminists, even though the first examples we have come across in this book are due to feminists. For instance, the Liberation Theology Marxists are usually ideological exegetes, although most secular Marxists believe they should approach the Scriptures the same way the last category of Feminists do. They think that their interpretation advances the revolution (and so benefits the oppressed social classes), and so they should attack the scriptural texts or Christianity or religion in general. Similar things can be said about other ideological exegetes.

The second caveat is that the question of how to relate to a prevailing societal view or even one that has not yet prevailed but that we are convinced of (e.g., liberal democracy, environmentalism, capitalism), is a difficult question and cannot be reduced to questions of exegesis (good or bad), much less of eisegesis.[7] It requires a much broader discussion. Here it is enough to observe that there is such a thing as ideological eisegesis. And it is important to observe that theological exegesis is not eisegesis.

---

[7] For a fuller discussion of this issue, see Clark, *MWC*, 531–538.

CHAPTER TWENTY-ONE

HISTORICAL RELIABILITY

The parts of the Bible that are intended to describe historical events do so reliably for Christian purposes (i.e., with reasonable historical accuracy), although modern historical method does not allow us to resolve many questions of how precisely.

Introduction to the chapter. In this book we are dealing with how to read the Old Testament in the light of the New. With some regularity that raises historical questions about both the Old and the New Testaments. Both purport to tell us what happened in the past. But can we rely on what they tell us—do they tell the truth?

Of course, as we have seen, the entire Bible does not narrate history, but some parts of it clearly intend to. Moreover, there are some different possible ways a narrative text could present historical facts, some of which are similar to our history books, some of which are quite dissimilar. In the special discussion on "Scriptural Interpretation and Literary Genre," we began to consider these issues.

The first chapters of Genesis are written in a genre that is debated. Some see them as historical or at least having an historical kernel. Some do not. Starting with chapter 12, most scholars see the text either as intended to be historical or at least as handing down material that was understood to be historical. Rather than trying to sort out the genre of the first eleven chapters, beyond what we have done in chapter 2 to consider Genesis 1, we will begin with Genesis 12 to discuss the relationship of scriptural historical narrative to modern history writing.

The limitations of historical evidence. At an earlier time, many held the view that history writing was making steady progress, and we would eventually be able to have history books that told us "how it actually happened." Some who discussed this area a century and more ago thought that history should be a science like that of the natural sciences. We should sooner or later be able to write history with the same precision or exactness and certainty as we write astronomy, or possibly even chemistry.[1] Such views have been largely abandoned. We cannot do anything like that very often, if ever, especially for ancient history.

Perhaps the chief reason this view has been retired is the development of scientific theory and of the philosophy of science. The scientific method as used in a discipline like chemistry is a study of recurrent phenomena and seeks to find established regularities in the way those phenomena occur ("laws" like Boyle's Law), or at least, in a discipline like astronomy, descriptions of relatively constant features of the phenomena being discussed, like the number, placement, and movement of the stars.

History does not have a subject matter like that. Rather it typically seeks to describe singular past events, people, or institutions, like the battle of Waterloo, the personality of Napoleon, or the nature of the Directory when it was ruling revolutionary France. To do that, history is written with certain kinds of evidence, and the nature of historical method is more like the methods of investiga-

---

[1]   J. B. Bury said in 1902 in his inaugural lecture as Regius Professor of Modern History at Cambridge: "History is a science, no less and no more." Speaking of the development of historical method he said, "The idea of a scrupulously exact conformity to facts was fixed, refined, and canonized." He added, "To clothe the story of human society in a literary dress is no more the part of a historian as a historian, than it is the part of an astronomer as astronomer to present in an artistic shape the story of the stars." (Fritz Stern, ed. *The Varieties of History* [Cleveland, OH: The World Publishing Company, 1956], 209–223). Carl Gustav Hempel, the logical positivist philosopher, was perhaps the last major voice for this kind of a position in his "The Function of General Laws in History," *Journal of Philosophy*, 39 (15 January 1942), 36.

tion in legal cases than like those of the physical sciences.

In ancient history as written by modern historians, some of the evidence is what could be described as physical evidence. We have remains of ancient buildings and other artifacts so we can to some extent see what they were like and understand them—if we can identify them, date them, and place their origin when significant. We have surface survey methods that give us information about patterns of settlement in early centuries—if we can interpret them well. We also have some letters and other documents of ancient people, and we can read what they said and how they said it. We have some official documents, records, and inscriptions. The greater part of the evidence we use, however, comes from literary historical records written by ancient writers intended to be descriptions or references to historical people and events.

The literary historical records almost always have discrepancies between them, sometimes major ones. Moreover, they commonly may agree on the main lines of an event, but disagree about the details. In addition, they very often evaluate the people and events in somewhat different ways. The hero of one account may be the villain in the next. And, as we will see, they often exhibit different literary approaches to the writing of history.[2]

Moreover, we have much less historical data for the ancient world than we do for modern times. That does not mean that we cannot tell, for instance, that Augustus Caesar existed, won the battle of Actium, and reigned until AD 14. But it does mean that we know much less about him than we know about, say, Queen Victoria. We know much more, however, about Augustus than we do about Ramesses II, who many think was the Pharaoh in the book of Exodus.

Correspondingly, we can evaluate with greater confidence the historicity of material about William Booth, the Victorian evan-

---

[2] See A. N. Sherwin-White, *Roman Society and Roman Law in the New Testament* (Oxford: Clarendon, 1963), 186–193, for a discussion of the challenges of working with sources in ancient history, focusing on Tiberius Caesar, the Roman emperor at the time of the crucifixion of Christ, and also evaluating the work of Herodotus as an historical source.

gelist who founded the Salvation Army, than we can the historicity of material about the Apostle Paul, and we can evaluate with
greater confidence the historicity of material about Paul than we
can that about Moses. By the time we go back to the first period of
Israelite history in the land of Canaan, we have very little data, at
least for much of the time and place we are interested in. For Ramesses II, at least in the Karnak region, we have a decent amount;
for Gideon in the Israelite highlands, we have none beyond the
text in Judges.[3]

The limitations of historical method. Depending on the historian,
we find significantly different historical evaluations of events and
people narrated in the Scripture. Langer's *Encyclopedia of World History*[4] has been a reference work in history and provides examples of
how modern history writing normally worked before the advent of
post-modernism. The story of David, for instance, in its main outlines, makes it into Langer's *Encyclopedia*. So does the Exodus, although the way it is described in the *Encyclopedia* is one that many
scholars would not accept. Many scholars would put the patriarchs
into a history as well, although Langer does not.

On the other hand, there is a school of contemporary historians commonly called the Minimalists who would not put any of this
into their historical writings. They think there is not enough truly historical evidence for the earliest periods of Israelite history to
see what scriptural texts narrate as other than fiction. Some of them

---

[3] Mark S. Smith, *The Early History of God: Yahweh and the Other Deities in Ancient Israel*,
2nd ed. (Grand Rapids, MI: Eerdmans, 2002), xxii: "Despite many gains, the basic
task [of research on Israelite deities and religion] remains largely a matter of interpreting and integrating small pieces of evidence drawn from rather disparate sources
. . . In my opinion, what vestiges we have provide barely enough material to write a
proper history of religion for ancient Israel. In general it is very difficult to garner little more than a broad picture of Israel prior to the eighth century [BC], and at times
the theses offered seem conjectural." For a review of the more ample, but still scanty
and uneven, sources for the study of New Testament history, see Martin Hengel, *Acts
and the History*, chap. 1.

[4] William L. Langer, *An Encyclopedia of World History*, 5th ed. (Boston: Houghton Mif-
flin, 1972).

hold the amazingly skeptical view that we cannot even tell if David or Solomon existed, primarily on the basis of their evaluation of the scantiness of the archaeological evidence. As many have observed, they flout the basic principle that absence of (archaeological) evidence is not evidence of the historical absence of something. Their views are nonetheless discussed, at times positively, in serious academic presentations.[5]

To keep perspective, events narrated in Scripture are not the only events that make it into some modern history books, but not into others. There are many events narrated by Herodotus, the Greek historian (fifth century BC) often called "the father of history," that are accepted as historically factual by some historians and not by others. The same is true of some of what Thucydides (fourth century BC) said, although he is considered one of the most reliable Greek historians. In fact, the most consistent problem of the historian dealing in modern history is sorting through the large quantity of potential evidence, while the most consistent problem of the historian working in ancient history is the lack of evidence and the existence of many "holes" ("*lacunae*") in the historical records. Our historical knowledge of ancient history is very uneven, and so the evaluation modern historians give of the conclusions we can draw from the data can vary considerably.

We have then many reasonably reliable sources for ancient history and we can write good ancient histories, but we can rarely tell with certainty whether any particular detail or event "actually happened" the way it was written, or sometimes actually happened at all. We do not have tools that can tell us exactly how the human authors were writing their history or exactly what their evidence was, and so we cannot go behind the text to tell exactly what hap-

---

[5] For works that effectively argue against the Minimalists, see K. A. Kitchen, *On the Reliability*; William G. Dever, *What Did the Biblical Writers Know and When Did They Know It: What Archaeology Can Tell Us about the Reality of Ancient Israel* (Grand Rapids, MI: Eerdmans, 2001); James K. Hoffmeier, *Israel in Egypt*; and Baruch Halpern "Erasing History: The Minimalist Assault on Ancient History," *Bible Review* 11/6 (1995), 26–35, 47; the first two writing in a "splendidly classical polemical fashion," as David Noel Freedman put it when speaking of Dever.

pened—even though some historians feel licensed to do so. We need to soberly accept the value but also the limitations of historical method.

In addition, ancient history as an academic discipline is by no means "hard science." There is a broad historical methodology that all contemporary academic historians would accept. There are additional principles and approaches that historians who work in ancient history would accept. But there are many disagreements among contemporary historians—they often operate on different principles and come up with different interpretations of both the material evidence and the literary sources—and there have been major shifts in approach. Since the advent of "post-modernism" among historians, some would even say that history writing has broken down as a discipline.[6]

The fact that some historians would not include events like the Exodus does not rule out their historicity, but it does indicate that the nature of the texts, or at least the historical evidence we have in some of these instances, differs from that for the Battle of Actium or Napoleon's defeat at Waterloo. A sound historian might give the judgment: we lack enough evidence to include much of what is said in the scriptural accounts (probably without thereby saying that he knows it did not happen), while another sound historian might disagree.

There are a variety of reasons for such judgments. Some historians might not be willing to accept these events because some of the

---

[6] "The state of historical studies at present represents a cacophony of voices produced by clashing stratagems and rival interests and allows for no single synthesis standing for all of us." Mark T. Gilderhus, *History and Historians: A Historiographical Introduction* (Upper Saddle River, NJ: Prentice Hall, 2010), 106. Jon D. Levenson, *Creation*, xxxi, "In a period of less than two decades since I left graduate school, the old verities that I learned have mostly been shaken, and no new historical consensus has emerged." For the view that this state of affairs is part of the broader "state of crisis in the humanities," see N. T. Wright, *The New Testament and the People of God* (Minneapolis, MN: Fortress, 1992), 31–32 and the references there. For a similar view but from the perspective of an anthropologist speaking about what is commonly called "the social sciences," in this case including history, see Clifford Geertz, *Local Knowledge: Further Essays in Interpretive Anthropology* (New York: Basic Books, 1983), 1–6.

scriptural accounts have to be centuries later than the events they recount, and they think we cannot rely on the historical accuracy of most texts written at such a distance. Or they might say we do not have enough confirmatory evidence from outside the scriptural texts, such as archaeological evidence or additional references in other sources. Or they might hold that the literary form of the narratives is not intended to be historical in the modern sense, so we cannot put the events in them into history books. Perhaps, however, the most important reason for abandoning the view that we are in the process of creating assured scientific history is the realization that history writing is more of an art than a science, and the judgments in both the ancient sources and in the modern historian writing on the basis of the sources will depend on skill in making good historical judgments.[7]

The limitation that the nature of the evidence puts upon the historical enterprise is one problem. The approaches of the various historians provide another. This comes into greater play as we move from simply trying to judge what the facts are to the attempt to write a synthesis of historical data such as a continuous history, or, even more so, an attempt to ascertain the causes of events, or, still more so, attempts to evaluate what people in the past have done or said.

To some extent the difficulty is inherent in any human attempt to understand a large amount of complex data and come up with a reasonable synthesis. We need to develop categories or concepts and make use of patterns of inference. We often find it helpful to make reasonable assumptions or use models of development or causality. Few historians avoid making evaluative judgments. All these could be described as non-factual elements of theory formation.

---

[7] Peter Stuhlmacher expressed dismay at the lack of objective results in the quote in footnote 1, p. 467. He then went on to express the point being made here, namely that the methods require non-factual elements, when he says, "The reasons for this are that historical study always contains an element of subjectivity and that the complex combination of methods which comprises historical study (text- and literary-criticism, form- and redaction-criticism, lexicography and the history of religions) can be quite variously used and accented."

Such elements, of course, can be used well or badly. In dealing with attempts to summarize biblical history or ancient history in general, however, the use of various principles or theories often seems to motivate many historians to move beyond what can be supported by the evidence.

More seriously, we have to deal with an increasing number of historians who use history to advance an anti-religious agenda or a moral ideology at odds with Christian teaching or at least write speculative historical reconstructions at odds with Christian teaching, often without always using good historical method. The following is a sampler of problematic procedures in common use (although not universally used):

- Ruling out supernatural intervention *a priori* so that all passages in which anything supernatural is referred to must be historically unreliable, literary adornment, later invention, etc. Many historians would use this criterion to say that there are miraculous or marvelous events in some narration, and such things do not happen, and so the narration is unreliable for providing historically reliable data. Or at their most gracious they would hold that we could not tell if such things did happen.[8] That would have to be recognized as ideological bias in the historian, since we have examples of well-confirmed miracles[9] and of many events that are extraordinary enough to convince onlookers that something

---

[8] Mark T. Gilderhus, *History and Historians*, 29, writes with condescension, "No modern scholar working in a reputable field can claim legitimately to possess the means by which to verify any statements about the role of divine influences in history and nature. As manifestations of faith, statements about God's purposes are not subject to proof by reason, logic, and evidence."

[9] See Ruth Cranston, *The Miracle of Lourdes* (New York: McGraw-Hill, 1955) for an account of some of the most well-established cases of miracles; see C. S. Lewis, *Miracles,* for a basic account of the reasonableness of belief in miracles, especially for clarifying that a miracle is not the violation of the laws of nature; and see Stanley L. Jaki, *Miracles and Physics* (Front Royal, VA: Christendom Press, 1989) for a discussion of miracles and the philosophy of science.

supernatural is happening.[10] Nonetheless professional historians commonly employ the principle.

- Adopting the view that since the Scriptures are faith documents (or even propaganda pieces) they cannot provide us reliable access to the events they are referring to, despite the fact that historians normally use faith and propaganda documents as useful and reliable historical sources. We cannot automatically throw out historical records that were written to support a message. If we did, we would have to reduce the ancient history section of Langer's *Encyclopedia* by a large percentage, well over a majority, perhaps almost completely—not to mention many, even a substantial majority, of the writings of most secular historians themselves.[11] Moreover, the critique often overlooks the common sense observation that few people who argue for or expound a position find it advantageous to falsify public facts.[12]

- Relying on the hermeneutics of suspicion, that is, the prin-

---

[10] Rodney Stark, *The Rise of Christianity: A Sociologist Reconsiders History* (Princeton, NJ: Princeton University Press, 1996), 90: "Modern scholars have too long been content to dismiss reports of miracles in the New Testament and other similar sources as purely literary, not as things that happened. Yet we remain aware that in tabernacles all over modern America, healings are taking place. One need not propose that God is the active agent in these 'cures' to recognize their reality both as events and as perceptions. Why then should we not accept that 'miracles' were being done in New Testament times too, and that people expected them as proof of religious authenticity?"

[11] Caird, *Language and Imagery*, chap. 12, holds that what makes an account historical is that it refers to an event that happened in the past, and that it is important to distinguish between the fact that something is asserted to have happened and the understanding of it. We may believe that the authors of scriptural writings were mistaken in their understanding of the events they referred to, but that does not vitiate the fact the authors actually referred to historical events and therefore their writings were a testimony to the historicity of those events.

[12] See Sherwin-White, *Roman Society and Roman Law*, 191–193; and Dever, *What Did the Biblical Writers Know*, 47: "They [the Revisionists] do not appreciate the fact that all literature in effect is fundamentally 'propaganda,' that is, self-conscious expression of a worldview, usually in the advocacy of a cause. That the Hebrew Bible is in that sense 'propaganda' is not in dispute among responsible scholars; the only question is whether or not such propaganda reflects anything of the real world of the time. And it inevitably does, otherwise it would not have been credible for those to whom it was addressed."

ciple that behind idealistic explanations of motivation, including religious ones, lies the real motivation, namely an attempt to do or acquire something for one's own advantage, most commonly to advance one's own power.[13] This principle, of course, itself provides a good basis for the suspicion that those who use it are just doing so to support their own "message" in a covert way (now sometimes referred to as "suspecting the hermeneutics of suspicion").[14]

- Failure to deal well with the issue of subject and object in evaluating historical narratives, and so proceeding by determining that the narrative structure or approach is the product of the writers (who therefore are writing historical fiction or an ideological piece) or their "communities" or "circles." This approach is often taken without adequately considering that the objective fact being described and the sources for knowing about it also have to be taken into account before we can ascertain the nature of the writer's contribution to the final product. If we do not have that data, our view of the writer's contribution is largely speculative or simply arbitrary.

- Partiality in the amount of evidence one requires to substantiate a particular view; for instance, for many exegetes it would take a huge, perhaps unattainable, amount of evidence to establish the authenticity of a miracle story reporting an event that actually happened, but it would require only an indication of plausibility to establish that a particu-

---

[13] For an example: the "Hebrew Scriptures consist mainly of the Scriptures of the temple cult. . . . the purpose of this cult was to legitimate rulers in Jerusalem, and this is what the Scriptures are mostly about." Robert B. and Mary P. Coote, *Power, Politics, and the Making of the Bible* (Minneapolis, MN: Fortress, 1992), 3. For an up-front statement that the hermeneutics of suspicion should be used to advance a Feminist agenda regardless of what the text says, see Elizabeth Schüssler Fiorenza, "Feminist Hermeneutics."

[14] See Levenson, *Hebrew Bible*, the second half of section II, for a critique of this approach, which he identifies as a sub-species of "historicism." See also the outworking of the hermeneutics of suspicion that N. T. Wright describes in Marcus J. Borg and N. T. Wright, *The Meaning of Jesus: Two Visions* (New York: HarperCollins, 1998), 17–18.

lar story was invented by the Jerusalem priestly caste or the early church leaders for purposes of their own.[15]

- Lack of discipline in scholarly speculation by a readiness to produce plausible theories and reconstructions that can never be controlled by the available evidence that we have and using them for accounts of Israelite history or early Christianity.[16]

- In New Testament studies, using the criterion that the only way to be sure that we have an authentic saying of Jesus is if we can show it to be distinctive of him, that is, dissimilar to known tendencies in Judaism before him or the Church after him—thus ensuring that it will never be established that the authentic Jesus learned anything from Judaism or that the Church faithfully learned anything from him.[17]

If we understand how modern history writing works, we should soon realize that we are not just confronted with the challenge of evaluating the historical reliability of scriptural texts or of other texts in ancient history. We are also confronted with the challenge of evaluating the historical reliability of modern historical writings. This includes writings of Scripture scholars who treat historical topics in the Bible, many of whom write with a skeptical, even anti-religious bias. A major part of the challenge in evaluating the historical reliability of Scripture texts is not only the unavoidable difficulties of any ancient

---

[15] The presentation of the position in footnote 9, p. 526 provides a good example.

[16] N. T. Wright, in *The Resurrection of the Son of God*, 18–19, put the point somewhat caustically by saying, "When traditio-historical study (the examination of hypothetical stages by which the written gospels came into existence) builds castles in the air, the ordinary historian need not feel a second-class citizen for refusing to rent space in them."

[17] As C. F. D. Moule put it in *The Origin of Christology* (Cambridge, UK: Cambridge University Press, 1977), 155–156, "It is impossible to find criteria by which a later and modified form of a tradition can be infallibly recognized or an earlier form infallibly restored. . . . No historian in his right mind would try to construct a portrait of a figure of the past solely from views, sayings or characteristics which he shared neither with his predecessors nor with his successors." Moule is, of course, indirectly commenting on volumes that have been written by reputable exegetes.

history but also the very avoidable orientations, especially ideologi-cal orientations, of many modern historians and Scripture scholars.[18]

Historical genres. In the second methodological discussion, we looked at the question of literary genre. We saw that to understand what a writing is trying to communicate we have to understand the literary form or genre. This turns out to be true when we evaluate historical writing as well. Ancient historical writing, including his-torical writing in the Scriptures, uses different genres than we find in most modern historical writing. We cannot deal with the question of the historical accuracy of the historical narratives in history with-out understanding the difference in genre or approach to writing history between the ancient documents and the modern scholarly writings that try to understand them.

To begin with a complication, there is more than one approach to the historical nature of narratives found in ancient historical sources. One can be illustrated by the way many scholars would in-terpret Homer's classical Greek epic, the *Iliad*. They would say that the *Iliad* probably has an historical reference, and from it we can learn some things about historical events. There was a Troy, Myce-naean "Greeks" attacked it, Troy did fall, and the main characters in the story quite likely existed over three millennia ago.

However, the *Iliad* is not straight history, but an epic poem—and probably one that was modified over time after the original author wrote (recited) it. If we were able to go back and observe the fall of Troy, in many respects it would not look the way Homer portrayed it. Homer was not interested in writing an historical ac-count of the sort that could be used in a modern history book. But he did think his poem was about something that happened, and many scholars today would defend that view.[19] Probably he also

---

[18] These difficulties are summarized in Pope Benedict XVI's Apostolic Exhortation, *Verbum Domini,* 35 as "the danger of dualism and a secularized hermeneutic."

[19] Many scholars have defended the core historicity of the events of *The Iliad* more vig-orously in recent years. For a survey of the evidence, see Edwin Yamauchi, "Homer and Archaeology" in Alan Millard and James K. Hoffmeier, ed., *The Future of Biblical Archaeology: Reassessing Methodologies and Assumptions* (Grand Rapids, MI: Eerd-

thought it captured the true significance of the events he narrated.

A later and different example is what is sometimes referred to as the Melian Dialogue. As already noted, Thucydides is considered one of the most reliable ancient Greek historians. In his history of the Peloponnesian war, he describes how the Athenians tried to persuade the inhabitants of the island of Melos to submit to them. He does so by reproducing the interaction in the form of a dialogue. The dialogue does not contain a stenographic report, much less a transcript of an audio recording, of what the actual negotiators on each side said, but it vividly conveys what was going on.

As Thucydides himself said in his introduction, he made use of set speeches, keeping to the general sense of what he remembered or was reported to him, but made the speakers say "what, in my opinion, was called for by each situation" (*The Peloponnesian War* I, 22). For an ancient historian, this was true history. For most modern historians this would most likely not be considered true history, at least not of the kind they would be open to writing (or publishing).

There is still another common form of ancient historical writing, what is called annals or chronicles (e.g., the Babylonian Chronicle or the annalistic framework of Kings and Chronicles, explicitly based on sources like the Chronicles of the Kings of Israel and of Judah).[20] The annals often focus on rulers and list facts with little

---

mans, 2004), 69–90. For current views of the historical background to the Trojan Wars, see Kenneth W. Harl, "The Legend of Troy" in *Great Ancient Civilizations of Asia Minor* (Chantilly, VA: The Teaching Company, 2001), 6.

[20] The records cited in the historical works of the Old Testament include "the Book of the Chronicles of the Kings of Judah" (1 Kings 14:29; 15:7, 23; 22:46); "the Book of the Chronicles of the Kings of Israel" (1 Kings 14:19; 15:31; 16:5, 14, etc.); "the Book of the Kings of Judah and Israel" (2 Chron 16:11; 25:26; 27:7; 28:26, etc.); the acts of King David in "the Chronicles of Samuel the seer," "the Chronicles of Nathan the prophet," "the Chronicles of Gad the seer" (1 Chron 29:29); the acts of Solomon in "the book of the acts of Solomon" (1 Kings 11:41) and in "the Chronicles of Nathan the prophet," "the prophecy of Ahijah the Shilonite," and "the visions of Iddo the seer" (2 Chron 9:29); the records of the acts of Rehoboam in "the chronicles of Shemaiah the prophet and of Iddo the seer" (2 Chron 12:15) and the acts of Abijah in "the story of the prophet Iddo" (2 Chron 13:22); "the books of the kings of Israel" (2 Chron 20:34), "the Book of the Wars of the LORD" (Num 21:14), and "the Book of Jashar" (Josh 10:13; 2 Sam 1:17).

development: King So-and-So lived so long and fought these wars and built these buildings and there was such and such a natural disaster during his reign (for one scriptural example of the style, see 1 Kings 15:1–8). There is also mention of deities to give those deities credit for events or to cite their justification for various actions. Apart from the mention of the deities, ancient annals come close to modern history, although, ironically, modern historians seem rarely interested in just listing facts, but much more so in their interpretations of the facts and in justifications of those interpretations.

These different kinds of ancient historical writing are only typical examples and in practice many ancient writings seem to be on a continuum between them. Moreover, ancient writers have what to modern historians is the distressing practice of writing different parts of their works with different historical styles or even worse of presenting a collage of sources written in different historical styles.[21] In addition, none of them, other than perhaps annalists, would think a sequential history that did not "clothe the story of human society in a literary dress," as Bury put it, was worth writing. They would probably even think it was uncivilized, or at least only worthy of scribal technicians who keep annals. The above list, however, illustrates the main features of the approaches we need to deal with.

There is a more contemporary example that allows us to see what is at issue. Allan Eckerd has written a series of books on the early history of the American Indians, *Narratives of America*. They read somewhat like novels in that they are narratives that contain dialogues. The narrative parts are written like the narratives in much modern history, although more vivid than most. The dialogues, however, are taken from the letters and writings of the period, but as dialogues they are not transcripts of what was actually said on a given occasion. Rather, they are reconstructions.[22] His books are there-

---

[21] Alter, *Genesis*, xlii: "It is quite apparent that a concept of composite artistry, of literary composition through a collage of textual materials, was generally assumed to be normal procedure in ancient Israelite culture."

[22] Eckerd begins in his first volume *The Frontiersmen* (Boston: Little Brown and Company, 1967): "This book is fact, not fiction." He further says, "In order to help provide continuity and maintain a high degree of reader interest, certain techniques normally

fore placed in the fiction section of most bookstores. They have, however, a reasonable claim overall to be accurate historically; they are complete with references to the historical sources on which they are based; and they would make a good introductory history text, better than most of those in the history section. Nonetheless they violate the canons of modern historical writing and so are exiled to the fiction section.

Modern history writing presents us with a different literary genre than ancient history writing (or Eckerd's *Narratives*). There are criteria for what goes into modern history books, some of which we could describe as "canonical" as Bury does (see footnote 4, p. 511), although most contemporary historians would not want to use that word. Perhaps the chief criterion comes from the goal: to describe past events the way they happened with descriptive accuracy and precision and perhaps also explain why they happened (though some modern historians do not think they should try to do that). A second criterion is consistency of genre. A history book can only contain writing that is intended to achieve the goal, and so fables, poetic descriptions, and dramatizations are not allowed. Much ancient history writing, including the historical writing in the Scriptures, would not have recognized these criteria as rules they had to follow, as we have seen.

There is another, often unspoken, but nevertheless pervasive criterion that is especially relevant to a study of the Scriptures, and that is the criterion of secularity. The modern genre of historical writing, at least in many parts of the world, is secular. It is not acceptable to include in a history book the assertion that the Resurrection of Christ happened, for instance, or that God actually spoke to Moses in the burning bush. Statements like that would get the book automatically slotted out of the history section of the bookstore or library into the theology or religion section.

At the same time, most history books will not contain denials of such events. They are usually non-committal on such things and

---

associated with the novel form have been utilized, but in no case has this been at the expense of historical accuracy." For the most part, his protests were to no avail.

often studiously ambiguous in describing them. The current domi-nant ideal for the modern historical genre is neutrality on religious assertions, although religious skepticism is very often acceptable while statements of religious belief now almost never are. This is an especially relevant observation when we consider that many biblical scholars see their work as a category of history and not as a branch of theology.[23]

Some contemporary historians would say that most ancient his-torical writing is not historical (or not *really* historical). It is more helpful, however, to say that people in the ancient world did not approach history the same way we do. We cannot deal with their histories the way we would approach a modern historical writing, but that does not mean they do not put us in contact with actual historical facts or that they were not intended to.[24] How they do so depends on the approach of each writing.

We cannot begin to evaluate the judgments about the historical nature of scriptural material if we do not recognize that for most modern historians, any attempt to recount what happened in the past by including something we know or might guess did not hap-pen in the way we have described it, for instance, by including a dia-logue that is only "called for by each situation," is not a truly histor-ical approach. The modern historical genre does not allow for that. Different views of the nature of true history writing, such as those of most of the biblical authors, do.

Christian historical evaluation. So how do Christians who under-stand the genre of modern history and accept it in its broad outlines

---

[23] The American biblical scholar Bruce Vawter put this bluntly in "The History of Isra-elite Religion: A Secular or Theological Subject?" *Biblical Archaeology Review,* 31/3, 42: "Our task must be an historical, not a theological, enterprise."

[24] As William Dever put it (*What Did the Biblical Writers Know,* 272), "it is unreasonable to demand that the ancient writers should have been modern, scientific and academic historians, or that they should have written the history we want." R. W. L. Moberly, *DTIB,* 212 made the point more fully by saying, "If ancient Israel's genres do not cor-respond to those of "history" as articulated in modern Western thought, they need be none the worse for that. The challenge is learning to recognize and appreciate the ancient conventions, and to relate them appropriately to our modern ones."

approach the historicity of the narrative accounts in the Scriptures?

They have to begin by recognizing that the scriptural narratives are written in a different historical genre than modern historians write in. All ancient historical writing is, as we have seen. Then they have to evaluate the views in the relevant modern historical literature. Then somehow they have to put the two together.

We can use the account of the life of Abraham that we discussed in chapter 6 of this book as one example of the historical question for scriptural writings. We read in Genesis 12 that Abraham moved from his family home in Haran in northern Mesopotamia (modern Harran in southern Turkey) to Canaan. Do we know that happened?

After all, the account we have is written in a book that was no doubt written down centuries later (almost certainly in a language Abraham did not use), and we have no confirmatory external evidence like an altar he erected in Canaan or an entry in Middle Kingdom Egyptian dynastic records that mentions him, much less one that says he moved to Canaan from Haran.[25] So some scholars will hold, we just do not know that it happened. Others will add that since it is written in a religious book designed to make a theological point, it was probably invented to fit the message the book was trying to convey, and therefore, following the "hermeneutics of suspicion," we should doubt that it did.

We can grant that we cannot prove or establish with empirical certainty that there was a nomadic pastoralist in the second millennium BC named Abram or Abraham who moved from Haran to Canaan. On the other hand, we cannot prove or establish with empirical certainty that it did not happen. Moreover we do have some evidence, namely, the account in the book of Genesis that is based on some traditions that were passed down in a careful way.

In addition, the account fits in with what we know of second millennium history in a way that could not have been invented by people centuries later who lived in significantly different circum-

---

[25] All that exists is a reference in an inscription of Pharaoh Shoshenq I to someone who might be our Abram.

stances, like the putative post-exilic authors of Genesis or the more likely author or authors in the early monarchical period.[26] Moreover, family history seems to be especially tenacious in the oral traditions of stable tribal societies.[27] Finally, the limited amount of historical material we have for the time and place means it is not surprising that we have no other evidence for Abraham.

Nonetheless we can be confident that everything in the patriarchal narratives did not happen just the way it was written down, much less that every line spoken by someone was based on a stenographic report. If we are trying to write a modern history of Old Testament Israel, we are trying to do something the human authors of the Old Testament were not trying to do. They were not trying to write entries for Langer's *Encyclopedia of World History*, even less a correct minimalist history. They likely felt free to alter the sequence of events for thematic intelligibility or make up dialogues that, in their opinion, were "called for by each situation" or speak with rhetorical emphasis so that their intended audience would understand the significance of something that did happen.

The authors of the narratives almost certainly did not invent historical narratives out of whole cloth, especially not the main lines of the events or developments that they recount. They did not, howev-

---

[26] See Gary A. Rendsburg, *The Redaction of Genesis*.

[27] See Dever, *What Did the Biblical Writers Know*, 179–180 for a discussion of the role of oral tradition in Old Testament history. Richard Bauckham, *Jesus and the Eyewitnesses: The Gospels as Eyewitness Testimony* (Grand Rapids, MI: Eerdmans, 2007), 1–1, 240–289, presents an extensive analysis of the role of oral tradition in the Gospels and the life of Jesus. The whole book is a defense of the view that the Gospels contain reliable eyewitness tradition. While it does not apply in the same way to the accounts of the patriarchs, the book does provide an added example of the reliability of various forms of oral tradition. One of his important sources is *Story as History— History as Story: The Gospel Tradition in the Context of Ancient Oral History* by Samuel Byrskog (Tübingen: Mohr/Siebeck, 2002). See also Paul Rhodes Eddy and Gregory A. Boyd, *The Jesus Legend: A Case for the Historical Reliability of the Synoptic Jesus Tradition* (Grand Rapids, MI: Baker Academic, 2007), chap. 6, for a presentation of the contemporary discussion of oral tradition. In addition, the discussion of the historical basis of the *Iliad* and the *Odyssey* treated in footnote 15, p. 529 provides an example of how tenacious oral recollections can be, even into a much later age that has very little recollection of the earlier period.

er, think they were required to describe, "how it actually happened" to the smallest detail. The historical sections of both the Old and New Testament are good historical sources, most often rather good ones for ancient history, but, as we have seen, not ones written in a modern historical genre.

If we look at the other end of the Scripture, the New Testament, we find that the situation is rather different. To be sure, the New Testament historical records present some of the same challenges we find in the patriarchal accounts, and do not present historians a seamless garment from which they can read off "what actually happened" to the smallest detail. Nonetheless, the crucifixion of Christ is probably the best-attested event in ancient history. Since the Resurrection is closely linked with the crucifixion there is also more evidence for it than most events in ancient history.[28] To be sure, there is a nest of interpretation questions connected with both events, and skeptical historians will entertain any explanation for the accounts of the Resurrection other than that the Resurrection happened. Nonetheless, as facts they are rather well-attested.

The historical data in both testaments contain discrepancies. But, as we have seen, all historical sources in ancient history do. A discrepancy, however, is not a logical contradiction. To be contradictory two statements have to be incompatible (one *cannot* be true without the other being false and vice versa), and what they assert has to be about the same object in the same respect. As logicians have observed, contradictions are notoriously hard to establish in anything other than formal disciplines like logic and mathematics. In the light of what has been said above about the difference in historical genres, establishing contradictions should also have to establish that the two statements have to have the same intent in the way their authors are speaking about historical facts (speaking exactly

---

[28] For two recent scholarly justifications of the historicity of the Resurrection, see Richard Swinburne, *The Resurrection of God Incarnate* (Oxford: Clarendon Press, 2003) and N. T. Wright, *The Resurrection of the Son of God*, Christian Origins and the Question of God, vol. 3 (Minneapolis, MN: Fortress, 2003), both professors at Oxford. See also the reference in footnote 7, p. 525 to Caird's useful background discussion of the historical nature of the New Testament accounts of the crucifixion (and Resurrection).

versus speaking loosely, speaking symbolically versus speaking literally, speaking for emphasis versus simply reciting facts, etc.).[29] Establishing a true contradiction between ancient historical sources is normally beyond our reach.

Orthodox Christians believe the Scriptures are inerrant, because they are inspired by God. God is their author, although he works through human authors. There are, however, different views of inerrancy. That is a subject beyond the scope of this book. Here, however, the focus is on historical accuracy.

We may have good theological reasons to hold one or another view of inerrancy. If, however, we are dealing with the limitations of our understanding—both limitations of our understanding of what the Scriptures mean to tell us about historical events and limitations in our confidence of the results produced by modern historical writers, especially in ancient history—we need to recognize that we can only go so far. We can, in other words, sit loosely to ideological arguments against inerrancy, while being confident that on the whole the Scriptures hold up reasonably well as historical documents (of the sort produced by ancient writers). We cannot, however, confidently defend every jot and tittle.

To put the point more simply, if someone says, Abraham did not go from Haran to Canaan, or Abraham never existed, we can ask with confidence the question: how do you know that? The answer will turn out to be inadequate to establish the point. If, however, we say that Abraham did go from Haran to Canaan, and we are trying to convince someone without Christian or Jewish belief, we will

---

[29] Robert Alter (*Genesis*, xliii), discussing contradiction in Old Testament writing, says, "There are many kinds of ambiguity and contradiction, and abundant varieties of repetition, that are entirely purposeful, and that are essential features of the distinctive vehicle of literary experience." R. W. L. Moberly (*Old Testament Theology*, 111), says much the same thing: "There is, in fact, a tricky conceptual question as to what constitutes a genuine contradiction, as distinct from a difference, a disagreement, a tension, or a paradox." His chapter 4 is a skillful treatment of the issue of contradictions in Scripture, especially in the light of Hebrew paratactic style. Martin Hengel (*Acts and the History*, 130), focusing less on the literary form and more on the question of historical accuracy, puts it this way, "The multiplicity of perspectives of historical onlookers produces very different horizons of knowledge."

not be able to assert that he did with historically convincing belief, much less empirical certainty. If, however, we say that Abraham existed, we can give some good historical reasons for why we think so, although not ones that amount to empirical certainty. Certainly here one has to rely on faith, but we can have reasonable confidence without certainty.

It is not accidental that the Hebrew word for "true" is often translated "reliable" or "faithful." Truth is something we can walk on or lean on and not fall into error. We do not need to know the exact historical facts about all past events to be able to have a reliable understanding of much that happened in the course of ancient history. And we do not need to know the exact historical accuracy—to the detail—of most events narrated in Scripture to be able to have confidence that on the whole the historical writings in Scripture give us a reliable understanding of the most important events that happened in God's dealing with the human race.[30]

Christian teaching practice. What then do we do with the account of Abraham in the book of Genesis? That depends on the genre we adopt. If we are writing a chapter in a book on ancient history, we may say that the account of Abraham in Genesis probably tells us about something that actually happened, but our modern historical method does not allow us to tell how much of it actually happened—we do not have much other evidence and we cannot always evaluate the genre of presentation well enough to evaluate everything in it. That should not, however, make us skeptical about whether it happened or not. It should simply have us accept the fact that we can only get so far and no farther in applying modern historical method to the material we have.

We have, however, an additional criterion to use, one different

---

[30] Some authors distinguish between "precision" and "accuracy." For a treatment of the accuracy of the gospel accounts in the face of differences in detail, i.e., degree of precision, see Darrell L. Bock, "Precision and Accuracy" in Hoffmeier and Magary, *op. cit.*, 367–382. A similar treatment in terms of "standard of accuracy" can be found in Swinburne, *op. cit.*, 36–37. A similar Patristic treatment can be found in Augustine, *De consensus evangelistarum*, II.12.29 and 21.51.

than modern secular historians have, and one different than ancient historians like Herodotus and Thucydides had. Where the fact that something happened is important to the truth of what is said in Scripture, we should accept it on the authority of the status of the Scripture as the Word of God. Fundamental to the scriptural teaching is the fact that God made a covenant with Abraham. It does not matter much if the list of children born to Abraham's concubine is completely accurate, but it does matter that God made a covenant with Abraham. That is an event on which the rest of God's working with the human race depends, and we cannot believe in the inspiration of Scripture in any coherent sense if we do not believe that.

If we reflect on the account of the covenant with Abraham, we should quickly be able to see that there is no way it could come from the process by which we know of most historical events. No one observed God making a covenant with Abraham—other than Abraham himself. God spoke to him, sometimes in a vision, sometimes probably without one. We have to believe that Abraham has reliably passed on revelation he personally received.

The content of Abraham's revelation seems to have been transmitted to his family and handed on from generation to generation. Eventually it was included in the canon of Scripture by a process of witness and spiritual discernment. If we do not accept that revelation, we have no historical method that can give us access to what God said—but there is no historical method that can call Abraham's testimony into question. There can only be a refusal to believe, the refusal that some have called negative faith and that really is a blind leap.

So how do we approach writing or speaking about Abraham? Because that depends on the genre we adopt, it in turn depends on the goal we have. If our goal is to publish in a secular academic journal or get a book into the historical section of a bookstore, we will need to follow the canonical requirements of modern secular historical writing, no matter how speculative or tedious the results may turn out to be.

If, however, we are doing Christian teaching, we simply present the material in the scriptural text as we find it—to the degree we can understand how it was intended to be taken. The text is, after all, evidence for what happened, unless of course it gives signs of being a tale and not an historical account. Moreover, we will get farther in our understanding of the events narrated in Scripture, even probably in our historical judgment of what happened, if we rely on what is said about them by the human authors who transmitted the material and were much closer in time and culture to those events than those modern scholars who provide us with speculative reconstructions.[31]

We may think it helpful to occasionally say that modern historical method or scholarship cannot tell us a great deal about something that is said in the Scriptures. In Christian teaching we should, however, present the material as it is given in the text. That is, after all, the way God allowed it to be given to us. If we follow the text in the spirit of how the text is written (as well as we can discern that), we can be confident that we are getting the truth God intended us to have.

---

[31] C. S. Lewis, a respected scholar in pre-modern English literature, said in "Fern-seed," *op, cit.,* 198 of the view that "Christ came very rapidly to be misunderstood and misrepresented by His followers, and has been recovered or exhumed only by modern scholars": "The idea that any man or writer should be opaque to those who lived in the same culture, spoke the same language, shared the same habitual imagery and unconscious assumptions, and yet be transparent to those who have none of these advantages, is in my opinion preposterous. There is an *a priori* improbability in it which almost no argument and no evidence could counterbalance."

CHAPTER TWENTY-TWO

Spiritual Transposition

When the old covenant order is changed to the new covenant order, the old covenant order is transposed to a spiritual medium, the medium of the Holy Spirit. The concrete elements of the old covenant order are transposed; and the provisions of the law are modified (spiritualized) according to the transposition (interpreted differently because fulfilled).

Introduction to the chapter. This is the final chapter of the second part. As such it does not treat so much an exegetical principle, like the previous chapters of the second part, but provides an overview of the result of the theological exegesis of how the New Testament treats the stages of God's plan.

Transpositions. The term "transposition" refers broadly to a change in position. Transpositions occur in a variety of ways. There are, for instance, simple transpositions. A melody is transposed into a different key. That is mainly a matter of changing the notes to a different scale, leaving everything else unchanged. Logical transposition involves moving the arrangement of the logical symbols in such a way that the logical relationships are not changed. Sometimes "transposition" is used to refer to a change in medium, as in pictorial art from fresco to mosaic.

It is transposition in medium that is the concern here. Someone creates a garden. Then someone else produces a drawing of that garden. If the drawing is good, a visitor could tell right away that it was "the same" garden. Yet the medium is radically different. In the one case it is rocks and bushes, grass and statues. In the other it is paper and pencil marks. In the one case it has a variety of colors. In the other it has various shades of grey.

Drawing a picture of a garden transposes the garden into a simpler medium. In order for that to work the same line on a paper has to do duty for more than one feature of the landscape. What in reality might be a cube made up of squares now becomes a collection of acute angles. They sometimes represent acute angles in the garden, like the angle of the stick leaning against the cube, but sometimes represent right angles, now represented by acute angles because the drawing uses the technique of perspective.

There is a yet greater transposition possible. The person who creates the garden might also create a map of the garden and put some useful information on it for people who want to find their way through the garden or maintain it. When we are given the map, even when we are familiar with the garden, we might not realize that it represents the garden without some serious investigation. Once we recognize that it is a map of the garden we know, we can see that it portrays "the same" garden. Paradoxically, it tells us some things about the garden that we could not tell by looking at the drawing or even by looking at the garden itself. We might, for instance, recognize for the first time that the garden is arranged in a swirl.

The transposition to a simpler medium might allow us to see, or see more readily, the nature of the garden. But it will not give us the experience of being in the garden and of its pleasantness. We can keep the map in our desk to refer to; we can put the drawing on the wall for decoration or to remind us of the garden; but we cannot go out into the map or drawing to have a conversation with someone or pluck the fruit that grows in the garden—unless in the way we might if we live in our imaginations more than most of us do or probably should.

Spiritual transposition. The new covenant order is not just a development of the old covenant order, although it is that in a certain way. It is certainly not a simple abolition of the old covenant
order, although the old covenant order is no longer necessary for
the fullest available relationship with God. Rather it is the transposition of the old covenant order into a new medium. To describe
the change, the Scripture often uses the contrast between the flesh
(the physical) and the spirit (the new covenant order is "not made
with hands"—Mt 14:58; 2 Cor 5:1; Col 2:11), and sometimes the
contrast between the earthly and the heavenly. For simplicity, we
might say that when the old covenant order is changed to the new
covenant order, the old covenant order is transposed to a spiritual
medium, the medium of the Holy Spirit.

Christians know that the Holy Spirit is a person. We "invoke"
him, speak to him, include him in doxologies. He has a mind (Rom
8:27). Yet the Scripture often speaks about him in a more imperson-
al way. He is a power at work in the world, and he operates in human
beings (e.g., Lk 4:14; 1 Cor 2:4; 12:7). He is often referred to as "the
Spirit," although it would be a grave mistake to fail to recognize that
he is the *Holy* Spirit, the Spirit *of God*. There are other spirits operating in the world, and they are often not beneficent.

What happens when an old covenant reality is transposed to the
medium of the Spirit? We can use a familiar example here. The old
covenant temple was a building on a mountain in the city of Jerusalem, with an inner room, the Holy of Holies, where God dwelled on
earth. To use the Old Testament idiom, that was where the earthly
footstool of God's throne was placed, with him seated in (invisi-
ble) glory above it. In front of it were various furnishings (a candlestick to see by, altars to place offerings on, basins for cleansing,
etc.). Around the temple building were various walls, curtains, and
barriers to protect the holy places, but also to keep people at a safe
distance. They could come closer depending on their position and
also their state of purity.

In the new covenant, the temple is not a building but first of all
a body of people. It is the Body of Christ, people joined with Christ,

the Church of Christ. The old covenant temple has been transposed from the medium of a physical place in which God dwelled to the medium of a people in whom God dwells because the Holy Spirit has been given to them. God is present in their midst by the Spirit, especially when they gather corporately. He is also present in each of them, especially when they turn to him "in their heart."

The difference of medium brings about some important changes. When the temple became spiritual in the sense that it was transposed to a spiritual medium, then the individual's access to God became freer and more direct. If Christians maintain a certain purity of life through their obedience to his commandments, then they can turn to him any time and have an access to him that is, in scriptural terms, close (near) or direct.

New covenant access is more direct because the Spirit within is a medium of communication. Since he is the Spirit of God, he brings the indwelling presence of God. Put differently, he puts us into contact with heaven, heaven understood as the place of God's presence, the place where God's throne is put because he rules the universe "from heaven." The Holy Spirit allows us to interact more immediately with God.

Each element of the old covenant order has been transposed into the new covenant order, the order of the Spirit. We have looked at many of these transpositions, especially as we have understood typological connections between the Old and New Testaments. Understanding them, however, as spiritual transpositions, transpositions that are made to the medium of the Spirit, allows us to see how the elements of the old covenant order are and should be applied to new covenant life.

For instance, in the old covenant it was obligatory for the judges and rulers of God's people to put to death people who had committed certain serious crimes. They deserved the death penalty. Left at large they would have corrupted the life of the old covenant people of God and even brought destruction upon it, not least because of the judgment of God. In the new covenant, physical death is not inflicted, as we have seen. Rather, serious criminals are put out of the community and avoided. Exclusion from the community is the new covenant equivalent of the old covenant death penalty.

Exclusion can be an authentic equivalent because of the change from old covenant order to new covenant order. In the old covenant as taught in the Pentateuch, the old covenant people were a nation living on a land, God's land. The new covenant people are still a nation, but they now no longer live together on a physical land. Although physically scattered in a diaspora, they live together in the Holy Spirit and in the Body of Christ, the land of the living. To put them out of the Christian community is the spiritual equivalent of putting them out of the land of Israel by putting them to death (1 Cor 5:3–5). The penal code of the old covenant is typologically fulfilled by the spiritual penal code of the new.

To use another example, old covenant people had an army. They most often used it to fight off or destroy their enemies who attacked them, but at times they used it to conquer neighboring nations. New covenant people do not have an army—unless they happen to also be a physical nation like the Byzantines or Medieval European nations were. They do, however, fight, and their weapons are not swords and shields, or bombs and tanks, but the Word of God and prayer (Eph 6:10–20).

Once again, this involves a transposition from a physical order to a spiritual one. Old covenant people had their bodies and physical weapons. New covenant people have their transformed, spiritualized, inner human being and spiritual weapons. To conquer pagan people by bringing them into subjection to Christ (evangelizing them) is the spiritual equivalent of conquering them and bringing them into subjection to the old covenant king of Israel. The wars of the old covenant people are spiritually fulfilled by evangelism and spiritual warfare—and these have the great advantage that they bring a benefit to the conquered without the by-product of damage and destruction.

The various elements of new covenant life are spiritual equivalents of elements of old covenant life. Physical (fleshly) things are not. The Church of the Holy Sepulcher in Jerusalem or Hagia Sophia in Istanbul or St. Peter's in Rome are not equivalents of the old covenant temple in Jerusalem, the unique place to have the fullest access to God on earth, even though they have been constructed to image the old covenant temple. The church of Christ is the spiritual equivalent. It is the spiritual equivalent because it performs the same function in God's plan, that is, to be a full dwelling place of God in this world. It also performs that function in a spiritually better or more spiritually effective way than the old covenant temple building did.

It is easy for us to consider that the new covenant order is weaker than the old covenant order. Dealing with an army or a panel of judges backed up by executioners is more immediately intimidating than what most Christians experience as new covenant enforcement. We are tempted to think that spiritual things are more immaterial and wispier than physical things. That, however, would be a great mistake. When Uzzah performed the forbidden action of putting out his hand and touching the ark, power came out and struck him dead instantly (2 Sam 6:6–7). When the woman with a hemorrhage put out her hand in faith to touch Christ, power came from him and healed her body in a way that no doctors could. The more spiritual something is, the more powerful it is to give life and death.

Unfortunately, many Christians lack conviction that their new reality is more powerful and impressive. They may be only nominal Christians or they may be active Christians with some level of Christian practice, but their connection to the Holy Spirit who brings about the transposition is so weak that they do not experience spiritual power and reality personally. They need more of an encounter with the baptizer in the Holy Spirit so they can experience a personal change, an inner ability to live the way Christ teaches and a genuine contact with the spiritual, heavenly realities that comes through the presence of the Spirit at work in them.

The Christian purpose for the old covenant order. Why then should a Christian read about the old covenant order in the Old Testament? The old covenant order is like a drawing in a simpler medium. It is a drawing, however, of a fleshly, earthly reality that was later brought into existence through Christ as a spiritual, heavenly reality. Because the medium of the old covenant is simpler, like a drawing or a map, we can see many things about the spiritual reality more clearly and often with more impact when we read the Old Testament. It instructs us typologically about what for Christians is now present.

As we have seen, each element of the old covenant order, both the elements of the ceremonial life and also the elements that go into the national life of the old covenant people, can instruct us about new covenant life. There is, however, something even more important typologically than each element, and that is the pattern (form) of old covenant life as a whole, especially as it is described for us in the law (the Pentateuch, here completed by the book of Joshua).

To make a comparison, someone might draw a picture of a ladder that is sitting in our yard. We might take that picture and show it to a shopkeeper and tell him that we want to buy a ladder like that. The elements of both ladders, the ladder in our yard and the ladder in the drawing, are very different in nature. We cannot climb anywhere by using the drawing, but we can communicate to the shopkeeper what we are looking for by using the drawing. He will recognize it as a ladder instantly.

The shopkeeper does not need to be told that each pair of horizontal lines represents a rung, that the pairs of horizontal lines are in a series and they are equidistant from one another, that there are vertical lines on each side that touch the ends of the horizontal lines, and that there are two curved lines on top of the vertical lines (that represent hooks that allow us to steady the ladder). Rather, he recognizes the pattern (the form) right away, and he can tell intuitively, without looking at each element and the relations between them and without thinking about it, that he is looking at the drawing of a ladder.

The pattern of human life in relationship with God is not familiar to us the way the pattern of ladders is. Moreover, a spiritual medium can be harder for us to understand than a physical medium. However, if we understand the sketch, the description, of old covenant life in the Pentateuch, the physical shape of a people living on a land with a temple in the capital city and surrounded by enemies, we can more easily understand the nature of the spiritual life of new covenant people, living in the Spirit, with a temple in their capital city in heaven, surrounded by spiritual enemies. If, in other words, we can see the pattern of old covenant life and how people lived it physically, we then can more readily come to understand and think about the spiritual realities of the new covenant life we participate in.

Of course we also need to know the reality and power of the Holy Spirit, given to us through the work of Jesus Christ and in him, by the blessed will of our Father who is in heaven.

APPENDIX: SELECT BIBLIOGRAPHY

NEW TESTAMENT INTERPRETATION OF THE OLD TESTAMENT

The below selection of books contains modern studies of the way the New Testament interprets the Old Testament, with special attention to how the texts convey spiritual truth.

Bauckham, Richard. *Jesus and the Eyewitnesses: The Gospels as Eyewitness Testimony*. Grand Rapids, MI: Eerdmans, 2007. A good overview of how the previous dominant scholarly approach to the origin of the Gospels misconceived their approach and overlooked the importance of eyewitness accounts in them.

Congar, Yves, O.P. *The Mystery of the Temple*. London: Burns and Oates, 1962. Originally published in 1958 in French. A study of one of the most important types in Scripture, the temple, and its meaning in the whole of Scripture by a French Catholic theologian.

Cullmann, Oscar. *Salvation in History*. New York: Harper & Row, 1967. Originally *Heil als Geschichte: Heilsgeschichtliche Existenz im Neuen Testament* (Tübingen: Mohr, 1965). A classic presentation of the salvation history approach to New Testament theology by a modern Protestant exegete.

Daniélou, Jean, S.J. *The Bible and the Liturgy*. Notre Dame, IN: University of Notre Dame Press, 1956; reprint: Ann Arbor, MI: Servant, 1979. Probably the best overall view of the use of Old Testament typology in Christian doctrine by an important patristic scholar. It focuses on the use of the Old Testament in the Catholic liturgy, but is largely ecumenically accessible. Daniélou's book *From Shadows to Reality* (Westminster, MD: Newman, 1960) provides supplementary material.

de Lubac, Henry, S.J., *The Sources of Revelation*. New York: Herder and Herder, 1968. The most accessible presentation of the influential approach to the spiritual senses in Scripture by an influential French Jesuit theologian.

Fairbairns, Patrick. *The Typology of Scripture*. Grand Rapids, MI: Kregel Publications, 1989. Originally published in 1845–47. A thorough treatment of typology in the Scripture in the Reformed tradition, and therefore a summary of traditional Reformed exegesis.

Goppelt, Leonhard. *TYPOS: The Typological Interpretation of the Old Testament in the New*. Grand Rapids, MI: Eerdmans, 1982. Originally published in 1939 in German. A thorough treatment of the typology in the New Testament by a German New Testament scholar.

Kinzer, Mark S. "Beginning with the End: The Place of Eschatology in the Messianic Jewish Canonical Narrative," in *Israel's Messiah and the People of God: A Vision for Messianic Jewish Covenant Fidelity*, edited by Jennifer M. Rosner, 91–125. Eugene, OR: Cascade Books, 2011. A helpful introduction to Messianic Judaism and to ways Jewish exegesis affects Christian teaching.

Levering, Matthew. *Christ's Fulfillment of Torah and Temple: Salvation According to Thomas Aquinas*. Notre Dame, IN: University of Notre Dame Press, 2002. An overview of Aquinas's view of the old covenant fulfillment in Christ. Aquinas' interpretation and his dealing with the connected theological issues have been very influential and touch on most of the important theological issues, even today.

Background to the Special Discussions

The following are some significant contemporary works in Scripture scholarship that provide background to the methodological discussions.

Alter, Robert. *The Art of Biblical Narrative.* New York: Basic Books, Inc., 1981. Alter's presentation on the literary nature of Old Testament narrative has been influential in giving rise to a new approach. He applied the method in commentaries on biblical books, beginning with *Genesis: Translation and Commentary.* New York: Norton, 1996.

Anderson, Gary A. *The Genesis of Perfection: Adam and Eve in Jewish and Christian Imagination.* Louisville, KY: Westminster John Knox, 2001. A study of the way Genesis 1–3 has been understood in Jewish and Christian exegetical tradition, and how various "gaps" in the scriptural text have given rise to theological positions.

Beale, G. K. *Handbook on the New Testament Use of the Old Testament: Exegesis and Interpretation.* Grand Rapids, MI: Baker Academic, 2012. A handbook of exegetical and interpretive practice for understanding the use of the Old Testament in the New.

Hahn, Scott W. *Kinship by Covenant: A Canonical Approach to the Fulfillment of God's Saving Promises,* Anchor Yale Bible Reference Library. New Haven, CT: Yale University Press, 2009. The currently fullest presentation of the idea of covenant in Scripture and the related scholarly literature, seeking to synthesize the material with a canonical perspective.

Hengel, Martin. *Acts and the History of Earliest Christianity.* Philadelphia: Fortress, 1980. A book that is not solely about Acts but also about the relationship between scriptural exegesis and historical method.

Kerr, Fergus. *Twentieth-Century Catholic Theologians: From Neoscholasticism to Nuptial Mysticism.* Oxford: Blackwell, 2007. A helpful and sometimes overlooked study of the way certain currents of romanticism have influenced modern theology (primarily Catholic, but not just Catholic) with background of how traditional theology approached the same topics.

Kitchen, K. A. *On the Reliability of the Old Testament.* Grand Rapids, MI: Eerdmans, 2003. Kitchen is a noted Egyptologist and provides the best available survey of the material from the ancient Near East that bears on the historical nature of the Old Testament texts. It was written to counter the Minimalist position (see footnote 1, p. 520) and makes a strong case for its thesis. It is, however, even more useful as an overall survey, partly because it is not restricted to Syro-Palestinian material. It is written in a "splendidly classical polemical fashion" (see footnote 1, p. 520) and so can be disorienting to some who are used to a different scholarly style.

Lewis, C. S. *Miracles: A Preliminary Study.* New York: MacMillan, 1947. A book that treats the meaning of miracles in Scripture, but in so doing makes use of what we now might call philosophical theology to present a profound theological understanding of how God works in creation.

Moberly, R. W. L. *Old Testament Theology: Reading the Hebrew Bible as Christian Scripture.* Grand Rapids, MI: Baker Academic, 2013. A book that provides a good presentation of "the canonical approach" or "canonical criticism" in action. It can be helpfully supplemented by Moberly's *The Theology of the Book of Genesis* (Cambridge, UK: Cambridge University Press, 2009).

O'Keefe, John J. and R. R. Reno. *Sanctified Vision: An Introduction to Early Christian Interpretation of the Bible.* Baltimore, MD: Johns Hopkins University, 2005. A study of the way the patristic authors interpreted the Scriptures, with a focus on understanding their methodology from the perspective of the patristic authors themselves

The Pontifical Biblical Commission, *The Jewish People and Their Sacred Scriptures in the Christian Bible.* Vatican City: Libreria Editrice Vaticana, 2002. http://www.vatican.va/roman_curia/congregations/cfaith/pcb_documents/rc_con_cfaith_doc_20020212_popolo-ebraico_en.html. An overview by an international body of

Catholic scholars of the Christian interpretation of the Old Testament, with special attention to Christian views of the Jewish people. It provides a summary, as of 2002, of much modern Scripture scholarship on the Christian views of the Old Testament and the Jews, with the stated goal of achieving a positive view of the Jewish people by Christians.

Reardon, Patrick Henry. *Chronicles of History and Worship: Orthodox Christian Reflections on the Books of Chronicles.* Ben Lomond, CA: Conciliar Press, 2006. An overview of the books of Chronicles that presents its purpose primarily as seeing David in relationship to the ongoing worship of Israel.

Second Vatican Ecumenical Council, Dogmatic Constitution on Revelation *Dei verbum* (November 18, 1965), and Benedict XVI, Apostolic Exhortation *Verbum Domini* (September 30, 2010). Two chief authoritative documents on the approach of the Catholic Church to Scripture. Both can be found on the Vatican website: *Dei verbum* at http://www.vatican.va/archive/hist_councils/ii_vatican_council/documents/vat-ii_const_19651118_dei-verbum_en.html.; *Verbum Domini* at http://w2.vatican.va/content/benedict-xvi/en/apost_exhortations/documents/hf_ben-xvi_exh_20100930_verbum-domini.html.

Swinburne, Richard. *Revelation: From Metaphor to Analogy.* Oxford: Clarendon Press, 2007. A study of the conceptual underpinnings of scriptural interpretation by a contemporary Oxford philosopher. It provides an overview of the material in modern analytical philosophy that is relevant to many of the questions treated here. It is one volume of his work in Christian apologetics.

Vanhoozer, Kevin J., ed. *Dictionary for Theological Interpretation of the Bible.* Grand Rapids, MI: Baker Academic, 2005. A comprehensive reference work to theological interpretation, written by authors with a variety of approaches.

COLLECTIONS OF PATRISTIC SCRIPTURAL COMMENTARY

Oden, Thomas C., ed. *Ancient Christian Commentary on Scripture.* Downers Grove, IL: InterVarsity Press, 1998–2010. A running commentary on both the Old and New Testament in the form of a catena of selections from patristic authors, one that gives a usable, even if sometimes uneven, overview of patristic exegesis.

The Liturgy of the Hours. New York: Catholic Book Publishers, 1975. The Roman Catholic prayer book in four volumes contains a one year and two year cycle of scriptural readings in the Office of Readings and in addition contains for those Scripture readings accompanying readings, mostly patristic, that function as a commentary on the whole Scripture. It is ecumenically accessible, especially the readings for Ordinary Time, Advent, and Easter, as distinguished from the proper of the saints. *The Office of Readings* (Boston, MA: St. Paul Editions, 1983) is one volume with only the Office of Readings.

OTHER BOOKS BY THE AUTHOR WITH FURTHER BACKGROUND

Redeemer: Understanding the Meaning of the Life, Death, and Resurrection of Jesus Christ. Ann Arbor, MI: Servant, 1992.

Man and Woman in Christ: An Examination of the Roles of Men and Women in Light of Scripture and the Social Sciences. Ann Arbor, MI: Servant, 1980; East Lansing, MI: Tabor House, 2006.

"Modern Approaches to Scriptural Authority," in Peter Williamson and Kevin Perrotta, eds. *Christianity Confronts Modernity.* Ann Arbor, MI: Servant, 1981.

Baptized in the Spirit. Pecos, NM: Dove, 1970; E. Lansing, MI: Tabor House, 2003.

Charismatic Spirituality: The Work of the Holy Spirit in Scripture and Practice. Cincinnati, OH: St. Anthony Messenger Press, 2004.

Catholics and the Eucharist: A Scriptural Introduction. Ann Arbor, MI: Servant, 2000. Chapter 1 contains a presentation on the nature of the Scripture.

Christian Tithing. East Lansing, MI: Tabor House, 2006.